E-Discovery and Data Privacy

E-Discovery and Data Privacy

A Practical Guide

Edited by

Catrien Noorda

Stefan Hanloser

Published by:
Kluwer Law International
PO Box 316
2400 AH Alphen aan den Rijn
The Netherlands
Website: www.kluwerlaw.com

Sold and distributed in North, Central and South America by:
Aspen Publishers, Inc.
7201 McKinney Circle
Frederick, MD 21704
United States of America
Email: customer.service@aspenpublishers.com

Sold and distributed in all other countries by:
Turpin Distribution Services Ltd.
Stratton Business Park
Pegasus Drive, Biggleswade
Bedfordshire SG18 8TQ
United Kingdom
Email: kluwerlaw@turpin-distribution.com

Printed on acid-free paper.

ISBN 978-90-411-3345-8

Printed and Bound by CPI Group (UK) Ltd, Croydon, CR0 4YY.

Summary of Contents

Summary of Contents

Summary of Contents

Table of Contents

Table of Contents

Table of Contents

Chapter 5.5
Estonia   **77**
Ants Nõmper and Jaanus Kasevits

Chapter 5.6
Finland   **87**
Erkko Korhonen

Table of Contents

Chapter 5.7
France   **99**
Charlotte Portmann

Chapter 5.8
Germany   **109**
Stefan Hanloser

Chapter 5.9
Greece   117
Maria Giannakaki

Table of Contents

Table of Contents

Table of Contents

Table of Contents

Chapter 5.20
Romania   **231**
Silvia Popa

Chapter 5.21
Serbia   **241**
Aleksa Anđelković

Chapter 5.22
Slovakia   **247**
Jana Habánová and Michal Lučivjanský

Chapter 5.23
Slovenia   **257**
Tomaz Petrovic

Table of Contents

Table of Contents

Chapter 6.5
Taiwan   **349**
Jill Niu and Katherine Juang

About the Editors

Catrien Noorda is Of Counsel in Howrey's Amsterdam office and a member of the Dutch Bar since 1994. Catrien specializes in intellectually property (IP) and information technology (IT) law and has particular expertise in data protection law. She has been advising numerous multinational corporations on their international data protection compliance strategies ever since the entry into force of the Data Protection Directive in 1995. Catrien is a member of the Association of IP Law, the Dutch Association of Advertising Law, and the Media Law Association. She is a member of the Association of Information Technology Lawyers and was a board member from 2004 through 2008. Catrien regularly publishes and lectures on IP and IT law subjects, especially in the field of data protection.

Stefan Hanloser is a senior associate with Howrey LLP, working out of the firm's Munich office. Dr Hanloser's practice focuses on privacy and data protection compliance. He advises national and multinational companies in a variety of sectors on the processing of personal data and the structuring of international data flows under European data protection law. Dr Hanloser has also a strong focus on the transfer of personally identifiable information for pretrial discovery purposes. Prior to joining the firm's Munich office, Dr Hanloser worked in the firm's office in Washington, D.C., and with an international law firm in Munich and New York. He has been a member of the German Bar since 2002. Dr Hanloser is a certified Data Protection Auditor (TÜV).

List of Contributors

Carlos de Almeida Sampaio is partner of Cuatrecasas, Gonçalves Pereira and head of the Intellectual Property, IT, and Data Protection Department. Carlos de Almeida Sampaio has a master in law from the University of Lisbon Law School, completed his post-graduate and J.D. studies in Brussels and Champaign-Urbana (University of Illinois), and has been a member of the Portuguese Bar since 1979. He regularly publishes IT and data protection articles and books and lectures on information technologies law in the post-graduation course of University of Lisbon Law School. Carlos de Almeida Sampaio advises numerous national and multinational corporations on both Portuguese and European IT and data protection legal issues and is a member of the Portuguese Information Technologies Association.

Daniela Ampollini is a senior associate at Trevisan & Cuonzo Avvocati, working out of the firm's Parma office. Daniela has been a member of the Italian Bar since 2001 and she specializes in IP and IT law. Daniela has considerable experience in data protection law. She has been advising numerous multinational corporations in industrial and intellectual property and IT law issues, both in litigation and contractual issues and compliance strategies. Daniela is a member of the International Trademark Association and a contributor to the Kluwer IP Cases and the Kluwer Patentblog. She is a regular contributor to national and international law journals and conferences on the subjects of IP and IT law.

Aleksa Anđelković LL.M, is an attorney at law at Moravčević Vojnović Zdravković oad, Belgrade, in cooperation with Schönherr Rechtsanwälte GmbH, Vienna. Aleksa Anđelković counsels clients in areas of Mergers & Acquisitions (M&A), regulatory, telecommunications, and competition law. He finished his LLM and specialization studies at Central European University in Budapest, with his thesis covering regulation of electronic communications in the EU and the practice and impact of the European Court of Justice on the liberalization of the telecommunication market. Aleksa Anđelković is the author of several articles on regulation of electronic communications, number portability, and data protection.

Fabienne Brison is partner at Howrey and a member of the Brussels Bar since 1988. Fabienne has in-depth knowledge and extensive practical experience in copyright, media, and new technologies. She is professor at the Vrije Universiteit Brussel and guest professor in the LLM's Intellectual Property at the HUBrussel and Intellectual Property & Competition Law at the University of Liège, and in the BBMM-training for Benelux models and trademark representatives. Fabienne is the Chair of the Belgian Association for Copyright, Vice-Chair of the Intellectual Property Council (Copyright Division), Chair of BeTech, and co-editor of the legal magazine *Auteurs & Media*. She is a CEPINA-approved arbitrator for domain-name .be disputes and an ICT-mediator.

Laura Cantero is an Associate at Howrey's Madrid office (Howrey Martínez Lage). Her experience in the area of data privacy covers providing advice to national and multinational companies on the processing of personal data, as well as drafting and auditing privacy policies related to the collection and processing of customer/patient data. She has also lectured in master's degrees courses on e-commerce and data protection issues involved therein. Besides, Laura's activity focuses on IP litigation and advice, and related subjects such as copyright, unfair competition, and advertising.

Dr Michael Cartier is a senior associate with the Litigation and Arbitration Team at Walder Wyss Ltd., Switzerland, working out of the firm's Zurich office. Dr Cartier mainly advises in dispute resolution and represents parties in both international and domestic arbitrations, before state courts, and in enforcement and legal assistance matters. He also advises on matters involving white-collar criminal law and corporate investigations with cross-border implications. Prior to joining Walder Wyss Ltd., Dr Cartier clerked at a Swiss court and worked for a trading company in Japan. He was admitted to the Swiss Bar in 2004.

Line Coll is a lawyer at Wiersholm and has been member of the Norwegian Bar Association since 2002. Wiersholm is one of Norway's leading law firms – an internationally oriented firm dedicated to business law, operational legal services, and litigation. Coll specializes in IT law and has particular expertise in data protection. She has been advising corporations on data protection matters since the implementation of the Data Protection Directive. She was secretary of the Norwegian Privacy Commission from 2007 to 2008. Coll has also been working at the University of Oslo as a researcher and lecturer within privacy and data protection, and has written several books and articles within this legal field.

Kaisa Fahllund is the Head of Hannes Snellman's Technology practice, covering both IP (Intellectual Property Rights) and TMT (Technology, Media and Tele-coms). Her fields of expertise include technology transfer, licensing and IP litigation as well as ICT agreements and transactions of all sizes and ICT related litigation. She also advises clients on issues relating to e-commerce, data protection, telecommunications, trade practices and marketing.

Justin George is a senior associate with Ravindran Associates. He graduated from the University of Exeter in the United Kingdom and was called to the Singapore Bar in 2007. Since commencing practice, Justin has specialized in IP/IT law and represents clients in both contentious and non-contentious matters. Justin has acted for clients in trademark, passing-off, breach of confidence, patent, and copyright litigation and has argued before the Registrar of Trademarks. Justin has also prosecuted criminal offences under the Trade Marks Act under the authority of the Attorney-General's Chambers and handles the enforcement programme for IP proprietors. On the commercial aspect of Justin's work, he advises clients on the data protection regime in Singapore, drafts and reviews media and information technology contracts and technology licensing agreements, and advises clients on regulatory issues.

Irena Georgieva is a senior attorney with Schönherr in cooperation with Advokatsko druzhestvo Andreev, Stoyanov & Tsekova in Sofia, Bulgaria. She specializes in corporate and regulatory law and in particular personal data protection, telecommunications and public procurements. Ms Georgieva has been involved in various data protection issues and advises Schönherr clients on international data transfer, registrations, and approval proceedings before the Bulgarian data protection authority as well as in outsourcing projects. She is a member of the Sofia Bar Association and a PhD candidate at the Groningen University, Netherlands.

Vivien Gertsch originally comes from Salzburg, Austria, where she also studied law. After her PhD she worked in several trust companies in the area of company law and tax law. She has received the Swiss diploma as tax expert. At the Liechtenstein University she was responsible for the training of trust officers and gave lectures in company and tax law for the last ten years. She also has diplomas as Liechtenstein trustee and CPA and in mediation. She is author of various publications about tax law, company law, and due diligence law/compliance.

Maria Giannakaki is an Attorney at Law in Athens, Greece, and is an associate in Karageorgiou & Associates law firm. She specializes in IT and IP law, as well as personal data protection law. Maria advises in all aspects of personal data protection law, including model contracts, Binding Corporate Rules (BCRs), employees monitoring, whistleblowing schemes, commercial communications, and e-discovery issues. As a data protection practitioner, she has participated in several global data protection compliance projects for multinational companies having presence in Greece. While Maria specializes in Internet and e-commerce law, she also advises on related topics of banking and financial services, consumers' protection, media, and marketing law and has considerable experience in drafting international commercial contracts.

Jasdev Singh Gill is admitted to practice in Malaysia and is the Managing Partner of Jasdev Chambers in Malaysia. He specializes in the area of IP, including copyright, trademarks, patents, designs, data protection, and trade secrets. Jasdev has been advising and has represented national and multinational companies from a wide variety of sectors on their IP matters as well as regulatory compliance issues. He is a co-contributor to the chapters on Malaysia in the book entitled *Intellectual Property Protection in Asia* published by LexisNexis. Jasdev is also a member of the Intellectual Property Committee of the Malaysian Bar.

Carina Gommers is senior associate at Howrey and has been a member of the Brussels Bar since 2002. She also is an affiliated junior researcher at the KULeuven (Centre for Intellectual Property Rights). Her practice covers all aspects of IP rights, including trademarks, copyright, patents, and design rights. She deals with contentious and non-contentious matters for a wide variety of clients across sectors. Carina has extensive experience regarding customs seizures as well as in regulatory affairs for pharmaceuticals. Carina also provides advice on compliance with the Belgian Data Protection Act and privacy issues, including drafting of e-mail and Internet policies. Her practice further focuses on litigation regarding unfair trade practices, including misleading advertising, enticement of clientele, passing off, price reductions, and other forms of commercial promotions.

Hazel Grant is a partner with Bristows, London, where her work regularly involves data protection compliance audits and coordinating advice on pan-European projects. Additionally, Hazel advises on data transfers (using both EU model contracts and binding corporate rules), government data sharing projects and responses to data security breaches. Her clients range from central government departments and agencies to global IT service providers. Hazel is an editor of the Encyclopedia of Data Protection and Privacy, a contributing editor (on data protection and freedom of information) for the Encyclopedia of Information Technology Law (both Sweet and Maxwell). She is a member of the editorial board of the Freedom of Information Journal.

Jana Habánová specializes in real estate development and transactions. She advises domestic and international real estate companies on their investments in Slovakia. Jana graduated in law from the Comenius University in Bratislava 2003 (JUDr. 2005) and obtained a master's degree in European studies from the University of Hamburg. She has been a member of the Slovak Bar since 2008.

Kinga Hetényi is the managing partner of Schönherr Hungary, where she also heads the M&A Practice Group. She is a Hungarian attorney with over fifteen years of experience. She has lead numerous M&A transactions, and has advised many multinational clients on corporate and labor law. Her expertise also includes IT/media and telecommunications law and distribution and agency law. After graduating from Eötvös Loránd University of Budapest in January 1995, she worked for nine years in the corporate department of the Budapest office of one of the largest international law firms and for one year at the Frankfurt office of the same law firm. In 2004 and 2005 she was the head of the legal department of the Hungarian subsidiary of a global FMCG company listed on the NYSE. In 2005 she joined the Hungarian law firm, which became the Budapest office of Schönherr in 2008.

Tomáš Hülle is an associate in Schönherr's Prague office. Tomáš focuses on intellectual property and information technology law, dispute resolution, and data protection. He has advised corporations on data protection issues, in particular with regard to the protection of their employees' private data. Tomáš regularly publishes in the field of unfair competition, intellectual property, and information technology law and is a member of several legal associations focusing on international arbitration.

Laura Ielciu has been a member of the Bucharest Bar since 2008. Her area of expertise includes civil law, EU law, and human rights law. In particular, Laura advises clients, both national and multinational companies, on Romanian data protection law compliance. Laura graduated in law from the Babes-Bolyai University in Cluj-Napoca in 2004 and obtained a master's degree in Comparative Law from the University of Strasbourg in 2010.

Zuzana Jiřištová specializes in IP and IT law, with particular focus on data protection law. Zuzana studied at Charles University in Prague, University of Turku, Finland, and University of Melbourne, Australia.

Katherine Juang is a senior associate at Lee and Li, Attorneys-at-Law and has been a member of the Taipei Bar Association since 2002. Ms Juang obtained a master's degree in law in Taiwan and her master's thesis dealt with the protection of medical information. She specializes in data protection compliance, IP law, competition law, pharmaceutical regulatory compliance, and environmental law. She has been advising various local and foreign clients on the compliance of their local and/or international data protection structure, and regularly participates in and contributes to the firm's seminars on data protection compliance.

Dr Stavros Karageorgiou is the managing partner of the law firm Karageorgiou & Associates and he is licensed to practice before the Supreme Court. Mr Karageorgiou specializes in corporate, commercial, and IT law and has a strong focus on data protection law. He has particular expertise in telecommunications and electronic banking and payment services. He has worked as a legal advisor at SWIFT s.c. La Hulpe and DIAS S.A. He collaborates with an international network of law firms and specialized consultants and advises national and multinational companies in a variety of sectors, including data protection, electronic banking, and telecommunication law.

Sukumar Karuppiah is admitted to practice in both Singapore and Malaysia and is a partner with Messrs Ravindran Associates in Singapore and Jasdev Chambers in Malaysia. His practice focuses on the development, protection, exploitation, and enforcement of IP rights, including copyright, trademarks, patents, designs, data protection, and trade secrets, covering diverse industries such as luxury consumer goods, software, electronics, food and beverage, pharmaceuticals, and entertainment. He contributed to the chapters on Singapore and Malaysia in the book entitled *Intellectual Property Protection in Asia* published by LexisNexis, which is updated annually.

Jaanus Kasevits is an associate lawyer in Raidla Lejins & Norcous' Tallinn office, specializing in matters related to IT and electronic communication and data protection. Jaanus gained his B.A. and M.A. degrees from the University of Tartu. He joined Raidla Lejins & Norcous in 2007 and has been a member of the Estonian Bar Association since 2010.

Gilbert S. Keteltas litigates complex commercial matters in United States courts. A recognized leader on eDiscovery strategies, he co-authored "Discovery of Electronic Evidence" Electronic Evidence Law and Practice (ABA, 2d Ed. 2008). He serves on the Advisory Board of Georgetown Law's Advanced eDiscovery Institute and is active in Sedona Working Group 1: Electronic Document Retention and Production. Mr Keteltas is a partner at Howrey LLP in Washington, D.C., and chairs its eDiscovery practice. He is a trusted advisor to global companies on the creation, deployment, and defence of eDiscovery response programs. Mr Keteltas received his J.D. from Georgetown Law and his B.S. in Industrial & Labor Relations from Cornell University.

Dr Mindaugas Kiškis is Associate Partner with the Law Firm LAWIN Lideika, Petrauskas, Valiūnas ir partneriai in Lithuania and is a Professor at the Mykolas Romeris University. He has been working in the fields of data protection and security, technology and media law, and IP since 1998. He has held a PhD since 2002 and was admitted to the Lithuanian Bar in 2003. He advises major multinational corporations in complex trans-border technology and data protection transactions and litigation; he also has significant international research and lecturing experience. He has published two textbooks, three monographs, as well as twenty-five articles on said topics in Lithuania and abroad.

Erkko Korhonen is an associate with Hannes Snellman Attorneys Ltd. Mr Korhonen works at the IP (Intellectual Property) and TMT (Technology, Media and Telecoms) group advising clients in the field of intellectual property law, data protection, e-commerce, media and marketing law, as well as ICT contracts and general contract law. Mr Korhonen has been advising corporations on their international data protection issues for several years.

Günther Leissler is an attorney at Schönherr Rechtsanwälte GmbH, Vienna. He specializes in data protection law, IT, and telecommunications. He frequently advises clients of Schönherr in Austria and Central and Eastern Europe (CEE) on all kinds of privacy and data protection matters, including outsourcing projects, installation of joint information and whistleblowing systems, as well as international data transfer issues. He regularly represents clients in their registration and approval proceedings before the Austrian data protection authority. Günther Leissler is the author of various articles on public law, especially on data protection and privacy law.

Claire Léonelli is Senior Associate at MOLITOR Avocats à la Cour and a member of the Paris Bar and Luxembourg Bar (List IV). Prior to joining MOLITOR, Claire was working in IP/IT departments of international law firms in Paris. She is now heading the IP, IT, and Media department of MOLITOR Avocats à la Cour. She has significant expertise in data protection law issues, and in particular in matters relating to the transfer of personal data outside Luxembourg. She is a member of AIJA (Association Internationale des Jeunes Avocats), APRAM (Associations des practiciens du droit des marques et des modèles), ECTA (European Communities Trade Mark Association), and ItechLaw.

Michal Lučivjanský is a paralegal at Schönherr Rechtsanwälte GmbH, Bratislava. Previously he worked as a legal assistant at Freshfields Bruckhaus Deringer, Bratislava. Michal is a student at the Faculty of Law, Comenius University in Bratislava, editor-in-chief of the faculty law journal, and a member of the executive board of the local European Law Students' Association group. In his future career he would like to focus on international relations and transactions.

Gonçalo Mendes da Maia is a partner with the leading Macau law firm MdME Lawyers | Private Notaries. He specializes in corporate, finance, construction, and infrastructure law, and represents major financial institutions, banks, developers, international luxury retailers, and gaming and construction companies, namely in matters related to IP and IT and data protection compliance. He is a member of the Portuguese and Macau Bar Associations.

Michel Molitor is one of the founding partners of MOLITOR Avocats à la Cour. He is the personal contact partner for many of the firm's national and international clients in numerous industry sectors. He has developed sound expertise on privacy and data protection compliance, in particular in the field of employment relationships and in the banking sector. He is an active member of the International Bar Association (IBA), the Association of Luxembourg Banking Lawyers (ALJB), the Association Luxembourgeoise pour l'Arbitrage (ALA), and of the Luxembourg Investment Fund Association (ALFI). He is also Vice-President of the Employment Law Specialist Association Luxembourg (ELSA) and a member of the European Employment Law Association (EELA).

Miklós Molnár is an associate with Schönherr in Budapest, where he specializes in competition law, M&A transactions, and general corporate work. In the past two years he has been involved in a number of significant transactions for both domestic and foreign clients of the firm. Mr Molnár joined the firm as an intern while finalizing his law studies at the Eötvös Loránd University of Budapest (ELTE) in August 2006. He will earn a further degree at the University Pázmány Péter Budapest, Deák Institute of Postgraduate Studies, in Competition Law in 2010. Previously, he studied competition law at the University of Salzburg and also studied at the Justus-Liebig University in Giessen.

Martin Nedelka is partner in Schönherr's Prague and Bratislava office. He is a member of the Czech, Slovak, and Brussels Bar. Martin specializes in competition law, regulatory matters (energy, telecommunications), and public procurement. Martin also focuses on data protection law.

Magdalena Nilsson is an associate at the Warsaw office of Schönherr. She has been a member of the Polish bar since 2006. Magdalena specializes in banking law and mergers and acquisitions. She has experience in advising international financial institutions and banks in connection with bank lending transactions as well as in banking regulations and supervision. She has also been involved in a wide range of share and asset acquisitions.

Jill Niu is a counsellor at Lee & Li, Attorneys-at-Law, the largest law firm in Taiwan. Her practice focuses on medical and healthcare laws (including compliance of privacy and data protection in conducting clinical studies and marketing programmes), employment and labour laws, corporate governance, and compliance and tax litigation. Ms Niu also acts as a counsel to a local association of multinational pharmaceutical firms and has been advising the association on the code of marketing practices, including privacy and data protection issues, from the perspective of clinical trial laws and regulations and the Personal Data Protection Act. She has been a member of the Taipei Bar Association since 1992.

Dr iur Ants Nõmper is a partner in Raidla Lejins & Norcous' Tallinn office and one of the top specialists in Estonia in the areas of IT and IP, data protection, and medical law. He gained his B.A. from the University of Tartu, an LLM from the University of Göttingen, Germany, and a PhD from the University of Tartu. Ants joined Raidla Lejins & Norcous in 1999. He has been a member of the Estonian Bar Association also since 1999. Ants is a lecturer of medical law at the University of Tartu. Throughout the years Ants has been actively involved in legislative drafting in Estonia (Human Gene Research Act, Health Insurance Act, Unemployment Insurance Act, etc.).

Rune Opdahl is a lawyer in Wiersholm and a member of the Norwegian Bar Association since 2006. Wiersholm is one of Norway's leading law firms – an internationally oriented firm dedicated to business law, operational legal services, and litigation. Opdahl specializes in IP and IT law and has particular expertise in copyright, data protection/privacy, and e-commerce. He primarily works with enterprises in the media, Internet, technology, telecom, and broadcasting industries. Opdahl has been involved in comprehensive investigations, e-discoveries, and other forensic data collections. He lectures on IP law subjects at the University of Oslo.

Tomaž Petrovič is a Slovenian attorney and partner of Filipov, Petrovič, Jeraj in partnerji in cooperation with Schönherr, where he specializes in dispute resolution and regulatory, public, and environmental law. His focus includes data protection law, telecommunications, and public procurement and other regulatory issues. He frequently advises the clients of Schönherr on all kinds of privacy and data protection matters, including outsourcing projects, installation of joint information and whistleblowing systems, as well as international data transfer issues. Tomaž Petrovič is co-author of articles on public law, including data protection and privacy law.

Przemysław Pietrzak is a partner at the Warsaw office of Schönherr. He has been a member of the Polish Bar since 1996 and has worked in Polish real estate and M&A transactions advising major international investors from all over Europe, North America, and Asia. Mr Pietrzak also regularly advises clients on Polish public procurement and construction law issues.

Silvia Popa is a senior associate with Schönherr si Asociatii SCA in Bucharest, Romania, having joined the practice in early 2006. Silvia has focused her practice on civil and administrative law and litigation. Silvia has been advising international and domestic clients on legal and data protection compliance matters, before and after Romania's accession to the EU. Silvia holds a Law Degree from the University of Timisoara in Romania and an LLM in European and International Law from the University of Amsterdam. Silvia has been a member of the Timis Bar in Romania since 2004.

Charlotte Portmann is a Senior Associate in Howrey's Paris office. Her practice covers all aspects of IP rights, including trademarks, design, copyright, and unfair competition issues. She deals with both contentious and non-contentious matters for a wide variety of clients in sectors such as beverages, consumer goods, and software. Her practice focuses on trademark prosecution and litigation as well as contractual matters and customs interventions. Moreover, she also has experience in data protection issues, such as whistleblowing and cross-border personal data transfers.

Dr Jürg Schneider is a managing associate in the Information Technology, Intellectual Property and Competition Team of Walder Wyss Ltd., Switzerland. Dr Schneider advises national and multinational companies on privacy and data protection compliance, in particular regarding the processing and international transfer of personal data. He also advises IT users as well as IT service providers and software publishers on legal aspects of information technology. Dr Schneider regularly lectures and publishes on IT law topics, in particular in the field of data protection. Prior to joining Walder Wyss Ltd., Dr Schneider worked at a Neuchâtel law firm and as a research assistant at the University of Neuchâtel. He was admitted to the Swiss Bar in 1995.

Dr Ueli Sommer is a partner of Walder Wyss Ltd., Switzerland. Dr Sommer heads the employment practice group. He has many years of experience in all aspects of employment law, including all data protection aspects in the employment field. Dr Sommer regularly lectures and publishes on employment and data protection topics. Dr Sommer is a board member of the European Employment Lawyers Association (EELA) and Co-Chair of the International Employment Committee of the International Section of American Bar Association (ABA). He was admitted to the Swiss Bar in 1995.

Sarmis Spilbergs is an associate with Klavins&Slaidins LAWIN based in Riga, Latvia. Mr Spilbergs, among others, specializes in product and services licensing, IT, e-commerce, telecommunications, personal data protection, and intellectual property law. He frequently advises large multinational companies in structuring their personal data flows (client, employee, supplier data) with other group companies worldwide, and ensuring compliance with local legislation. Mr Spilbergs has also assisted with registration of personal data processing with the competent authorities, performed review and adaptation of model contracts and advised on applicable requirements towards consent clauses for data subjects. His LLM and bachelor's thesis were both related to personal data protection in the online environment. Mr Spilbergs was admitted to the Latvian Bar in 2008.

Mirena Taskova is an attorney with Schönherr in cooperation with Advokatsko druzhestvo Andreev, Stoyanov & Tsekova in Sofia, Bulgaria. She has extensive experience with numerous national and international companies in various aspects of processing and transfer of personal data, as well as on real estate matters. Ms Taskova is a member of the Sofia Law Bar Association.

Álvaro Velázquez is a senior associate at Howrey Martínez Lage in Madrid. Mr Velázquez has extensive experience in litigating IP rights, including patents, designs, trademarks, copyrights, and domain names, before civil commercial, criminal, and administrative courts. He also litigates and advises with regard to unfair competition, advertising, labelling, and data protection issues for international clients across a range of sectors, including pharmaceuticals, life sciences, telecoms, and engineering, also coordinating with other jurisdictions in cross-border issues. Mr Velázquez regularly teaches IP law and related matters in several specialized seminars and master's degree programmes coordinated by Spanish universities and post-graduate law schools.

Markus H. Wanger was born in 1955, followed legal studies at the University of Innsbruck, and obtained Dr.iuris in 1981. He is a founder and senior partner of WANGER Advokatur and Chairman of the Trust Company WANGER Wirtschaft-streuhand AG, both in Vaduz and Liechtenstein. He is also a Fellow of the Chartered Institute of Arbitrators, London, and Court Judge of Arbitrations for Sports (CAS/TAS), Lausanne, former President of the Liechtenstein Association of Trustees, he is a member of the Board of Examination for lawyers, Vaduz, and was lecturer for Liechtenstein Company law at HTW Chur, Hochschule fur Technik und Wirtschaft. He is the author of various publications on Liechtenstein and international law. Among others, he wrote a commentary on Liechtenstein trademarks and compendiums on foundations, arbitration, trust, and taxes, and is co-author of *Foundations in Europe* (Bertelsmann Verlag, 2000), and *Stiftungen in Theorie, Recht und Praxis, Handbuch für ein modernes Stiftungswesen,* (Duncker & Humblot, Berlin, 2005). He is an author of various publications in law gazettes and magazines and frequent lecturer on Liechtenstein law at, among others, the Offshore Symposium at Jesus College, Oxford.

Liad Whatstein is the head of the litigation department of Dr Shlomo Cohen & Co. and has been a member of the Israel Bar since 1991. Mr Whatstein graduated with distinction from the Tel Aviv University and the London School of Economics and was the associate editor of the *Tel Aviv University Law Review*. He currently serves as the Chairman of the Intellectual Property Committee of the Israeli Bar Association and is a frequent speaker on IP and IT matters. Mr Whatstein has vast experience in some of Israel's most complex and widely publicized IP and IT conflicts. He has been successfully representing numerous international clients in the IP and IT field and is constantly acclaimed by international directories for his achievements and skills.

Peter Zorin has been an associate with Schönherr since 2009. He specializes in data protection law. He has helped with research on various articles on public law, especially on data protection and privacy law. He previously worked for the European Court of Justice, Slovenian language division, Jurist linguist, Luxembourg/Luxembourg (2008–2009).

Chapter 1

Introduction

*Catrien Noorda**

Over the past ten years the amount of electronically stored information (ESI) within corporations has increased dramatically. Given a US discovery model that expressly recognizes the importance of the preservation, collection, and production of ESI, multinational corporations are more and more confronted with the conflict between US e-discovery and national laws protecting ESI. Laws protecting ESI are for the largest part based on the right of individuals to protection of their privacy. However, they can also be based on banking secrecy or local laws simply blocking the transfer of data for discovery purposes. A party that is confronted with a request to produce ESI is often placed in a dilemma: satisfy compulsory US discovery obligations or comply with the local laws. US courts do not have much empathy for victims of this dilemma, and failure to produce evidence can result in losing the case. On the other hand, companies that ignore their local laws because of the importance of litigation may face severe sanctions. In October 2009, the Berlin Data Protection Commissioner imposed on the German railways company Deutsche Bahn a fine of Euros (EUR) 1.123 million for, *inter alia*, monitoring employees' workplace access to external e-mail accounts.[1]

This book aims to provide multinational companies with some insight on the US e-discovery model – why it is important to comply, the obstacles they may

---

* Howrey LLP, Amsterdam, the Netherlands.
1. Press release of the Berlin Data Protection Commissioner of 23 Oct. 2009.

encounter in various jurisdictions where they may be located, the sanctions risked, and practical solutions where conflicts arise.

To this end, first the US e-discovery model will be explained (Chapter 2), and second the European Data Protection Directive and the way in which it restricts data processing for discovery purposes will be discussed (Chapter 3). Chapter 4 discusses the Hague Convention on the Taking of Evidence. Chapters 5 and 6 contains overviews of the local data privacy and other restricting laws of most European Union (EU) jurisdictions and deals with the laws in some countries in the rest of the world.

Chapter 2
US E-discovery

*Gil Keteltas**

Central component of US E-discovery

I. THE EVOLUTION OF E-DISCOVERY IN THE UNITED STATES

Pretrial discovery is a central component of litigation in the United States. US discovery typically involves, among other things, extensive disclosure (or 'production') of documents by all parties to the litigation. In many cases, these document productions are voluminous. Discovery has taken on added complexity in today's litigation environment, where over 90% of information generated by corporations is electronically stored information (ESI).[1] As a result of changes to federal and state procedural rules in the United States, the production of ESI has become a fact of life for US lawyers.

While ESI is now ubiquitous, it can be difficult to identify all sources of ESI that are relevant in specific litigation. ESI is inherently different than paper records. It is easy to generate, duplicate, and circulate. It is also inexpensive to save or archive. Single computers, thumb drives, or backup tapes can hold volumes ranging from millions to tens of millions of pages. Storage of ESI is typically not

---

*   Gil Keteltas, Howrey LLP, Washington, D.C.
1. *In re Bristol-Myers Squibb Sec. Litig.*, 205 F.R.D. 437, 440 n. 2 (D.N.J. 2002). See also *Best Practices Recommendations & Principles for Addressing Electronic Document Production*, in THE SEDONA PRINCIPLES: SECOND EDITION, 1 (June 2007) ('While twenty years ago, PCs were a novelty and email was virtually nonexistent, today more than 90% of all information is created in an electronic format').

Catrien Noorda & Stefan Hanloser, *E-Discovery and Data Privacy*, pp. 3–12.

ESI STORAGE USUALLY NOT CENTRALIZED [handwritten]

centralized. Relevant ESI may be found on multiple desktop and laptop computers, numerous servers, loose and portable storage media such as DVDs, and a range of handheld devices such as cell phones and PDAs. Moreover, data can be lost by actions of individual employees or by automated processes used to manage and reduce the volume of data retained by a corporation.[2]

51 20 PRODUCTION [handwritten] As a result, production of relevant ESI in litigation requires that it first be properly identified and preserved (typically at the outset of litigation), collected, and reviewed. Also, ESI cannot simply be printed and turned over to an opponent. It must be produced in a reasonably usable electronic format that, usually, will include data that would not necessarily be apparent from the printed page (including user-specific data, such as the name of the author, the precise folder and computer on which the document was found, and the date the document was last accessed).[3] These difficulties may be magnified in government investigations where the scope of the investigation may not be apparent at the start (or may change in the course of the investigation).[4]

II.   THE RULES OF E-DISCOVERY

2006 change to Fed. Rules of Civil Procedure [handwritten]

While discovery in US litigation historically focused on paper records, in December 2006, the Federal Rules of Civil Procedure were amended to address ESI. The amendments were intended to 'confirm that discovery of electronically stored information stands on equal footing with discovery of paper documents'.[5] The rules do not define 'electronically stored information,' but the phrase was intended to 'cover all current types of computer-based information', and to be 'flexible enough to encompass future changes and developments'.[6]

A.   WHAT IS ESI?

obvious ESI [handwritten]

It is noteworthy that relevant ESI can be obvious (e.g., e-mail, word processing documents, spreadsheets), but it can also involve less obvious and, arguably, more

---

2. See Rice, P., ELECTRONIC EVIDENCE: LAW AND PRACTICE (ABA Publishing, 2nd edn., 2008), 2–8.
3. Fed. R. Civ. P. 34. See also Fed. R. Civ. P. 34(b) advisory committee's note ('If the responding party ordinarily maintains the information . . . in a way that makes it searchable by electronic means, the information should not be produced in a form that removes or significantly degrades this feature').
4. Willenken, K., 'How to Handle Hard Drives in Government Probe', THE NATIONAL LAW JOURNAL, 26 Mar. 2010 ('In the absence of court supervision or rules, and given the tendency of government investigations to change focus over time, a responding company cannot hope to identify and preserve every byte of relevant electronically stored information. There is an element of fortune-telling inherent in every preservation effort'.).
5. Fed. R. Civ. P. 34(a) advisory committee's note.
6. Fed. R. Civ. P. 34(a) advisory committee's note ('The wide variety of computer systems currently in use, and the rapidity of technological change, counsel against a limiting or precise definition of electronically stored information').

fleeting forms of information, including, when relevant, data temporarily stored by computers for minutes or even seconds. For example, in *Columbia Pictures v. Bunnell*, owners of movie and television rights claimed that the defendant was facilitating unauthorized distribution of their materials over the Internet.[7] In discovery, plaintiffs sought server logs from the random access memory (RAM) of computers in the United States and the Netherlands. The defendant argued that this information was ephemeral and therefore could not be electronically *stored* information.   *ESI WHICH MUST BE PRESERVED*

The potential sources of ESI that must be preserved are those sources that are relevant to the litigation. Depending on the facts, claims, and defences, a party may have to consider sources including online collaboration rooms, instant messaging chat logs, social networking sites, thumb drives, and tiny memory cards. 'While a litigant is under no duty to keep or retain every document in its possession once a complaint is filed, it is under a duty to preserve what it knows, or reasonably should know, is relevant in the action, is reasonably calculated to lead to the discovery of admissible evidence, is reasonably likely to be requested during discovery, and/or is the subject of a pending discovery request'.[8]

In addition, a party subject to a duty to preserve is also required to preserve uniquely relevant information even if it believes that information is not reasonably accessible (e.g., because it is stored on legacy media [tapes] that the company is no longer able to read, or can only read at great expense). The obligation to preserve can exist even where the company may not ultimately have an obligation to produce the information.   *PRESERVATION*

Preservation decisions must be reasonable at the time they are made based on the specific facts, claims, and defences at issue in the litigation. Decisions should also be documented so they can be defended years later (if necessary).   *DECISIONS*

B.   DISCOVERY IN US LITIGATION

To understand why the preservation, collection, review, and production of ESI have become such dominant issues in US litigation, one needs to consider the key differences between US litigation and litigation outside the United States.

---

7. *Columbia Pictures Indus. v. Bunnell*, No. CV 06-1093 FMC (JCx), 2007 US Dist. LEXIS 46364 (C.D. Cal. 29 May 2007), *review denied*, 245 F.R.D. 443 (C.D. Cal. 2007). See also *Healthcare Advocates, Inc. v. Harding*, 497 F. Supp.2d 627 (E.D. Pa. 2007) (court implicitly concluded that information temporarily stored in cache files was discoverable).
8. *Jeanblanc v. Oliver T. Carr Co.*, No. 91-0128 (JHG), 1992 US Dist. LEXIS 10765, *5 (D.D.C. 24 Jul 1992) (quoting *Wm. T. Thompson Co. v. General Nutrition Corp., Inc.*, 593 F. Supp. 1443, 1447 [C.D. Cal. 1984]). See also THE SEDONA FRAMEWORK, *id.* at 5 ('The main focus of ESI discovery is the content and not the container. That is, any kind of relevant ESI in any computer system is fair game. This includes all forms of ESI [e-mail, word processing, spreadsheets, etc.] as well as all types of ESI systems [e-mail servers, file servers, database systems, etc.]. If ESI content is relevant to a dispute, then it is a potential target of discovery, regardless of format or location'.).

Gil Keteltas [handwritten: LITIGATION OUTSIDE U.S.] [handwritten: BEGINNINGS OF LITIGATION]

Outside the United States, litigation typically begins with a complaint that sets forth detailed allegations of specific facts. Pretrial discovery is limited, with few documents changing hands. And depositions in which a witness must respond to hours of questioning based, in many cases, on the documents exchanged in discovery are also limited. Cases are often tried by judges who determine the facts. The data of individual employees are rarely mined or disclosed in litigation. Indeed, in many countries, the privacy of individual data is viewed as a human right.

In contrast, discovery in US litigation is a right, and key information must be provided to an opponent even without a request from the opponent.[9] US discovery rules permit discovery of all information relevant to a claim or defence in pending litigation (with the exception of information protected from disclosure by an applicable privilege, such as the attorney-client privilege). And relevance is broadly defined to include evidence admissible in court as well as evidence that is 'reasonably calculated to lead to the discovery of admissible evidence'.[10] A party receiving a discovery request must produce all relevant material within the company's possession, custody, or control (which may include material held by foreign-based entities who are not formal parties to the litigation).[11]

The Rules of Civil Procedure that govern litigation in US federal courts 'do not require a claimant to set out in detail the facts upon which he bases his claim. To the contrary, all the Rules require is "a short and plain statement of the claim" that will give the defendant fair notice of what the plaintiff's claim is and the grounds upon which it rests.'[12] Once this 'notice pleading requirement' is met, procedural rules provide for the facts to be developed through broad discovery.

A foreign entity might also be subject to a third-party discovery subpoena where the US court has jurisdiction over the third party (or where appropriate Hague Convention procedures are followed). Under federal law, a third-party subpoena can 'command each person to whom it is directed to attend and give testimony or to produce and permit inspection, copying, testing, or sampling of

[handwritten: 3rd PARTY SUBPOENA]

---

9. For example, without waiting for an opponent's discovery request a party must provide, among other things, 'a copy – or a description by category and location – of all documents, electronically stored information, and tangible things that the disclosing party has in its possession, custody, or control and may use to support its claims or defenses, unless the use would be solely for impeachment'. Fed. R. Civ. P. 26(a)(1)(A)(ii).

10. Fed. R. Civ. P. 26(b).

11. In addition, when a duty to preserve records is triggered, that duty covers data within the company's possession, custody, or control.

12. *Conley v. Gibson*, 355 US 41, 47 (US 1957). See also Fed. R. Civ. P. 8(a)(2). These pleading requirements are still the subject of dispute and discussion, as made clear in US Supreme Court cases decided in the past few years. See *Ashcroft v. Iqbal*, 129 S. Ct. 1937, 1949 (US 2009) ('the pleading standard Rule 8 announces does not require "detailed factual allegations", but it demands more than an unadorned, the-defendant-unlawfully-harmed-me accusation'); *Bell Atl. Corp. v. Twombly*, 550 US 544 (US 2007) (requiring 'enough facts to state a claim to relief that is plausible on its face').

[handwritten: 3rd parties prot protected from undue burd & exp]

designated books, documents, electronically stored information, or tangible things in the possession, custody or control of that person'.[13]

Still, third parties are subject to protection from undue burden and expense, and must be permitted reasonable time to object or respond to a subpoena.[14] A person's status as a non-party is typically afforded special weight in evaluating burden.[15] And courts may be more likely to credit the burdens of addressing international privacy concerns in considering the burdens of third-party subpoenas.

III. US DISCOVERY AND INTERNATIONAL PRIVACY LAWS

[handwritten: TENSION B/T U.S. & INT'L PRIVACY]

Where ESI is located outside the United States, the very steps that US procedural rules require may run afoul of data protection requirements in the country where the ESI resides. The tension between US discovery rules and international data privacy protections is well documented[16] and has meaningful practical implications. The US case law shows that a breakdown in any step of the ESI discovery process can trigger motions for sanctions, which could range from monetary sanctions to complete dismissal of a party's case (where, for example, the party willfully destroyed relevant and important documents). Indeed, in some cases failures of preservation, collection, and review seemingly eclipse the main dispute between the parties. But the disclosure of information in a US litigation or investigation could violate the blocking statute of the country in which the data is found and subject the disclosing party to sanctions, including civil penalties or even criminal penalties.

A.   US Approach toward Foreign Privacy Laws

US courts often do not share foreign sensibilities concerning data privacy or the importance of foreign blocking statutes. For example, in rejecting claims that

---

13. Fed. R. Civ. P. 45(a)(1)(C)(emphasis added).
14. The 2006 amendments to Rule 45 clarified the concept of undue burden in the context of electronically stored information: '[a] person responding [to a subpoena] need not provide discovery of electronically stored information from sources that the person identifies as not reasonably accessible because of undue burden or cost'. Fed. R. Civ. P. 45. But this provision envisions the burden imposed by large volumes of information that are difficult to access, or legacy data formats that require special processing or review tools.
15. See Fed. R. Civ. P. 45(c)(1); *N.C. Right to Life, Inc. v. Leake*, 231 F.R.D. 49, 53 (D.D.C. 2005).
16. Losey, Ralph C., Introduction to E-Discovery: New Cases, Ideas, and Techniques (1st edn., 2009) 366 ('Electronic discovery has become the front line of the conflict between the US legal system and the rest of the world. Whenever a foreign company is sued in the US, it becomes subject to discovery requests, which today means primarily discovery of the information kept in its computers [ESI]. When the information is in the company's computers in its home country, or involves non-US employees who enjoy fundamental privacy rights that we do not, a conflict of law issue arises'.).

disclosure of information held by a Malaysian bank would violate Malaysian secrecy requirements, a US magistrate judge observed that the party resisting discovery did not provide 'any authority regarding the likelihood of prosecution, conviction, or imposition of the maximum sentence or fine, if a party is compelled to disclose information pursuant to a court order'.[17]

But the US view that foreign data protection rules are 'paper tigers'[18] is being tested by emerging enforcement activity. For example, a French attorney was convicted for violating the French Blocking Statute,[19] which bars a party from 'requesting, seeking, or disclosing in writing, orally or in any other form, documents or information of an economic, commercial, industrial, financial or technical nature for the purposes of constituting evidence in view of foreign judicial or administrative proceedings'.[20] But even this conviction is likely to be distinguished by US courts given unique allegations that the French attorney misled a witness to obtain information for use in a foreign proceeding.

And while US courts have shown little interest in enforcing foreign blocking statutes, foreign data protection authorities have not embraced the US litigation model that permits the wide-ranging search, review, and production of data (including personal data).[21]

B.   INFORMATION LOCATED OUTSIDE THE UNITED STATES MAY BE SUBJECT TO DISCOVERY IN US LITIGATION

There are a number of scenarios in which a non-US entity may face US discovery demands. The first and most obvious is where the entity is a party to US litigation. Even as to parties to litigation, there may be distinctions made between those who

---

17. *Gucci Am., Inc. v. Curveal Fashion*, No. 09 Civ. 8458 (RJS)(THK), 2010 US Dist. LEXIS 20834 (S.D.N.Y., 8 Mar. 2010). See also *Accessdata Corp. v. Alste Techs GmbH*, No. 2:08cv569, 2010 US Dist. LEXIS 4566 (D.Utah, 21 Jan. 2010) (rejecting unsupported claim that disclosure of information would constitute a major breach of German privacy law). This assumption of lax enforcement is not limited to US courts. See *Heidberg v. Grosvener*, (1993) Q.B., 324, 325 (U.K.) (litigant had no reasonable basis to fear prosecution under French blocking statute 'where there was no evidence that any person had ever been prosecuted for breach' of the statute).
18. The phrase 'paper tiger' comes from a Chinese phrase meaning something that appears threatening but is really harmless. See <http://en.wikipedia.org/wiki/Paper_tiger>.
19. *In re Advocat 'Christopher X'*, Cour de Cassation, French Supreme Court, 12 Dec. 2007, Appeal n 07-83228.
20. French Penal Law No. 80-538 (16 Jul. 1980).
21. See THE SEDONA CONFERENCE FRAMEWORK FOR ANALYSIS OF CROSS-BORDER DISCOVERY CONFLICTS: A PRACTICAL GUIDE TO NAVIGATING THE COMPETING CURRENTS OF INTERNATIONAL DATA PRIVACY AND E-DISCOVERY, 2008 Public Comment Version, 1–2 (available at <www.thesedonaconference. org>, hereafter 'The Sedona Framework') (discussing the conflict between US discovery and foreign data privacy rules); Art. 29 Data Protection Working Party, Working Document 1/2009 on pretrial discovery for cross-border civil litigation (11 Feb. 2009) (00229/09/EN7WP) (WP 158) at 2 (discussing the 'tension between the disclosure obligations under US litigation or regulatory rules and the application of the data protection requirements of the EU').

seek the benefits of a US court as plaintiffs versus those who involuntarily are brought into US courts (and fight jurisdiction). In other words, where the foreign entity is a plaintiff in the United States and seeks the protections of a US court, claims that it should not be subject to discovery under US procedural rules will certainly be rejected by the court.

In *Reino de Espana v. American Bureau of Shipping*,[22] the Kingdom of Spain sued in federal court in the Southern District of New York to recover damages in connection with an oil spill off the coast of Spain. The defendant sought discovery of e-mail communications and other electronic records. Spain claimed that such records no longer existed, that its production was sufficient, and that privacy laws precluded further production from individual government computers.

The Court rejected Spain's arguments and found that privacy laws were not a barrier to production. The Court noted:

> This litigation is in the Southern District instead of a court in Spain. Discovery is governed by the Federal Rules of Civil Procedure, not Spanish privacy laws and government privileges. It was incumbent upon Spain to identify and preserve relevant documentation related to its claims. The failure to conduct discovery in accordance with the Federal Rules and this Court's rules is sanctionable.[23]

After finding that the missing records were directly relevant to the claims at issue, and that Spain had 'failed to place a timely and adequate litigation hold in its agencies and ministries', the Court entered monetary sanctions and considered (but did not order) an adverse inference instruction.[24] Where a foreign entity does not seek out the benefits of the US court system, but is sued in the United States, discovery is still likely (although it may be delayed pending resolution of the question of whether the court has jurisdiction over the foreign party). But jurisdictional claims can take time to litigate. And even a foreign entity with a strong jurisdictional defence takes a significant risk if it does not take steps to preserve potentially relevant information while jurisdictional matters are litigated (presuming that the court has even stayed discovery while the jurisdictional matters are litigated).[25]

---

22. No. 03 Civ. 3573, 2006 WL 3208579 (S.D.N.Y. 3 Nov. 2006).
23. *Ibid.*, at note 19.
24. *Reino de Espana v. Am. Bureau of Shipping*, No. 03 Civ. 3573, 2007 US Dist. LEXIS 41498, *25 (S.D.N.Y. 6 Jun. 2007). An adverse inference instruction varies by circumstance, but typically involves an instruction to a jury that it may presume that information that was lost or destroyed would be harmful to the case of the party that lost or destroyed the information.
25. See *In re NTL, Inc. Sec. Litig.*, 244 F.R.D. 179 (S.D.N.Y. 2007) ('Defendant NTL Europe does not seriously contend that plaintiffs' failure to seek a preservation order should let defendant NTL Europe off the hook of its preservation obligations'.). *But see Fortis Corporate Ins., SA v. Viken Ship Mgmt. AS*, 2007 WL 3287357 (N.D. Ohio 2007) (refusing to sanction foreign corporation for its failure to preserve, but observing that '[p]erhaps in the fullness of time foreign-based companies doing business in the United States will be held to the same "litigation holds" and other devices now routinely applied by litigants here to make sure pertinent documents and other materials are retained and produced. And perhaps they should be held to the

In *Columbia Pictures Indus. v. Bunnell*,[26] the defendants operated a website, utilizing servers in the Netherlands that allowed users to find and download files over a peer-to-peer network. Owners of movie and television rights brought this copyright infringement action alleging that the defendants facilitated unauthorized distribution of copyrighted programming over the Internet. The plaintiffs sought a discovery order requiring the preservation of server logs from computers in the United States and the Netherlands. The defendants claimed that information on those logs was ephemeral (and not electronically *stored* information) and need not be preserved. They also asserted that the blocking statute of the Netherlands prohibited preservation or production of such data.

The court rejected these arguments and, on the subject of the blocking statutes, explained that 'even if the Netherlands' statute applies and is read to prohibit defendants' preservation or production of the Server Log Data, it is well settled that foreign blocking statutes do not deprive an American court of the power to order a party subject to its jurisdiction to produce (let alone preserve) evidence even though the act of production may violate that statute'.[27] The Court specifically highlighted that the dispute over production of information did not relieve plaintiffs of their 'obligation to preserve' the server logs.

Some parties attempt to avoid jurisdictional questions by seeking documents located outside the United States from a company located in the United States. For example, a US company may be a party to a lawsuit (or a recipient of a third-party subpoena). The opposing party may pursue documents located outside the United States, possibly in the possession of a related corporation. These cases can present a thorny issue because a party must preserve, search, and produce information within its possession, custody, or control.[28] 'If the producing party has the legal right or the practical ability to obtain the documents, then it is deemed to have "control", even if the documents are actually in the possession of a non-party'.[29]

---

same standards in an era of ever-expanding global trade. Increasingly negligence on the other side of the globe can cause injury locally'.).

26. 2007 US Dist. LEXIS 63620 (C.D. Cal. 24 Aug. 2007), *review denied Columbia Pictures, Inc. v. Bunnell*, 245 F.R.D. 443 (C.D. Cal. 2007) ('[T]he Magistrate Judge properly found that Defendants had failed to meet their burden in establishing that Netherlands law would prohibit retention of the Server Log Data or production of an encrypted, anonymous version of that data to Plaintiffs'.).

27. *Ibid.*, at note 49.

28. Fed. R. Civ. P. 16, 26 and 45(a)(1)(C).

29. See, e.g., *Gerling v. Int'l Ins. Co. v. Commissioner,* 839 F.2d 131, 141 (3d Cir. 1988) ('Where the relationship is thus such that the agent-subsidiary can secure documents of the principal-parent to meet its own business needs and documents helpful for use in the litigation, the courts will not permit the agent-subsidiary to deny control for purposes of discovery by an opposing party'.); *In re Flag Telecom Holdings, Ltd. Sec. Litig.,* 236 F.R.D. 177, 180 (S.D.N.Y. 2006), citing *Riddell Sports Inc. v. Brooks,* 158 F.R.D. 555, 558 (S.D.N.Y. 1994); *Yong Ki Hong v. KBS Am, Inc.,* No. 05-Civ.-1177, 2006 US Dist. LEXIS 89700, *18 (E.D.N.Y. 12 Dec. 2006) ('the KBS Defendants . . . are to produce any responsive documents in their possession, custody or control, whether these documents are located in the United States or Korea. This includes documents that may not be in their possession, but which they have the legal right or practical

[handwritten annotation: DIFFERENT COURT RULINGS ON QUESTION OF DISCOVERY & control]

Location of the information does not determine control, and a party can have control over documents located abroad.[30]

Numerous courts have wrestled with the question of whether discovery of foreign documents can be had through a US corporation. Where the US entity has the practical ability to obtain documents from a foreign relative in the ordinary course of business, some courts have found control for the purposes of requiring the US entity to produce the foreign records.[31] Others, however, have held that the control is not determined by practical ability to access documents but must be based on the legal right to obtain documents.[32] Although certainly not the prevailing view, one state court has declared that corporate relationships alone constitute 'sufficient control for purposes of requiring discovery'.[33]

These questions become more difficult where global networks are interconnected. Employees may share and access information in virtual collaboration rooms. Information of one entity may be accessible to employees in the United States, either by design or because steps were not taken to prevent access. These are questions that corporate relatives with potential discovery exposure in the United States should weigh in setting up their networks.[34] Moreover, a corporation seeking to resist discovery on the grounds that it does not have control over

[handwritten annotation: CONSIDERATION IN NETWORK SET]

---

ability to obtain'.); *In re Uranium Antitrust Litigation*, 480 F. Supp. 1138 (D. Ill. 1979) (defendants ordered to produce documents located outside the United States).

30. *Ibid.*, See also *In re Marc Rich & Co., A.G.*, 707 F.2d 663, 667 (2d Cir.), *cert. denied*, 463 US 1215 (1983); *Cooper Indus., Inc. v. British Aerospace, Inc.*, 102 F.R.D. 918, 920 (S.D.N.Y. 1984).

31. See, e.g., *SEC v. Credit Bancorp, Ltd.*, 194 F.R.D. 469 (S.D.N.Y. 2000) ('One of the circumstances which warrants a finding of control is where a corporate entity has the ability in the ordinary course of business to obtain documents held by another corporate entity'); *Cooper Industries v. British Aerospace*, 102 F.R.D. 918 (S.D.N.Y. 1984) (refusing to require application of Hague Convention procedures, the Court explained that '[t]he documents plaintiff seeks all relate to the planes that defendant works with every day; it is inconceivable that defendant would not have access to these documents and the ability to obtain them for its usual business').

32. *In re Citric Acid Litig.*, 191 F.3d 1090 (9th Cir. 1999) ('[W]e conclude – consistent with all of our sister circuits who have addressed the issue – that the legal control test is the proper standard under Rule 45. . . . Ordering a party to produce documents that it does not have the legal right to obtain will oftentimes be futile, precisely because the party has no certain way of getting those documents'.). *In re Nortel Networks Corp. Sec. Litig.*, 2004 US Dist. LEXIS 19129 (S.D.N.Y. 23 Sept. 2004) (rejecting production of Canadian documents though US relative where plaintiffs were unable 'to identify any enforceable obligation' of the Canadian entity to provide access to the information and where an agreement between the Canadian and US entities left the question of access to the discretion of the Canadian firm).

33. *Strom v. American Honda Motor Co.*, 423 Mass. 330, 667 N.E.2d 1137 (1996) (finding sufficient legal control when 'the information sought is in the possession or custody of a wholly owning parent [or virtually wholly owning] or wholly owned [or virtually wholly owned] subsidiary corporation, or of a corporation affiliated through such a parent or subsidiary').

34. *Nortel Networks, ibid.* (rejecting the contention that discovery should be allowed because the US entity could electronically access documents in the possession of the Canadian entity on the grounds that the assumption was speculative and 'without foundation, and that any electronic communications software is not designed to permit such access by the American firm').

the documents at issue will likely bear the burden of establishing that defence to production.[35]

IV.   OUTLOOK

This book should provide the practitioner a basis to understand where US discovery requirements may conflict with country-specific blocking statutes or other data protection requirements. Armed with this information, a practitioner will be prepared to put in place protections that may permit controlled disclosure of information, to negotiate limits to discovery with an opponent, or to advocate that a court limit discovery to minimize international data protection concerns. This information should also be useful to corporations that are considering how to manage the cross-border flow or accessibility of information.

---

35. *Cf. In re Parmalat Sec. Litig.*, 2005 US Dist. LEXIS 12554 (S.D.N.Y. 28 Jun. 2005) (Court overruled objections to production where the record did not establish that documents were 'unobtainable by subpoena or other compulsory process').

Chapter 3

EU Data Privacy Regulations

*Catrien Noorda and Stefan Hanloser**

I.   INTRODUCTION

The concept of data privacy aims at protecting an individual against any potential harm that could derive from a detrimental processing of information related to the individual. Whether or not a processing of personal information is detrimental, and thus may be objected to by the individual, basically depends on the role the individual plays in social and economic life. The indispensable interaction between an individual and the environment requires a mandatory set of permissible data processing, which is beyond the individual's self-determination in data privacy matters. When it comes to the legitimate processing of an individual's data within an e-discovery process, the focus lies on these statutory permissions, since for practical reasons consent to the intended data processing can hardly be obtained from all individuals whose personal data are affected.

II.   REGULATORY FRAMEWORK

Often a request for the production of information includes personal data that are stored by different legal entities in various countries around the world. As a

*   Howrey LLP, Amsterdam, the Netherlands; Dr Stefan Hanloser, Howrey LLP, Munich, Germany.

Catrien Noorda & Stefan Hanloser, *E-Discovery and Data Privacy*, pp. 13–27.
© 2011 Kluwer Law International BV, The Netherlands.

consequence, the responding party, that is, the party that receives a request for the production of information, has to comply with the data privacy laws in several jurisdictions. Whereas it is generally understood that data privacy laws can vary considerable, it is a common misunderstanding that the data protection laws of the Member States of the European Union (EU) are fully harmonized.[1] Certain standards for the protection of personal data are in fact laid down in the EU Data Protection Directive of 24 October 1995[2] and in the E-Privacy Directive of 12 July 2002.[3] However, the answer of whether a specific processing of personal data is permissible in an EU Member State can never be found in the EU Data Protection Directive but only in the Member State's domestic data protection law. As a matter of fact, the statutory prerequisites for lawful data processing, both from a procedural and a material point of view, vary considerably among the Member States, let alone the different enforcement practices by the data protection supervisory authorities and courts.[4]

Regarding the regulatory data protection framework in Europe, it is worth noting that with the entry into force of the Lisbon Treaty[5] on 1 December 2009, the Charter of Fundamental Rights (CFR)[6] was given binding legal effect. Article 8 of the Charter recognizes the right to the protection of personal data, which may only be processed fairly for specified purposes and on the basis of the consent of the person concerned or some other legitimate basis laid down by law. Everyone has the right of access to data that have been collected concerning them, and the right to have the data rectified. Compliance with these rules shall be subject to control by an independent authority. The CFR is based, *inter alia*, on the European Convention on Human Rights (ECHR).[7] In two landmark decisions, the European Court of Human Rights held that the right to privacy as laid down in Article 8 of the ECHR does equally apply at the workplace and in private life.[8] As a consequence, European employees may have an expectation of privacy vis-à-vis their employer.

---

1. As of August 2010, there are twenty-seven EU Member States: Austria, Belgium, Bulgaria, Cyprus, the Czech Republic, Denmark, Estonia, Finland, France, Germany, Greece, Hungary, Ireland, Italy, Latvia, Lithuania, Luxembourg, Malta, the Netherlands, Poland, Portugal, Romania, Slovakia, Slovenia, Spain, Sweden, and the United Kingdom.
2. Directive 95/46, Protection of individuals with regard to the processing of personal data and on the free movement of such data, 1995 O.J. (L 281) 31 (EC).
3. Directive 2002/58, Processing of personal data and the protection of privacy in the electronic communications sector – Directive on privacy and electronic communication, 2002 O.J. (L 201) 37 (EC), as amended by the Directive 2009/136 of 15 Nov. 2009, 2009 O.J. (L 337) 11 (EU).
4. As a consequence, for the purposes of this practical guide, the ardent discussion of whether the EU Data Protection Directive only sets minimum standards, which allow a stricter transposition by the Member States, or aims at fully harmonizing the data protection law in the EU does not matter.
5. Treaty of Lisbon amending the Treaty on European Union and the Treaty Establishing the European Community of 13 Dec. 2007, 2007 O.J. (C 306) 1 (EU).
6. Charter of Fundamental Rights of the European Union of 12 Dec. 2007, 2007 O.J. (C 303) 1 (EU).
7. Convention for the Protection of Human Rights and Fundamental Freedoms of 4 Nov. 1950.
8. ECHR 23 Nov. 1992, 13710/88 (Niemitz *v.* Germany); ECHR 25 Jun. 1997, 20605/92 (Halford *v.* United Kingdom).

This is particularly important since e-discovery investigations within companies mostly relate to employees' e-mails and electronic files and to their communications and work products. Before monitoring or searching employees' communication or files, their privacy rights must be considered.

III.   ARTICLE 29 WORKING PARTY

In order to promote the uniform interpretation of the EU Data Protection Directive, its Article 29 provides for the establishment of a Working Party. The Article 29 Working Party is an independent advisory body on European privacy and data protection law. It is composed of data protection officials from the EU Member States, the EU Data Protection Supervisor, and the European Commission. The Working Party's opinions and guidelines expressed in its Working Papers are not binding on the national data protection authorities but have persuasive authority. To give an example, in its decision[9] on the structuring and management of whistleblower hotlines under the Sarbanes-Oxley Act by European affiliates of US companies in compliance with European privacy and data protection law, the Austrian Data Protection Commission explicitly adopted the key principles developed by the Working Party in its Working Paper 117 on 'the application of EU data protection rules to internal whistle-blowing schemes'. Therefore, the European data protection authorities, when required to decide on data processing related to discovery requests, are likely to follow the Working Party's guidelines. And parties to US litigation are likely to invoke the Working Party's guidelines when arguing over the extent to which European privacy and data protection law permits or restricts the transfer of personal data to the United States for litigation purposes.

IV.   RELEVANT PROVISIONS OF THE EU DATA
               PROTECTION DIRECTIVE

A.   SCOPE OF APPLICABILITY

According to its Article 3, the EU Data Protection Directive applies to the processing of personal data that takes place wholly or partly by automatic means, and to the processing that takes place otherwise than by automatic means if the personal data form part of a filing system or are intended to form part of a filing system. The reasoning behind this is that data contained in an automated processing or a structured file are more easily accessible and therefore the potential threat to privacy is more imminent.

A 'processing' of personal data is defined in Article 2 of the Directive as 'any operation or set of operations which is performed upon personal data, whether or not by automatic means, such as collection, recording, organization, storage,

---

9. Decision of 5 Dec. 2008, <www.ris2.bka.gv.at/Dsk/> (in German only).

adaptation or alteration, retrieval, consultation, use, disclosure by transmission, dissemination or otherwise making available, alignment or combination, blocking, erasure or destruction'. Therefore, the term covers virtually any activity in respect of personal data and will in any event include personal data in the employees' e-mail accounts or electronic files if identified, preserved, collected, and transferred within an e-discovery process.

Article 2 of the Directive defines 'personal data' as any information relating to an identified or identifiable natural person (the 'data subject'). As the Working Party has made clear in its Working Paper 136 of 20 June 2007,[10] the term personal data has to be interpreted broadly. Amongst others, personal data are not restricted to private e-mail correspondence but may also comprise business e-mail correspondence. In contrast, a piece of information does not qualify as personal data if it does not relate to an identifiable individual. Thus, the applicability of the local law implementing the Directive can be avoided by anonymizing the personal data. Making data anonymous means that the person cannot be identified, whether by the controller or by any other person, taking account of all the means likely reasonably to be used either by the controller or by any other person to identify that individual. If it is still possible to identify the individual, but the identity is disguised, for instance by encoding and keeping the corresponding identifiers separate, data are not anonymized but pseudonymized. In the case of pseudonymization, data protection rules apply, but the risks at stake are lower so that the application of these rules becomes more flexible.[11]

B. APPLICABLE DATA PROTECTION LAW; CONFLICT OF LAWS

The EU Data Protection Directive provides that each EU Member State shall apply the national provisions it adopts pursuant to this Directive to the processing of personal data where the processing is carried out in the context of the activities of an establishment of the controller in the territory of the EU Member State. The Directive further provides that when the same controller is established in the territory of several EU Member States, the controller must take the necessary measures to ensure that each of these establishments complies with the obligations laid down by the applicable national law. According to Recital 19 of the Directive, the legal form of such an establishment is not relevant in this respect and an establishment could also be simply a branch office. The location of the server containing the electronic files is not relevant for the applicable law. Thus, the domestic data protection laws of those EU Member States apply where establishments, which are involved in the e-discovery process, have their seats. This means that if a multinational corporation has subsidiaries or branches in several Member States and the e-discovery process relates to e-mail accounts and data files of

---

10. Opinion 4/2007 on the concept of personal data.
11. Working Paper 136, 21.

employees working in several establishments, the corporation has to comply with the laws of each EU Member State of each such establishment.

C.   CONTROLLER: PROCESSOR RELATIONSHIPS

The responsibility for data processing under the EU Data Protection Directive lies with the so-called 'controller'. According to Article 2 of the Directive, the controller is the natural or legal person, public authority, agency, or other body that alone or jointly with others determines the purposes and means of the processing of personal data. The data controller has to be distinguished from the so-called 'processor', which is defined in Article 2 of the Directive as a natural or legal person, public authority, agency, or other body that processes personal data on behalf of the controller. Information technology (IT) service companies hosting the e-mail servers of a company often qualify as processors within the meaning of the Directive. It may also be that one entity within a group of companies manages the e-discovery process on behalf of other group companies. Such an entity would also qualify as a processor on behalf of the other members of the group. Pursuant to the Directive, Member States have to provide that the carrying out of processing by way of a processor must be governed by a contract in writing or equivalent form stipulating that the processor shall only act on instructions from the controller and shall implement appropriate technical and organizational measures to protect the data against loss, destruction, unauthorized disclosure or access, and other unlawful processing.

It may sometimes be difficult to determine whether a party is a controller or a processor. In this respect the Working Paper 169 of 16 February 2010, which contains a detailed analysis of the concepts, provides guidance.[12]

D.   DATA PROTECTION PRINCIPLES

Pursuant to Article 6 of the EU Data Protection Directive, personal data must be:
  (a) processed fairly and lawfully;
  (b) collected for specified, explicit and legitimate purposes and not further processed in a way incompatible with those purposes;
  (c) adequate, relevant and not excessive in relation to the purposes for which they are collected and/or further processed;
  (d) accurate and, where necessary, kept up to date;
  (e) kept in a form which permits identification of data subjects for no longer than is necessary for the purposes for which the data were collected or for which they are further processed.

---

12. Opinion 1/2010 on the concepts of 'controller' and 'processor'.

Catrien Noorda and Stefan Hanloser

The principle under (a) means that, for instance, data may not be collected with the use of false pretences. Principle (b) means that data always have to be processed for a purpose and may not be processed or stored 'just in case'. Especially the principle under (c) is relevant in e-discovery investigation processes. It means that it is not allowed to hand over an entire e-mail file to a court or another party in the litigation, but that a selection has to be made – for instance, by using keywords. The principle under (e) may cause problems in some EU Member States as storage periods of personal data may be limited by law while removing data after the lapse of a storage period may be contrary to the US obligation to preserve electronic evidence. This problem might be overcome by explicitly specifying future litigation as a purpose for the processing in documentation in respect of the processing (such as notifications, e-mail policies, and information statements to the employees).

E. LEGITIMATE PROCESSING

The criteria for making data processing legitimate are mentioned in Article 7 of the EU Data Protection Directive, which provides that EU Member States shall provide that personal data may be processed only if:

(a) the data subject has unambiguously given his consent; or
(b) processing is necessary for the performance of a contract to which the data subject is party or in order to take steps at the request of the data subject prior to entering into a contract; or
(c) processing is necessary for compliance with a legal obligation to which the controller is subject; or
(d) processing in necessary in order to protect the vital interests of the data subjects; or
(e) processing is necessary for the performance of a task carried out in the public interest or in the exercise of official authority vested in the controller or in a third party to whom the data are disclosed;
(f) processing is necessary for the purposes of the legitimate interests pursued by the controller or by the third party or parties to whom the data are disclosed, except where such interests are overridden by the interests [. . .] or[13] fundamental rights and freedoms of the data subject which require protection under Article 1 (1).

In practice, data processing as part of a US e-discovery process will mostly have to be based on the grounds mentioned under (a) or (f). The ground mentioned under (c) seems to be relevant as well, but, in the Article 29 Working Party's opinion, this ground can only serve as a basis for e-discovery if the legal obligation

---

13. In the English translation of the Directive there is a typo at this point; in all other languages it reads 'or', not 'for'.

18

to comply with e-discovery requests follows from a national law in the relevant Member State.[14]

1.　　　Employee Consent

According to Article 2 of the Directive, 'the data subject's consent' means any freely given, specific, and informed indication of the data subject's wishes by which he or she signifies agreement to personal data relating to him or her being processed. The Article 29 Working Party has taken the view that 'where as a necessary and unavoidable consequence of the employment relationship, an employer has to process personal data it is misleading if it seeks to legitimize this processing through consent'.[15] According to the Working Party, 'reliance on consent should be confined to cases where the worker has a genuine free choice and is subsequently able to withdraw the consent without detriment'. This means that the employees must be offered a reasonable alternative without the intended processing of their data should they initially refuse or later withdraw consent. Thus, consent will in most instances not be the appropriate basis for e-discovery investigations since the responding party cannot offer to its employees the option to exclude their e-mail accounts or folders from the e-discovery process upon their wish.

2.　　　Legitimate Interests

If consent is not a valid basis for processing as part of e-discovery investigations, this will have to be based on the legitimate interest ground as provided in Article 7 (f). This, first of all, means that the controller should have a legitimate interest to process the data as part of an e-discovery investigation. The interests involved with the litigation to which the discovery relates will mostly amount to such a legitimate interest. This legitimate interest should further be proportionate to the invasion of the individual's privacy. This means that it is only allowed to carry out the processing that is strictly necessary to observe the legitimate interests involved. In addition, the principle of subsidiarity has to be complied with. This principle entails that if the legitimate interests can be observed in a way that is less detrimental to the privacy interests of the individual, the less detrimental way has to be followed. Principles of proportionality and subsidiarity in practice will mean that the individuals will have to be informed of the investigation and of the progress in advance, that keywords have to be used in searching the data, that the data should be anonymized or pseudonymized as much as possible, that data should be sufficiently safeguarded, and that the persons involved with the investigation should be limited and bound by confidentiality obligations.

---

14. Working Paper 117, Opinion 1/2006 on the application of EU data protection rules to internal whistleblowing schemes in the fields of accounting, internal accounting controls, auditing matters, fight against bribery, and banking and financial crime.
15. Working Paper 48, Opinion 8/2001 on the processing of personal data in the employment context.

3.   Special Categories of Data

Article 8 of the Directive provides for stricter rules in respect of certain special categories of data. Special categories of data are data revealing racial or ethnic origin, political opinions, religious or philosophical beliefs, trade union membership, and the processing of data concerning health or sexual orientation. These data may be processed for certain specific purposes in the field of employment law as authorized by national law, for the vital interests of the individual or by certain specific institutions with a philosophical, religious, or trade union aim. Otherwise, these categories of data may only be processed with the consent of the individual or when necessary for the establishment, exercise, or defence of legal claims. As set out above, consent is usually not a valid basis for processing as part of e-discovery, but it could, of course, be argued that the processing as part of e-discovery is necessary for the establishment, exercise, or defence of legal claims.[16] However, again the principles of proportionality and subsidiarity apply, which means that only the special categories of data may be processed if they are adequate, relevant, and not excessive in relation to the defence of legal claims, which means that they should be left out as much as possible by using keywords, disregarding, if possible, correspondence of works council or trade union members and correspondence with company medical staff.

F.   TRANSPARENCY

Transparency is an important principle underlying the EU Data Protection Directive. According to Article 10 of the Directive, when personal data are collected from the employee, the controller or his or her representative must provide the data subject with at least the following information, except where the data subject already has it:

(a) the identity of the controller and of his representative, if any;
(b) the purposes of the processing for which the data are intended;
(c) any further information such as
  – the recipients or categories of recipients of the data,
  – whether replies to the questions are obligatory or voluntary, as well as the possible consequences of failure to reply,
  – the existence of the right of access to and the right to rectify the data concerning him
  in so far as such further information is necessary, having regard to the specific circumstances in which the data are collected, to guarantee fair processing in respect of the data subject.

---

16. This is also in line with Working Paper 158, which provides that the same basis can serve as a basis for the transfer of data outside the EU.

According to Article 11 of the EU Data Protection Directive, if the personal data have not been obtained from the data subject, but from a third party, the controller or his or her representative must, in principle, provide the data subject with at least the following information, except where the data subject already has it (at the time of undertaking the recording of personal data or if a disclosure to a third party is envisaged, no later than the time when the data are first disclosed):

(a) the identity of the controller and of his representative, if any;
(b) the purposes of the processing;
(c) any further information such as
   – the categories of data concerned,
   – the recipients or categories of recipients,
   – the existence of the right of access to and the right to rectify the data concerning him
   in so far as such further information is necessary, having regard to the specific circumstances in which the data are processed, to guarantee fair processing in respect of the data subject.

The transparency requirement also applies to the monitoring and screening of employees' private electronic communications by e-mail or on the Internet at the workplace. The monitoring and screening is a matter of data processing so that the employees need to be informed in advance, that is, before their accounts or folders are accessed for the identification and preservation of responsive information within an e-discovery process. One option for safeguarding transparency is the implementation of a policy for the use of electronic communication means for private communication purposes. The policy can address the monitoring and screening of private electronic communications by e-mail or on the Internet so that the employees are made aware of the processing of their personal data by their employer.

G.   Rights of Data Subject

According to Article 12 of the Directive, every data subject should be given the right to obtain from the controller (amongst others):

(a) without constraint at reasonable intervals and without excessive delay or expense:
   – confirmation as to whether or not data relating to him are being processed and information at least as to the purposes of the processing, the categories of data concerned, and the recipients or categories of recipients to whom the data are disclosed,
   – communication to him in an intelligible form of the data undergoing processing and of any available information as to their source,
(b) as appropriate the rectification, erasure or blocking of data the processing of which does not comply with the provisions of the EU Data Protection

Directive, in particular because of the incomplete or inaccurate nature of the data;

(c) notification to third parties to whom the data have been disclosed of any rectification, erasure or blocking carried out in compliance with (b), unless this proves impossible or involves a disproportionate effort.

H.   TRANSFER OF PERSONAL DATA TO THIRD COUNTRIES

The EU Data Protection Directive prohibits, in principle, data export to countries that are not EU Member States or members states of the European Economic Area (EEA)[17] and lack – from the point of view of the European Commission or the national data protection authorities (DPAs) – an adequate level of protection. Currently the following countries are considered by the European Commission to provide an adequate protection level: Argentina, Canada, Faeroe Islands, Guernsey, Isle of Man, Jersey, and Switzerland.[18] The United States, with its sector-specific privacy laws, does not fulfil the EU standards for an adequate level of protection. The relevant paragraphs of Articles 25 and 26 of the Directive read as follows:

Article 25
Principles

(1) The Member States shall provide that the transfer to a third country of personal data which are undergoing processing or are intended for pro-cessing after transfer may take place only if, without prejudice to com-pliance with the national provisions adopted pursuant to the other provisions of this Directive, the third country in question ensures an adequate level of protection.

---

17. As of August 2010, there are thirty EEA member states: the twenty-seven EU Member States and three EFTA member states: Iceland, Liechtenstein, and Norway. The three EFTA member states have implemented the Directive 95/46, cf. Agreement on the EEA, Art. 7; Decision of the EEA Joint Committee No 83/1999 of 25 Jun. 1999.

18. Argentina (Commission Decision 2003/490 of 30 Jun. 2003, Adequate Protection of Personal Data in Argentina, 2003 O.J. [L 168] 19 [EU]), Canada (Commission Decision 2002/2 of 20 Dec. 2001, Adequate Protection of Personal Data Provided by the Canadian Personal Informa-tion Protection and Electronic Documents Act, 2002 O.J. [L 2] 13 [EC], however, limited to data recipients subject to the Canadian Personal Information Protection and Electronic Documents Act of 13 Apr. 2000), Faeroe Islands (Commission Decision 2010/146 of 5 Mar. 2010, Adequate protection provided by the Faeroese Act on processing of personal data, 2010 O.J. [L 58] 17 [EU]), Guernsey (Commission Decision 2003/821 of 21 Nov. 2003, Adequate Protection of Personal Data Provided in Guernsey, 2003 O.J. [L 308] 27 [EU]), Isle of Man (Commission Decision 2004/411 of 28 Apr. 2004, Adequate protection of personal data in the Isle of Man, 2004 O.J. [L 151] 48 [EU], corrigendum, 2004 O.J. [L 208] 47 [EU]). Jersey (Commission Decision 2008/393 of 8 May 2008, Adequate protection of personal data in Jersey, 2008 O.J. [L 138] 21 [EU]) and Switzerland (Commission Decision 2000/518 of 26 Jul. 2000, Adequate Protection of Personal Data Provided in Switzerland, 2000 O.J. [L 215] 1 [EC]).

(2) The adequacy of the level of protection afforded by a third country shall be assessed in the light of all the circumstances surrounding a data transfer operation or set of data transfer operations; particular consideration shall be given to the nature of the data, the purpose and duration of the proposed processing operation or operations, the country of origin and country of final destination, the rules of law, both general and sectoral, in force in the third country in question and the professional rules and security measures which are complied with in that country.

The DPAs may, however, authorize sets of data transfers to recipients in third countries if appropriate contractual clauses provide adequate safeguards to the data subjects. The standard contractual tool for securing the intra-group transfer of huge quantities of human resources and customer data are Binding Corporate Rules (BCRs). BCRs are enforceable codes of conduct for privacy and data protection compliance to which each member of the corporate group subscribes. In contrast to a multitude of mutual data transfer agreements between the corporate members in the EU and overseas – for instance, the Standard Contractual Clauses (SCCs) authored by the European Commission – BCRs are a single set of rules. They are tailor-made for the specific needs of the corporation and reflect its specific group structure and intra-group data flows. However, within the e-discovery context, BCRs can only pave the way for a transfer of personal data to the United States but cannot legalize the onward transfer to the requesting party or the US court.[19]

However, under the EU Data Protection Directive, personal data may be transferred to data recipients in the United States if the recipient has notified the US Department of Commerce that it adheres to the 'Safe Harbour Privacy Principles'[20] and the Frequently Asked Questions (FAQs).[21] There are only approximately 300 legal entities that have acknowledged the Principles and the FAQs.[22]

As an alternative, Article 26 of the Directive provides for specific derogations:

Article 26
Derogations

(1) By way of derogation from Article 25 and save where otherwise provided by domestic law governing particular cases, Member States shall provide that a transfer or a set of transfers of personal data to a third country which

---

19. Working Paper 74 of the Art. 29 Working Party of 3 Jun. 2003 on 'Transfers of personal data to third countries: Applying Article 26 (2) of the EU Data Protection Directive to Binding Corporate Rules for international data transfers'.
20. See Annex I, Safe Harbor Privacy Principles Issued by the US Department of Commerce on 21 Jul. 2000, to Commission Decision 2000/520, Adequacy of the Protection Provided by the Safe Harbour Privacy Principles and Related Frequently Asked Questions Issued by the US Department of Commerce, 2000 O.J. (L 215) 8 (EC).
21. See Annex II, Frequently Asked Questions (FAQs), to Commission Decision 2000/520.
22. Among others Amazon.com, Inc., Apple, Inc., Google Inc., Hewlett-Packard Company, PepsiCo, Inc., Microsoft Corporation (<www.export.gov/safehrbr/list.aspx>).

does not ensure an adequate level of protection within the meaning of Article 25 (2) may take place on condition that:

(a) the data subject has given his consent unambiguously to the proposed transfer; or

(b) the transfer is necessary for the performance of a contract between the data subject and the controller or the implementation of precontractual measures taken in response to the data subject's request; or

(c) the transfer is necessary for the conclusion or performance of a contract concluded in the interest of the data subject between the controller and a third party; or

(d) the transfer is necessary or legally required on important public interest grounds, or for the establishment, exercise or defence of legal claims; or

(e) the transfer is necessary in order to protect the vital interests of the data subject; or

(f) the transfer is made from a register which according to laws or regulations is intended to provide information to the public and which is open to consultation either by the public in general or by any person who can demonstrate legitimate interest, to the extent that the conditions laid down in law for consultation are fulfilled in the particular case.

The applicability of these derogations has been clarified by the Article 29 Working Party in its recently published Working Paper 158.

I.   WORKING PAPER 158

On 11 February 2009, the Article 29 Working Party adopted Working Paper 158 concerning pretrial discovery for cross-border civil litigation.[23] The Working Paper aims at reconciling the 'demands of the litigation process in foreign [non-EEA] jurisdictions' with European data protection obligations. The Working Paper covers the retention, preservation, and archiving of data for litigation purposes (referred to in Europe as 'processing'), and discovery of such data in US civil litigation. It expressly does not address '[d]ocument production in US criminal and regulatory investigations' or '[c]riminal offences in the US relating to data destruction'.

The most significant statements made by the Working Party in its Working Paper can be summarized as follows:

– The Working Paper recognizes that the transfer of personal data for litigation purposes to the United States is not illegal per se under the EU Data Protection Directive. But such data transfers must follow specific

---

23. Working Paper 158 of the Art. 29 Working Party of 11 Feb. 2009 on pretrial discovery for cross-border civil litigation.

requirements of the Data Protection Directive to comply with European privacy and data protection law.

- If personal data are relevant to a pending, imminent, or reasonably foreseeable litigation, they may be retained until the termination of the proceedings.
- The Directive permits the transfer of personal data to a country with an inadequate data protection level – for instance, the United States under European standards – if the transfer is necessary or legally required for the establishment, exercise, or defence of legal claims in court, however, in the Working Party's view, only if there is one single transfer of all relevant data.
- Non-responsive documents that contain personal data should be culled in the EU Member State and irrelevant personal data on responsive documents should be redacted in the Member State so that only relevant personal data are actually transferred to the United States and disclosed to the requesting party.
- The data subject's freely given, specific, and informed prior consent to a later data processing for litigation purposes can only be expected in rare cases – for instance, if the individual is involved in the litigation – and will not typically be a basis for finding that the 'processing' of personal information in Europe is legitimate.
- An obligation imposed by a non-EU legal statute or regulation will not usually justify data processing within the EU (unless, for example, an individual Member State recognizes an obligation to comply with an order of a foreign court).
- If the identity of the data subject is irrelevant, data should be anonymized or pseudonymized.
- The Working Party finally recognizes that a request under the Hague Convention on the taking of evidence[24] is a valid ground for a data transfer to the United States in compliance with the Directive.

The Working Paper assesses the handling of data in litigation in two different areas: (1) the general legal requirements for the retention of personal data by the responding party during the preservation phase and the later transfer of such data to the requesting party during the production phase; and (2) the specific legal requirements for a data export to third countries that lack – from the point of view of the European Commission or the national DPAs – an adequate level of protection (like the United States with its sector-specific privacy laws).

General Requirements for the Retention and Transfer of Personal Data
Whenever litigation or regulatory investigations and proceedings are reasonably anticipated by a legal entity, no matter whether the entity is the initiator or the target of litigation, it has a duty to preserve the potentially relevant data, that is,

---

24. Hague Convention on the Taking of Evidence Abroad in Civil and Commercial Matters of 18 Mar. 1970.

protect the data from destruction or alteration. Under the EU Data Protection Directive, the retention of data constitutes 'processing' and requires justification under Article 7 of the Directive. This is the same with the later transfer of personal data to the requesting party, which is also deemed to be data processing under European data protection law.

The data subject's consent to data processing for litigation purposes under Article 7(a) of the EU Data Protection Directive can only be expected in rare cases. In practice, the boiler-plate declarations of consent signed by employees or customers are often insufficient to cover data processing in legal proceedings with a third party. In addition, the Working Party casts doubt on whether employees can give their consent voluntarily if asked to do so by their employer once litigation is anticipated or even pending.

Since, in the Working Party's view, an obligation imposed by a foreign statute or regulation does not typically qualify as a 'legal obligation' within the meaning of Article 7(c) of the Directive, discovery obligations under the Federal Rules for Civil Procedure cannot justify data processing within the EU either.

But under Article 7(f) of the Directive, personal data may be processed if legitimate interests necessitate the processing, unless such legitimate interests are overridden by the interests or fundamental rights and freedoms of the data subject. The Working Party gives some guidance on how to balance the conflicting interests under Article 7(f) of the Directive: If the personal data are irrelevant, the responding party cannot claim any legitimate interests in processing such data for litigation purposes. Therefore, if the identity of the data subject is irrelevant, data should be anonymized or at least pseudonymized, the Working Party argues. Non-responsive documents that contain personal data should be filtered out in the EU Member State and irrelevant personal data on responsive documents should be redacted in the Member State so that only relevant personal data are transferred to the United States and disclosed to the requesting party. In practice, the disclosing party is required to seek the requesting party's agreement: (i) for the production of anonymized or pseudonymized documents or data; and (ii) for the redaction of irrelevant personal data on responsive documents.

Specific Requirements for the Export of Personal Data to the United States
Rightly, the Working Party singles out Article 26(1)(d) of the Directive, which explicitly permits the transfer of personal data to a country with what the EU characterizes as an 'inadequate data protection level' – for instance, the United States – if the transfer is necessary or legally required for the establishment, exercise or defence of legal claims (in court).[25] This provision is, in fact, key to the reconciliation of e-discovery rules and European privacy and data protection law. However, the Working Party restricts this beneficial provision to cases '[w]here the transfer of personal data for litigation purposes is likely to be a single transfer of all relevant information', without even giving an explanation for this potentially burdensome limitation. As an alternative, only a subscription to the

---

25. In the English translation of the Directive the restriction 'in court' was left out by mistake.

Safe Harbour Programme, the implementation of BCRs, or the signing of SCCs could be an option to legalize a data export to the United States.

The Working Party's reference to the Hague Convention is of little practical relevance since a Letter of Request procedure is seen as 'unduly time consuming and burdensome'[26] and some European countries, such as Germany, Italy, and Spain, do not 'execute Letters of Request [for] pre-trial discovery'.

---

26. *Société Nationale Industrielle Aérospatiale v. US Dist. Ct.*, 482 US 522, 542 (1987).

Chapter 4

Hague Convention on the Taking of Evidence Abroad

*Stefan Hanloser**

I.   INTRODUCTION

The Hague Convention on the Taking of Evidence[1] affects pretrial discovery in a US litigation – that is, the discovery of evidence after the filing of a claim but before the final hearing on the merits – if the production of documents, electronically stored information, or tangible things that are located in a foreign Contracting State to the Hague Convention[2] is requested under Rule 34(a) of the Federal Rules of Civil Procedure.[3] The Hague Convention is often seen by the responding party, which is confronted with the request for the production of information, as a last resort to evade or at least delay exterritorial discovery. The idea behind this

*   Dr Stefan Hanloser, Howrey LLP, Munich, Germany.
1.   Hague Convention on the Taking of Evidence Abroad in Civil and Commercial Matters of 18 Mar. 1970.
2.   As of August 2010, there are fifty Contracting States to the Convention: Argentina, Australia, Barbados, Belarus, Bosnia and Herzegovina, Bulgaria, People's Republic of China, Croatia, Cyprus, Czech Republic, Denmark, Estonia, Finland, France, Germany, Greece, Hungary, Iceland, India, Israel, Italy, Korea, Kuwait, Latvia, Liechtenstein, Lithuania, Luxembourg, Mexico, Monaco, Netherlands, Norway, Poland, Portugal, Romania, Russian Federation, Seychelles, Singapore, Slovakia, Slovenia, South Africa, Spain, Sri Lanka, Sweden, Switzerland, Macedonia, Turkey, Ukraine, United Kingdom, United States, Venezuela.
3.   Federal Rules of Civil Procedure (2009).

Catrien Noorda & Stefan Hanloser, *E-Discovery and Data Privacy*, pp. 29–34.
© 2011 Kluwer Law International BV, The Netherlands.

strategy is that if the rather burdensome procedure under the Hague Convention was the exclusive and mandatory channel for obtaining evidence that is located abroad, it would necessarily delay the whole discovery process. And even worse (or better, depending on whether one assumes the perspective of the requesting or responding party), many Contracting States to the Hague Convention have declared that they will not execute Letters of Request 'issued for the purpose of obtaining pre-trial discovery of documents as known in Common Law countries'.[4] As a consequence, documents located in these countries would be inaccessible if the Hague Convention was the only way for obtaining evidence abroad.

II.   SCOPE OF APPLICATION

The Hague Convention can only prove as an obstacle to pretrial discovery within its scope of application.

A.   MATERIAL SCOPE OF APPLICATION

Under Article 1 of the Hague Convention, a judicial authority of a Contracting State may request the competent authority of another Contracting State, by means of a Letter of Request, to obtain evidence, or to perform some other judicial act in civil or commercial matters. It derives from Article 3(e)–(g) of the Convention that 'obtaining evidence' includes examining persons on statements of the subject matter, putting questions to persons to be examined, and inspecting documents or other property, both land and chattels.

The term 'taking evidence' undoubtedly covers the taking of evidence *in* a foreign country, that is, the questioning of a witness or the inspection of documents

---

4. Under Art. 23 of the Hague Convention, a Contracting State may, at the time of signature, ratification, or accession, declare that it will not execute Letters of Request issued for the purpose of obtaining pretrial discovery of documents as known in common law countries. As of August 2010, there are twenty Contracting States that made an unreserved declaration under Art. 23 of the Convention: Argentina, Australia, Croatia, Germany, Greece, Hungary, Iceland, Italy, Lithuania, Luxembourg, Monaco, Poland, Portugal, Romania, South Africa, Spain, Sri Lanka, Macedonia, Turkey, and Ukraine. In order to prevent so-called 'fishing expeditions', that is, requests for documents to find out what documents might be in the other party's possession or control, fifteen Contracting States have made a limited declaration under Art. 23 of the Convention, stating that they will not execute Letters of Request issued for the purpose of obtaining pretrial discovery of documents as known in the common law countries to the exclusion of 'documents clearly enumerated in the Letters of Request and of direct and close connection with the subject matter of the litigation', 'particular documents specified in the Letter of Request, and which are likely to be in his [i.e. the responding party's] possession', 'documents[, which] have been reasonably identified according to the dates, the contents or other information', 'documents which the court, which is conducting the proceedings believes to be in his [i.e. the responding party's] possession, custody or power', etc.: People's Republic of China, Cyprus, Denmark, Estonia, Finland, France, India, Korea, Mexico, Netherlands, Norway, Sweden, Switzerland, United Kingdom, and Venezuela.

or other property in the territory of another country. It is, however, debatable whether evidence is also taken abroad if a US court orders, under Rule 34(a)(1) of the Federal Rules of Civil Procedure, a party over whom it has *in personam* jurisdiction to produce documents or tangible things that are located abroad. In the *Aérospatiale* case it was unanimously confirmed both by several European countries in their *amici curiae* briefs[5] and by the US Supreme Court that the production of documents and tangible things located in a foreign country is within the scope of the Hague Convention. The US Supreme Court held that 'the text of the Convention (...) does [not] purport to draw any sharp line between evidence that is "abroad" and evidence that is within the control of a party subject to the jurisdiction of the requesting court'.[6]

B.   PERSONAL SCOPE OF APPLICATION

In the *Aérospatiale* case, the Court of Appeals contended that if it has jurisdiction over a litigant, 'the Hague Convention does not apply to the production of evidence in th[e] litigant's possession, even though the documents and information sought may physically be located within the territory of a foreign signatory to the Convention'.[7] As a consequence, if the evidence was sought from another party to the lawsuit, the Convention would be inapplicable and would not provide the exclusive and mandatory procedures for obtaining documents and information located within the territory of a foreign Contracting State.

---

5. *Société Nationale Industrielle Aérospatiale v. US Dist. Ct.*, *Amicus curiae* brief of the Federal Republic of Germany, 25 I.L.M. 1475, 1539, 1541 (1986): 'Ordering without using the Convention the production in the United States of evidence located within the territory of a signatory to the Convention violates that foreign country's sovereignty when its legal system places the power to take evidence solely and exclusively with its courts. Having personal jurisdiction over a party does not authorize American courts to apply the Federal Rule of Civil Procedure in disregard of the Convention'.; *Amicus curiae* brief of the Government of Switzerland, I.L.M. 25 (1986): 1475, 1549, 1551 'If a US court unilaterally attempts to coerce the production of evidence located in Switzerland, without requesting governmental assistance, the US court intrudes upon the judicial sovereignty of Switzerland. Use of the Convention will satisfy the requirement of both nations by providing the needed evidence to the US litigant through a procedure consistent with Swiss law an sovereignty'; *Amicus curiae* brief of the Republic of France, I.L.M. 1475, 25 (1986): 1519, 1521 'The court below erroneously affirmed an order permitting United States litigants seeking evidence situated in France to disregard Convention procedures so long as the persons from whom the discovery is sought are parties to the litigation and subject to the American court's *in personam* jurisdiction'.
6. *Société Nationale Industrielle Aérospatiale v. US Dist. Ct.*, 482 US 522, 541 (1987).
7. *In re Société Nationale Industrielle Aérospatiale*, 782 F.2d 120, 124 (8th Cir. 1986), citing *In re Anschütz & Co. GmbH*, 754 F.2d 602, 615 (5th Cir. 1985): 'We hold that the Hague Convention is to be employed with the involuntary deposition of a party conducted in a foreign country, and with the production of documents or other evidence gathered from persons or entities in the foreign country who are not subject to the court's *in personam* jurisdiction. The Hague Convention has no application at all to the production of evidence in this country by a party subject to the jurisdiction of a district court pursuant to the Federal Rules'.

Stefan Hanloser

This statement was contested in the *amici curiae* briefs urging reversal of the Court of Appeals' decision. The United States and the Securities and Exchange Commission opposed the Court of Appeals' decision stating that '[t]he Hague Evidence Convention prescribes procedures by which litigants [sic] (...) may obtain evidence from abroad'.[8] The Swiss government took the position that '[t]he Convention plainly applies to the discovery of all evidence located in a contracting state, even if a US court has personal jurisdiction over the party from whom the evidence is sought. To conclude otherwise would deprive the Convention of one of its essential purposes'.[9] The German government pointed out that the '[e]xperience with the application of the Convention shows that the vast majority of discovery requests were directed to parties [sic], mostly corporate defendants'.[10] The French government argued that 'the (...) rationale – that the Convention does not apply if the target of the discovery demand is itself a party to the litigation – is at odds with the language and the negotiating history of the Convention. The holding below frustrates the Convention's objective of reducing tensions between nations with different judicial systems precisely in those cases where the potential for conflicts is the greatest: evidence situated abroad is invariably at issue where (...) one or more of the parties is a foreigner with no ties to the Unites States other than the participation in commerce'.[11]

In line with the *amici curiae* briefs, the US Supreme Court held that 'the text of the Convention draws no distinction between evidence obtained from third parties and that obtained from the litigants themselves; (...). (...) the Hague Convention does "apply" to the production of evidence in a litigant's possession'.[12]

III.   PROCEDURE; LETTERS OF REQUEST
        (LETTERS ROGATORY)

In civil or commercial matters a judicial authority of one Contracting State may send a Letter of Request – also known as Letter Rogatory – to the Central Authority of another Contracting State that is designated to receive Letters of Request and to transmit them to the domestic judicial authority that is competent to execute them, that is, to obtain evidence or to perform some other judicial act. The Letter of Request shall specify: (i) the authority requesting its execution and the authority requested to execute it; (ii) the names and addresses of the parties to the proceedings

---

8. *Société Nationale Industrielle Aérospatiale v. US Dist. Ct.*, Amicus curiae brief of the United States of America and the Securities and Exchange Commission, 25 I.L.M. 1475, 1504, 1507 (1986).
9. *Société Nationale Industrielle Aérospatiale v. US Dist. Ct.*, Amicus curiae brief of the Government of Switzerland, 25 I.L.M. 1475, 1549, 1551 (1986).
10. *Société Nationale Industrielle Aérospatiale v. US Dist. Ct.*, Amicus curiae brief of the Federal Republic of Germany, 25 I.L.M. 1475, 1539, 1542–1543 (1986).
11. *Société Nationale Industrielle Aérospatiale v. US Dist. Ct.*, Amicus curiae brief of the Republic of France, 25 I.L.M. 1475, 1519, 1522 (1986).
12. *Société Nationale Industrielle Aérospatiale v. US Dist. Ct.*, 482 US 522, 541 (1987).

and their representatives; (iii) the nature of the proceedings for which the evidence is required; and (iv) the evidence to be obtained or other judicial act to be performed.

In principle, the judicial authority that executes a Letter of Request applies the methods and procedures to be followed under its domestic law. However, the requesting authority may ask in the Letter of Request for a special method or procedure to be followed. The executing authority accommodates the request unless it is incompatible with its domestic law or is impossible of performance by reason of its internal practice and procedure or by reason of practical difficulties. Upon request of the requesting authority, the executing authority informs the parties to the litigation and their representatives directly about the time when, and the place where, the proceedings will take place so that they may be present.

A Letter of Request shall be executed expeditiously. If the Central Authority considers, however, that the request does not comply with the provisions of the Hague Convention, it promptly informs the requesting authority about its objections.

IV.   NO 'RULE OF FIRST RESORT'

Whereas it is generally accepted that the Hague Convention applies to the production of evidence that is located abroad,[13] it is a highly debated topic whether the Hague Convention provides the exclusive and mandatory procedures for such exterritorial discovery. The US Supreme Court held in its *Aérospatiale* decision in 1987 that US courts are not required to first resort to the Hague Convention whenever discovery is sought from a foreign litigant.[14] The Court contended that neither the preamble nor Articles 1 and 15–17 of the Convention speak in mandatory terms, which would purport to describe the procedures for all permissible transnational discovery and exclude all other existing practice.[15] The Court also argued that, 'if the Convention had been intended to replace completely the broad discovery powers that the common-law courts in the United States previously exercised over foreign litigants subject to their jurisdiction, it would have been most anomalous for the common-law contracting parties to agree to Article 23 [of the Convention], which enables a contracting party to revoke its consent to the treaty's procedures for pre-trial discovery'.[16] The Court also pointed out that Article 27 plainly states that the Convention does not prevent a Contracting State from using more liberal methods of rendering evidence than those authorized by the Convention.[17] The Court therefore rejected 'a new rule of law that would

---

13. See *supra* II.A.
14. *Société Nationale Industrielle Aérospatiale v. US Dist. Ct.*, 482 US 522, 541 (1987).
15. *Société Nationale Industrielle Aérospatiale v. US Dist. Ct.*, 482 US 522, 534–535 (1987).
16. *Société Nationale Industrielle Aérospatiale v. US Dist. Ct.*, 482 US 522, 536–537 (1987).
17. *Société Nationale Industrielle Aérospatiale v. US Dist. Ct.*, 482 US 522, 538 (1987); Art. 27(c) of the Convention provides: 'The provisions of the present convention shall not prevent a

require first resort to the Convention procedures whenever discovery is sought from a foreign litigant. (...) In many situations the Letter of Request procedure authorized by the Convention would be unduly time consuming and expensive, as well as less certain to produce needed evidence than direct use of the Federal Rules'.[18] However, 'American courts (...) should exercise special vigilance to protect foreign litigants from the danger that unnecessary, or unduly burdensome, discovery may place them in a disadvantageous position'.[19] Accordingly, US courts tend to adhere to the Restatement (Third) of Foreign Relations of the United States, section 442(1)(c),[20] which provides a 'five-factor test' for balancing the US court's interest in ordering a person subject to its jurisdiction to produce documents with the interests of the foreign sovereign.[21]

V.   CONCLUSION

A responding party might invoke the Hague Convention for tactical reasons but will know that US courts are reluctant to apply it in extraterritorial discovery proceedings. A responding party should therefore focus on the Restatement's 'five-factor test' and argue accordingly.

Contracting State from – (...) permitting, by internal law or practice, methods of taking evidence other than those provided for in this Convention'.

18. *Société Nationale Industrielle Aérospatiale v. US Dist. Ct.*, 482 US 522, 542 (1987); cf. also dissenting opinion of Justice Blackmun, 482 US 522, 548 (1987): 'I fear the Court's decision means that courts will resort unnecessarily to issuing discovery orders under the Federal Rules of Civil Procedure in a raw exercise of their jurisdictional power to the detriment of the United States' national and international interests'.

19. *Société Nationale Industrielle Aérospatiale v. US Dist. Ct.*, 482 US 522, 546 (1987).

20. Restatement (Third) of Foreign Relations of the United States § 442(1)(c) provides: 'In deciding whether to issue an order directing production of information located abroad, and in framing such an order, a court or agency in the United States should take into account the importance to the investigation or litigation of the documents or other information requested; the degree of specificity of the request; whether the information originated in the United States; the availability of alternative means of securing the information; the extent to which noncompliance with the request would undermine important interests of the United States; or compliance with the request would undermine important interests of the state where the information is located'.

21. *Minpeco, S.A. v. Conticommodity Servs., Inc.*, 116 F.R.D. 517, 522–530 (S.D.N.Y. 1987); *Volkswagen v. Valdez*, 909 S.W.2d 900, 902 (Tex. 1995); *Weiss v. Nat'l Westminster Bank PLC*, 242 F.R.D. 33, 42–58 (E.D.N.Y. 2007).

Chapter 5.1

Austria

*Günther Leissler**

I.   INTRODUCTION

Pretrial discovery or e-discovery in terms of structured collecting, processing, and submitting of electronically stored business information is yet rather uncommon in Austria. So far a specific legal framework for e-discovery does not exist, nor is there e-discovery-related judicature in place. However, recently in Austria, e-discovery-related search for electronic information, not least the term 'e-discovery' itself, became better known.

    Although Austria has no specific legal framework dealing with e-discovery, any kind of request for information in the spirit of mutual pretrial disclosure or e-discovery in its widest sense will potentially conflict with applicable Austrian data protection law. While e-discovery requests typically aim for disclosure of business-relevant information (often including the disclosure of employee data), Austrian data protection law principally prevents personal data from being disclosed. As in most other countries, the outcome of this conflict depends on a balance check where the interests of the requesting company are balanced against those of the individuals affected by this request (the data subjects). In order to gain an impression of the Austrian data protection authority's view, recently representatives of several companies made flying visits in order to discuss their views with the authority. However, so far the Austrian data protection authority did not issue

---

*   Günther Leissler, Attorney at Law at Schönherr Rechtsanwälte GmbH, Vienna, Austria.

Catrien Noorda & Stefan Hanloser, *E-Discovery and Data Privacy*, pp. 35–42.
© 2011 Kluwer Law International BV, The Netherlands.

any guidelines or informal statements on how to handle e-discovery requests in Austria. So at this stage it can be summarized that the principles of Austrian data protection law apply to e-discovery in the same way as to any other processing or transferring of personal data.

II.   AUSTRIAN DATA PROTECTION LAW: BACKGROUND

In Austria the European Data Protection Directive[1] was implemented by the Federal Data Protection Act 2000 (*Datenschutzgesetz 2000* – the 'DPA')[2] on 17 August 1999, which replaced the former Federal DPA1978. The DPA was last revised on 1 January 2010, where, however, no e-discovery-related provisions had been amended. In its early stages data protection was nearly below perception of the Austrian public. Although the implementation of the DPA in 1999 enhanced the development of Austrian data protection law, it was not until recent years that the importance of Austrian data protection law significantly increased. This development was boosted by a manifold pertinent media coverage dealing with data protection issues that really touched the public, such as improper disclosure of employee data, exaggerated closed-circuit television (CCTV) monitoring, or improper handling of health data. This led to an 'upward spiral': the more that news of breaches of data protection law was reported, the more people got interested in data protection issues, which led to an overall awareness-raising with respect to data protection and, not least, data protection law in Austria.

A.   AUSTRIAN DATA PROTECTION LAW: SCOPE OF THE DPA

While the main principles of Austrian data protection law certainly do not differ much from those of other European countries, it is nevertheless an Austrian specification that Austrian data protection law applies to both legal entities as well as natural persons.[3] The DPA therefore applies to 'personal data' in the broadest sense, including any information relating to an identified or identifiable person or a legal entity.[4] In the context of e-discovery this means that the DPA will not only apply to any individuals being potentially affected by an e-discovery request (such as employees and customers), but also to the Austrian-based company as the responding party. Therefore it can be assumed that in the context of pretrial or e-discovery, nearly all kinds of requests for information will affect 'personal data' within the meaning of the DPA, no matter whether they relate to information about individuals or solely to corporate data. Thus, the principles of the DPA will frequently have to be observed when it comes to answering e-discovery requests.

---

1. Council Directive 95/46, Protection of individuals with regard to the processing of personal data and on the free movement of such data, 1995 O.J. (L 281) 31 (EC) (Privacy Directive).
2. Bundesgesetz über den Schutz personenbezogener Daten (Datenschutzgesetz 2000 – DSG 2000), BGBL I nr 165/1999 idgF.
3. Article 1 DPA refers to the term 'everyone' without distinguishing between natural persons and legal entities.
4. Section 4 para. 1 DPA.

B.   AUSTRIAN DATA PROTECTION LAW: LEGITIMACY OF PROCESSING
       PERSONAL DATA

In a nutshell, Austrian data protection law is nothing but a balancing of interests. The interests of one party seeking personal data are weighed against the interests of those being affected (who are, in terms of the DPA, the data subjects). As a general rule it can be stated that any processing of personal data is prohibited unless it is expressly legally permitted. Of course, the DPA provides for several statutory 'permissions' that allow the processing of personal data. In practice, the most important of these permissions are: (i) statutory permissions; (ii) express consent given by the affected individual; and (iii) 'overriding legitimate interests' of the data controller. However, even when personal data are validly processed on the grounds of one of these permissions, the DPA additionally asks for proportionality. This fundamental principle prevents excessive data processing in relation to its purpose. In the light of e-discovery this means that, for example, if an e-discovery request targets the content of specific documents but not the persons who drafted the documents or its addressees, disclosure of these documents on a personal basis will be prohibited. Also, if an e-discovery request targets documents being relevant for only a short period of time, it will not be permitted to disclose this information over an annual period of time. In short: Disproportionality will invalidate any processing of personal data. This principle should be self-understood; however, in practice it can frequently be observed that data are often processed in an exaggerated manner simply due to the fact that it is easier to process and transfer data 'packages' en bloc than to filter and select those data categories that are really of relevance for the intended purpose.

C.   AUSTRIAN DATA PROTECTION LAW: EMPLOYEE DATA

Virtually every e-discovery request will potentially require the disclosure of employee-related information such as e-mail, file notes, or phone call logs. Especially with respect to employee communication data, such as e-mail and phone call log files, not only the aforementioned data protection regulations will apply but also some labour-law-specific considerations have to be taken into account.[5] In Austria an employee is entitled to make use of his or her work equipment for private purposes as long as his or her employer does not explicitly prohibit such private usage. This leads to the fact that commonly not only business-related mails but also private correspondence is stored on employee accounts. So if the responding party wants to disclose employee correspondence for the purpose of answering an e-discovery request, Austrian labour law will potentially require consultation of the works council or, if no works council is in place, explicit consent of the affected employee. This leads to further inconveniences as Austrian courts and also the Data Protection Commission often doubt that employees really are in the position to give

---

5. Additionally, such data are protected by the secrecy of the communications as stated in the Austrian Telecommunications Act and the related provisions in the Austrian Criminal Code.

their consent without any restraints when asked by their employer. Having said so, the responding party might therefore think twice about whether employee data has to be disclosed on a personal basis or whether respective disclosure on an anonymous or at least pseudonymous level might be sufficient.

D.   A<small>USTRIAN</small> D<small>ATA</small> P<small>ROTECTION</small> L<small>AW</small>: C<small>USTOMER</small> D<small>ATA</small>

E-discovery requests might often target customer-related information. It is in the nature of things that those customers are frequently not involved in the upcoming litigations nor are they in the position to affect or control the intrusiveness and extent of their data disclosure. In the light of the aforementioned principles of balancing of interests and proportionality, this means that also any disclosure of customer-related information has to be limited to the extent absolutely necessary. Again, the responding party should therefore carefully consider whether revelation of customer data really has to be done on a personal basis or whether anonymous or pseudonymous data would be sufficient.

E.   A<small>USTRIAN</small> D<small>ATA</small> P<small>ROTECTION</small> L<small>AW</small>: S<small>UPERVISORY</small>
                    A<small>UTHORITIES</small>; E<small>NFORCEMENT</small>

No matter what kind of data are processed in Austria, they will be subject to the supervision of the Austrian Data Protection Commission *(Datenschutzkommission* (DSK)). If the DSK detects data being processed in breach of the DPA, this might lead to administrative fines of up to Euros (EUR) 25,000 and, although not very likely, even to prison sentences of up to a year. Additionally, the offender might face civil action or claims under Austrian competition law and, needless to say, a risk of loss of reputation due to bad media coverage.

    However, due to the fact that e-discovery still plays a rather minor role in Austrian data protection practice, the DSK did not deal with e-discovery-specific misconduct so far. Nevertheless, there is a risk that the DSK will certainly trace complaints about illegitimate data transfers in the course of e-discovery requests, which could very likely lead to the aforementioned sanctions.

III.   PRETRIAL DISCOVERY AND DATA PROTECTION IN
                AUSTRIA: GENERAL

Though not very surprising, it has to be stated that foreign legal statutes do not qualify as 'statutory permissions' within the meaning of the DPA.[6] In other words,

---

6. Compare Art. 29 WP 158 of 11 Feb. 2009 on pretrial discovery for cross-border civil litigation; also compare Art. 29 WP 117 of 01 Feb. 2006, where it is stated (in conjunction with whistle-blowing) that an obligation imposed by a foreign legal statute may not qualify as a legal

statutory civil litigation rules in the United States or the United Kingdom can neither impose legally valid obligations on Austrian individuals or companies nor can they legitimate the processing of personal data under the DPA. In addition, Austria did not sign the Hague Convention on the Taking of Evidence,[7] so that Letters of Request based upon the Hague Convention will not form valid legitimate reasons for the disclosure of personal data either. Also, Austrian local law does not provide a sufficient legal basis for answering e-discovery requests. Yet, the Austrian Code on Civil Procedure provides for scenarios where litigants can be obliged via court order to provide relevant documents to the court.[8] However, in a nutshell, it can be summarized that those provisions relate to pending proceedings and are not comparable to pretrial litigation rules as they exist in the United Kingdom and the United States. Therefore disclosing personal information in the course of an e-discovery request cannot be properly based upon 'statutory permissions' within the meaning of the DPA.

A. PRETRIAL DISCOVERY AND DATA PROTECTION IN AUSTRIA: CONSENT

Having said so, consent might form another legal ground for the processing of personal data. However, in the context of e-discovery this might be no more than theory. First, valid consent has to meet very strict formal requirements. Second, the consenting data subject is entitled to revoke his or her consent at any time without giving reason, which leads to the fact that pretrial disclosure based upon consent stands on rather shaky grounds.[9] Third, in most cases it will simply not be feasible to ask all individuals involved, which might be several hundreds of customers, for their consent. So consent will very unlikely provide a solid basis for the handling of e-discovery requests.

B. PRETRIAL DISCOVERY AND DATA PROTECTION IN AUSTRIA: OVERRIDING LEGITIMATE INTERESTS

A clearly more interesting starting point will therefore be processing of personal data upon overriding legitimate controller interests. In principle, trying to comply with e-discovery requests will certainly be within the 'legitimate interests' of the

---

obligation by virtue of which data processing in the EU would be made legitimate. Although not expressly stated in its hitherto decisions about whistleblowing in Austria, the Austrian Data Protection Commission nevertheless shared this view and based its approvals rather upon 'overriding legitimate controller interests' but not on the US Sarbanes-Oxley Act.
7. The Hague Convention on the Taking of Evidence Abroad in Civil and Commercial Matters of 18 Mar. 1970 (Hague Convention).
8. Section 303 CoCP.
9. Decision 4 Ob 179/02f of the Austrian Supreme Court, dated 19 Nov. 2002.

responding party. In this respect the DPA explicitly allows the processing of personal data upon 'overriding legitimate interests' of the data controller if this is required for establishing, exercising, or defending legal claims in court.[10] Although the aim of this provision is primarily to put litigants into the position to defend their positions in the course of already-pending litigations, it might nevertheless be validly arguable that complying with UK or US pretrial litigation rules is also covered by this exemption if the Australian company is affected by the litigation. This provision is essential for any data processing in the context of e-discovery, as it not only allows the processing of non-sensitive but also of sensitive data.[11] However, even if this approach can validly be argued, it nevertheless adds up in balancing the interests of the corresponding party as the data controller against the rights for privacy of the data subjects. This balancing check has to be done on a case-by-case basis, where, in a nutshell, the intrusiveness and the volume of the intended data disclosure have to be weighed against the relevance of the data for the upcoming litigation.

C.   PRETRIAL DISCOVERY AND DATA PROTECTION IN
       AUSTRIA: SUMMARY

In summary, all of these considerations show that there is a potential conflict between Austrian data protection law and e-discovery requests. In order to ease this conflict the corresponding party will generally be very well advised to limit the disclosure of information to anonymized data whenever possible. Another approach might be to encrypt the data where a third-party provider holds the key. In that scenario the data will be disclosed only on a pseudonymized level and the data will be decrypted only under well-founded circumstances.

D.   PRETRIAL DISCOVERY AND DATA PROTECTION IN
       AUSTRIA: REGISTRATION OBLIGATIONS

In the context of e-discovery, an Austrian-based company, when responding to an e-discovery or pretrial request, will frequently act as a data controller within the meaning of the DPA. This means not less than full responsibility and liability for any disclosure of personal data that comes along with responding to an e-discovery request.

In this respect the responding party (as the data controller) has to take care for the required filings with the Austrian authorities. First, any processing of personal data in Austria has to be registered with the Austrian Data Processing Register

---

10.   Section 8 para. 3 Sen 5 DPA; s. 9 para. 9 DPA.
11.   WP 158: establishment, exercise, or defence of legal claims under Art. 8(e) of the Data Pro-
      tection Directive might form appropriate ground for the processing (even) of sensitive data for
      the purpose of e-discovery.

(*Datenverarbeitungsregister* – DVR), which forms an organizational unit of the Austrian Data Protection Commission. As a general rule, processing of personal data can be started while the respective registration proceedings are still pending. However, for certain data categories, such as criminal or sensitive data, prior finalization of the registration proceedings is required. Second, in specific cases, such as international data transfers to third countries, the Data Processing Commission additionally has to give its approval. Such approval always has to be obtained before the data are transferred. So whenever it comes to answering e-discovery requests, the responding party will have to consider carefully the data categories involved in order to determine whether the registration has to be completed before any information is disclosed and, if required, it will be well advised to enter into the respective approval proceedings in due time.

E.   PRETRIAL DISCOVERY AND DATA PROTECTION IN AUSTRIA:
          INTERNATIONAL DATA TRANSFERS

Responding to pretrial requests will frequently require transferring data from Austria to other countries, very often to the United Kingdom or the United States. While UK-targeted data transfers will qualify as data transfers within the European Union (EU) and therefore do not have to comply with specific requirements under the DPA, any data transfers to non-EU countries (besides Switzerland) are subject to specific restrictions. As said, data transfers to third countries deemed to have 'inadequate' data protection standards require prior approval by the Austrian Data Protection Commission. Valid legal grounds for such data transfers might basically be produced through consent of the data subjects, appropriate Model Clauses, approved Binding Corporate Rules (BCRs), or a valid 'Safe Harbour' registration in case the requesting party is a US-based company. However, the handling of each of these alternatives is rather cumbersome, and (besides Safe Harbour) the responding party will always end up in tedious approval proceedings before the Austrian Data Protection Commission. It is therefore of key importance to understand that establishing, exercising, or defending legal claims in court not only forms valid legal reason for the disclosure of personal data but also for data transfer to third countries. In that case not even approval by the Data Protection Commission will be required. So if the responding party can validly argue that the intended data transfer is in line with establishing, exercising, or defending legal claims in court, this will put it in the position to circumvent tedious approval proceedings.

Another approach to avoid approval proceedings could be found in data transfers from the Austrian responding party to another EU-located entity where 'filtering' of the requested information takes place. This approach would be in line with the recommendation of the Article 29 Working Party, where the 'filtering' services of someone 'with sufficient knowledge of the litigation process' and who does not have a role in the litigation but has the sufficient level of independence and trustworthiness to reach proper determination of the relevance of the personal data might be appropriate.[12] However, a welcomed 'side effect' of this approach would be that any subsequent data transfers from this entity to the United States would not be subject to the DPA, and therefore would not be subject to approval requirements before the Austrian Data Protection Commission.

F.   PRETRIAL DISCOVERY AND DATA PROTECTION IN
          AUSTRIA: TIME MANAGEMENT

Appropriate timing is crucial. Not only does the processing of specific data categories (such as criminal or sensitive data) require finalized registration with the Austrian Data Processing Register, also approval proceedings have to be completed before the data are transferred to third countries. All in all, such registration and approval proceedings can easily take several months, sometimes even up to half a year. Of course, this potentially conflicts with the usually tight time frames for appropriate handling of e-discovery requests. Therefore strategically well-positioned notification and approval proceedings are crucial. As said, approval requirements might be circumvented on the basis of exercising or defending legal claims. If disclosure of criminal or sensitive data is unavoidable, registration requirements can nevertheless be mitigated when such data are processed only on a pseudonymized level. In that case the responding party will be in the position to start the data processing even before the registration is finalized.

IV.   CONCLUSION

E-discovery assigns new tasks for Austrian data protection law. However, e-discovery can be handled successfully despite the protective and rigid character of Austrian data protection law if advantage is taken of the law's loopholes in an advised manner.

---

12. WP 158.

Chapter 5.2

Belgium

*Fabienne Brison and Carina Gommers**

I.   DISCOVERY

A.   NATIONAL 'DISCOVERY' ORDERS

1.   In General

Belgian procedural law does not contain specific rules on discovery. On the contrary,

Article 870 of the Belgian Judicial Code stipulates that every party needs to prove what it alleges. In addition, parties are the master of the proceedings and the court has a more passive role.[1]

However, the subsequent Article 871 of the Belgian Judicial Code immediately provides an opportunity for the court to order a party to the litigation to produce evidence in its possession. In addition, Article 877 of the Belgian Judicial Code stipulates that a court can order the production of evidence by a party to the litigation or even a third party when there exist important, precise, and corresponding presumptions that that party has such evidence in its possession

*   Fabienne Brison, partner at Howrey LLP, professor at the Vrije Universiteit Brussel (ECOR, LSTS, and SMIT), the Hogeschool-Universiteit Brussel, and guest professor at the University of Liège; and Carina Gommers, senior associate at Howrey LLP and affiliated junior researcher at the Katholieke Universiteit Leuven.
1.   Brussels Court of Appeal, 18 Dec. 2008, <www.juridat.be>.

Catrien Noorda & Stefan Hanloser, *E-Discovery and Data Privacy*, pp. 43–55.
© 2011 Kluwer Law International BV, The Netherlands.

and that it can prove a relevant fact. Such orders are similar to discovery in the sense that a court orders a party, upon request of another party, to produce certain documents and/or information.[2] However, other than in respect of US-style discovery, such a court order would relate to specific documents or information. 'Fishing expeditions' are not allowed.

2. Specific Procedures

In addition, specific procedures exist that are also similar to discovery orders. We refer in this respect to the possibilities in intellectual property litigation of applying for a *saisie-description*[3] and for an order to provide certain documents and/or information relating to, for example, the origin of infringing goods.[4]

3. Enforceability

Deceptively destroying, altering, or hiding evidence that is subject to a national 'discovery' order is criminally sanctioned pursuant to Article 495*bis* of the Belgian Criminal Code.

Furthermore, most national 'discovery' orders will be requested with a penalty payment in application of Article 1385*bis* of the Belgian Judicial Code. If the court orders the discovery under penalty payment, the party not complying with the order needs to pay that penalty to the requesting party. If no penalty payment is foreseen in the order, the party requesting the discovery can attempt to obtain damages from the party not complying with the 'discovery' order under the general rules of tort law. But in that case, the requesting party would need to substantiate the fault, causal link, and the actual damages suffered. Article 882 of the Belgian Judicial Code confirms this, since it explicitly provides that parties or third parties, who, without any lawful justification, withhold from submitting the evidence as ordered by the judge can be ordered to pay damages.

B.   DISCOVERY ORDERS FROM ABROAD, INCLUDING THE
         UNITED STATES

Belgium does not have any specific blocking statutes that would prohibit compliance with a discovery order from a court abroad. In the past, protection against foreign discovery orders was sought before the Belgian courts, requesting the Belgian courts to prohibit a party to initiate or pursue discovery proceedings

---

2. For a more detailed overview of these possible national 'discovery' orders, see: P. Van Leynseele, 'Pour un modèle belge de la procédure de Discovery?', J.T. (1997): 225.
3. Articles 1369*bis*/1 to 1369*bis*/10 of the Belgian Judicial Code.
4. Article 53 § 3 of the Belgian Patent Act of 28 Mar. 1984, Art. 86*ter* § 3 of the Belgian Copyright Act of 30 Jun. 1994, and Arts 2.22.4 and 3.18.4 of the Benelux Treaty on Intellectual Property Rights (with respect to trademarks and industrial design rights).

abroad. The Dendermonde Commercial Court ruled that a Belgian court does not have jurisdiction to rule on a possible abuse of judicial proceedings abroad: once the discovery had been ordered by a foreign court, the legitimacy thereof had been confirmed by that court that enjoys jurisdictional immunity.[5] The Brussels Court of Appeal, however, ruled in summary proceedings that it had jurisdiction and could grant interim measures, such as a suspension of the discovery order, if it has jurisdiction to hear the case on the merits.[6] The Brussels Court of Appeal deemed irrelevant that the requested interim measures were destined to be executed abroad.[7]

If such order would come from within the European Union (EU), the Council Regulation Number 1206/2001 of 28 May 2001 on cooperation between the courts of the Member States in the taking of evidence in civil or commercial matters should be applied.

If the discovery order comes from outside of the EU, the Hague Convention of 1 March 1954 on civil procedure is applicable in Belgium.

II. BELGIAN DATA PROTECTION LAW

The Belgian Data Protection Act was enacted on 8 December 1992 (hereinafter the 'BDPA').[8] The BDPA was later amended by the Act of 11 December 1998 to implement the European Data Protection Directive[9] (hereinafter the 'Directive') in Belgium. The Royal Decree of 13 February 2001 further implements the BDPA (hereinafter the 'Royal Decree').[10]

A. GENERAL RULES

1. Scope of Application

a. Material Application

i. 'Personal Data'
Article 1, section 1 of the BDPA stipulates, in conformity with the Directive, that the term 'personal data' refers to any information relating to an identified or

---

5. See Dendermonde Commercial Court, 3 Jan. 2000, R.W. (2000–2001): 1095–1097.
6. See Brussels Court of Appeal, 21 Oct. 2005, TBH (2006): 970.
7. *Ibid.*
8. See <www.privacycommission.be/en/static/pdf/wetgeving/privacy-act-september-2009.pdf> for an English translation of the BDPA.
9. Directive 95/46/EC of the European Parliament and of the Council of 24 Oct. 1995 on the protection of individuals with regard to the processing of personal data and on the free movement of such data.
10. See <www.privacycommission.be/en/static/pdf/wetgeving/royal-decree-2001-september-2009.pdf> for an English translation of the Royal Decree.

identifiable natural person, in particular through an identification number or one or more specific factors characterizing his or her physical, physiological, mental, economic, cultural, or social identity.

Information is considered a broad concept, not limited to facts but also including perceptions, such as a sound or an image.[11]

ii.   Processing

Article 1, section 2 of the BDPA defines, in conformity with the Directive, what constitutes processing of personal data: any (set of) operation(s) performed upon personal data, whether or not performed by automated means, such as collection, recording, organization, storage, alteration, retrieval, consultation, use, disclosure by transmission, dissemination or otherwise making available, combination, alignment, blocking, erasure, or destruction.

Processing done by a natural person in the course of a purely personal or household activity is excluded from the scope of application of the BDPA.[12]

b.   Territorial Application

According to Article 3*bis* of the BDPA, the BDPA is applicable on processing of personal data when:

(i) the processing is carried out in the context of effective and genuine activities of an establishment of the controller in the Belgian territory or in a place where, by virtue of international public laws, Belgian law applies; or

(ii) the processing is done by using equipment located in Belgium, unless such equipment is solely used for transiting data through Belgium.

2.   Applicable Rules

a.   Situations in Which Personal Data Can Be Processed

i.   In General

Article 5 of the BDPA stipulates that personal data may only be processed if:

- the data subject has unambiguously given his or her consent;
- it is necessary for the performance of a contract to which the data subject is party or in order to take steps at the request of the data subject prior to entering into a contract;
- it is necessary for compliance with a legal obligation to which the controller is subject;
- it is necessary in order to protect the vital interests of the data subject;

---

11. J. Dumortier, 'Privacybescherming en gegevensverwerking', *Vlaams Jurist Vandaag* (1993): 6.
12. Article 3 § 2 of the BDPA.

- it is necessary for the performance of a task carried out in the public interest or in the exercise of official authority vested in the controller or in a third party to whom the data are disclosed; or
- it is necessary for the purposes of the legitimate interests pursued by the controller or by the third party or parties to whom the data are disclosed, except where such interests are overridden by the interests of the fundamental rights and freedoms of the data subject.

Of the above possible situations in which personal data can be processed, we consider that unambiguous consent and the necessity for the purposes of the legitimate interests pursued by the controller are relevant in case of discovery orders. In the latter case, care should be taken that the fundamental rights and freedoms of the data subject do not override the interests of the controller, since in that case there would no longer be a justification to process the personal data.

Relying on consent is problematic when the data subjects are employees (see section II.B below).

ii.   For the Processing of Sensitive Data
Articles 6 to 8 of the BDPA provide stricter rules for the processing of so-called sensitive data, that is, data relating to race or ethnic origin, political opinions, religious or philosophical beliefs, trade union membership, sex life, as well as medical and judicial data. The BDPA requires, for instance, that for the processing of such data (except the judicial data[13]), consent does not only need to be unambiguous, but also in writing. Some question whether this extra criterion for consent, going beyond what was required by the Directive, can be upheld in the long term.[14]

*b.   Conditions in Which the Processing of Personal Data
Is Legitimate*

In addition, Article 4, section 1 of the BDPA provides that processing is only legitimate when the personal data are:

- processed fairly and lawfully;
- collected for specified, explicit, and legitimate purposes and not further processed in a way incompatible with those purposes;
- adequate, relevant, and not excessive in relation to the purposes for which they are collected and/or further processed;

---

13. Article 8 of the BDPA describes under which conditions data relating to judicial and administrative proceedings can be processed, for example, when the processing is done by lawyers or legal counsel and insofar as necessary to protect the interest of their clients. Article 8 does not indicate that processing would be permissible if the data subject has given his or her unambiguous and/or written consent.
14. D. De Bot, Art. 6 Wet Persoonsgegevens, in X., *Personen- en familierecht, Artikelsgewijze commentaar met overzicht van rechtspraak en rechtsleer*, Kluwer, Mechelen, 1 Sep. 2001, looseleaf.

- accurate and, where necessary, kept up to date; every reasonable step must be taken to ensure that data which are inaccurate or incomplete, having regard to the purposes for which they were collected or for which they are further processed, are erased or rectified; and
- kept in a form that permits identification of data subjects for no longer than is necessary for the purposes for which the data were collected or for which they are further processed.

c.   *Notification Duty*

For any *automated* processing of personal data, Article 17 of the BDPA provides that, prior to the processing, a notification should be filed by the controller[15] or his or her representative with the Supervisory Authority in Belgium, that is, the Commission for the Protection of Privacy (hereinafter 'the Belgian Privacy Commission').[16] Such notification can be filed online on the Belgian Privacy Commission's website.[17]

The Royal Decree, however, provides that no notification should be filed for some processing, such as for payroll administration (provided that the conditions of Article 51 of the Royal Decree are met) or for customer and supplier management (insofar as the conditions of Article 55 of the Royal Decree are met).

d.   *Rights of the Data Subject*

Articles 9 to 12 of the BDPA enumerate the rights of the data subject, namely:

- the information right (what kind of information needs to be given to the data subject, for example, the name and address of the controller and the purposes of the processing, and when);
- the access rights (and their conditions);
- the right to correct and/or delete (and its conditions); and
- the opt-out right in case of direct marketing.

In case of an e-discovery order, the controller needs to take note of these rights of the data subject and respect them. This implies, for instance, that in case of collection of data from the data subject, the data subject has, pursuant to Article 9, section 1 of the BDPA, a right to receive certain information (e.g., the purpose of processing) ultimately at the moment upon which the data are obtained, unless the data subject already has such information. In case of collection of data from a third

---

15. The controller is pursuant to Art. 1 § 4 of the BDPA and in conformity with the Directive, the natural or legal person, factual association, or public authority that alone or jointly with others determines the purposes and means of the processing of personal data. The Art. 29 Working Party provides further guidance on the concepts of 'controller' and 'processor' in Working Document 169, issued on 16 Feb. 2010.
16. Commission for the Protection of Privacy, rue Haute 139, 1000 Brussels, T: +32 2 213 85 40, F: +32 2 213 85 65, e-mail: commission@privacycommission.be.
17. <www.privacycommission.be>.

party, the obligation to provide information arises at the time of recording the data or when communication thereof to a third party is considered, unless the data subject already has such information.

e.   *Transfer to Third Countries*

Article 21, section 1 of the BDPA provides that personal data that are undergoing processing after transfer may in principle only be transferred outside the EU insofar as the third country provides an adequate level of protection. It is up to the European Commission (EC) to determine which countries ensure an adequate level of protection.

Article 21, section 2 of the BDPA further stipulates that transfer of personal data outside the EU for certain types of processing and in some circumstances may be prohibited by a Royal Decree, after having received the opinion of the Belgian Privacy Commission and in compliance with Article 25 of the Directive.

In addition, Article 22 of the BDPA allows the transfer of personal data outside the EU to countries not ensuring an adequate level of protection in one of the following cases:

- the data subject has given his or her unambiguous consent for the transfer;
- the transfer is necessary for the performance of an agreement between the data subject and the controller or for the performance of pre-contractual arrangements made on request of the data subject;
- the transfer is necessary for the conclusion or performance of an agreement between the controller and a third party that is in the interest of the data subject;
- the transfer is necessary or mandatory due to an important public interest or for the establishment, exercise, or defence of a legal claim;
- the transfer is necessary for the protection of the vital interests of the data subject; or
- the transfer is done from a public register that, according to the laws or regulations, is intended to inform the public and that can be consulted by anyone who can demonstrate a legitimate interest, insofar as the conditions for consultation in that particular case have been complied with.

With respect to e-discovery, we consider that two of the above-mentioned cases are relevant. First, one could rely on the unambiguous consent of the data subject.[18] Second, one could argue that the transfer is necessary or mandatory due to an important public interest or for the establishment, exercise, or defence of a legal claim.

Finally, Article 22 *in fine* of the BDPA provides for the possibility of a transfer to third countries not ensuring an adequate level of protection in cases where an agreement ensuring adequate protection and binding both the sending and the receiving party governs the transfer. This agreement should describe, for example,

---

18. This is problematic when the data subject is an employee (see s. II.B below).

the categories of personal data that will be processed, the purpose of the transfer, the recipients, and the security measures that will be taken to limit the risk of unauthorized access.

In Belgium, such an agreement needs to be enacted in a Royal Decree, after having received an opinion from the Belgian Privacy Commission.[19] The authorization by Royal Decree is, however, not necessary when the agreement is identical to the Standard Contractual Clauses (SCCs) drafted by the EU,[20] since these ensure an adequate level of protection in any event.[21]

The EC has drafted two types of SCCs for a transfer from controller to controller: Commission Decision 2001/497/EC of 15 June 2001 on SCCs for the transfer of personal data to third countries, under Directive 95/46/EC, and Commission Decision 2004-915/EC of 27 December 2004 amending Decision 2001/497/EC as regards the introduction of an alternative set of SCCs for the transfer of personal data to third countries. In addition, the EC also drafted SCCs for the transfer from a controller to a processor: Commission Decision 2010/87/EU of 5 February 2010 on SCCs for the transfer of personal data to processors established in third countries under Directive 95/46/EC, replacing with effect from 15 May 2010 the Commission Decision 2002/16/EC of 27 December 2001 that previously provided the SCCs for the transfer from a controller to a processor.

Information about the possible transfer of the personal data should be included in the notification to be filed with the Belgian Privacy Commission (see section II.A.2.c above).

f.   *Possible Liabilities*

Data subjects can file a complaint with the Belgian Privacy Commission for any incorrect processing. The Commission will then act as a mediator to reach an amicable settlement (Article 31 of the BDPA).

Under Belgian law, the liabilities for non-compliance with the BDPA are the following:

- Data subjects can initiate proceedings before the President of the District Court when processing of their personal data is not done correctly (Article 14 of the BDPA). Data subjects, however, need to contact the controller prior to initiating such proceedings (Article 14, section 5 of the BDPA). The President of the District Court can subsequently order that certain personal data be corrected or removed.
- The controller is liable for any damages suffered by data subjects due to incorrect processing or any other violation of the BDPA, unless the controller is able to prove that the damage was caused by a fact for which he or

---

19. Article 22 *in fine* of the BDPA.
20. See para. 4.I.H above.
21. This is confirmed on the Belgian Privacy Commission's website: <www.privacycommission. be/en/in_practice/grensoverschrijdende_doorgifte_van_persoonsgegeven/#N100EF>.

she cannot be held accountable (Article 15*bis* of the BDPA), for example, *force majeure*.[22]

The BDPA provides criminal sanctions for incorrect processing by the controller:

- a penalty of Euros (EUR) 550 up to EUR 110,000 for:
- the communication of personal data without mentioning that the data subject objected thereto; or
- not implementing sufficient security measures when working with a processor.

To avoid this sanction the controller must:

(1) choose a processor providing sufficient guarantees in respect of technical security measures and organizational measures governing the process to be carried out;
(2) ensure compliance with those measures by including those in a contract with the processor;
(3) provide in the same contract the liability of the processor to the controller;
(4) stipulate in the same contract that the processor shall act only on instructions of the controller and that the obligations of the controller to implement appropriate technical and organizational security measures to protect personal data against accidental or unlawful destruction, accidental loss, alteration, unauthorized disclosure or access – in particular when data is transmitted over a network – and against all other unlawful forms of processing, are also incumbent on the processor; and
(5) ensure that the contract is in writing or in an electronic form (for the purpose of keeping proof) (Article 32 of the BDPA).
    - a penalty of EUR 550 up to EUR 550,000 for any violation of Articles 4 through 10, sections 1, 17, 19, and 22 (Article 39 of the BDPA[23]);
    - In case of criminal sanctions, the court can order that the judgment should be published in one or more newspapers (Article 40 of the BDPA).
    - In case of criminal sanctions, the court can also order the forfeiture of certain equipment used to process the data as well as prohibit the controller to process data directly or through an intermediary during up to two years as from the judgment (Article 41 of the BDPA).

---

22. D. De Bot, Art. 15*bis* Wet Persoonsgegevens, in X., *Personen- en familierecht, Artikelsgewijze commentaar met overzicht van rechtspraak en rechtsleer,* Kluwer, Mechelen, 1 Sep. 2001, loosleaf.
23. As indicated above, these Articles concern, for example, the conditions of legitimate processing and the rights of the data subjects.

Fabienne Brison and Carina Gommers

B.   PARTICULAR RULES REGARDING EMPLOYEES' E-MAIL

Since e-mail[24] can be qualified as correspondence between natural persons and can contain information about such persons, the principle is that a third party cannot take note of the content thereof without the authorization of all parties involved. This is the mere application of the BDPA, however confirmed, wholly or partly, in different other regulations.

First, Article 314*bis* of the Belgian Criminal Code criminally sanctions anyone who deliberately reads private communications, such as an e-mail (non-professional), to which he or she is not party, insofar as this is done during the transmission thereof. The Correctional Court of Leuven considered that Article 314 is applicable when e-mail messages are stored on a server, insofar as the recipient has not yet activated his or her mailbox and had a possibility to open and read the e-mail.[25]

Second, Article 124 of the Belgian Electronic Communications Act of 13 June 2005 in addition sanctions anyone who:

– intentionally takes note of the existence of information of any kind that has been sent electronically, not being the addressee and not having received permission of all parties involved in the communication;
– intentionally identifies persons involved with the transmission and the content of that information;
– intentionally takes note of the data regarding the electronic communication not relating to him- or herself; or
– alters, deletes, publishes, saves, or uses information, identification, or data received either intentionally or unintentionally.

However, Article 128 of the Belgian Electronic Communications Act provides an exception to this prohibition for the registration of electronic communication performed in legal business transactions in order to prove a commercial transaction or another business communication, on the condition that the parties to the communication were informed of the registration, as well as the precise purposes and the duration thereof, prior to that registration. The Act also indicates that the registered data should be destroyed once the term to initiate proceedings against the transaction has expired.

The Ghent Court of Appeal decided that an e-mail of the defendant sent to a third party could be admitted as evidence, since the foregoing articles had not been contravened.[26] The Court ruled that the BDPA was not breached since the e-mail in question did not contain personal data. With regard to Article 109*ter* D of the

---

24. We emphasize that professional e-mails can also be protected by the right to privacy (see in this respect ECHR, 16 Dec. 1992, *Publ. ECHR A*, n°251-B).
25. Corr. Leuven, 4 Dec. 2007, *T. Strafr. 2008/3*, 223–226.
26. Ghent, 16 Jun. 2004, *Soc. Kron.* 2005, 48–53.

Belgian Telecommunications Act of 21 March 1991,[27] the Court considered that this only related to the existence of the telecommunication and not to the content thereof. Still, according to the Court, it only sanctioned, under the therein enumerated conditions, that third parties control who, at what time, from where, or with whom the telecommunications means are used.

Third, further specific rules apply to the processing of employees' e-mail, which can be found in the Collective Employment Agreement Number 81 of 26 April 2002[28] (hereinafter the 'CEA 81').

As a rule, the CEA 81 provides that monitoring of employees' e-mail can only be done bearing in mind the rules as set forth in the BDPA, and the principles of finality, proportionality, and transparency.

The principle of finality implies that interception and inspection of e-mail is only allowed insofar as it serves one of the following purposes:

- preventing unlawful or defamatory facts, facts contrary to public morals, or facts that could harm the dignity of another person;
- protecting the economical, commercial, and financial stakes of the company, which are confidential, and also preventing practices contrary to such stakes;
- safeguarding the safety and/or good technical operation of the information technology (IT) network systems of the company, including the control on costs thereof as well as the protection of the installations of the company; or
- respecting the *bona fide* compliance of the company policy and rules for the use of online technologies.

Although it depends on the specific circumstances, e-discovery investigations in our opinion typically fall under the first two or the last bullet.

The interception and inspection should also be proportional, meaning that the interference with the privacy of the employees should be limited to the extent necessary. The CEA 81 further clarifies that, in principle, only global general data can be collected by the company. 'Global data' are, for example, the number of e-mails sent per 'working post' and the size of these e-mails, but not the identification of the employee who sent such e-mails.

If individualization of e-mails is done, meaning the processing of the global data to data that can be linked to an identified or identifiable person, a direct or indirect procedure has to be followed depending on the purpose of such individualization:[29]

(i) For the three first purposes mentioned above a direct individualization is possible. This implies that if the company becomes aware of an irregularity during the processing of the global data, the company can

---

27. The Arts 109*ter* C until 109*ter* E of the Belgian Telecommunications Act of 21 Mar. 1991 (published in the *Belgian State Gazette* of 27 Mar. 1991) are the precursors of Arts 124 and 125 of the of the Belgian Electronic Communications Act.
28. Published in the *Belgian State Gazette* of 29 Jun. 2002.
29. See Art. 15 of the CEA n° 81.

immediately individualize the data in order to track down the identity of the responsible person(s).

(ii) For the last purpose mentioned above, an indirect procedure needs to be followed, which implies a prior information phase to the employees concerned.

This prior information phase is destined to inform the employees that an irregularity has been discovered and that the global data will be individualized if such irregularity is again discovered. In the indirect individualization procedure, the responsible employee is also invited by the company for a meeting prior to any decision or evaluation that can have an effect on the employee in question.

Finally, the principle of transparency results in an obligation for the employer to inform the employees both collectively (via the works council if there exists one in the company) and individually.[30]

The information should be explicit, effective, clearly understandable, and accurate.

Fourth, we can mention the Collective Employment Agreement Number 68 of 16 June 1998 regarding camera surveillance.[31]

III. APPLICATION OF BELGIAN DATA PROTECTION IN DISCOVERY PROCEEDINGS

A. NATIONAL 'DISCOVERY' ORDERS

If a Belgian court orders a national 'discovery', personal data will most likely be processed. The personal data to be processed could be identification data (e.g., names, addresses, or telephone numbers) and could also include sensitive data (e.g., health-related data or judicial data).

If the BDPA is applicable (see above), the parties to the litigation should take care that the processing of the personal data is in compliance with the BDPA. One possibility to legitimately process personal data, excluding judicial data, in case of a national 'discovery' order is to request the consent of the data subjects.[32] This might be complicated and, insofar as employee data are concerned, insufficient.[33] Employees are considered not to be in a position to fully give free consent. This is confirmed in Article 27 of the Royal Decree that prohibits processing of sensitive personal data, such as health-related data, even if written consent is obtained, when the controller is the employer of the data subject.

---

30. See Arts 7 and 8 of the CEA n° 81.
31. Published in the *Belgian State Gazette* of 2 Oct. 1998.
32. Articles 5 a), 6 § 2 a), and 7 § 2 a) of the BDPA.
33. Employees are considered not to be in a position to fully give free consent. This is confirmed in Art. 27 of the Royal Decree that prohibits processing of sensitive personal data, such as health-related data, even if written consent is obtained, when the controller is the employer of the data subject.

Another justification could be the necessity of processing the personal data to comply with a legal obligation of the controller,[34] and in case of sensitive data, the necessity of the processing of such data in order to determine, exercise, or defend a right in judicial proceedings.[35]

The controller could finally also try to rely on the necessity to process personal data for the purposes of its legitimate interests or of the parties to whom the data are disclosed. In that case, such interests need to be balanced against the interests of the fundamental rights of the data subject.[36]

The other applicable rules set out above regarding the conditions in which the processing is legitimate and the rights of the data subject should also be complied with. Finally, a notification should be filed with the Privacy Commission insofar as the processing is done wholly or partly automated.

B.   DISCOVERY ORDERS FROM ABROAD

For discovery orders from abroad, we consider that the same rules apply and, in addition, the rules regarding transfer of personal data to third countries need to be complied with.

In Belgium, Working Party Document 158 on pretrial discovery for cross-border civil litigation can be followed for guidance. It confirms that there exist three possible justifications for the processing of personal data in case of a discovery order from abroad: consent, necessity for compliance with a legal obligation, and necessity for the purposes of a legitimate interest,[37] and that data can be transferred to determine, exercise, or defend a right in legal proceedings. It further emphasizes that controllers have an obligation to limit the discovery of personal data to such data that are objectively relevant for the litigation[38] and that the rights of the data subjects should be respected.[39] It finally reiterates the rules on the transfer to third countries.[40]

---

34. Article 5 c) of the BDPA.
35. Articles 6 § 2 f) and 7 § 2 i) of the BDPA.
36. Article 5 f) of the BDPA.
37. Working Document 158 on pretrial discovery for cross-border civil litigation of 11 Feb. 2009, 8–9.
38. *Ibid.*, 10.
39. *Ibid.*, 11–12.
40. *Ibid.*, 13.

Chapter 5.3

Bulgaria

*Irena Georgieva and Mirena Taskova**

I.   INTRODUCTION

The Bulgarian legal system is unfamiliar with pretrial discovery and, in particular, e-discovery. Furthermore, the practice of the Bulgarian courts and competent authorities shows that they do not often have to resolve complex cross-border cases where discovery issues may have to be dealt with. Notwithstanding the above, the clash between the common law pretrial discovery requirements and the domestic data protection regulation exists in theory, due to the fact that the principles underlying the relevant Bulgarian legal framework do not differ much from those in the other European Union (EU) Member States.

A.   PRETRIAL DISCOVERY IN BULGARIA: GENERAL

'Pretrial discovery' as a means for collecting evidence is not regulated in the Bulgarian civil procedure legislation. According to the Bulgarian Code of Civil Procedure[1] (CCP), '[t]he contested facts relevant to the resolving of a case and the

---

*   Irena Georgieva and Mirena Taskova, Attorneys at Law at Schönherr in cooperation with Advokatsko druzhestvo Andreev, Stoyanov & Tsekova, Sofia, Bulgaria.
1.   Promulgated in the State Gazette No. 59/20.07.2007, effective 1 Mar. 2008, last amended SG No. 13/16.02.2010.

Catrien Noorda & Stefan Hanloser, *E-Discovery and Data Privacy*, pp. 57–65.
© 2011 Kluwer Law International BV, The Netherlands.

links there between have to be proved'.[2] In addition, the CCP stipulates that *'[a]ny motions by the parties for admission of evidence regarding facts which are irrelevant to adjudication of the case*, as well as any untimely motions for admission of evidence, would be *denied by the court* by a ruling' (emphasis added). In practice, the goal of pretrial discovery to collect as much evidence as possible and then to sift out the relevant evidence for the case is rather uncommon and seems to be impracticable for Bulgaria. However, no 'blocking statutes' are in place that may potentially hinder in Bulgaria the cooperation with foreign court authorities in civil litigation proceedings, unless such cooperation interferes with other specific legislative restrictions (as discussed hereunder).

B.   PRETRIAL DISCOVERY IN BULGARIA: HAGUE CONVENTION ON THE TAKING OF EVIDENCE

As a signatory to the Hague Convention on the Taking of Evidence,[3] Bulgaria cooperates with other jurisdictions on foreign litigants' requests for collecting evidence. Consequently, where any discovery is being sought in Bulgaria the Hague Convention (and in addition the Council Regulation (EC) Number 1206/2001[4]) will be considered as a 'first resort' requirement.

In the Hague Convention Ratification Act,[5] Bulgaria has declared – on the basis of Article 23 of the Hague Convention – that it will not execute any court requests for pretrial discovery of documents, as applicable in the common law countries. It must be emphasized that according to the Bulgarian Ministry of Justice,[6] this reservation[7] is considered as a sufficient legal ground on which any pretrial discovery request may be rejected. Currently, this remains a live issue mainly for the US trial procedures, as in 2003 the United Kingdom has also made a reservation under Article 23.[8]

---

2. Article 153 of the CCP.
3. The Hague Convention on the Taking of Evidence Abroad in Civil and Commercial Matters of 18 Mar. 1970 (Hague Convention).
4. Council Regulation (EC) No. 1206/2001 of 28 May 2001 on cooperation between the courts of the Member States in the taking of evidence in civil or commercial matters.
5. Act on the ratification of the Convention on the taking of evidence abroad in civil and commercial matters, promulgated SG N 83/21 Sep. 1999.
6. The Bulgarian Ministry of Justice is appointed to be the central authority, which receives Letters of Request from the judicial authority of other Contracting States and transmits them to the authority competent to execute them, as required under Art. 2 of the Hague Convention.
7. Under Article 23 of the Hague Convention.
8. The United Kingdom's declaration (from 2003) on Art. 23 is to the effect that it '[w]ill not execute Letters of Request issued for the purpose of obtaining pre-trial discovery of documents...'. The declaration provides furthermore for a more detailed description of the phrase 'Letters of Request issued for the purpose of obtaining pre-trial discovery of documents'.

C.　　　　　PRETRIAL DISCOVERY IN BULGARIA: *AÉROSPATIALE* CASE AND ITS
　　　　　　REFLECTION IN BULGARIA

As explained above, the Bulgarian authorities would deem the Hague Convention reservation as the relevant ground on which the US pretrial discovery requests must be declined. Nevertheless, the practice of the US courts and in particular the milestone decision under the *Aérospatiale* case[9] must be taken into consideration. In 1987 the US Supreme Court held that the Hague Convention requisites are not obligatory for trial procedures in the United States, and the litigants could use the domestic procedures without following the sophisticated standardized procedure of the Hague Convention. It is stated in the decision that the 'Letters of Request-procedure' is a recommendable but not exclusive order for collecting evidence from abroad. The conclusions of *Aérospatiale* are being followed by most of the US courts, and the latter request the procedure under the Hague Convention to be observed on an exceptional basis.[10] Moreover, the recent US court practise in cases such as *Columbia Pictures Indus.*,[11] as well as other emblematic cases from the near past,[12] not only supports the decision in *Aérospatiale*, but also rules out arguments that foreign data protection legislation may be a valid restriction on the processing or transfer of any data to the United States.

Due to the fact that the Bulgarian authorities are not frequently facing cross-border discovery cases, the US court practise already recognizable in other European countries is not yet taken into consideration by the litigators in Bulgaria. However, every litigator must be aware of the above practice, which actually diminished the effect of the Bulgarian reservation under Article 23 of the Hague Convention and might prevent reliance on the national data disclosure restrictions. After Working Paper 158 on pretrial discovery for cross-border civil litigation,[13] it should be expected for Bulgaria to start analysing in detail the collision between its legislation and the pretrial discovery activities and to prepare its position in dealing with future cross-border litigation cases.

C.　　　　　PRETRIAL DISCOVERY IN BULGARIA: EFFECT OF WORKING
　　　　　　PAPER 158

Despite the proposal discussed in February 2009 that the countries having made declarations under Article 23 have to abandon such reservations in the name of the

---

9. *Société Nationale Industrielle Aérospatiale v. US Dist. Ct.*, 482 US 522, 542 (1987).
10. To this effect are the conclusions of the Compendium of reported post-*Aérospatiale* cases citing the Hague Evidence Convention compiled for the American Bar Association by McNamara/ Hendrix/Charepoo (June 1987–July 2003).
11. *Columbia Pictures Industries v. Justin Bunnell*, Case No. CV 06-1093 FMC(JCx), 2007 U.S. Dist.
12. *Gerling Global Reinsurance Corp. of Am. v. Low*, 186. F. Supp. 2d 1099, 1113 (E.D. Cal. 2001); *BREIN Foundation v. UPC Nederland B.V.*, 194741/KGZA-05-462/BL/EV (2005), etc.
13. Working Paper 158 of 11 Feb. 2009, published by the European 'Working Party on the Protection of Individuals with regard to the Processing of Personal Data'.

prompt taking of evidence in cross-border civil cases, most of these countries – including Bulgaria – are not willing to do so. Still, Working Paper 158 has initiated a process of facilitating pretrial discovery by inviting the interested parties 'to enter a dialogue with the Working Party'.[14] In addition, evaluating the consequences of the *Aérospatiale* case and the ensuing US court practise, Working Paper 158 declares the procedure under the Hague Convention to be just one of the possible ways for collecting evidence for the needs of the pretrial discovery.

II. DATA PROTECTION LAW IN BULGARIA

Bulgaria demonstrated its intention to harmonize the Bulgarian legislation with the EU at a very early stage[15] by taking the necessary steps to secure the same level of data protection in Bulgaria as in the EU Member States. The protection of personal data is regulated by the Personal Data Protection Act (PDPA)[16] that entered into force in the beginning of 2002. The PDPA implemented the Convention 108[17] as well as the Privacy Directive 95/46/EC[18] and represents a typical civil law act. After Bulgaria's accession as a Member State,[19] all amendments and supplements to the Act are based on the necessity for full compliance of the PDPA with the EU data protection legislation and for complete protection of the person's personal data.

A. DATA PROTECTION LAW IN BULGARIA: EMPLOYEES' PERSONAL DATA

In accordance with the Labour Code[20] and the PDPA, any employer may collect personal data from its employees upon registering as a data controller with the Bulgarian Commission for Personal Data Protection (CPDP). However, the employer may collect data for specifically defined legal purposes only if the processing is necessary for the fulfilment of obligations under an agreement to which the employee is a party, or if the employee has given his or her explicit consent.

The e-discovery procedure might involve processing of e-mails of the employees. As per the Constitution of the Republic of Bulgaria, the confidentiality

---

14. Conclusion of Working Paper 158, last sentence.
15. Predating its accession to the EU.
16. Promulgated, SG No. 01/04.01.2002; last amended SG No. 42/05.06.2009.
17. Council of Europe Convention for the protection of individuals with regards to automatic processing of personal data, 1981 (Convention 108).
18. Council Directive 95/46, Protection of individuals with regard to the processing of personal data and on the free movement of such data, 1995 O.J. (L 281) 31 (EC) (Privacy Directive).
19. Accession of Bulgaria and Romania to the EU, dated 1 Jan. 2007; Accession Treaty signed 25 Apr. 2005.
20. Promulgated, SG No. 26/01.04.1986; last amended SG No. 77/01.10.2010.

and freedom of correspondence are inviolable.[21] Furthermore, the Criminal Code provides for sanctioning of criminal offences related to the inviolability of the messages (including messages by electronic means). Therefore, the review of employees' correspondence could be considered as a breach of the Bulgarian legislation.

On the grounds of the PDPA, the processing of the employees' e-mails could be done after their explicit consent. If the employee agreed and signed internal rules of the employer providing for such processing, then additional consent of the employee is not necessary. In any case, if the employer is already registered as a data controller but the data subject to processing are not data about which the possibility to process has been registered in the CPDP's registers, actions for making an update of the registers have to be undertaken. Notwithstanding the above, the CPDP shows lack of any substantial practice or control over the employees' data processing.

B.   DATA PROTECTION LAW IN BULGARIA: ELECTRONIC COMMUNICATION

The Electronic Communications Act[22] (ECA) has transposed in Bulgaria the obligatory directions of the E-Privacy Directive[23] and thus establishes strict rules about confidentiality with respect to the processing of personal and traffic metadata. The explicit consent of the sender and the recipient is a *conditio sine qua non* for the tapping, recording, storage, or other types of interception or surveillance of electronically exchanged communication[24] (and the related traffic metadata) by any other person different from the sender and the recipient.[25]

The ECA provides for some exceptions from the above restriction, where the transposition of the relevant provisions of the E-Privacy Directive is not precise and impedes the interpretation of the legal text to a great extent. The lack of any practice of the CPDP or of the other competent authorities casts doubts over the scope of these exceptions.

---

21. Exceptions to this rule are permissible solely upon authorization from the judiciary, where this is necessitated for detection or prevention of grave crimes.
22. Promulgated, SG No. 41/22.05.2007; last amended SG No. 27/09.04.2010.
23. Directive 2002/58/EC of the European Parliament and of the Council of 12 Jul. 2002 concerning the processing of personal data and the protection of privacy in the electronic communications sector (E-Privacy Directive).
24. The ECA provides also for detailed elaboration on the rights of the undertakings providing public electronic communications networks and/or services to collect, process, and use data on users where such data are designated directly for the provision of electronic communications services.
25. Except for certain cases, explicitly provided by law.
    Further, with one of the last amendments of the ECA (which faced strong public disagreement), the Bulgarian legislator has widened the possibilities for storage of different kinds of traffic metadata (generally) concerning phone and e-mail services. The metadata is stored for the purposes of detection and investigation of serious criminal offences. However, processing and storage of data under the ECA should be always in compliance with the strict requirements of the PDPA. Processing of content is generally prohibited.

In the first place, the E-Privacy Directive explicitly provides that the technical storage necessary for the conveyance of communications must not be affected by the main restrictions on data processing. The ECA establishes a similar exception, which, however, is applicable only to undertakings providing electronic communications networks and/or services. This means that the usage of any 'Software as Service'[26] (SaaS) providers for the organization of any kind of electronically stored information (ESI) is in general prohibited.[27]

Other possible exceptions from the restrictions include the cases where[28] (1) 'the sender and recipient of the communications [have been] informed prior to the recording about the recording, the purposes thereof and the duration of the storage, as well as of their right to refuse such recording';[29] or (2) 'the recording [has been] necessary and [has been] provided for in a law for the purpose of securing *evidence of the conclusion* of commercial transactions' (emphasis added).[30]

Exception (2) presents a narrow transposition of the text of the E-Privacy Directive, where also the phrase 'or of any other business communication'[31] is not posed into the respective ECA provision. This means that the storage of electronic data would be allowed without the consent of the users only for the purposes of proving evidence about the conclusion of one commercial transaction.

As a general conclusion, the ECA provides for a deficient regulation, as compared to the EU standards, which are not only vague to meet the e-discovery requirements, but are too restrictive to be suitable for any reasonable storage of electronic communications by third parties, different from the Electronic Communications Services (ECS) providers. No significant practice throwing light on these ECA provisions exists at present.[32]

II.   PRETRIAL DISCOVERY AND DATA PROTECTION IN BULGARIA: GENERAL

Being a direct transposition of the Privacy Directive, the PDPA implements all of its restrictions and prerequisites that could obstruct e-discovery, as well as all

---

26. SaaS providers are generally considered as non-ECS (electronic communications services) providers, due to the fact that they do not provide conveyance of signals to electronic networks.
27. The adequacy of the level of personal data protection provided by the cloud computing services (incl. SaaS) is outside the subject matter of this paragraph.
28. Article 247 of the ECA.
29. Exception (1) is established following the general rules under the PDPA. The logistic difficulties that might arise in this case for the purposes of e-discovery will not be further explored.
30. The recorded communications and related traffic data could be stored for a period not longer than the period within which usage of the said communications and data is permitted.
31. Article 5, 2 of the Directive on Privacy and Electronic Communications: 'Paragraph 1 shall not affect any legally authorized recording of communications and the related traffic data when carried out in the course of lawful business practice for the purpose of providing evidence of a commercial transaction or of any other business communication'.
32. The administrative sanctions (in case the act does not constitute a criminal offence) for any violations of the above restrictions may amount up to BGN 10,000 (approx. EUR 5 000).

existing provisions that can somehow facilitate any possible discovery process in Bulgaria.

A.   PRETRIAL DISCOVERY AND DATA PROTECTION IN BULGARIA: APPROVAL PROCEDURE

One of the main obstacles in satisfying pretrial discovery requests – even where the Hague Convention requirements are not followed – is the data protection restrictions. Practically, the observance of the personal data rules under the relevant legislation and the time-consuming approval procedure before the CPDP have rendered it impossible to grant a discovery in due term. Some data protection and labour provisions reflecting employees' rights as well as the electronic communication regulations provide for additional barriers in front of the e-discovery process.[33]

B.   PRETRIAL DISCOVERY AND DATA PROTECTION IN BULGARIA: PROCESSING; MANDATORY DELETION

The PDPA contains the well-known and broad definition of 'personal data', which covers each and every single piece of information that might identify a certain person. Personal data can only be processed (by the broad meaning of this term[34]) by data controllers registered with CPDP, supported if necessary by data processors,[35] and strictly for the purposes provided by law, upon the control of CPDP. In the light of the e-discovery goals it should be outlined that any corporate and/or other information connected with the regular course of business of one company that is capable of identifying certain individuals (e.g., clients, employees, third parties) would be considered personal data protected by the PDPA. One of the significant impediments for the realization of any e-discovery requests in Bulgaria is the obligation for deletion of personal data upon fulfilment of the particular purposes of the processing. Exceptions to this obligation under the PDPA do exist, but are not useful for e-discovery goals.[36]

---

33. Alongside the legislative conflicts, other issues must also be taken account of in the process of carrying out e-discovery activities (e.g., lack of unanimous system for electronic storage of information in Bulgaria; lack of suitable servers; metadata storage differences; the availability of means for a proper transformation of Bulgarian-language e-documents, etc.).

34. Processing of personal data shall mean any operation or set of operations that can be performed with respect to personal data, whether by automatic means or otherwise, such as collection, recording, organization, storage, adaptation or alteration, retrieval, consultation, use, disclosure by transmission, dissemination, provision, updating or combination, blocking, deletion, or destruction.

35. The definitions of 'data controller' and 'data processor' are fully transposed as stipulated in the Privacy Directive.

36. In cases of transfer of personal data to another controller, if the respective purposes for processing are identical the data could remain undestroyed. Additionally, the controller may store

C.   PRETRIAL DISCOVERY AND DATA PROTECTION IN BULGARIA:
                 INTERNATIONAL DATA TRANSFER

The transfer of personal data is a statutory bar that might also hinder the e-discovery process. The PDPA envisages several conditions that should be observed prior to the transfer of personal data, where the control of the CPDP is of particular significance. An adequate level of data protection[37] is required for data transfer to 'third countries',[38] where the approval of the CPDP takes a certain amount of time due to the inspection that may be executed. The transfer of data to the United States has a substantial effect on e-discovery activities. The CPDP is very sensitive to that subject matter. Even in the exceptional cases where data transfer could be legally made without any analyses and/or approval of the CPDP,[39] the latter still has to review all of the documentation provided by the controller. Before granting an approval, the CPDP might investigate the entire data processing and transfer between a Bulgarian exporter and a US importer and the purposes thereof. Safe Harbour registration of the US-based data recipient and/or the use of appropriate Standard Contractual Clauses (SCCs) could be appointed as conditions precedent for the CPDP's approval.[40]

Finally, the sanctions envisaged in the PDPA for violation of privacy provisions under the PDPA also affect e-discovery, where the penalties that could be imposed to the personal data controller are amounting up to Bulgarian Lev (BGN) 100,000 (approx. EUR 50,000). In cases of a second violation, a sanction of double the amount will be imposed.

D.   PRETRIAL DISCOVERY AND DATA PROTECTION IN BULGARIA:
                 FACILITATING PROVISIONS

The PDPA envisages for strict, clearly determined alternative conditions on the sole basis of which the personal data may be processed. Some of these conditions can potentially be further applied in allowing e-discovery, namely the assurance of explicit consent of the individual to whom the personal data relates; the processing of data as a legally binding obligation to the data controller; the processing is necessary for the purposes of the legitimate interests pursued by the controller

---

for a longer time the processed personal data as anonymous for historical, scientific, or statistical purposes with the prior permission of the CPDP.
37. The adequacy of the level of protection of personal data afforded by a third country has to be assessed by the CPDP by considering all circumstances related to the data transfer operation or the set of data transfer operations, including the nature of data, the purpose and duration of its processing, the legal basis, and the security measures provided in such third country.
38. 'Third country' means any country that is not a member of the European Union and is not a country signatory to the European Economic Area Agreement.
39. As described in para. D hereunder.
40. Based on this regulation, cloud computing services are also hardly possible to be used for e-discovery purposes.

or by a third party to whom the data are disclosed; and the performance of a task carried out in public interest. Unfortunately, apart from the 'explicit consent' alternative,[41] the legal practice of the CPDP is not sufficient to secure a predictable interpretation of the other alternatives. Therefore, definite conclusions for the legal ground on which e-discovery data processing could be allowed are not possible. The processing of sensitive data for the purposes of establishment, exercise, or defence of legal claims, as one of the exceptions provided by law, could be considered also as a factor enabling the e-discovery process, where the subject matter of the collected evidence constitutes sensitive data.

By way of exception from the general requirements of the law related to the international data transfer (as discussed in paragraph C above), and in favour of e-discovery, the transfer of data to third countries could be facilitated[42] if the particular controller has the explicit written consent of the person whose data would be transferred; the transfer is necessary to comply with a legal obligation or to establish, exercise, or defend legal claims; an adequate level of protection is assured; or certain appropriate SCCs are in place.

The strict interpretation of the above paraphrased provisions of the PDPA shows that the presence of any of these would be a sufficient condition for the CPDP to allow personal data to be transferred from Bulgaria to any third country. However, the constant practice of the CPDP demonstrates that the latter prefers to review the whole documentation provided by the data controller and in particular scrutinizes cases of data transfer to the United States (as described in paragraph C above).

II.   CONCLUSION

Due to the lack of material cross-border cases, the dilemma with the legislations' collision by performing any e-discovery procedures on a domestic level is neither explored in detail so far nor have any attempts been made to solve it by the Bulgarian litigators. Moreover, the emphasis of the data protection restrictions relevant for e-discovery activities is mainly on the transfer of personal data to third parties (and especially to the United States), where the control of the competent Bulgarian authorities is rigorous. Most of the other concerns presented in this chapter do not have actual impact on practice and thus remain rather theoretical.

---

41. Considered as rather inappropriate and difficult to be accomplished for the e-discovery goals.
42. That is, no analyses and/or approval by the CPDP needed.

Chapter 5.4

Czech Republic

Martin Nedelka[*]

I.   INTRODUCTION

As in other European Union (EU) countries, the European Data Protection Directive was implemented in the Czech Republic. Better protection of individuals' personal data made collecting and transferring data to most countries outside of the EU more difficult. This chapter provides an overview of the conditions for personal data collection, processing, and transfer in case of pretrial discovery.

II.   CZECH DATA PROTECTION LAW: BACKGROUND

The grounds of data protection in the Czech Republic are set out by the Charter of Fundamental Rights and Freedoms, which is part of the Constitution.[1] Article 10 paragraph 3 states: 'Everyone has the right to be protected from unauthorized gathering, public revelation or other misuse of their personal data'. The constitutional right to privacy is further developed by the Personal Data Protection

---

[*]   Dr Martin Nedelka LL.M., Mgr. Tomáš Hülle, Mgr. Zuzana Jiřištová, Schönherr v.o.s., Prague, Czech Republic.
1.   Constitutional Act No. 2/1993 Coll. as amended. An English translation is available at the website of the Constitutional Court of the Czech Republic, <www.concourt.cz/view/1419>, 2 Dec. 2009.

Catrien Noorda & Stefan Hanloser, *E-Discovery and Data Privacy*, pp. 67–76.
© 2011 Kluwer Law International BV, The Netherlands.

Martin Nedelka

Act (PDPA).[2] The PDPA entered into force on 1 June 2000. One of main reasons for its enactment was the obligation to harmonize the Czech legal order with the European Data Protection Directive.[3]

Under the PDPA, the Office for Personal Data Protection (the Office)[4] was established as a central administrative authority, that is, as an independent administrative body that does not fall within the authority of any ministry. The Office is entrusted with competence in the area of personal data protection and also acts as a supervisory authority in the same area.

A. CZECH DATA PROTECTION LAW: SCOPE OF THE PDPA

The PDPA protects the privacy of the individual against unauthorized interference by stipulating the requirements under which it is possible to collect and process personal data. The PDPA applies for data collection and processing in the private as well as in the public sector. Apart from the term 'personal data', which is defined as any information that identifies or enables the identification of a data subject, for example, a photograph or unique e-mail, the PDPA also introduces the term 'sensitive data', whose processing is subject to a higher degree of scrutiny. Sensitive data are personal data that reveal, for example, nationality, biometric records, or trade union membership.

B. CZECH DATA PROTECTION LAW: PRINCIPLES OF DATA COLLECTION AND PROCESSING

The PDPA states that the subject who collects and processes personal data is a controller and enumerates the requirements that must be fulfilled for legal collection and processing. Section 4 paragraph j) of the PDPA defines a controller as 'any entity that determines the purpose and means of personal data processing, carries out such processing, and is responsible for such processing'.

The personal data may be processed only with the consent of the data subject. The PDPA enumerates a number of exemption clauses, which enables, for example, protection of vital interests of the data subject without his or her prior consent. In most cases, however, consent is necessary. The controller must specify the purpose, means, and manner of the personal data to be processed in advance. The controller may collect and process only personal data that are absolutely

---

2. Act No. 101/2000 Coll., on the Protection of Personal Data and on Amendment to Some Acts, as amended. An English translation is available at the website of the Office for Personal Data Protection, <www.uoou.cz/uoou.aspx?menu=4&submenu=5>, 2 Dec. 2009.
3. Directive 95/46/EC of the European Parliament and of the Council of 24 Oct. 1995 on the protection of individuals with regard to the processing of personal data and on the free movement of such data.
4. The official name in Czech is 'Úřad pro ochranu osobních údajů'. Official website at <www.uoou.cz/uoou.aspx>, 2 Dec. 2009.

necessary for the specified purpose and only for the period in which the personal data are absolutely needed.[5]

All obligations imposed on the controller during personal data collection and processing aim toward finding a balance between the constitutional right of individuals to be protected against unauthorized gathering, public revelation, or other misuse of their personal data on the one side, and the needs of the controller to collect and process the personal data on the other side.

C.   CZECH DATA PROTECTION LAW: NOTIFICATION OBLIGATION

The controller must notify the Office of the intent to process personal data. The notification is made in writing before processing begins. The Office has thirty days from the delivery to decide whether it will start proceedings. If proceedings are not started, the notification is acknowledged and the controller may start the processing. If the personal data are part of data files publicly accessible on the basis of a special act or when such personal data are needed for exercising rights and obligations following from a special act, or the processing has a philosophical, religious, or trade union aim, the notification obligation to the Office does not apply.[6]

D.   CZECH DATA PROTECTION LAW: CONTROLLER RESIDES
               OUTSIDE OF THE EU

In addition to the controller, personal data may also be processed by the processor. The processor is a body that processes personal data on behalf of the controller on the grounds of a written agreement.[7] The controller's obligations also apply to the processor.[8] The distinction between controller and processor is important when the controller resides outside of the EU, for example, in the United States. In that case, the controller must authorize a processor. Section 3, paragraph 5, subsection b) of the PDPA states:

> [...] a controller who is established outside the territory of the European Union carries out processing in the territory of the Czech Republic, unless where it is only a personal data transfer over the territory of the European Union. In this case, the controller shall be obliged to authorize the processor in the territory of the Czech Republic according to the procedure stipulated in section 6.
>
> If the controller carries out processing through its branches established in the territory of the European Union, he must ensure that these branches will

---

5. Section 5 of the PDPA.
6. Section 16 of the PDPA.
7. Section 4 of the PDPA.
8. Section 7 of the PDPA.

process personal data in accordance with the national law of the respective Member State of the European Union.

E.   CZECH DATA PROTECTION LAW: EMPLOYEE'S E-MAILS AND
     ELECTRONIC FILES

Almost any (legal) file consists not only of documents but also of different kinds of communication, usually e-mails. The e-mails constitute an integral part of the file, and therefore they may be demanded in a pretrial discovery request. In the Czech Republic, an employee's e-mails have the same level of protection as regular correspondence written in hard copy. The confidentiality of e-mails is an individual's constitutional right;[9] therefore, employers should be exceptionally cautious when accessing an employee's e-mail.

Under section 316, paragraph 1 of the Labour Code,[10] employees must not use the employer's computers and communication devices for their private needs without the employer's consent. The employer is authorized to control in an appropriate way compliance with this prohibition. There are two interpretations of the term 'control in an appropriate way'. Nevertheless, employees must always be informed about the possibility of monitoring. Under the stricter interpretation, the employer may only monitor the number of incoming/outgoing e-mails and under no circumstances is it allowed to scan the content of the e-mails. The second interpretation understands the given term not only as counting the number of e-mails, but also as monitoring the content of the work-related e-mails in an appropriate and reasonable way.[11]

Without any regard for which interpretation prevails in the future, two recommendations might be useful. First, the employer should inform all employees about the monitoring of the e-mails. A safe way of doing this is by including a clause on monitoring in the employment contract. Nowadays it is unreasonable to expect that employees will not use their work e-mail account for private needs. The employer is recommended to accept internal rules governing the private use of the e-mail account and to order the employees to distinguish and indicate private e-mails from other e-mails that may be accessed by the employer, for example, in case of the employee's illness or pretrial discovery request.[12] This distinction might be done simply by creating a 'Private' folder in each employee's e-mail account.

---

9. The Charter of Fundamental Rights and Freedoms states in Art. 13: No one may violate the confidentiality of letters or the confidentiality of other papers or records, whether privately kept or sent by post or by some other means, except in the cases and in the manner designated by law. The confidentiality of communications sent by telephone, telegraph, or by other similar devices is guaranteed in the same way.
10. Act No. 262/2006 Coll. Labour Code, as amended.
11. Václav Bartík, Eva Janečková, *Ochrana osobních údajů v aplikační praxi*. Linde Praha, 2009, 149.
12. Václav Bartík, Eva Janečková, *Ochrana osobních údajů v aplikační praxi*. Linde Praha, 2009, 150.

F.   CZECH DATA PROTECTION LAW: STORAGE OF PERSONAL DATA FOR
       DISCOVERY PURPOSES

Under section 5, paragraph 1, subsection e) of the PDPA, personal data may be stored for a period that is absolutely necessary to fulfil the purpose of personal data collecting.[13] If the purpose stated in the controller's notification on intent to collect personal data is 'pretrial discovery', the data may be stored for an indefinite period of time. If the notification does not include 'pretrial discovery' as one of the purposes, and the other notified purposes were already fulfilled, and nevertheless the controller wishes to store the documentation containing personal data, the possible solution might be making the documentation anonymous.

G.   CZECH DATA PROTECTION LAW: TRANSFER OF PERSONAL
       DATA ABROAD

Even if personal data are legally collected and processed, the successful pretrial discovery claim faces one more obstacle: the transfer of personal data outside of the Czech Republic.

Personal data may be freely transferred only between countries of the EU. If personal data are transferred to a third country, stricter rules apply.

Third countries (non-Member States of the EU) may be divided into two groups: countries that have the same standard of personal data protection as the EU, and countries that do not. Transfers to countries in the first group can be made without the cooperation of the Office, whereas transfers to countries in the second group require the authorization of the Office. As the legal regulations on data protection in the United States are very different compared to the EU, the transfer of data from the Czech Republic to the United States must usually be authorized by the Office.

Under section 27, paragraph 4, when considering the application for authorization, the Office must:

> [...] examine[s] all circumstances related to the transfer of personal data, in particular the source, final destination and categories of personal data which are to be transferred, the purpose and period of the processing, with regard to available information about legal or other regulations governing the personal data processing in a third country.

Stated simply, the office must balance the individual's constitutional right to be protected against unauthorized gathering, public revelation, or other misuse of his or her personal data against the need to transfer the personal data.

Furthermore, there are some concepts that enable avoidance of the Office's authorization. The first concept, based on the above-mentioned relation between the controller and processor, applies for multinational companies with a complex

---

13.   Official webpage of the Office, <www.uoou.cz/uoou.aspx?menu=14&loc=331>, 4 Dec. 2009.

structure. For example, if a parental company residing in the United States (controller) concludes an agreement with a subsidiary residing in the Czech Republic (processor) on the processing of personal data, the transfer may be conducted via the agreement. However, the processor may not process the data for purposes or to controllers other than those stated in the agreement.[14]

Binding Corporate Rules (BCRs) are another way of simplifying the transfer of personal data abroad. The BCRs must be introduced within the whole company for each and every subsidiary and must comply with the standard of personal data protection in the EU. BCRs may be used only for transfers within the company.[15]

The transfer of personal data outside of the company (onward transfer) may be performed on the basis of the third concept: Standard Contractual Clauses (SCCs). SCCs are clauses authorized by the EU Commission[16] and their text may not be altered. If SCCs are added to the agreement between two subjects transferring personal data, the Office's authorization is not necessary.[17]

In addition to these three concepts, transfers from the Czech Republic to the United States may be accomplished on the basis of a so-called 'Safe Harbour'. Companies that receive certification that they comply with Safe Harbour Privacy Principles may also transfer data from the Czech Republic without the Office's authorization. Nevertheless, due to the complexity of the legal regulation, when transferring personal data to the United States and Canada, consulting individual cases with the Office is highly recommended.[18]

H.   CZECH DATA PROTECTION LAW: SANCTIONS AND ENFORCEMENT

Severe sanctions are established in the PDPA against infringers of personal data protection. Each data subject who finds or presumes that the controller or the processor is carrying out processing of his or her personal data that is in contradiction with the protection of the personal life of the data subject or with the law, in particular if the personal data are inaccurate regarding the purpose of their processing, the data subject can ask the controller or processor for an explanation or require the controller or processor to remedy the situation. This can mean in

---

14. Official website of the Office, <www.uoou.cz/uoou.aspx?menu=41&submenu=46>, 3 Dec. 2009. Václav Bartík, Eva Janečková, *Ochrana osobních údajů v aplikační praxi*. Linde Praha, 2009, 176.
15. Václav Bartík, Eva Janečková, *Ochrana osobních údajů v aplikační praxi*. Linde Praha, 2009, 177.
16. Commission Decision of 15 Jun. 2001 on Standard Contractual Clauses for the Transfer of Personal Data to Third Countries, under Directive 95/46/EC, Commission Decision of 27 Dec. 2001 on Standard Contractual Clauses for the Transfer of Personal Data to Processors Established in Third Countries, under Directive 95/46/EC, Commission Decision of 27 Dec. 2004, Amending Decision 2001/497/EC, as Regards the Introduction of an Alternative Set of Standard Contractual Clauses for the Transfer of Personal Data to Third Countries.
17. Václav Bartík, Eva Janečková, *Ochrana osobních údajů v aplikační praxi*. Linde Praha, 2009, 178.
18. Official website of the Office, <www.uoou.cz/files/rk_26-07-00.pdf>, 3 Dec. 2009.

particular blocking, correction, supplementing, or liquidation of personal data. If the explanation is found sufficient by the controller or processor, they will try to remove the infringing state. If the controller or processor does not accept the data subject's request, the data subject is entitled to appeal directly to the Office. Nevertheless, the above-mentioned procedure is not an obstacle for the direct commencing of procedures before the Office. If any damage occurs during the possession of personal data or anyhow differently connected to the procedure, the general regulations of the Civil Code and damages shall apply. The same also applies with regard to non-monetary damages to the data subject.

As stated above, the Office's control activities are performed on the basis of a control plan or on the basis of incentives and complaints. If a person entitled by an office (the 'controlling person') finds that obligations imposed by the PDPA have been breached, the inspector shall determine which measures shall be adopted in order to eliminate the established shortcomings and set a deadline for their elimination. If the destruction of such personal data is ordered, this data will be blocked until the destruction is executed. The other measures depend on the infringer and his or her legal nature. The measures are different for entrepreneurs and natural persons. Measures that can be taken against an infringer who is an entrepreneur include a fine of up to Czech Koruna (CZK) 10,000,000 (approx. EUR 384,615). When the Office decides on the amount of the fine, it should take into account the seriousness, manner, duration, and consequences of the breach and the circumstances of the breach. Personal data are also protected by the Criminal Code;[19] anybody who violates its provisions shall be punished by imprisonment of up to eight years.

Nevertheless, entrepreneurs are not liable for a potential violation of the PDPA if they prove that they have made their best reasonable efforts to prevent the breach of their legal obligation. The Office must commence the proceeding within one year as of the day when it became aware of the breach, but not later than within three years as of the day when the breach was committed.

Moreover, a disciplinary fine of up to CZK 25,000 (approx. EUR 961) may be imposed on a person who fails to provide the Office with the required co-operation during the performance of an inspection. A delay in taking measures imposed for reparation of discovered facts within the prescribed deadline is considered as a failure to provide co-operation. This fine can be imposed repeatedly.

Practical overview and recent development

A case regarding video recording of suspects occurred in 2008 before the Office. A reporter whose building was repeatedly damaged set up a camera that recorded the suspects the next time they damaged the building. These suspects were charged but found not guilty based on an insufficient amount of evidence. The reporter was

19. Act No. 40/2009 Coll., Criminal Code, as amended.

punished by a fine of CZK 3,000 (approx. EUR 115) based on the finding that he did not obtain approval from the two suspects for their recording.[20]

In 2010 the Court decided on a case in which a newspaper in Kroměříž published the personal data of the aggrieved party to a criminal proceeding. The newspapers were not aware of the fact that the personal data belonged to the aggrieved party because this party was simultaneously acting as a witness in the proceedings. The Office imposed a very low fine of CZK 3,000 (approx. EUR 115) based on the relevant circumstances.

In March 2010 the Office imposed a fine of CZK 2,300,000 (approx. EUR 88,461) on the Czech Office for Drug Control (the 'CODC') for unlawful collection of information. The CODC was collecting information about patients from all drugstores in the Czech Republic and processing that information into its central database. Nevertheless, the CODC did not state the purpose, means, or manner of collecting and did not ask the patients for their approval. The CODC also had not implemented any means for protection of such information. As a result, the Data Protection Act was violated by this collecting.[21]

III.   PRETRIAL DISCOVERY IN THE CZECH
         REPUBLIC: BACKGROUND

Czech civil procedure[22] does not recognize pretrial discovery or any similar mutual disclosure of case-related facts. The Czech court may order the other party or even a third person to provide a case-related document; however, this document must be specified. It is not possible to require an inexplicit number of documents that are specified only by the fact they are related to the case. The documents are specified by the party that seeks to use the document as proof. In rare cases, the court specifies the document. Generally, the parties to the dispute use only documents that they have in their possession as proof.

A.   PRETRIAL DISCOVERY IN THE CZECH REPUBLIC: HAGUE
         CONVENTION ON THE TAKING OF EVIDENCE

The Czech Republic is a party to the Hague Convention on the Taking of Evidence[23] (Hague Convention) and a member of the EU. In relations within the EU, except Denmark, the regulation on cooperation between the courts of the

---

20. ČT 24 available at <http://www.ct24.cz/domaci/21162-natocil-vandaly-na-kameru-na-usvedceni-zabery-nestacily-presto-ma-za-ne-zaplatit-pokutu/>, 7 Jul. 2008.
21. Ihned available at <http://domaci.ihned.cz/c1-41378370-ustav-pro-kontrolu-leciv-dostal-pokutu-nezakonne-sbiral-data-pacientu/>, 16 Mar. 2010.
22. Act No. 99/1963 Coll. Civil Procedure Code, as amended, Part 2, Ch. II Evidence.
23. Convention of 18 Mar. 1970 on the Taking of Evidence Abroad in Civil or Commercial Matters.

Member States in the taking of evidence[24] has priority over the Hague Convention. In relations outside of the EU (and Denmark), the Czech courts and public authorities find the Hague Convention mandatory and are expected to resort to the Hague Convention, unless there is another bilateral treaty on the same matter.[25]

Article 23 of the Hague Convention enables countries to 'declare that they will not execute Letters of Request issued for the purpose of obtaining pretrial discovery of documents'. The Czech Republic did not make any such declaration and therefore pretrial discovery requests to the Czech courts and authorities should be handled smoothly. Currently,[26] the Czech Ministry of Justice does not file any request for pretrial discovery.[27] Though it is highly improbable, there was no pretrial discovery request targeted to the Czech Republic. The Ministry's declaration is probably due to the fact that the Czech courts and authorities have not yet been involved in a pretrial discovery request; in other words, there has not yet been a need to involve any court or public authority due to non-cooperation of the requested subject.

B.   PRETRIAL DISCOVERY IN THE CZECH REPUBLIC: BLOCKING STATUTES

Pretrial discovery requests directed to the Czech Republic are not blocked by any statutes or proceedings relating merely to foreign applicants. Section 124 of the Civil Procedure Code[28] prevents all participants to the procedure (i.e., foreign as well as Czech participants) from obtaining information protected by a legal obligation to maintain secrecy. A typical example of the statute stipulating the obligation is the Act on Protection of Secret Information and Secret Capacity.[29]

---

24. Council Regulation (EC) No. 1206/2001 of 28 May 2001 on cooperation between the courts of the Member States in the taking of evidence in civil or commercial matters.
25. Czech responses to the questionnaire on the execution of the Hague Convention on the Taking of Evidence Abroad in Civil or Commercial Matters, available at <http://hcch.e-vision.nl/upload/wop/2008czechrepublic20.pdf>, 5 Dec. 2009.
26. The questionnaire to the Hague Convention was filled out in 2008.
27. Czech responses to the questionnaire on the execution of the Hague Convention on the Taking of Evidence Abroad in Civil or Commercial Matters, available at <http://hcch.e-vision.nl/upload/wop/2008czechrepublic20.pdf>, 5 Dec. 2009.
28. Article 124 of the Civil Procedure Code states: The evidence must be carried out in the manner that preserves the duty to maintain confidentiality of secret facts protected by a special act and the duty to maintain confidentiality provided by law or recognized by the state. In these cases, the examination may be carried out only if the examined person has been relieved of the duty to maintain confidentiality by the competent authority or by the person in whose favour the duty is; this rule shall analogously apply where the evidence is carried out otherwise than by way of examination.
29. Act No. 412/2005 Coll. on Protection of Secret Information and Secret Capacity, as amended.

The Act constitutes the basis of the protection for information vital to the statehood and security of the Czech Republic.[30]

IV.   PRETRIAL DISCOVERY VERSUS DATA PROTECTION IN THE CZECH REPUBLIC: CONCLUSION

There is nothing in the Czech legal framework that would forbid execution of pretrial discovery requests from common law countries. Nevertheless, the right balance must be found between pretrial discovery requests and the constitutional rights of the data subject.

The execution of the pretrial discovery request coming from the United States and involving Czech personal data may be divided into two stages. In the first stage, required documents are collected, and in the second stage, the documents with personal data are transferred to the second party.

In the first stage, the company collecting the documents that include personal data must ensure that the personal data in the documents are collected in accordance with the PDPA. This means that the personal data must be collected by a company as the competent controller, which notifies the Office of its intent to collect the personal data and that receives the consent of the data subject or meets legal conditions for the collection of the personal data without the data subject's consent. If the company (controller) does not meet the requirements of the PDPA, the documents including personal data must not be collected, unless they are made anonymous.[31]

If documents are successfully collected and still include personal data, the second stage – the transfer – will follow. The transfer of personal data to the United States, the country with the widest pretrial discovery, needs to be authorized by the Office, or it must be conducted by means of one of the four concepts described above. When choosing the right legal framework for the transfer, it should be considered that only the concepts of SCCs and Safe Harbour are applicable to onward transfer.

The execution of pretrial discovery requests from the United States for documents containing personal data may be in some cases administratively demanding, but it is not impossible.

---

30. Czech responses to the questionnaire on the execution of the Hague Convention on the Taking of Evidence Abroad in Civil or Commercial Matters, available at <http://hcch.e-vision.nl/upload/wop/2008czechrepublic20.pdf>, 5 Dec. 2009.
31. Working Paper 158 of 11 Feb. 2009 published by the Working Party on the Protection of Individuals with Regard to the Processing of Personal Data.

Chapter 5.5

Estonia

*Ants Nõmper and Jaanus Kasevits**

I.   LEGAL FRAMEWORK IN ESTONIA FOR PRODUCTION
           OF DOCUMENTS

Much like most other European countries, the legal system in Estonia does not
recognize a discovery regime – the mutual disclosure of case-related facts by the
parties to the litigation – as known in common law countries. However, the law
does set out provisions that make it possible to obtain documents from relevant
parties based on both procedural and substantive law.

During litigation, the exchange of documents between litigants is closely
controlled by the court, as by default litigants are only expected to produce documents that support their case. The court may oblige litigants or third parties to
produce documents on its own initiative or based on a request of a party to the
dispute. It is important to emphasize that the amount of information to be obtained
this way is very limited and cannot be compared to the amount of information that
could be obtained between litigants in a discovery procedure. It is not a widespread
practice for the courts in Estonia to order parties to produce documents on their
own initiative, and effectuating such requests by a party to the litigation is subject
to strict conditions. If a person requests that the court orders submission of a

*   Ants Nõmper and Jaanus Kasevits, Raidla Lejins & Norcous law office.

Catrien Noorda & Stefan Hanloser, *E-Discovery and Data Privacy*, pp. 77–85.
© 2011 Kluwer Law International BV, The Netherlands.

document by another person (be it a party to the litigation or a third party not involved therein), the person requesting the document must in the request:

(1) describe the document and its content; and
(2) describe the reason why the requesting party believes the document to be in the possession of the other party.

Estonian courts generally interpret these requirements rather strictly, making it difficult for the parties to the dispute to obtain documents that they cannot identify clearly, thereby limiting the possibility of general, wide-scope requests.

The Estonian Law of Obligations Act stipulates that a party who has a legitimate interest in examining a document that is in the possession of another party may demand that the possessor of the document allow the document to be examined, if the document:

(1) has been prepared in the interests of the party who wishes to examine the document; or
(2) sets out a legal relationship between such party and the possessor of the document or the preparation of a transaction between those parties.

In a 2009 decision[1] the Estonian Supreme Court explicitly stated that a discovery proceeding is not allowed under the above provisions. In a 2008 decision[2] the Supreme Court ruled that the provision of the Law of Obligations Act described above does not provide a party requesting documents with the right to request documents to be handed over to its possession. Instead, documents may be inspected at their location or, in case of a substantial reason, elsewhere as prescribed by law.

II. BLOCKING STATUTES

Estonia does not have any 'blocking statutes' that would specifically prohibit the transfer of documents or information to foreign states. Furthermore, the Estonian Code of Civil Procedure stipulates that unless otherwise provided by law or a treaty, an Estonian court shall provide procedural assistance in performance of a procedural act at the request of a foreign court if, pursuant to Estonian law, the requested procedural act belongs to the jurisdiction of the Estonian court and is not prohibited. A procedural act may also be performed or a document may be issued pursuant to the law of a foreign state if this is necessary for the conducting of proceedings in the foreign state and the interests of the participants in the proceeding are not damaged thereby. In practice, procedural assistance provided by Estonian courts to foreign courts is of varying effectiveness. There is no well-developed practice on how requests for assistance should be interpreted and carried out by Estonian courts and therefore often such proceedings become subject to

---

1. The decision is not publicly available due to procedural restrictions.
2. 16 Jan. 2008 Decision No. 3-2-1-132-07, s. 14.

appeals in Estonian courts, fuelled by lack of common interpretation by Estonian judges.

III.   HAGUE CONVENTION ON THE TAKING OF
         EVIDENCE ABROAD

Estonia has joined the Hague Convention on the Taking of Evidence Abroad (hereinafter the Convention). When joining the Convention, Estonia declared based on Article 23 of the Convention that it will execute a Letter of Request for production of a document or a copy thereof, if the Letter of Request corresponds to the following requirements:

(1) a proceeding has been initiated (this does not include a distinction between pretrial and trial proceedings; pretrial proceedings are enough for this requirement to be fulfilled);

(2) documents have been reasonably identified by date, content, or other information (via this requirement Estonia basically sets out that Estonia does not allow discovery proceedings); and

(3) the Letter of Request describes circumstances that give reason to believe the documents are in the party's ownership, possession, or are known to the party.

IV.   DATA PROTECTION AND PERSONAL DATA

A.   Overview of Data Protection Principles in Estonia

Although European directives regarding data protection do allow European Union (EU) Member States a margin of appreciation for different options in a number of areas, Estonia has not used this option extensively. Instead, in most aspects, the Estonian approach in adopting the directives has been to closely follow the wording of the EU regulations in national legislation. The following provides a general overview of the Estonian data protection law:

Definition of personal data – personal data are any data concerning an identified natural person or a natural person who can be identified, regardless of the form or format in which such data exists.

Definition of processing of personal data – processing of personal data is any act performed with personal data, including the collection, storage, disclosure, retention, or destruction thereof or several of the aforementioned operations, regardless of the manner in which the operations are carried out or the means used.

Legal ground for processing of personal data – as a general rule, processing of personal data is permitted only with the consent of the data subject. However, the law does provide a number of exceptions to this rule, allowing personal data to be processed without the consent of the data subject. Consent is not required if the data are processed (these are alternative, not cumulative): (1) based on a provision arising from the law; (2) for the performance of a task prescribed by a treaty or directly applicable legislation of the Council of the European Union or the European Commission; (3) in individual cases for the protection of the life, health, or freedom of the data subject or another person if obtaining the data subject's consent is impossible; or (4) for performance of a contract entered into with the data subject or for ensuring the performance of such a contract (does not apply if the data to be processed are sensitive personal data).

General principles applicable to processing of personal data – Estonian law sets out seven general principles with which the processing of personal data must comply. These principles, *inter alia,* stipulate that personal data may be only collected

– in an honest and legal manner;[3]
– for the achievement of determined and lawful objectives;[4] and
– to the extent necessary for the achievement of determined purposes;[5] and
– with the consent of the data subject or with the permission of the competent authority.[6]

In addition:

– personal data must be up-to-date, complete, and necessary for the achievement of the purpose of data processing;[7]
– the data subject must be notified of data collected concerning him or her and granted access thereto;[8] and
– security measures must be applied in order to protect personal data from involuntary or unauthorized processing.[9]

With regard to usual, everyday data processing activities, these offer little practical use, since these activities are usually well regulated by other specific provisions of the law and their interpretations have been well developed in practice. However, in the context of – at least in Estonia – rather rare discovery and cross-border litigation cases, these principles may assume a central role, as in such cases the need to interpret specific provisions of the law against the background of general principles arises.

Treatment of electronic information – no specific difference is made between electronic and non-electronic information, both with regard to what kind of

---

3. Principle of legality.
4. Principle of purposefulness.
5. Principle of minimalism.
6. Principle of restricted use.
7. Principle of high quality of data.
8. Principle of individual participation.
9. Principle of security.

data constitutes personal data and also what kind of activities can be construed as processing personal data.

B.   PRESERVATION OF ELECTRONICALLY STORED INFORMATION

One of the several conflict areas between discovery proceedings and data protection law stems from the fact that in order to facilitate discovery, common law countries place a duty on parties to identify and retain all relevant electronically stored information (ESI) under their control whenever litigation or regulatory investigations are anticipated. If the ESI includes any personal data, then under data protection law such activities are to be construed as processing of personal data. At the same time, data protection law stipulates that personal data may only be processed on specific legal grounds for determined purposes and only to the extent necessary for such purposes (abovementioned principles of purposefulness and minimalism); that is, there are no legal grounds to process personal data at random for an unlimited time in preparation for a possible litigation in a foreign state. This conflict can be overcome by processing personal data in such a way that it is based on any of the following legal grounds under which data are processed (these are alternative, not cumulative):

(1) based on explicit consent provided by the data subject(s);
(2) based on a provision arising from the law;
(3) for the performance of a task prescribed by a treaty or directly applicable legislation of the Council of the European Union or the European Commission;
(4) in individual cases for the protection of the life, health, or freedom of the data subject or another person if obtaining the data subject's consent is impossible; and
(5) for performance of a contract entered into with the data subject or for ensuring the performance of such a contract (does not apply if the data to be processed are sensitive personal data).

In practice, the most likely legal grounds to be considered in case of a need to retain data for discovery purposes are items 1 (data subject's consent) and 5 (performance of contract) of the above list.

C.   EMPLOYEES' PERSONAL DATA

Conditions under which an employer has a right to access and search employees' e-mail accounts and electronic files in Estonia are not clearly set out in Estonian law. The principal provision regulating this is subsection 11 of Article 28(2) of the Estonian Employment Contract Act, which states that 'an employer is obliged to respect the privacy of an employee and to inspect the performance of employment duties in a manner which does not violate the fundamental rights of an employee'. Exact limits on what can be construed as respecting the privacy of employees and not violating their fundamental rights is left to be determined on a case-by-case basis. This means that, in general, employers in Estonia have the right to access and search employees' e-mail accounts and electronic files and do not require employees' consent for this, as long as the e-mails and files are located on (or made available via) the employer's computers and the employer applies reasonable measures to avoid any personal and non-work-related e-mails or files to be included in the processing. The latter is necessary, since the processing of employees' personal e-mails and files could easily be construed as not respecting the privacy of employees. To mitigate this risk, employers in Estonia sometimes supplement their employment contracts with a provision stating that only work-related e-mails and files are allowed to be processed on the employer's computers. It is clear that in practice such an obligation is rarely followed exactly by employees, but this is not a problem for employers. The purpose of such a provision is foremost not to ensure that no private e-mails or files are found on employer's computers, but rather to provide a legal ground for (or at least an argument in support of) searching an employer's computers without performing encumbering processes needed to filter out private e-mails and files, since based on this provision an employer may have a reasonable cause to believe no private e-mails or files are present on the computers.

D.   TRANSFER OF PERSONAL DATA ABROAD

Under Estonian law, the general principle is that personal data may only be transferred abroad to countries that provide an adequate level of data protection. The following states are automatically deemed as having an adequate level of data protection: EU Member States, European Economic Area (EEA) member states, the United States with regard to recipients that have joined the Safe Harbour framework, and countries specifically named by the European Commission as providing an adequate level of data protection. Transferring personal data to these countries is not subject to any provisions specifically regulating the transfer of personal data abroad – such transfers are regulated on the same basis as data processing within Estonia.

The above does not mean that personal data may not be transferred at all to countries not deemed to provide an adequate level of data protection. Such transfers can be carried out, but only based on any of the following three exceptions provided by law (these are alternative, not cumulative):

(1) *Specific permission granted by the Estonian data protection authority.* To obtain such a permission, the data controller (person wanting to transfer personal data abroad) must confirm to the data protection authority that it will ensure the protection of personal data in the destination state and must demonstrate the means with which this is achieved. Usually this means that the person sending the data (usually Estonian affiliate) and the person receiving the data (parent company abroad) must execute an agreement based on standard contractual clauses, which the person sending the data will then submit to the Estonian data protection authority as confirmation

that data will be adequately protected. On average, obtaining such a permission should take about a month, if no complications arise.

(2) *Consent of data subjects (persons whose personal data are included in the ESI).* The law stipulates that such a consent has to be based on the free will of the data subject, but this does not mean that an employee cannot provide a consent to his or her employer. Employment relations between the relevant persons are in practice by themselves not enough to give rise to an argument that an employee's consent is not based on free will. With regard to employment relations, such a consent may be given both in the employment contract (for possible future discovery proceedings) and also separately afterward. If an employee refuses to provide consent and none of the other grounds for transferring personal data abroad apply (which in the average case is unlikely), then the data may not be transferred outside of Estonia.

(3) *Two additional specific exceptions provided by law.* Personal data may be transferred to countries not providing an adequate level of data protection if: (1) in a specific case if it is necessary for the protection of the life, health, or freedom of the data subject or another person, on the condition that it is impossible to obtain consent from the data subject, or (2) if a third party requests information obtained or created in the process of performance of public duties and the requested data do not contain any sensitive personal data and access to the data has not been restricted for any other reasons. Because of their nature and mostly narrow wording, application of these two exceptions in practice is rare.

The above regulation can be a source of conflict between the process of discovery and the local data protection regulation, since the former is aimed at transferring data outside of Estonia while the latter in large part makes an effort to obstruct that in respect of certain states. In practice the problem is mitigated by the fact that most discovery proceedings require ESI to be transferred to US companies that have joined the Safe Harbour framework, thereby not being subject to general Estonian data protection requirements regulating cross-border data transfers. However, in the event data are transferred to governmental bodies (for instance, a court as part of litigation), Safe Harbour does not provide a solution. Article 26.1d of the Directive providing that data may be transferred to countries outside of the EU if such is necessary for the exercise of legal claims, and which is the basis for Working Party Paper 158, is not implemented in Estonia.

On the other hand, the Inspectorate does follow Working Party opinions, so it will likely find a practical solution when confronted with this gap in practice.

E.   COMMON PRACTICAL SOLUTIONS TO THE LEGAL PROBLEMS
      DESCRIBED ABOVE

It is important to note that because of the small size of Estonia, many of the legal hurdles described above are often solved by practical means. Compared to an average EU Member State or to the United States, Estonia is a small country, by both population (less than 1.5 million) and area. This directly affects the nature of business of the Estonian affiliates of large international companies in Estonia (in connection with whom the likelihood of discovery proceedings in Estonia is the greatest). The affiliates are usually small and their activities in Estonia are well defined, because of which often it is not cost effective for them to implement their own information systems. Instead they frequently simply use their US-based (and Safe Harbour) parent company's information systems over the Internet. In addition to cost benefits, these kinds of arrangements have the legal benefit of moving any personal data outside of Estonia already upon their entry into the system, at which moment processing of the personal data is no longer subject to the Estonian data protection law. Such practices are usually not that widespread in countries larger than Estonia, since in these the presumably larger amounts of data make such overseas data exchange difficult. However, in Estonia, this is an option often considered by those companies whose business processes allow it.

F.   ENFORCEMENT OF DATA PROTECTION LAW

Enforcement of Estonian data protection law is carried out by the Estonian Data Protection Inspectorate. Violations of the requirements for the processing of personal data stipulated in the law are treated as misdemeanours and are punishable by a fine of up to approximately Euros (EUR) 32,000. In addition to misdemeanours, the Estonian Criminal Code stipulates one criminal offence regarding personal data – illegal disclosure of sensitive personal data, enabling access to such data, or transfer of such data for personal gain or if significant damage is caused thereby to the rights or interests of another person that are protected by law. Such an offence in punishable by a pecuniary punishment or up to one year of imprisonment.

Generally, the imposition of penalty payments and fines in Estonia is rather rare (although it is becoming more widespread) and in practice the Inspectorate usually only applies such measures if a data controller violates the law and does not bring its activities into compliance even after a precept or a warning has been issued by the Inspectorate.

V.   CONCLUSION

On a general level Estonian data protection regulation follows closely the guidelines provided by European law, without making much use of the discretionary possibilities provided to Member States in the European directives. As such, the conflict areas between discovery proceedings and data protection in Estonia are similar to those that can be found in other European countries. Although most of these conflicts can be solved with reasonable efforts in

Estonia once the need arises in connection with discovery proceedings, it is beneficial to analyse two key areas in advance when structuring Estonian affiliates' relations with their parent companies: should the need arise, on what conditions can ESI be retained and, once this is done, what are the options to transfer the ESI to the destination state?

Chapter 5.6

Finland

*Erkko Korhonen**

I.   FINNISH DATA PROTECTION LAW

In Finland the protection of personal information is based on the provisions of the
Finnish Constitution (731/1999) regarding the right to privacy. According to the
Finnish Constitution, detailed provisions on the protection of personal data
have to be included in an act, which is done through the Personal Data Act (PDA)
(523/1999, the 'PDA'). The PDA implements Directive 95/46/EC[1] (the 'Directive').

A.   FINNISH DATA PROTECTION LAW: DEFINITION OF PERSONAL DATA

For the purposes of evaluating the relationship between pretrial discovery and data
protection, the essential definitions contained in the PDA have to be assessed.
The term 'personal data' is defined in the PDA as 'any information on a private
individual and any information on his or her personal characteristics or personal
circumstances, where these are identifiable as concerning him or her or the

---

*   Erkko Korhonen, Hannes Snellman Attorneys Ltd., Helsinki, Finland.
1.   Directive 95/46/EC of the European Parliament and Council of 24 Oct. 1995 on the Protection of
Individuals with Regard to the Processing of Personal Data and on the Free Movement of Such
Data.

Catrien Noorda & Stefan Hanloser, *E-Discovery and Data Privacy*, pp. 87–97.
© 2011 Kluwer Law International BV, The Netherlands.

members of his or her family or household'.[2] This definition has to be interpreted in the sense that as a starting point, all information concerning a private individual is personal data.

It makes no difference for the applicability of the PDA whether an individual has provided the personal data by him- or herself or whether the personal data have been gathered otherwise in relation to an individual, for example, as an employee. However, the PDA does not apply to the processing of personal data by a private individual for purely personal purposes or for comparable ordinary and private purposes.

B.　　　　　FINNISH DATA PROTECTION LAW: COLLECTION, PROCESSING, AND USE OF PERSONAL DATA

The 'processing of personal data' means the collection, recording, organization, use, transfer, disclosure, storage, manipulation, combination, protection, deletion, and erasure of personal data, as well as other activity involving personal data. Any processing of personal data should always be based on the specific grounds contained in the PDA. Thus, also retention and use of personal data for the purposes of, and in connection with, a pretrial discovery process require that at least one of the grounds laid down in the PDA is met. These grounds are equivalent to those listed in Article 7 of the Directive (see Chapter 4.E).

The PDA provides for specific requirements for the processing of sensitive personal data. These include, *inter alia*, personal data relating to race or ethnic origin, social, political, or religious affiliation, trade union membership, criminal acts, the state of health, and criminal sanctions. Sensitive personal data may be processed, for example, if processing of data is necessary for preparing or filing a lawsuit or for responding to or deciding such a lawsuit.

C.　　　　　FINNISH DATA PROTECTION LAW: TRANSFER OF PERSONAL DATA

Transfers of personal data from Finland to other European Union (EU) Member States or within the European Economic Area (EEA) are generally permitted without further approval, provided that such transfers fall within the legitimate purposes of processing of the personal data. Except in the event one of the exceptions, as presented below, applies, personal data may not be transferred outside the EU/EEA countries, unless the recipient country is considered to provide an

---

2. The requirement that personal data 'relate to' an individual was considered by the Data Protection Board in the case of TTVK (Dno. 2/936/2005). The Board stated that an Internet protocol (IP) address can be regarded as personal data. Although an IP address alone does not identify a person, together with other means it can identify a person.

adequate level of data protection.[3] The exceptions to the above restriction include cases where:

(1) the data subject has expressly consented to the transfer of his or her personal data outside the EU/EEA. Such a consent must be explicit and unambiguous and given in full awareness of all the relevant factors relating to the proposed transfer;

(2) the transfer is necessary to enter/perform a contract between the data subject and the data controller or in order to take steps before entering into such a contract;

(3) the transfer is necessary for the conclusion or performance of a contract concluded between the data controller and a third party in the interest of the data subject;

(4) the transfer is necessary or called for by law for securing an important public interest or for establishment, exercise, defence, or decision of legal claims;

(5) the transfer is necessary in order to protect the vital interests of the data subject;

(6) the transfer is made from a register from which the access to data, either generally or on special grounds, is expressly provided by law;

(7) the data controller, by means of contractual terms or otherwise, gives adequate guarantees for the protection of privacy and the rights of the individual and the European Commission has not concluded that such guarantees are inadequate. This exception enables the use of Binding Corporate Rules (BCRs) to effect intra-group transfers, provided that all group companies accept such rules as binding and that the rules are approved by the data protection authorities prior to when transfers of personal data are effected; or

(8) the transfer is effected by the use of the Standard Contractual Clauses (SCCs) approved by the European Commission under Article 26.4 of the Directive (95/46/EC).

It should be noted that if the transfer of personal data is based on either paragraph 6 or 7 above, a data controller is obliged to make notification to the Data Protection Ombudsman thirty days prior to the planned transfer. Furthermore, it should be noted that a data controller does not have any obligation to obtain approval from the Data Protection Ombudsman; the notification regime in Finland is thus not an approval regime.

---

3. With respect to transfers of personal data to a recipient in the United States, an adequate level of data protection is ensured if the US recipient of data is committed to comply with the Safe Harbour Privacy Principles on the protection of privacy, approved by the US Department of Commerce and the European Commission.

D.   FINNISH DATA PROTECTION LAW: APPLICATION AND ENFORCEMENT OF THE PDA

The PDA applies to the automated processing of personal data. It also applies to non-automated processing of personal data, if the data are part of or are intended to become a part of a personal data file. With respect to the scope of application of Finnish law, the PDA applies to processing of personal data, if the controller is established in the territory of Finland, or if he or she is otherwise subject to Finnish law. The PDA also applies if the controller is not established in the territory of a Member State of the EU, but it uses equipment located in Finland in the processing of personal data, except where the equipment is used solely for the transfer of data through the territory. In the latter case the controller has to designate a representative established in Finland.

The enforcement authorities are the Data Protection Ombudsman and the Data Protection Board. The Ombudsman promotes good processing practice and issues directions and guidelines in order to ensure that conduct contrary to the PDA is not continued or repeated. If necessary, the Ombudsman refers the matter to the Board or reports the matter for prosecution. In addition, the Ombudsman decides matters brought to the Ombudsman's attention by data subjects by ordering data controllers to grant rights of access to the data subject or to rectify an error. The Board deals with questions of principle relating to the processing of personal data when these are important for the application of the PDA, or for making decisions in matters of data protection.

The decisions of the Ombudsman and the Board are subject to appeal in accordance with the provisions of the Finnish Administrative Judicial Procedure Act (586/1996). The Ombudsman and the Board may only impose financial penalties for a personal data violation under the PDA. A person who intentionally or grossly, negligently, and contrary to the provisions of the PDA:

(1) violates the provisions relating to the drawing up of the description of the file, defining the purpose of the processing of the personal data, the information on processing of personal data, the rectification of the file, of the right of the data subject to prohibit the processing of personal data, and the notification to the Data Protection Ombudsman;
(2) provides false or misleading data to a data protection authority in a matter concerning a personal data file;
(3) violates the provisions on the protection and destruction of personal data file; or
(4) breaches a final order issued by the Data Protection Board and thus compromises the protection of the privacy of the data subject or his or her rights, shall be sentenced for a personal data violation.

The penalties for a personal data file offence, for breaking into a personal data file, and for violation of the secrecy obligation are provided for in the Finnish Penal Code (39/1889). The penalties range from a fine to one year in prison. The fine is determined on the basis of the defendant's daily income – that is, as day-fines, the minimum number of which is one and the maximum number is 120. Prosecutions for criminal offences are brought before the Finnish District Courts and may lead to fines or imprisonment. Claims for damages by data subjects are also brought before the Finnish District Courts as independent claims or integrated with criminal proceedings.[4] Between 2004 and 2007, there have been in total thirty-two cases in the Finnish District Courts in which a defendant was found guilty of personal data file offences.

E.   FINNISH DATA PROTECTION LAW: EMPLOYEE'S E-MAILS AND IDENTIFICATION DATA

The use of an individual's personal data as part of e-discovery is not only governed by data protection law. It is also governed by the Act on the Protection of Privacy in Electronic Communications (516/2004, as amended, the 'E-Privacy Act'). Furthermore, it is governed by the Finnish Act on the Protection of Privacy in Working Life (759/2004, the 'WLA'). In addition, it is governed by the Finnish Constitution (731/1999) and the general principle of secrecy of confidential communications guaranteed therein, stating that 'the secrecy of correspondence, telephony and other confidential communication is inviolable'. Pursuant to the Finnish Constitution, an employer is not permitted to jeopardize this secrecy of employees' confidential messages. It should finally be noted that also the Finnish penal code contains a provision regarding unlawful message interception.

The E-Privacy Act provides that, amongst others, all messages, identification data, and location data are confidential. Identification data are defined as data that can be associated with a subscriber or user (for example, an employee) and that are processed in communications networks for the purposes of transmitting, distributing, or providing messages. Identification data include, amongst others, data regarding routing, duration, and time of communication as well as duration of connection and amount of data transferred during connection. Identification data are regarded as personal data if they can without considerable efforts be associated with an individual employee.

Consequently, identification data are viewed as comparable to communication and thus such data enjoy similar basic rights relating to the 'privacy of communication' as, for instance, e-mails.[5] The confidentiality of communication also applies to identification data generated through the browsing of websites.

---

4. According to the Penal Code, for example, transfer of personal data outside the EU or EEA in violation of the PDA may be considered as a personal data file offence, provided that such transfer violates the privacy of the data subject or causes him or her other damage or significant inconvenience.
5. It should be noted that through recent amendment (entered into force on 1 Jun. 2009) to the E-Privacy Act, corporate subscribers (e.g., employers) have been granted a restricted right to process identification data of employees' e-mails (information on the recipients and senders of an employee's e-mails), under certain circumstances, in order to identify suspected disclosures of business secrets and illegal uses of the communication network or fee-based information society services, provided that these acts are likely to cause significant damage or harm or that the

Erkko Korhonen

The WLA contains specific provisions regarding data protection in employment relations. Under the WLA, the employer is granted some restricted rights to get information on and gain access to the employee's e-mail communication, but these rights only apply to e-mails intended to be received by the employer and only in cases where an employee is temporarily or permanently prevented from performing his or her duties. In other words, the employer's rights never apply to the employees' personal, private communication.

It should be noted that the applicable provisions vary depending on the status of the employment relationship – that is, whether there is a current employment at hand (i.e., the employee is currently employed by the employer) or whether the employee has, for example, terminated his or her employment relationship (i.e., the employee is a former employee of employer) and is therefore permanently prevented from performing his or her duties.

1. Current Employees

The Finnish legislation is primarily aimed at ensuring that the employer's business will suffer no harm even though the employee is temporarily or permanently absent from work. There are neither legal provisions nor Finnish legal practice regarding the employer's right to access the e-mails of its current employees (the provisions under the WLA concern the employer's right to retrieve and open the employee's e-mails during a temporary or permanent absence).

However, with regard to the communication by the employee at the workplace, which is part of his or her work performance, the employer shall have a right to supervise such communication and review the content of such communication. If the employee sends, for example, work-related e-mail to the customer, it is not possible for the employee to deny printing the message and disclosing it to the employer. It is the employer's full right to review the e-mail message sent to the customer by the employee.

On the basis of the above-mentioned facts, it can be stated that the current employees of the employer do not have a right to refuse to allow the employer to access and review the employee's work-related electronic communication. Under the Finnish legislation, it may well be that a refusal could be regarded as a breach of work performance and duties of the employee. However, it should be borne in mind that the employer's right to access electronic communication (for example, e-mails) of its current employees relates only to work-related communication whereas the personal messages of the employees are private and confidential.

---

disclosed business secrets are of significant importance to the corporate subscriber or its partner. Corporate subscribers are thus allowed to process identification data relating to employees' e-mail communications, such as information on the sender and recipient of the e-mail, but not the content of the e-mail messages. However, certain preconditions for processing need to be met prior to initiating processing (e.g., a mandatory reporting to the Data Protection Ombudsman and access to a company's business secrets should be limited, the propriety of data security measures should be taken care of, and the employees should be provided with written instructions on the use of the networks).

Therefore, the private messages should be separated from the work-related messages belonging to the employer.

It should be also noted that the protection of privacy of employees' confidential messages does not mean that the employees necessarily should be allowed to send other than work-related messages within the employer's mailing system.[6]

2. Former Employees

According to the WLA, if the employee is permanently prevented (that is, if the employment relationship is terminated) from performing his or her duties *and his or her consent cannot be obtained,*[7] the employer shall have a right with the assistance of the system administrator (named party) and on the basis on the information related to *the sender, the recipient,* or *the title of the e-mail,* to find out if the former employee has sent or received work-related e-mails. The information contained in the e-mail must be essential to the employer's business – that is, under the WLA, the information must be essential to the employer in order to complete negotiations, serve customers, or safeguard the employer's operations otherwise.

Neither the legislation nor the preparatory works of the legislation contain explicit guidance regarding the situation when the former employee refuses to give the consent for the employer to retrieve and open the e-mails of the employee during the permanent absence of the employee. However, an interpretation has been presented in the Finnish legal literature according to which it must be the employer's right to retrieve and open the e-mails of the employee during the employee's permanent absence even without the consent of the employee – that is, the intention of the legislator could not have been to give the employee a possibility by refusing to give the consent to permanently deny the access to the employee's work-related e-mail communication after the termination of the employment relationship.

The prerequisites for the retrieval of the e-mail(s) during the employee's permanent absence are the following:

(a) The former employee managed tasks independently on behalf of the employer and it is not possible to obtain the information by any other system maintained by the employer; and

(b) It is evident, on account of the former employee's tasks, that e-mails belonging to the employer have been sent or received.

---

6. According to the WLA, the use of e-mail and other data networks is subject to the cooperative procedures under the Finnish Act on Cooperation within Undertakings (334/2007). This means, *inter alia,* that the introduction of policies and principles used regarding the use of e-mail and other data networks must be discussed between the employer and either the employees or the representatives of employees. The aforesaid applies to corporations that employ at least thirty people in Finland.

7. According to the preparatory works of the legislation, consent cannot be received, for example, due to the death or serious illness of the employee.

In addition, the employer must ensure that finding out the matters attended by the former employee and safeguarding the operations of the employer are not possible by other means.

If the retrieval of an e-mail does not lead to the opening of the message (i.e., the message is of personal nature or not essential to the employer), the employer must draft up a report: (i) that is signed by the parties taking part in the retrieval process; (ii) in which are stated the reasons for retrieval; and (iii) the time of retrieval; and (iv) that identifies those who performed the retrieval.

According to the WLA, the e-mail(s) may be opened with the assistance of the system administrator and in the presence of another person, provided that: (i) based on the information retrieved it is evident that the information belongs to the employer; and (ii) it is essential to the employer to receive information contained in the e-mail(s) in order to complete negotiations concerning the employer's operations or to serve customers or safeguard the employer's operations; and (iii) the message sender and the recipient cannot be contacted for the purpose of establishing the content of the message or for the purpose of sending it to an address indicated by the employer.

A report must be also prepared of an opened message identifying: (i) the message opened; (ii) the reason for its opening; (iii) the time it was opened; (iv) the persons performing the opening; and (v) the persons to whom the information on the content of the opened message was given.

The reports regarding the retrieval and opening of e-mails must be provided to the former employee. The information of the sender or the content of the message may not be processed more excessively than is necessary for the purposes of retrieval or opening of the e-mail. The parties processing the information must be subjected to confidentiality obligation and they must have undertaken not to use the information for their benefit.

II. PRETRIAL DISCOVERY IN FINLAND: BACKGROUND

In Finland, as in other Nordic countries in general, the parties' obligation to disclose a document, or other information, in a trial is much more limited in scope and in its objectives than in common law countries. The disclosure obligation concerns only documents that can be assumed to have significance as evidence in a case.[8]

One of the main differences under Finnish law concerning the obligation to disclose documents, in comparison to the common law countries, is the requirement for the party requesting the disclosure to specify the requested document. This might, in practice, prove difficult. The difference relates to the objective of Finnish regulation, that is, acquisition of sufficient evidence, as in the common law

---

8. The Finnish Code of Judicial Procedure (1.1.1734/4), Ch. 17, Provision 12.

countries, for example, in the United States, the objectives of the discovery institution relate also, amongst others, to the elaboration of the claim. In Finland, only a court of law may order a document to be delivered to the court. This order may be made regardless of whether the document is in the possession of the litigant or a third party.

A. PRETRIAL DISCOVERY IN FINLAND: BLOCKING STATUTES

The cooperation with foreign courts or public authorities in litigation or regulatory investigations and proceedings is not restricted under Finnish law. There are no 'blocking statutes' that would prohibit the transfer of information abroad.

B. PRETRIAL DISCOVERY IN FINLAND: HAGUE CONVENTION ON THE TAKING OF EVIDENCE

Finland has made a reservation in accordance with Article 23 of the Hague Convention on the Taking of Evidence (1970).[9] According to the reservation, Letters of Request issued for the purpose of obtaining pretrial discovery of documents are only executed if they require a person: (a) to state what documents relevant to the proceedings to which the Letter of Request relates are, or have been, in his or her possession, custody, or power; or (b) to produce any documents specified in the Letter of Request that are likely to be in his or her possession, custody, or power. Therefore, a Letter of Request addressed to a Finnish court for a pretrial discovery of documents, of the scope as it is known in the common law countries, is not likely to succeed. The reservation is closely linked to the relevant Finnish legislation concerning the disclosure of documents. As stated above, the difficulty of the Finnish system relates to the limited scope of the obligation to disclose documents, and to the practical difficulty of specifying the requested documents.

However, in practice, the party who possesses the relevant documents may not be reluctant to disclose the requested documents. This is due to the fact that in order to present, or to answer to, claims, the party has to present all of the relevant documents. Further, a party is likely, in order to support its argumentation, to comply with the procedural orders given by the court in question. The practical difficulty of a common law court requesting the party to disclose documents relates to the Finnish data protection legislation, as presented above. Therefore, even if the party is willing to cooperate in accordance with the common law pretrial discovery processes, this might be, in whole or in part, prohibited under the Finnish data protection legislation.

---

9. Hague Convention on the Taking of Evidence Abroad in Civil or Commercial Matters of 18 Mar. 1970.

III. PRETRIAL DISCOVERY VERSUS DATA PROTECTION

A. GROUNDS FOR PROCESSING OF PERSONAL DATA FOR PRETRIAL DISCOVERY PURPOSES

Personal data can be processed for discovery purposes, if: (i) a data subject (i.e., the person to whom the personal data pertains) has given his or her consent thereof; or (ii) if the Data Protection Board has issued permission for the same; or (iii) if processing of data is necessary for drafting or filing a lawsuit or for responding to or the deciding of such a lawsuit.

Whilst consent is a ground for processing under the PDA, it would not in many cases provide a viable basis for processing. This is due to the fact that it is required that consent is given voluntarily and that a data subject is informed exactly about what he or she consents to.

The permission of the Data Protection Board will be granted, for example, in the event the processing aims to realize a legitimate interest of the data controller or the recipient of the data, provided that such processing does not compromise the protection of the privacy of the individual or his or her rights. It should be noted that this prerequisite for processing 'for the purposes of a legitimate interest' is in many other EU countries and under the Directive on data protection (95/46/EC) considered as a general ground for processing and thus does not require any additional permission. The Finnish legislation is in this respect substantially more stringent, as the processing based on 'the purposes of a legitimate interest' requires permission of the Board, a procedure that may be time consuming.

Furthermore, personal data may be processed on case-by-case basis for the purposes of drafting or filing a lawsuit or responding to or the deciding of such a lawsuit.[10] According to the interpretation of a representative of the Data Protection Ombudsman, personal data may be processed in the discovery process, provided, however, that this processing is limited only to personal data that are necessary for the lawsuit. Thus, the capture and production of all content of an e-mail server without prior filtering of relevant content would not be permitted. In addition, this ground for processing requires that there actually is or will be a lawsuit. Therefore, general retention of data that also contains personal data for discovery purposes cannot be based on this ground.

The PDA explicitly permits the transfer of personal data to a country outside the EU/EEA, for instance to the United States, if the transfer, for example, is necessary for purposes of drafting or filing a lawsuit or for responding to or the deciding of such a lawsuit.

---

10. In fact, this ground for processing concerns processing of sensitive personal data. However, according to an unofficial interpretation of the Office of Data Protection Ombudsman, also processing of other than sensitive personal data – that is, 'normal' personal data – may be based upon that ground.

IV.   CONCLUSION

Finnish data protection legislation, as well as electronic privacy legislation, places certain restrictions on the processing and transfer of personal data based on requests relating to e-discovery procedures. However, taking these restrictions into account, it is possible to process personal data for the purposes of the e-discovery process.

Chapter 5.7

France

*Charlotte Portmann**

I.   INTRODUCTION

In France, e-discovery requirements are likely to challenge conflicting obligations
deriving from the 1970 Hague Convention on the Taking of Evidence and the
French blocking statute of 26 July 1968 on the disclosure of documents and information of an economic nature. In addition, conflicts follow from the French Data
Protection Act.

II.   DISCOVERY FRAMEWORK AND COMMUNICATION
            OF DOCUMENTS UNDER FRENCH LAW

In France, there is no discovery process. Each party in litigation has to spontaneously provide the exhibits and documents upon which they rely in their briefs.[1]
The judge will see to it that exhibits are exchanged in due time between the parties.
Upon request a judge can order a party to produce a specific case-related document
it detains or that is detained by a third party, provided there is no legal reason
preventing its disclosure such as privacy right or business secrecy.[2]

---

*   Charlotte Portmann, Howrey LLP, Senior Associate, Paris, France.
1. Article 132 of Code of Civil Procedure: '*the party who refers to an exhibit has to disclose it to the
    other party in the proceeding. Such a disclosure shall be spontaneous*'.
2. Articles 138 to 142 of Code of Civil Procedure.

Catrien Noorda & Stefan Hanloser, *E-Discovery and Data Privacy*, pp. 99–107.
© 2011 Kluwer Law International BV, The Netherlands.

III.   THE HAGUE CONVENTION ON THE TAKING
         OF EVIDENCE

On 30 December 1974, France initially filed a declaration under Article 23 of the Hague Convention[3] that it will not execute Letters of Request issued for the purpose of obtaining pretrial discovery of documents as known in common law countries, which then prevented any pretrial discovery.

Afterward, through a declaration dated 24 December 1986,[4] which entered into force on 19 January 1987, France limited said reservation in the sense that it no longer applies when the requested documents are listed limitatively in the Letter of Request and have a direct and precise link with the case matter.

In a ruling dated 18 September 2003,[5] the Paris Appeal Court gave some guidelines on how to construe this kind of Letter of Request and the subsequent application of the reservation under the Hague Convention: listing of the documents is restrictive as far as the latter are identified within a reasonable degree of specificity in relation to certain criteria such as date, nature, or author. In the case at hand, the Court held that the Letter of Request complied with the requirements of the Hague Convention since it was sufficiently specified in time and extent, even if it covered a broader period than the one relating to the litigious facts and corresponding to the litigious assignment of shares.

Therefore, a Letter of Request addressed to a French authority as part of pretrial discovery will be implemented subject to the appraisal by the judge of its compliance with this general requirement of specific identification.

France considers the application of the Hague Convention mandatory insofar as a Letter of Request is issued by another contracting state's jurisdiction and shall be executed within the French territory and reciprocally.[6] This position is contrary to the one adopted by several other contracting states, such as the United States, which held in the famous *Aerospatiale* decision that resort to the Hague Convention is optional.[7]

As regards European Union (EU), EC Regulation 1206/2001[8] will prevail over the Hague Convention.

France has besides enacted a specific law, presented as a blocking statute, in order to ensure the exclusive application of the Hague Convention.

3. Published by decree n°75–250 of 9 Apr. 1975, JO 17/04/1975, 3980
4. Published by decree n°89–43 of 24 Jan. 1989, JP 28/01/1989, 1300,
5. Paris Appeal Court, 18 Sep. 2003, *Ladreit de Lacharriere v. Monsieur le Commissaire aux assurances de l'Etat de Californie*, RG N°2002/18509, Juris-Data 2003-234028.
6. See Summary of responses to the questionnaire of May 2008 relating to the evidence convention, with analytical documents, and Response France to 2008 Evidence Convention, available on the HCCH website. <www.hcch.net/index_fr.php?act=publications.details&pid=4397&dtid=33>
7. *Société Nationale Industrielle Aérospatiale v. United States District Court*, 482 U.S. 522, 544 n. 28 (1987).
8. EC Regulation n°1206/2001 of 28 May 28 on cooperation between the courts of Member States in the taking of evidence in civil or commercial matters.

IV.   FRENCH BLOCKING STATUTE

A.   French Blocking Statute: General Overview

Even though France is not the only country[9] that has adopted a blocking statute to prohibit the transfer of the information to foreign courts or public authorities, the French Act 80-538 of 16 July 1980[10] is very well known.

The main objective of this law was to prevent 'fishing expeditions' and render compulsory the resort to the Hague Convention as exclusive means for seeking evidence.

Article 1 provides that:

> Subject to international treaties or agreements, it is forbidden for any French national, French resident or any representative of legal entity established in France, to communicate whether in writing, orally or by any other means, documents or information of an economic, commercial, industrial, financial or technical nature to foreign public authorities if such communication is likely to attempt to French sovereignty, security or fundamental economic interests or public order.

Article 1*bis* provides under the same reservation of the existence of international treaties or agreements to exclude requests made under the Hague Convention, and in addition to laws and regulations in force, that:

> It is forbidden for any person to ask, seek for or communicate, in writing, orally or by any other means, documents or information of an economic, commercial, industrial, financial or technical nature leading to the gathering of evidence with a view to foreign judicial or administrative procedures or within the frame of such procedures.

This twofold prohibition is thus very broad and includes discovery by any means including e-discovery. Criminal penalties laid down in Article 3 for breach of this prohibition are up to six months' imprisonment and a fine up to Euros (EUR) 18,000.

B.   French Blocking Statute: Enforcement

Till a recent decision issued in 2007, this blocking statute has been rarely enforced, which led to questioning its scope and efficiency especially before US courts where this legal excuse was not taken into consideration in the absence of real enforcement in practice.

---

9. Such as Switzerland, the United Kingdom, Australia, Canada, and so forth.
10. Initial law n°68–678 of 26 Jul. 1968, limited to shipping trade, has been extended and amended by law n°80–538 of 16 Jul. 1980 on the communication of economic, commercial, or technical information to physical persons or legal entities, published in JO 17 Jul. 1980, 1799.

Even though in three cases where Article 1*bis* of the blocking statute has been invoked by French companies to refuse the communication of information requested,[11] the criminal penalties have never been applied until the decision of the Paris Appeal Court issued on 28 March 2007.[12]

The Court sentenced a French lawyer to a EUR 10,000 fine for breach of Article 1*bis* of the blocking statute, for having collected economic information to be used as evidence in a case pending before a US court. The Supreme Court upheld said decision on 22 December 2007[13] considering that the informal approach by the French lawyer toward a former employee of MAAF, a French insurance company, to gather information on the circumstances under which said company decided to purchase the foreign company constituted a breach of the blocking statute. Indeed, said collecting of evidences for use in foreign judicial proceeding was not made in accordance with the requirements of the Hague Convention.

Even though the circumstances of the case were very specific, most of the authors agree that it will in any case lead French companies to reassess the risks they are liable for on both sides: from a French perspective, in case of transmission of information covered by the blocking statute, since the risk of conviction is no longer theoretical, and from a US perspective, in case of refusal to communicate said information, and then encourage to use the Hague Convention as a means of discovery abroad.[14]

On the other hand, it has to be noted that in relation to administrative proceedings, there has been a relaxing in the application of the blocking statute and corresponding exchange of information. Article L.821-5-2 of the Commercial Code now provides that said blocking statute does not apply to the French accounting authority when it concludes agreements with its foreign counterparts.

---

11. Nanterre First Instance Court, summary judgment, 22 Dec. 1993, RG n°93-4436, Juris-Data n°1993-050136: dismissal under the ground of Art. 1*bis* of the blocking statute of communication of information's request made by former president of Lebanon, all the more than Lebanese judicial authority could use if needed the international rogatory commission; Versailles Appeal Court, 16 May 2001: dismissal of the request to communicate economic documents from Renault to Romanian company, if the appeal lodged against said decision was dismissed, the Supreme Court considered the reference to the blocking statute overmuch (Civ.2, 20 Nov. 2003, n°01-15633). Paris Commercial Court, 20 Jul. 2005, Juris-Data n°2005-288978: the Court considered that the order issued by a judge from the Southern New York district that required a French bank to give accounting and financial documents, without using the Hague Convention, is in breach of the blocking statute and contrary to the economic and financial French public order.
12. Paris Appeal Court, 28 Mar. 2007, RG n°06/06272, Juris-Data n°2007-332254.
13. Supreme Court, Criminal chamber, 12 Dec. 2007, n°07-83228.
14. M. Danis, 'Sanction de la communication illicite de renseignements à une autorité judiciaire étrangère', *JCP E* n°35, 28 Aug. 2008, 2016; D. Barlow, 'La loi du 26 juillet 1968 relative à la communication de documents et renseignements d'ordre économique : un état des lieux', *JCP E* n°43, 25 Oct. 2007, 2330; M. J. Gottridge & T. Rouhette, 'France puts some muscle behind its blocking statute', *New York Law Journal*, Vol. 239, No.82, 29 Apr. 2008; The Sedona Conference Framework for analysis of cross border discovery conflicts – A practical guide to navigating the competing currents of international data privacy and discovery, August 2008, 21.

V. FRENCH DATA PROTECTION ACT: DATA
    PROCESSING, DATA FILES, AND INDIVIDUAL
    LIBERTIES ACT 78-17 OF 6 JANUARY 1978[15]

Apart from the Hague Convention and the blocking statute aforementioned, attention should also be paid to the French Data Protection Act. Communication of personal data for use in cross-border discovery has to comply with the principles laid down in said Act. The French Data Protection Authority (National Commission for Data Protection and the Liberties – 'CNIL') is the supervisory authority.

The criminal offences for breach of said Act are substantially more severe than the ones provided in case of breach of the blocking statute: fine of up to EUR 300,000 and five years of imprisonment. The fines currently pronounced by the French Data Protection Authority vary from EUR 5,000 to EUR 50,000.[16]

A. FRENCH DATA PROTECTION ACT: GENERAL OVERVIEW

Under the French Data Protection Act, as in the Directive, the term 'personal data' is defined as any information relating to an identified or identifiable individual, that is, who can be identified, directly or indirectly, by reference to an identification number (e.g., social security number) or to one or more factors specific to him or her (e.g., fingerprints, name, and so forth). Processing means any operation or set of operations in relation to such data whatever the mechanism used and then includes, *inter alia,* collection, storage, use, disclosure by transmission, and deletion.[17] Transfer of personal data abroad covers any situation where data are transferred through one device to another or through a network and are aimed to be subject to a processing in the recipient country (for instance, centralization intragroup of the management human resources databases).

The processing of personal data shall comply with the following legal criteria set down in Articles 6 and 7:

- data shall be obtained and processed fairly and lawfully, for specified, explicit, and legitimate purposes; adequate, relevant, and not excessive compared to the purposes; accurate, complete, and updated; stored for a period no longer than is necessary for the purposes for which they are processed; and

---

15. Act n°78-17 of 6 Jan. 1978 as amended by the Act of 6 Aug. 2004 relating to the protection of individuals with regard to the processing of personal data and by the Act of 12 May 2009 relating to the simplification and clarification of law and lightening of procedures – English version available on French data protection authority's website: <www.cnil.fr/fileadmin/documents/en/Act78-17VA.pdf>.
16. Article 226–18 of Criminal Code.
17. Article 2 of 6 Jan. 1978 Act.

– processing must have received the data subject's unambiguous consent or benefit from a statutory permission (e.g., performance of a contract or compliance with legal obligation, pursuit of the data controller's or the data recipient's legitimate interest).

The processing of sensitive personal data as defined in Article 8 is prohibited unless the exceptions listed in the Data Protection Act apply.[18]

Any data processing has to be notified to the data protection authority unless exemptions apply provided for by said authority.[19] The rights granted to data subjects are listed in

Articles 38 and further and mainly concern the right to object (Article 38), the right of information and access to data (Article 39), and the right of rectification (Article 40).

As regards access to an employee's email, in light of secrecy of private correspondence, the French Supreme Court since a major ruling relating to Nikon in 2001 has adopted a general principle pursuant to which the employer is not allowed to have access to an employee's emails or files stored in the company's computer hard drive if they are identified as personal unless the employee is present during the investigation or is specifically called to attend to such an investigation.[20]

Data transfers outside the EU are provided for in Articles 68 to 70. In substance, the data controller cannot transfer personal data to a State that does not provide an adequate level of protection, unless the data subject has given his or her unambiguous consent or statutory permissions are likely to be applicable (e.g., for establishment, exercise, or defence of legal claims, and so forth),[21] or permission from the data protection authority has been granted on the basis of sufficient safeguards such as Standard Contractual Clauses (SCCs) or authorized Binding Corporate Rules (BCRs). Permissions are usually obtained within a delay of two months. If the recipient is a US-based entity that adheres to Safe Harbour Privacy Principles, transfer may also occur.

---

18. Express consent of the data subject unless otherwise stipulated by law or data made public by the data subject itself; the protection of human life; establishment, exercise, or defence of legal claim; medical research.
19. To date, fourteen exemptions have been granted in various sectors, such as exemption n°7 regarding processing constituted for purposes of external information and communication.
20. French Supreme Court, Social chamber, 2 Oct. 2001, n°99-42942 (personal e-mails identified as such by the employee);18 Oct. 2006, n°04-48025 and 30 May 2007, n°05-43102 (filed deemed to be professional since not identified by the employee as personal, for instance, in the subject matter of the e-mail); 17 Jun. 2009, n°08-40274 (unless a specific risk or event, the employer can only open the messages identified as personal by the employee in his or her presence).
21. See Art. 69 for other statutory permissions (protection of the data subject's life; protection of the public interest; consultation of a public register; performance of a contract or fulfilment of quasi-contractual obligations; conclusion or performance of a contract for the benefit of the data subject).

B.   FRENCH DATA PROTECTION ACT: RECOMMENDATION OF THE FRENCH DATA PROTECTION AUTHORITY ON TRANSFER OF PERSONAL DATA WITHIN THE FRAME OF US DISCOVERY

Given the growing number of motions being filed for transfer of personal data to the United States within the frame of discovery proceedings, and following the working document on pretrial discovery for cross-border civil litigation issued by the Article 29 Working Party in February 2009,[22] the French data protection authority recently published a specific recommendation dedicated to this issue. It gave some guidelines that can be useful to data controllers while trying to reconcile e-discovery requirements with those of the Data Protection Act.[23]

Said recommendation addresses the points discussed in the following sections.

1.   Responsibility for Processing

Pursuant to Article 5 of the French Data Protection Act, the data controller may be the French or foreign entity established on French territory or the foreign entity using means of processing located on French territory. Within the frame of discovery, said person will decide on the transfer of personal data and then on the purpose and means of processing.

2.   Legitimacy of Processing for Litigation Purposes

Pursuant to Article 7 of the French Data Protection Act, grounds that can legitimate a transfer of personal data are the following: (i) compliance with the Hague Convention and 1968 Act; (ii) legitimate interest of the data controller provided this is not incompatible with the interests or fundamental rights of the data subject, who will benefit in any case from a right to object on legitimate grounds while being informed of the processing;[24] (iii) in exceptional cases, the data subject's freely given, informed, and specific consent. Such consent is deemed to be freely given when it has been obtained without any pressure or risk of retaliation, which seems unlikely regarding an employee.

3.   Proportionality of Data

In order for the data collected within the frame of discovery to be adequate, relevant, and not excessive in relation to the purpose for which they are processed, the

---

22.   Working Document WP 158 adopted on 11 Feb. 2009, available at <http://ec.europa.eu/justice_home/fsj/privacy/docs/wpdocs/2009/wp158_en.pdf>.
23.   Deliberation n°2009-474 of 23 Jul. 2009 bearing recommendation regarding transfer of personal data within the frame of American judicial procedures so-called 'discovery', published in JO 19 Aug. 2009- N°190.
24.   Article 38 of the French Data Protection Act.

French data protection authority recommends resort to several techniques: (i) filtering with keywords carried out locally in the country where the personal data are found; (ii) trusted third party who will appraise the relevance of the data; (iii) providing the personal data in an anonymous or pseudonymized form so as to avoid giving data irrelevant in the litigation; (iv) stipulative court orders issued by the American judge, which will specify the conditions under which the data will be transferred and how they will be secured and kept confidential. If transfer of personal data is necessary, data must be exhaustive and accurate and limited to the identity, functions, and contact details of the concerned person, and to the elements strictly related to the pending litigation.

4.   Duration of Storage and Data Recipients

Data used within the frame of discovery shall be stored for the duration of the procedure, and can only be given to data recipients especially entrusted with the role to collect said data for this specified purpose.[25]

5.   Information of Data Subject

Information shall be given by the data controller to the data subject that personal data are being processed for litigation prior to the implementation of the processing. In the event of data collected by a third party, the data controller will inform the data subject as soon as reasonably practicable after the data are processed. In some cases, when preliminary measures are needed to prevent destruction of evidence, informing of the data subject may occur only after the adoption of said measures.[26]

6.   Security Measures

The data controller shall take all adequate precautions to ensure the data security, at all steps of the processing, especially as regards data storage. If external service providers are used, the data controller shall ensure that they are bound with strict confidentiality obligations.[27]

---

25. Articles 6 and 34 of the French Data Protection Act.
26. Articles 6 and 32 of the French Data Protection Act.
27. Articles 34 and 35 of the French Data Protection Act; Recommendation n° 2005-213 of 11 Oct. 2005 regarding modalities of electronic storage.

7.   **Formalities Regarding Transfer of Personal Data to the
United States**

Such transfer must comply with the above-mentioned requirements set down in
Articles 68 and 69. The data protection authority distinguishes two hypotheses and
specifies the following:

- if the personal data are located in France and directly transferred to the
  United States for litigation purposes:

In case of single transfer of relevant information, exemption of Article 69-3[28] can
justify the transfer, which then does not need to be authorized but only notified to
the authority.

In case of repetitive and massive transfer, such a transfer can only occur if the
data recipient complies with one of the following conditions: (i) US-based entity
adhering to Safe Harbour Privacy Principles; (ii) signature of SCCs; (iii) implementation of BCRs.

- if the personal data have already been transferred in the United States for a
  legitimate purpose previously authorized (e.g., centralization of the human
  resources databases of French subsidiary of an American group):

If such data are further transferred to a judicial authority, the data controller will
have to provide adequate protection to the data given to American authorities and
to the adverse party through the implementation of relevant tools such as a stipulative court order taking into account the protection of personal data.

If such data are further transferred to a party in litigation or a third party,
adequate contractual clauses shall be entered into with the party receiving the
information.

VI.   CONCLUSION

Even if the requirements laid down in French law may appear burdensome, their
compliance will ensure legitimate transfer of personal data abroad within the frame
of discovery.

---

28. Article 69-3°: the meeting of obligations ensuring the establishment, exercise, or defence of
     legal claims.

Chapter 5.8

Germany

*Stefan Hanloser**

I.   INTRODUCTION

There is an inherent tension between mandatory pretrial discovery requirements
and data protection law since discovery promotes the disclosure of data whereas
data protection is intended to prevent such disclosure. In Germany, this tension is
likely to become a real conflict – with practical implications for German companies that are doing business in the United States or that have their parent company,
a subsidiary, or an affiliate in the United States – since pretrial discovery is virtually unknown in Germany whereas data protection is one of the cornerstones of
German civil and public law.

II.   GERMAN DATA PROTECTION LAW: BACKGROUND

Germany is rightly said to have one of the strictest data protection regimes in the
European Union (EU), if not in the world. In fact, the world's first data protection
act was passed in the German federal state of Hesse on 7 October 1970. A federal
data protection act, the Bundesdatenschutzgesetz (BDSG), entered into force on

---

*   Dr Stefan Hanloser, Howrey LLP, Munich, Germany.

Catrien Noorda & Stefan Hanloser, *E-Discovery and Data Privacy*, pp. 109–116.
© 2011 Kluwer Law International BV, The Netherlands.

1 January 1978 and has been revised several times since then.[1] The European Data Protection Directive[2] was implemented in May 2001 and the most recent amendments came into effect on 1 September 2009. The public awareness for privacy and data protection in Germany, both in the public and private sectors, was sharpened by the Constitutional Court's landmark decision on a census law in 1983 when the individual's 'right of informational self-determination', that is, the freedom to 'determine the disclosure and use of ones data', was established.[3]

A.   GERMAN DATA PROTECTION LAW: PERSONAL DATA

The BDSG applies to 'personal data' only. Corporate data, business information, or technical know-how that does not relate to an identified or identifiable natural person is not protected.[4]

In the pretrial discovery context, it is important to note that employees are no less protected in Germany than any third parties. The responding party – that is, the litigant that receives a request for the production of information from the requesting litigant – may not rely on any privilege when it comes to the transfer and disclosure of its employees' personal data. In addition, the German courts and authorities interpret the term 'personal data' very broadly. Therefore, not only bank and credit card details or medical records are protected against pretrial disclosure. Corporate e-mails written by an identifiable employee, for instance, yield personal data, that is, the existence of an employment contract and the employee's capacity as author of the e-mail. This is the same with a call log of a company's telephone system that provides information about the outgoing and incoming calls since it contains information about employees' communication patterns and job performances in general. And even meeting minutes contain personal data since they record the attendance of participants and the content of their statements.[5]

In short, it is no exaggeration to say that virtually each and every pretrial discovery affects personal data in one form or another and requires a legal assessment under the BDSG.

---

1. Bundesdatenschutzgesetz (BDSG – Federal Data Protection Act), 14 Jan. 2003, BGBl. I 66.
2. Council Directive 95/46, Protection of individuals with regard to the processing of personal data and on the free movement of such data, 1995 O.J. (L 281) 31 (EC).
3. 15 Dec. 1983 Bundesverfassungsgericht (German Constitutional Court) 1 BvR 209/83 et al., NJW 1984, 419.
4. The transfer and disclosure of business information or technical know-how to a litigant may be restricted or excluded by non-disclosure or confidentiality agreements. This contractual protection of business information or technical know-how is, however, not the subject matter of this chapter on privacy and data protection law.
5. The examples are taken from the Working Paper 136 of 20 Jun. 2007 of the Art. 29 Working Party.

B.   GERMAN DATA PROTECTION LAW: EMPLOYEES' E-MAILS

Specific restrictions apply to the discovery of employees' private e-mail correspondence. If the employer explicitly allows or factually tolerates the private use of the business e-mail addresses by its employees, the secrecy of communication provisions (*Fernmeldegeheimnis*) of the Telecommunications Act[6] provide another obstacle for the e-discovery process. If the employer has not requested and obtained the employees' prior consents for screening their private electronic correspondence, the employer would breach the secrecy of communication vis-à-vis its employees when running an automated keyword search on the company's e-mail servers for case-relevant information, which could encroach on the employees' private e-mails.[7] If the employees' private or mixed private/business e-mails cannot clearly be identified and separated from their business-only e-mails, all e-mails are deemed to be 'private' and therefore protected by the secrecy of communication against keyword searches by the employer. As a consequence, companies that do not prohibit and actually prevent the private use of their business e-mail addresses must collect their employees' consents before screening their mail servers. Usually, the employees are ultimately asked to either consent to a surveillance of their private communication in line with the company's electronic communications policy or to confirm in writing that they will refrain from using their business e-mail addresses for private communication.

C.   GERMAN DATA PROTECTION LAW: DATA COLLECTION, PROCESSING, AND USE

Personal data may be collected, processed, and used only if the conditions of a statutory permission are met, or if the individual whose personal data is affected, that is, the 'data subject', has given his or her unambiguous consent. In short: collecting, processing, and using data is generally prohibited unless it is exceptionally permitted by law or valid consent.

Collection is the gathering of data on the data subject. Processing is the storage, modification, transfer, disclosure, blocking, and erasure of personal data. Use

---

6. Telekommunikationsgesetz (TKG – Telecommunications Act), 22 Jun. 2004, BGBl. I 1190, § 88.
7. In a recent decision, the Frankfurt Administrative Court restricted the employees' secrecy of communication to private e-mails that are stored on the company's e-mail server and that have not been retrieved by the respective employee yet. The Court held that the protected communication process ends once the recipient has received the message; 6 Nov. 2008 Verwaltungsgericht Frankfurt/Main, 1 K 628/08.F, CR 2009, 125. Even though the Constitutional Court adopted this distinction for the surveillance of communication by public authorities (16 Jun. 2009 Bundesverfassungsgericht, [2 BvR 902/06, NJW 2009, 2431), it is still advisable for companies to ask for their employees' prior consents even for retrieved e-mails, which are stored in <pst> files on the employees computers, in order to be on the safe side.

is any utilization of personal data other than processing, no matter for what purpose.

D.   GERMAN DATA PROTECTION LAW: DATA CONTROLLER;
            DATA PROCESSOR

The data controller is the legal entity that has to ensure that the collection, processing, or use of personal data – either by itself or by a data processor on its behalf – is in line with the BDSG. In a controller-processor relationship, the controller makes the decisions whereas the processor acts upon the controller's instructions. If a controller assigns data-related processes and decisions to another legal entity, such entity does not qualify as an instructed processor but becomes a data controller itself with genuine responsibilities under the BDSG.

Since the data transmission between a controller and its processor within the EU Member States or member states of the European Economic Area (EEA) is not restricted under German data protection law, groups of companies use these different roles for a strategic structuring of their data flows under the applicable data protection laws. Therefore, in a pretrial discovery project, it is not sufficient to find the group members that store relevant information; it must also be determined whether they actually store the information on their own behalf as data controllers or on behalf of other group members as data processors.

E.   GERMAN DATA PROTECTION LAW: TRANSFER ABROAD

In accordance with the European Data Protection Directive, the BDSG has express rules for the transfer of personal data abroad. The transfer of personal data to EU Member States or to member states of the EEA is not restricted. The transfer of personal data to countries outside the EEA is only permitted if an equivalent level of data protection is ensured by implementing a sufficiently strict contractual agreement or binding guidelines between the parties of the data transfer. If personal data are to be transferred to the United States, which is deemed to be a country without an equivalent level of data protection, the US-based recipient of the data can also self-certify under the Safe Harbour Programme.

F.   GERMAN DATA PROTECTION LAW: CONFLICT OF LAWS

The BDSG governs any collection, processing, or use of personal data in Germany no matter whether the data processor is located in Germany or abroad. If the data processor has, however, its corporate seat in an EU Member State or in a Member State of the EEA, the BDSG does not apply unless a German branch of the data processor collects, processes, or uses the data in Germany.

Since multinational companies tend to store their data at various locations worldwide, determining the applicable data protection law at the beginning of an e-discovery project becomes more and more challenging for the litigants and their legal advisors. Cloud computing makes the decision even more difficult.

G.   GERMAN DATA PROTECTION LAW: SUPERVISORY
          AUTHORITIES; ENFORCEMENT

The data protection regulations for the private sector are enforced by the sixteen German federal states.[8] Monetary penalties of up to Euros (EUR) 300,000 can be imposed for each violation of privacy provisions under the BDSG. Up to two years of imprisonment can be awarded if material privacy provisions of the BDSG were breached for personal gain or with the intention to harm others.

In 2008, thirty-five members of the *Lidl* retailers group were fined EUR 1.462 million for illegally spying on their employees.[9] In October 2009, the Berlin Data Protection Commissioner imposed on the German railways company Deutsche Bahn a fine of EUR 1.123 million for, *inter alia*, monitoring employees' workplace access to external e-mail accounts.[10]

III.   PRETRIAL DISCOVERY IN GERMANY: BACKGROUND

The mutual disclosure of documents and data is unknown in Germany. The litigants only produce those documents in court that support their case. If one party refers to a specific document in its pleadings, the court can order that the document be lodged with the court, no matter whether it is in the possession of a litigant or a third party.[11] Specific remedies apply for the enforcement of intellectual property rights and copyrights.

A.   PRETRIAL DISCOVERY IN GERMANY: BLOCKING STATUTES

The cooperation with foreign courts or public authorities in litigation or regulatory investigations and proceedings is not restricted under German law.

---

8. On 9 Mar. 2010, the Court of Justice of the European Union held that by making the data protection authorities subject to the scrutiny of the federal states, Germany incorrectly transposed the requirement that those authorities perform their functions 'with complete independence' under Art. 28(1) of the European Data Protection Directive, Case C-518/07, *European Commission v. Germany,* 2010 O.J. (C 113) 3 (EU). Therefore, the data protection supervisory authorities will have to be restructured in some federal states in order to achieve 'complete independence'.
9. Press release of the Ministry of the Interior of Baden-Württemberg of 11 Sept. 2008.
10. Press release of the Berlin Data Protection Commissioner of 23 Oct. 2009.
11. *Zivilprozessordnung* (ZPO – Code of Civil Procedure), 5 Dec. 2005, BGBl. I 3202, § 142.

In particular, there are no 'blocking statutes' that prohibit the transfer of information abroad.[12]

B.   PRETRIAL DISCOVERY IN GERMANY: HAGUE CONVENTION ON THE TAKING OF EVIDENCE

The Hague Convention on the Taking of Evidence[13] is often seen by the responding party, which is confronted with a request for the production of information, as a last resort to evade or at least delay pretrial discovery. The Hague Convention requires a Letter of Request sent by a judicial authority of the requesting Member State to the competent authority of the addressed Member State to obtain evidence that is intended for use in the judicial proceedings.[14] Germany has declared[15] that it will not execute such Letters of Request 'issued for the purpose of obtaining pretrial discovery of documents as known in Common Law countries'.[16] As a consequence, a Letter of Request addressed to a German authority for pretrial discovery of documents would be inevitably a dead end.

The US Supreme Court held in its *Aérospatiale* decision in 1987, however, that US courts are not required to first resort to the Hague Convention whenever discovery is sought from a foreign litigant since the Letter of Request procedure is unduly time consuming and expensive.[17] Therefore, a well-advised German litigant might invoke the Hague Convention for tactical reasons but will know that US courts are reluctant to apply it in pretrial discovery proceedings.

IV.   PRETRIAL DISCOVERY VERSUS DATA PROTECTION IN GERMANY: BACKGROUND

In February 2009, the European Working Party on the Protection of Individuals with Regard to the Processing of Personal Data[18] published its Working Paper 158

---

12. In contrast to this liberal approach to cross-border cooperation with foreign courts and public bodies, stricter rules apply to 'private' or consular depositions of witnesses in Germany. In an exchange of diplomatic letters with the United States, the German Foreign Office requires, for instance, that depositions are only taken on the grounds of a US embassy in Germany unless the witness explicitly agrees to a questioning at his or her home or on his or her business premises.
13. Hague Convention on the Taking of Evidence Abroad in Civil and Commercial Matters of 18 Mar. 1970.
14. Article 1 et seq. of the Hague Convention.
15. Issue 5 of 'Bekanntmachung über das Inkrafttreten des Haager Übereinkommens über die Beweis-aufnahme im Ausland in Zivil- oder Handelssachen' (Enactment Notice), 21 Jun. 1979, BGBl. II 780.
16. Article 23 of the Hague Convention.
17. *Société Nationale Industrielle Aérospatiale v. US Dist. Ct.*, 482 US 522, 542 (1987).
18. The Working Party is an independent advisory body on European privacy and data protection law. It is composed of data protection officials from EU Member States. The Working Party's opinions and guidelines expressed in its Working Papers are not binding on the national data

on pretrial discovery for cross-border civil litigation.[19] Since then, the responding party can hardly maintain that the transfer of personal data for litigation purposes to the United States is illegal per se under the BDSG. However, data transfers must follow specific requirements to comply with German data protection law.

A.   PRETRIAL DISCOVERY VERSUS DATA PROTECTION IN GERMANY: RETENTION AND TRANSFER OF PERSONAL DATA

Whenever litigation or regulatory investigations and proceedings are reasonably anticipated by a legal entity, no matter whether the entity is the initiator or the target of litigation, it has a duty to preserve the potentially relevant data, that is, protect it from destruction or alteration. The retention of data constitutes a 'processing' and requires justification under the BDSG. This is the same with the later transfer of personal data to the requesting party, which is also deemed to be data processing under German data protection law.

The data subject's consent to data processing for litigation purposes can only be obtained in rare cases. The boiler-plate declarations of consent commonly used in Germany seldom cover data processing in legal proceedings with a third party. In addition, some German data protection authorities contest that employees can give consent voluntarily if asked by their employers.[20]

Under section 28(1.2) of the BDSG, personal data may be processed if legitimate interests necessitate the processing and if such legitimate interests are not overridden by the interests of the individual whose data are affected. The Working Party gives some guidance on how to balance the conflicting interests: If the personal data are irrelevant for the case, the responding party cannot claim any legitimate interests in processing such data for litigation purposes. In a first step, non-responsive documents that contain personal data must be filtered out in the EU Member State, that is, Germany. In a second step, irrelevant personal data on responsive documents should be redacted in Germany so that only relevant personal data are transferred to the United States and disclosed to the requesting party. Whereas in the past, potentially responsive documents were transferred to the United States for review in a wholesale fashion, on-site reviews in Germany by US attorneys will increase so that irrelevant personal data are no longer exported in breach of section 28(1.2) of the BDSG.

---

protection authorities but are persuasive authority. The European data protection authorities, when required to decide on data processing related to US-style e-discovery, are likely to follow the guidelines set out in WP 158. And the requesting party will bring the new guidelines to the US court's attention when challenging a responding party's blunt statement that European privacy and data protection law prohibits the transfer of personal data to the United States for litigation purposes.
19. Working Paper 158 of 11 Feb. 2009.
20. Resolution of the Düsseldorfer Kreis of 23/24 Apr. 2009. In its explanatory memorandum of the latest amendment of the BDSG, the German parliament, however, explicitly mentions the consent given by an employee, BT-Drucks 16/13657, 35.

B.   PRETRIAL DISCOVERY VERSUS DATA PROTECTION IN GERMANY: EXPORT OF PERSONAL DATA TO THE UNITED STATES

Section 4c(1.4) of the BDSG explicitly permits the transfer of personal data to a country with what the EU characterizes as an 'inadequate data protection level', for instance, the United States, if the transfer is necessary or legally required for the establishment, exercise, or defence of legal claims in court. This provision is key to the reconciliation of e-discovery rules and German privacy and data protection law. Since non-responsive documents have already been filtered out and irrelevant personal data on responsive documents have been redacted, the remainder is in fact legally required for the establishment, exercise, or defence of legal claims before a US court.

V.   CONCLUSION

Even though Germany has a very strict data protection regime, it is flexible enough to accommodate the legal requirements of a US-style pretrial discovery.

Chapter 5.9

Greece

*Maria Giannakaki**

I.   INTRODUCTION

Multinational companies with operations in the United States and a presence in
Greece are subject to pretrial discovery rules that may require processing, disclosure, retention, and transfer of personal data in US civil litigation proceedings.
These requirements extend to any electronically stored information (ESI),[1] such as
electronic documents and files, e-mails, accounting databases, and other ESI such
as metadata and raw data that could be relevant to the case ('e-discovery'). Such
information that is subject to an e-discovery request is likely to contain personal
data relating to employees or third parties and raises serious concerns with regard
to the data subject's fundamental rights, in particular the right to privacy and
personal data protection.

II.   GREEK DATA PROTECTION LAW: BACKGROUND

The Greek legislation ensures a high level of protection of the fundamental rights
and freedoms of natural persons and in particular of their right to privacy and
lawful collection, processing, and transfer of their personal data. Data subjects'

---

*   Maria Giannakaki, Karageorgiou & Associates Law Firm, Athens, Greece.
1.   Amendment to the Federal Rules of Civil Procedure, effective 1 Dec. 2006.

Catrien Noorda & Stefan Hanloser, *E-Discovery and Data Privacy*, pp. 117–124.

right to 'informational self-determination' is a constitutional right, including the right to determine the disclosure and use of one's data.[2] The European Data Protection Directive[3] was implemented in the Greek legislation by Act 2472/1997 ('Data Protection Act'), while Act 3471/2006 implemented the European Directive[4] on the protection of personal data and privacy in the electronic telecommunications sector.

A. GREEK DATA PROTECTION LAW: PERSONAL DATA

The Data Protection Act applies only to 'personal data', to information relating to an identified or identifiable natural person. Corporate data, business information, or technical know-how[5] that does not relate to an identified or identifiable person is not protected under the Greek data protection law.[6]

According to the Data Protection Act, as applied by the Greek courts, the definition of personal data is very broad. It includes any and all information relating to the data subject. Employees' personal data include 'employment records' with all types of data and documents relating to an employee requested by labour law (with respect to salaries or social security and so forth), as well as data related to the employment relationship which are necessary for the organization and control of the company (corporate e-mail communications, call logs, Internet use, monitoring through closed-circuit television systems ('CCTV'), or data collected through whistleblowing schemes.

Pretrial discovery requests involve the processing of personal data, and Greek companies that are doing business in the United States or have a parent company, a subsidiary, or an affiliate in the United States, before disclosing such data, should ensure that the Data Protection Act requirements are met.

B. GREEK DATA PROTECTION LAW: EMPLOYEES' E-MAILS

Employees are no less protected in Greece than any other third party. The Greek Data Protection Authority has issued a Directive[7] that gives the guidelines and boundaries for the processing of employees' personal data, according to which it

---

2. Articles 5A and 9 of the Greek Constitution
3. Council Directive 95/46 on the protection of individuals with regard to the processing of personal data and on the free movement of such data, 1995 O.J. (L 281) 31 (EC).
4. Council Directive 2002/58 on the protection of personal data and privacy in the electronic telecommunications sector, 2002 O.J. (L 201).
5. The transfer and disclosure of business information or technical know-how may be restricted or excluded by non-disclosure or confidentiality agreements.
6. Such privileged information may be protected under Greek legislation regarding business and professional secrecy, bank secrecy, medical confidentiality, and so on.
7. Directive No. 1830/20.9.2001 (115/2001), <www.dpa.gr/portal/page?_pageid=33,23367&_dad=portal&_schema=PORTAL>.

would only be in exceptional circumstances that employee monitoring, would be considered necessary and justified.

More specifically, employees in Greece have the right and the legitimate expectation to a certain degree of privacy even in their workplace. This right should be balanced with other legitimate interests of the employer and particularly the employer's right to run the business efficiently and the right to protect the business from the liability or the harm that employee actions may create. The disclosure and data transfer of employees' data is permitted only if their business communication and/or Internet usage is clearly identified from the personal one. As a consequence, employers who want to monitor their employees' business e-mails should separate the personal communication of their employees:

(a) by giving employees the option to use two separate e-mail accounts: one for professional and one for purely private purposes, which will not be monitored;
(b) by allowing them to make use of their professional e-mail for personal purposes, by marking personal communications 'Private' or 'Personal' to indicate that the e-mail includes personal information and therefore should not be monitored; or
(c) by installing a number of computers not connected to the firm's network and without the right to use other forms of electronic storage (e.g., memory sticks). These computers could be accessible to employees at work for a limited period of time for personal communication. The employer could then monitor, disclose, and transfer all other communications deemed to be professional.

Further to the provision of a personal sphere in their employees' professional life, employers should seek for employees' express written consent for the collection, processing, transfer, and disclosure of their professional e-mail communication. This consent should be provided by employees following the provision of adequate information about the data collection and its purpose. Employees' data should be used only for the purpose for which they have been collected for. The Supreme Administration Court[8] ruled that employees' consent to the processing, disclosure, and transfer of their personal data by their employer is provided only for the purposes of the employment relationship. Therefore, when their consent to the collection of their personal data has been provided only for reasons relating to their working relationship, in case of a pretrial request employers should seek from their employees a specific consent related to the pretrial disclosure requested.

C.   GREEK DATA PROTECTION LAW: DATA COLLECTION
        AND PROCESSING

Personal data should be collected, processed, and used only if the conditions of the Data Protection Act are met. Any processing of personal data, including processing

---

8. SAC Decision 94/2003.

for litigation purposes as part of the pretrial discovery procedure, should meet a requirement of legitimacy under the Data Protection Act. Grounds for legitimate processing include the data subjects' unambiguous consent, the compliance with a legal obligation, and a legitimate interest that evidentially prevails over the rights of data subjects under condition that their fundamental rights are not affected.

D.   GREEK DATA PROTECTION LAW: DATA CONTROLLER AND DATA PROCESSOR

The data controller is the legal entity who determines the scope and the means of the processing of personal data, and who can be any natural or legal person, public authority or agency, or any other organization. In short: the data controller has to ensure that the collection, processing, or use of personal data is in line with the Data Protection Act. In practice, the data controller usually assigns to another legal entity, the data processor, the processing of personal data and the execution of some or all data-related processes. The data processor acts upon the controller's instructions. If a data controller grants to a legal person the authority to decide on the scope or the means of the outsourced activities, this legal person is qualified as a data controller, not a data processor.

In a pretrial discovery project relating to groups of companies, it is rather important to define the legal entity or entities who act as data controllers and those who act as data processors. The provisions of the Data Protection Act apply when processing is carried out by a controller or a processor established in the Greek territory or in a place where Greek law applies by virtue of public international law or by a controller (not a processor) who is not established in a third country (not a European Union (EU) Member State or European Economic Area (EEA) member) who, for the purposes of personal data processing, makes use of equipment situated in the Greek territory, unless such equipment is used only for purposes of transit through such territory.

E.   GREEK DATA PROTECTION LAW: TRANSFER OF DATA ABROAD

In accordance with the European Data Protection Directive, the Greek Data Protection Act has express rules for the transfer of personal data abroad. In general, data can be transferred freely:

    (a) within the EU Member States, and
    (b) to third countries that have been recognized by the European Commission (EC) as guaranteeing an adequate level of protection or to companies certified under the Safe Harbour Programme.

The Data Protection Authority interprets the word 'free' as authorization free. Even though the Authority's' authorization is not necessary for data transfers within the EU and to countries providing an adequate level of protection, a notification to the Authority is still required.

In addition to the above, the transfer of personal data to a non-EU Member State is exceptionally allowed following an authorization granted by the Data Protection Authority, provided that one or more of the following conditions occur:

(a) the data subject has consented to such transfer;
(b) the transfer is necessary for the establishment, exercise, or defence of a right in court;
(c) the transfer is necessary for the performance of a co-operation agreement with the public authorities of the other country, provided that the controller provides adequate safeguards with respect to the protection of the data subjects' privacy;
(d) data are transferred between a data controller established in the EU and a data importer based outside the EU on the basis of model contractual clauses approved by the EC.

Especially for multinational organizations, the authorization of the Data Protection Authority for the transfer of personal data outside the EU within their group of companies can be facilitated with the adoption of Binding Corporate Rules (BCRs). According to the Article 29 Working Party, if a set of BCRs is adopted, the Group of Companies should file an application for approval to the leading authority[9]

F.   CONFLICT OF LAWS

Multinational companies tend to collect personal data from all jurisdictions and store them in one country. Usually, these data are hosted on multiple servers and are accessible via the web ('cloud computing'). This practice, apart from the questions of safety and confidentiality of the data collected and transferred, also raises the issue of determination of the data protection law that is applicable to such data.

G.   PENALTIES

Any breach of the provisions of the Data Protection Act carries consequences of an administrative, criminal, and civil nature. The establishment and operation of a filing system, as well as making any changes to the terms and conditions on which a license was granted, without making a proper notification to the Greek Data Protection Authority, constitutes a criminal offence that carries imprisonment of up to one year and a fine ranging from Euros (EUR) 2,934 to EUR 14,673.

Administrative fines include warnings, fines ranging from EUR 880 to EUR 146,735, temporary or permanent revocation of license, destruction of a filing

---

9. As defined in WP Document 117/2006.

system or interruption of processing and destruction, and return or engaging (blocking) of the relevant files.

With regard to civil liability, the data subject must be fully compensated for loss he or she has suffered due to acts or omissions of a natural or legal person.

In 2009, the Data Protection Authority imposed a fine of EUR 20,000 on a Greek company for the illegal implementation and functioning of a whistleblowing scheme without employees' consent, without submitting a prior notification to the Authority for the collection of employees' data and their transfer to the parent company in the United Kingdom.[10] Moreover, the Authority decided that the implementation of a CCTV system in the company's premises aiming at the continuous monitoring of its employees was illegal and asked the data controller to abstain from this monitoring and destroy all files that were created.[11]

III. PRETRIAL DISCOVERY IN GREECE

Pretrial discovery of documents and data is unknown in Greece. Disclosure is limited to evidence needed for the scope of the trial and it is for the party to the litigation to offer evidence in support of its case. Should the other side require that information, the burden is upon that party to be able to know and identify it. Only if one party refers to a specific document in its pleadings can the court order that the document be lodged with the court. Specific remedies apply for the enforcement of intellectual property rights, copyrights, as well as data falling under the secrecy of correspondence.

A. PRETRIAL DISCOVERY IN GREECE: BLOCKING STATUTES

The mutual disclosure of documents and the cooperation with foreign courts or public authorities in litigation or regulatory investigations and proceedings are not restricted under Greek law. In particular there are no 'blocking statutes' that prohibit the transfer of information abroad, apart from the exception in Article 458 (2) of the Greek Code of Penal Procedures (Article 457,458) that prevents the Greek court's cooperation with a foreign one when the action refers to a person who cannot be extradited, or is prosecuted for reasons not relating to penal crimes (i.e., political ones).

Even though there are no blocking statutes to pretrial discovery, Greek affiliates of multinational companies should facilitate multinationals' compliance with US discovery obligations but also ensure that personal data are protected in accordance with the Data Protection Act. To our knowledge, pretrial discovery issues have never been brought before the courts or the Data Protection Authority. However, according to the data protection legislation and in the light of the

---

10. Decision 14/2008 of the Data Protection Authority.
11. Decision 4/2009 of the Data Protection Authority.

Opinion of the WP a. 29,[12] ('WP Opinion'), the consistency with the data protection legislation may be based on the grounds discussed in the following section.

B.   LEGITIMACY OF DATA COLLECTION AND PROCESSING

1.   **Data Subject's Consent**

According to the WP Opinion and the Data Protection Act, as specified by the Data Protection Authority,[13] consent is unlikely to provide an appropriate ground for processing. In most cases data subjects, such as customers and employees, cannot be considered to have freely consented to the processing of their data in relation to a pretrail US litigation. Moreover, it is difficult for companies to produce clear evidence that data subjects have provided an ex-ante valid consent for all potential pretrail requests.

2.   **Compliance with a Legal Obligation:**
                     The Hague Convention

Under the Greek law, an obligation imposed by a foreign statute or regulation may not be considered as a legal obligation by virtue of which data processing in the EU would be made legitimate.

For the disclosure of evidence abroad, in civil and commercial cases, Greece has signed the Hague Convention on the Taking of Evidence abroad in civil or commercial matters of 1970.[14] The Hague Convention requires a Letter of Request sent by a judicial authority of the requesting Member State to the competent authority of the addressed Member State to obtain evidence that is intended for use in the judicial proceedings.

Many Member States, including Greece, have declared that means of giving or providing evidence should be executed in compliance with the Greek law. Therefore, Greece declared that it will not execute Letters of Request issued for the purposes of obtaining pretrial discovery of documents. Consequently, under the Greek law, Letters of Request do not constitute a 'legal obligation' justification.

3.   **Pursuit of a Legitimate Interest**

Under the Data Protection Act and the WP Opinion, compliance with pretrial discovery requirements may be found to be necessary for the purposes of a legitimate interest pursued by the data controller provided that the data subject's fundamental rights and freedoms are protected. In pretrial discovery cases this

---

12.   WP 158 – Working Document 1/2009 on pretrial discovery for cross-border civil litigation, adopted on 11 Feb. 2009.
13.   Directive No. 1830/20 Oct. 2001 (115/2001).
14.   In Greece applicable by Law No. 3287/2004.

legitimate interest is the ability of an organization to promote or defend a legal right. However, the application of the 'legitimate interest' justification requires a case-by-case balance of data subjects' rights against the company's need for access to information.

In addition to the aforementioned requirements, data collection and processing should be made in accordance with the principle of purpose and proportionality and following the submission of a notification and authorization (in cases where sensitive data are processed) to the Data Protection Authority.

Moreover, data should be kept for a period of time necessary for the purposes for which the data have been collected. Data controllers and data processors should take all technical and organizational measures for the security and confidentiality of data and companies should also provide data subjects with accurate and adequate information and make sure that they can exercise their rights of access and rectification.

Furthermore, in order to promote compliance with the EU data protection legislation, companies should establish procedures for conducting an initial review of documents of their companies in Greece. All data that are irrelevant or unnecessary to the case should be removed or anonymized to the extent possible.

C.   PRETRIAL DISCOVERY IN GREECE: LEGITIMACY OF DATA TRANSFER

Where the transfer of personal data for pretrial purposes is likely to be a single transfer of all relevant information, Article 9, paragraph d of the Data Protection Act would be a possible ground for the transfer. More specifically, Article 9 paragraph d explicitly permits the transfer of personal data to a country that it is not a Member State of the EU and does not ensure an adequate level of protection, in cases where the transfer is necessary for the establishment, exercise, or defence of a right in court. This provision is a key for the balance of the conflicting interests between the parties involved in litigation, who have a legitimate interest in accessing information that it is necessary to make or defend a claim, and the rights of the individuals whose personal data are being sought.

Where a significant amount of data is to be transferred, the use of Safe Harbour procedure, BCRs, or Standard Contractual Clauses (SCCs) should be considered.

IV.   CONCLUSION

Even though the data protection regime in Greece is very strict, it does not prohibit data transfers for pretrial discovery purposes. However, it is necessary to balance the legitimate interest in accessing information that is necessary to make or defend a claim with the rights of the individuals whose personal data are sought.

Chapter 5.10

Hungary

*Kinga Hetényi**

I.   INTRODUCTION

Data protection is a serious issue in Hungary. Although the Hungarian data secrecy law only relates to natural persons, legal entities are frequently affected through the secrecy interests of their employees. Cooperation between Hungarian courts and authorities and other countries is beyond bilateral agreements. Although pretrial discovery is yet unknown in Hungary, proper handling of personal data is acknowledged to be a top-priority issue in Hungarian international business.

II.   DOMESTIC BACKGROUND: HUNGARIAN DATA PROTECTION LAW

Hungary has a very strict data protection regime. The relevant Data Protection Act (Avtv[1]) came into force in 1992 and was amended in December 2007 for the last time. The European Data Protection Directive was implemented in 2005,[2] one year after Hungary joined the European Union (EU). Besides this 'core' Act, other laws

---

*   Kinga Hetényi, Attorney at Law, and Molnár Miklòs, Associate at Schoenherr Hetényi Ügyvédi Iroda, Budapest, Hungary.
1.   Act LXIII of 1992, A személyes adatok védelméről, és a közérdekű adatok nyilvánosságáról.
2.   Council Directive 95/46 on protection of individuals with regard to the processing of personal data and on the free movement of such data; implemented into the Avtv on 1 Jun. 2005.

Catrien Noorda & Stefan Hanloser, *E-Discovery and Data Privacy*, pp. 125–130.
© 2011 Kluwer Law International BV, The Netherlands.

provide for data protection provisions as well, such as the Act on E-trading,[3] the Act on Personal Data in Healthcare,[4] and the Act on Name and Address in Research and in Direct Marketing.[5] Whenever it comes to assessing questions of Hungarian data protection law, the written statements of the Commissioner of Data Protection (ombudsman) are frequently of key importance.

A.   PERSONAL DATA

As said, the Avtv only relates to natural persons. Business secrets of legal entities are covered by the personal rights provisions of the Civil Code.[6] The Avtv's definition of personal data has to be understood rather broadly, which means it covers every single piece of data, or conclusion arising from a piece of data, as long as it can be linked with an identified natural person. The Avtv differentiates between personal data and special (sensitive) data, where the latter covers, *inter alia*, health condition, political interest, or membership in representation organizations. Within the framework of a corporate entity, most privacy-related questions come along with the personal data of its employees. Considering the broad definition of personal data, it can be stated that besides data such as name, address, or insurance number – which obviously must be qualified as personal data – also work-related data such as e-mail, phone numbers, and Internet protocol (IP) addresses or website addresses fall within the definition of personal data, and, with this, within the scope of the Avtv.

B.   COLLECTING AND MANAGING OF THE DATA

Hungarian data protection laws provide for a differentiation between 'managing' and 'processing' of data, where 'processing' is merely a technical term, and as such forms part of the 'data managing' process. However, managing or processing[7] (including every single operation on the data, for example, using, storing, forwarding, and so forth) is only permitted if: (i) prescribed by law or decree; or if (ii) the affected individual has given his or her consent. The consent has to be given upon appropriate information provided to the data subject about the key factors of the data controlling process. The consent has to be given in writing if sensitive data

---

3. Act CVIII of 2001, az elektronikus kereskedelmi szolgáltatások, valamint az információs társadalommal összefüggő szolgáltatások egyes kérdéseiről.
4. Act XLVII of 1997, az egészségügyi és a hozzájuk kapcsolódó személyes adatok kezeléséről és védelméről.
5. Act CXIX, a kutatás és a közvetlen üzletszerzés célját szolgáló név- és lakcímadatok kezeléséről.
6. Act IV of 1959, Polgári Törvénykönyv.
7. The wording of the Avtv differs from the Directive in this respect. The Directive uses 'data processing' for the entire procedure in relation to the personal data, whereas the Avtv's data processing describes only a technical part of the processing procedure, the 'data managing'.

are to be processed. However, for the sake of securing evidence, consent should also be in writing if non-sensitive data are going to be processed.

C.   MANAGING AND PROCESSING OF THE DATA

As set out above, data processing forms merely a technical part of the data managing process. It can be performed by an entity (the 'data processor') that can be different from the data manager. In that scenario a written data processing agreement is required, and the data manager is liable for his or her instructions given to the data processor. However, the data processor is – within the framework of his or her business and the confines set by the data manager – liable for processing, altering, deleting, forwarding, and publishing of the data. Further, the data manager is liable for any damage caused by misconduct of the data processor.

D.   SUB-PROCESSING, GROUP OF UNDERTAKINGS

One of the specialties of the Hungarian data protection regime is the prohibition of data sub-processors. Consequently a data processor is not allowed to pass on substantive decisions related to the data managing process. With this, the data processor is not allowed to subcontract his or her data processing obligations to a third person. For a single data manager it is yet possible to enter into agreements with other data processors, but in that scenario contractual relationships have to be established between the data manager and each of the data processors. Another specific Hungarian data protection issue is the fact that a corporate group (consisting of a group of undertakings) is not qualified as a uniform data manager but rather as a group of data managers (the undertakings of the group). This leads to the fact that personal employee data can only be forwarded within this group if the respective data protection requirements are met. The legal statements of the Data Commissioner frequently strengthen this point of view (which, however, is rather inconvenient, especially for parent companies located outside of Hungary).

E.   TRANSFER ABROAD

The Avtv provides for specific requirements for data transfers abroad. Forwarding personal data within the European Economic Area (EEA) has to be qualified as data transfer within Hungary.[8] Forwarding data into countries outside the EEA requires: (i) an explicit consent of the data subject; or (ii) a legal provision and an equivalent level of protection in the third country. For transferring personal data to the United States, as a country without an equivalent level of data

---

8.   See under 'Conflict of Laws'.

protection, the US-based entity receiving the data has to self-certify itself under the 'Safe Harbour' Programme.[9]

F.   CONFLICT OF LAWS

The Avtv covers the managing as well as processing of data within the territory of Hungary. Therefore any data processing has to comply with the Avtv even when the data manager is located abroad and only the data processor has his or her seat in Hungary. The Avtv is all the more applicable if the data manager is located in Hungary with only the data processor being abroad. In any case the data manager is liable for any misconduct of the data processor.

The data protection regulations are enforced by the Data Protection Commissioner and the Hungarian courts. However, the Commissioner is not entitled to issue mandatory regulations (i.e., he or she cannot impose fines). The Commissioner can rather call up the entity to remedy the breach of the Avtv and publish the initiating of the investigation and the investigated party. The Commissioner is empowered to order the data to be deleted, to discontinue the misconduct, and to suspend improper forwarding of data. Respective court orders can end up, for example, in obligation of giving appropriate information, deleting data, correcting data, or paying damages.

III.   PRETRIAL DISCOVERY

Similar to other continental law regimes, the mutual disclosure of documents and data (including data stored electronically) is unknown in Hungary.[10] The litigants only disclose documents and data if they have been referred to in a proceeding and only insofar as it supports their own case – that is, each party submits only what can be used for them as evidence which is relevant for their claims.[11]

A.   BLOCKING STATUTES

Cooperation between Hungarian and foreign courts and authorities is very much possible. The basis for that cooperation is several legal acts dealing with proceedings before courts and authorities. In addition, international organizations (basically in the field of competition law, like the ICN or ECN) try to smooth international work between Hungarian and foreign authorities.

---

9. 2000/520/EC.
10. Hungarian data protection does not provide a differentiation between physically or electronically stored data.
11. Provisions of Act III of 1952 on Polgári Perrendtartás (Act on Civil Proceeding).

B.　　　　PRETRIAL DISCOVERY IN HUNGARY: HAGUE CONVENTION
　　　　　ON THE TAKING OF EVIDENCE

Hungary implemented the Hague Convention[12] in 2004[13] (as Member State of the
EU since 1 May 2004) and appointed the 'Ministry of Justice'[14] for supervising and
fulfilling legal aid requests issued by another contracting party. According to the
convention for obtaining evidence by a judicial authority of a Member State, a
'Letter of Request' has to be sent to the competent authority of the other Member
State, in case of Hungary to the Ministry of Justice.

As did many other Contracting States, Hungary also took advantage of
Article 23 of the Convention and declared that 'Hungarian authorities will not
execute requests, which were issued within the framework of a proceeding, known
under the name "pre-trial discovery" of documents'.[15] This has the effect that such
a request addressed to Hungarian authorities will not be accepted.

This was confirmed by the Data Protection Commissioner in his annual report
for 2007, where he stated that the Convention does not oblige undertakings to
accomplish pretrial discovery requests.[16]

C.　　　　PRETRIAL DISCOVERY AND DATA PROTECTION IN HUNGARY

In the light of the aforesaid, data transfers (especially to the United States) frequently occur on only very specific occasions in Hungary. First, US authorities
might collect data about passengers travelling to the United States, or about
international bank transfers within the framework of a programme related to unco-
vering terrorism financing. Second, the Securities and Exchange Commission
(SEC)[17] is collecting data about Hungarian undertakings within a framework of
mutual legal aid. However, those data transfers are principally based on legal
provisions respectively on unilateral obligation engagements of the US authorities
or on agreements with the EU.

Finally, data transfers frequently occur between Hungarian subsidiaries and
their US-based parent companies. As the Hungarian data protection regime principally permits data transfers into third countries (i.e., not EEA countries), it is
permissible for a subsidiary to submit personal data (those of employers, customers, etc.) to its parent company within the framework of the Avtv (which

---

12. The Hague Convention on the Taking of Evidence Abroad in Civil and in Commercial Matters
    of 18 Mar. 1970.
13. Act CXVI of 2004 on the Convention on the Taking of Evidence Abroad in Civil and in
    Commercial Matters.
14. Name often changed since then.
15. § 3 (b) Act CXVI of 2004.
16. Az adatvédelmi biztos Beszámolója 2007 (Annual Report of the Data Protection Commissioner
    2007).
17. The SEC is collecting data within the framework of the act on corrupt foreign procedures and of
    the act on the stock exchange.

basically means that appropriate consent of the data subject is required). For the collecting of data, a legitimate interest of the data manager has to be in place. However, it might certainly be arguable that the status of litigation of the parent company forms a legitimate interest of data managing and processing. The more problematic aspect might be to validly separate data being relevant for the litigation from other potentially collected data. In that respect it has to be considered that data may only be collected to the extent that is necessary for achieving the legitimate processing interest. In any case, valid consent of the data subjects, respectively the affected employees, is required for transferring their personal data to the US-resident parent company.

IV.   CONCLUSIONS

E-discovery is still unknown in Hungary, which is why Hungarian data protection law does not provide for specific e-discovery provisions. E-discovery requests in terms of pretrial discovery cannot be validly based upon the Hague Convention either. Therefore dealing with e-discovery requests in Hungary has to be done within the general framework of Hungarian data protection law, which means that the Avtv requirements for third-country data transfers will frequently have to be satisfied.

Chapter 5.11
Italy

*Daniela Ampollini**

I.   INTRODUCTION

In Italy litigants have very limited tools available to access documents in the
hands of their adversaries, apart from some exceptions in industrial and
intellectual property litigation. The Italian system has nothing comparable to
the US pretrial discovery. Added to that, Italy has implemented the comprehensive regulatory framework for protecting personal data introduced by the
European Data Protection Directive 95/46/EC. This was implemented in Italy
by Law Number 675 of 1996, which was subsequently amended and finally
incorporated into the so-called Italian Data Protection Code of 2003 (DPC –
'*Codice in materia di protezione dei data personali*'), rendering 'discovery' even
more complex under Italian legislation.

*   Daniela Ampollini, Trevisan & Cuonzo Avvocati, Italy.

Catrien Noorda & Stefan Hanloser, *E-Discovery and Data Privacy*, pp. 131–142.
© 2011 Kluwer Law International BV, The Netherlands.

II.   DOMESTIC BACKGROUND: DISCOVERY
                   FRAMEWORK IN ITALY

A.   PRETRIAL DISCOVERY IN ITALY

1.   'Discovery'

A 'US-style' discovery is non-existent under Italian law. There are some limited instruments to obtain evidence from the other party and 'disclosure' of case-related facts whereby courts may order parties to produce one or more specific case-related documents upon the other parties' requests.

In general, Article 210 of the Civil Procedural Code (CPC) establishes that a party can ask the judge to order the adversary in litigation, or a third party, to exhibit documents or any other matters that are deemed to be necessary for the proceedings.

In intellectual and industrial property litigation, an instrument often defined by Italian practitioners as 'discovery' (although distant from the US discovery framework), is provided for under Article 121 of the Italian Industrial Property Code (IP Code) and Article 156*bis* of the Copyright Law Number 633 of 1941. According to these provisions, the party that provides serious evidence supporting the reasonableness of its claims and that identifies documents, elements, or information available to the other party may ask the court to order the adversary to exhibit this information. In addition, a party may ask the court to order the other party to provide elements for the identification of the persons involved in the production and distribution of the goods or services alleged to be infringing the intellectual property (IP) rights in suit. It also provides that the court, in issuing the above orders, shall take adequate measures to safeguard confidential information.

The above-described measures cannot be ordered *ex officio* by the court but must be requested by the interested party and may or may not be granted at the discretion of the judge. More important, no specific enforcement tool or sanction is established against parties who refuse to comply with the orders, apart from the general negative inferences the court will likely draw in relation to parties not complying with court orders.

2.   The Right to Information on Origin and Distribution Network of Goods Or Services Infringing Industrial Property Or Copyrights

New Articles 121*bis* IP Code and 156*ter* Copyright Law have improved the system in respect of collection of information from the adversary in industrial and IP litigation. Pursuant to these provisions, a party has the right to ask the judge (both in preliminary proceedings and proceedings on the merits) to order the opposing party or a third party to provide information on origin and distribution networks of the goods or services that allegedly infringe IP rights; the provision of this information will take place by means of a deposition during an oral hearing before the court. The requesting party should provide specific details such as the persons to be examined and the relevant subject matter of the questions to be posed. Furthermore, the motion should be 'justified' and 'in accordance with the principle of proportionality'. Any person who without justification refuses to answer the questions submitted by the court or, when under examination, provides false information shall be subject to criminal sanctions foreseen under Article 127(1)*bis* IP Code and Article 171*octies* Copyright Law, respectively – namely, they may be subject to imprisonment for a maximum of three years.

B.   BLOCKING STATUTES

In Italy, as far as civil litigation is concerned, co-operation with foreign courts or other public authorities in litigation is not restricted by 'blocking statutes' prohibiting the transfer of information to be used as evidence abroad.

C.   HAGUE CONVENTION ON THE TAKING OF EVIDENCE ABROAD

Italy is a party to the Hague Convention on the Taking of Evidence Abroad in Civil or Commercial Matters (hereinafter: Hague Convention) of 18 March 1970, entered into force in 1972, which instituted a uniform procedure for the issuance of 'Letters of Request', that is, petitions from a court in one state to a designated central authority in another state, requesting assistance from that authority in obtaining relevant information located within its borders. However, Article 23 of the Convention provides that 'a contracting party may at the time of signature, ratification or accession, declare that it will not execute letters of request issued for the purpose of obtaining pre-trial discovery of documents as known in common law countries'. Like many other Member States, Italy filed a declaration under the above-cited Article 23. Therefore, Italy does not allow the production of any information, regardless of substance, if that information is required for purposes of pretrial discovery in a common law country, such as the United States. As a consequence, a Letter of Request under the Hague Convention addressed to an Italian authority for pretrial discovery of documents would lead to no result.

However, a way around this has been provided in the 1987 decision of the US Supreme Court in *Societé Nationale Industrielle Aerospatiale v. US District Court for the Southern District of Iowa* of 1987, ruling that the use of the Convention was a 'permissive supplement' for other means of obtaining evidence located abroad so that US courts when confronted with an international discovery dispute are not forced to resort to the Hague Evidence Convention but may consider whether the Convention governs the evidence-taking procedure on a case-by-case basis.

An example of how the *Aerospatiale* precedent was applied to a case involving discovery to be carried out in the Italian territory is the case *Hagenbuch v. 36B Sistemi Elettronici Industriali S.r.l.* of 12 September 2005. The US District Court for the Northern District of Illinois granted the motion of an American patent holder to proceed with discovery under the federal rules of a document kept in Italy by an Italian corporation and denied the Italian defendant's motion for a protective order, in which it was, *inter alia,* alleged that the Hague Convention should be used. Referring to the teaching of *Aerospatiale,* the Court decided that: (i) the Italian defendant's employees' testimony that the defendant cannot infringe the plaintiff's patent is insufficient to support the defendants' allegation that the discovery request is overbroad and intrusive; (ii) Italy's disfavour against American pretrial discovery expressed in its declaration pursuant to Article 23 of the Hague Convention is less important than the interest in just, speedy, and inexpensive determination of litigation; (iii) the Hague Convention procedure is more difficult and time consuming than the American discovery procedure. The Court then held that, taking into account that the party moving for application of the Hague Convention carries the burden of showing that the latter Convention applied and given that this burden was not met by the Italian defendant, American discovery rules applied.

It is understood that this trend has been largely followed, while only a minority post-*Aerospatiale* cases decided in favour of the Convention. In light of the above, although Italy as a civil law country does not recognize the American discovery procedure, an American company in a commercial litigation filed with a US court against an Italian company is likely to be successful in compelling production of documents kept in Italy, notwithstanding the Italian reservation under Article 23 of the Hague Convention.

III.	PRIVACY LAW AS AN OBSTACLE TO PRETRIAL DISCOVERY REQUESTS
A.	ITALIAN PRIVACY LAW: SCOPE OF APPLICATION AND 'PERSONAL DATA'

Article 5 of the DPC provides that the Italian Code applies to the processing of personal data, including data held abroad, where the processing is performed by any entity established in Italy, as well as to the processing of personal data that is performed by an entity established in a country outside the European Union (EU), and where equipment, whether electronic or otherwise, situated in Italy is used in connection with the processing unless such equipment is used only for purposes of transit through the territory of the EU. If the Code applies, the data controller shall designate a representative established in the State's territory with a view to implementing the provisions concerning processing of personal data.

In implementing Directive 95/46, Italy adopted an approach stricter that the minimum mandated by EU law in respect of the definition of personal data. According to Article 4 (1) (b) of the DPC, 'personal data' shall mean any information relating to natural or legal persons, bodies, or associations that are or can be identified, even indirectly, by reference to any other information, including a personal identification number. Accordingly, the processing of not only the data of individuals, but also those of any legal subject, including companies, falls within the scope of application of the DPC.

B.   ITALIAN PRIVACY LAW: NOTIFICATION

Notification of the processing to the Italian Data Protection Authority is not required by the DPC as a general rule. It is, however, provided that prior notification be made in a number of specific cases listed in Article 37 DPC. These in substance coincide with cases of processing of 'sensitive data' (see paragraph C below). However, the processing of the sensitive data of the employees generally held by employers (such as limited health data or data relating to membership in work councils) is not included in the types of processing that need to be notified to the Data Protection Authority.

C.   ITALIAN PRIVACY LAW: CONSENT OF THE DATA SUBJECT AND
                      INFORMATION RELATING TO THE PROCESSING TO BE PROVIDED TO
                      THE DATA SUBJECT – EXCEPTIONS

Under Articles 13 and 23 of the DPC, processing – that is, collection, retention, and any kind of use (including modification and destruction) – of personal data is in principle allowed only based on the freely given and express consent of the data subject, provided that the data subject has previously received notice that clearly identifies the specific manner in which the processing will be carried out and the purposes thereof; the notice must contain a list of mandatory information, *inter alia,* the details of the data controller, the details of the entities to which the data will be communicated, and the right of the data subject to at any time withdraw consent and request the cancellation of the data. Consent may also be collected in an oral form, although the data controller must be able to support it with documentary evidence – for instance, by noting the consent given in forms, minutes, and so forth. Consent must be given in written form in case of 'sensitive data', that is, data concerning racial or ethnic origin; religious, philosophical, or other beliefs; political opinions; membership of parties, trade unions, associations, or organizations of a religious, philosophical, political, or trade-unionist character; as well as personal data disclosing health and sex life.

Article 24 of the DPC contemplates exceptions that apply to the requirement of consent. In particular, consent is not necessary, *inter alia*:

(i) when the processing is necessary to comply with an obligation imposed by a law, regulations, or EU legislation (Article 24(1)(a) DPC);

(ii) when the processing is necessary for the performance of obligations of a contract to which the data subject is a party, or in compliance with specific requests made by the data subject prior to entering into a contract (Article 24(1)(b) DPC);

   (iii) when the processing concerns data relating to economic activities that are processed in compliance with the legislation in force as applying to business and industrial secrecy (Article 24(1)(d) DPC);

   (iv) for processing other than dissemination, when the processing is necessary for carrying out the criminal investigations allowed to legal counsels or to establish or defend a claim in court, provided that the data are processed exclusively for said purposes and for no longer than is necessary therefore and in compliance with the provisions on business and industrial secrets (Article 24(1)(f) DPC); and

   (v) for processing other than dissemination, when the processing is necessary to pursue a legitimate interest of either the data controller or a third-party recipient in the cases specified by the Italian Data Protection Authority on the basis of the principles set out under the law, also with regard to the activities of banking groups and subsidiaries or related companies, unless said interest is overridden by the data subject's rights and fundamental freedoms, dignity, or legitimate interests (Article 24(1)(g) DPC).

Even when consent is not necessary, the data subject must always receive a notice containing specific information on the manners and purposes of the processing, prior to the collection of the data. Under Articles 13 (4) and 13 (5) of the DPC, in case of data collected from third parties – that is, not directly from the data subject – a notice to the data subject is to be provided at the time of recording of the data and no later than the time of the first communication of the data. However, if the data collected from third parties are processed for the purposes outlined in Articles 24 (1) (a) and 24 (1) (f) of the DPC (see paragraphs i and iv above), no prior notice to the data subject is required.

D.   ITALIAN PRIVACY LAW: RETENTION OF DATA

Article 11 (1) (e) of the DPC provides that the personal data may be retained by the data controller in a form that permits identification of the data subject for no longer than is necessary for the purposes for which the data were collected or subsequently processed. There is therefore no specific time limit for the retention of the data, but rather a general principle according to which, based on the specific circumstances, the data may not be kept for longer than is necessary to the specific processing that is lawfully carried out thereof.

E.   ITALIAN PRIVACY LAW: RIGHT TO REQUEST THE CANCELLATION OF THE DATA AND TO OPPOSE THE PROCESSING

The data subject has the right to at any time withdraw the consent given for the processing of its data as under Article 7 of the DPC the data subject can at any time, *inter alia*, request that the data controller cancel its data. Furthermore, with particular regard to cases in which processing is allowed even without consent, Article 7(4) of the DPC provides that the data subject always has the right to oppose the processing of its data 'for legitimate reasons'.

F.   ITALIAN PRIVACY LAW: SECURITY MEASURES

The Italian DPC provides for rather strict rules to safeguard the security of the data. Articles 31 – 36 of the DPC in particular provide for a detailed list of minimum security measures that must be applied by the data controller. This list, in case of data processed with the use of electronic instruments, includes computerized authentication, implementation of authentication credentials management procedures, use of an authorization system, regular update of the specifications concerning the scope of the processing operations that may be performed by the individual entities in charge of the management and/or maintenance of the electronic means, protection of electronic means and data against unlawful data processing operations, unauthorized access and specific software, implementation of procedures for safekeeping backup copies and restoring data and system availability, as well as the keeping by the data controller of an updated document incorporating the security policy adopted (an exception applies to the latter requirement in case of subjects that do not process sensitive data or do so in a limited manner).

G.   ITALIAN PRIVACY LAW: TRANSFER OF THE DATA OUTSIDE THE
                  TERRITORY OF THE EU

Articles 43 and 44 of the DPC govern the transfer of the data abroad and provide that transfer to a country outside the EU is generally allowed based on consent of the data subjects. Consent is, however, not required, *inter alia:*

   (i) when the transfer is necessary for safeguarding a substantial public interest that is referred to by laws or regulations (Article 43 [1] [c] DPC); and
   (ii) when the transfer is necessary for carrying out the criminal investigations allowed to legal counsels or to establish or defend a claim in court, provided that the data are processed exclusively for said purposes and for no longer than is necessary therefore and in compliance with the provisions on business and industrial secrets (Article 43 [1] [e] DPC);

Furthermore, under Article 44 (1) (b) of the DPC, consent is not required in all cases in which the country of the recipient has been considered by the European Commission (EC), according to the provisions of Directive 95/46, to guarantee a sufficient level of protection of personal data. As regards the United States, which is generally considered to be a country not guaranteeing a sufficient level of protection, the European Commission has recognized that the principles contained in the so called 'Safe Harbour' scheme published by the US Department of Commerce constitute a sufficient level of protections. Therefore, in case the US recipient company self-certifies under the Safe Harbour scheme, no requirement of consent applies for the transfer of data to the United States.

Consent is also unnecessary under Article 44 (1) (a) of the DPC in cases where the Data Protection Authority is satisfied that an adequate level of protection of the data is granted by means of specific contractual obligations binding the recipient of the data or so-called 'Binding Corporate Rules' (BCRs) in force within the relevant corporate group within which the transfer is effected. It is expressly provided that the data subject may enforce the DPC rules in cases where the relevant contractual or BCR provisions are breached.

H.　　　　　　Italian Privacy Law: Employees' E-mails

The monitoring and searching of employees' e-mails is a rather sensitive topic in the Italian legal system. Article 4 of the law on freedom and dignity of workers and their right of representation in the workplace (Law Number 300/1970) provides that workers have a right not to be monitored from a distance when they are at work, either by means of audiovisual or other appliances able to from a distance identify or record the activity of workers. It is well established, also in the case law of the Italian Data Protection Authority, that searching employees' e-mails falls within the definition of distance monitoring. Article 4 of Law Number 300/1970, however, allows such activity to take place when it is necessary for 'organizational, production or security reasons in the workplace'. In this case, however, the work council must be involved and, if the council does not agree, a motion to the work inspectorate will have to be filed.

Furthermore, the guidelines issued by the Italian Data Protection Authority (Number 81/2007 of 1 March 2007) must be complied with. These clarify the general rules that employers must apply in managing the e-mail accounts and Internet access of employees. Specific consideration is given to whether and to what extent the searching of the employees' e-mail accounts and the use of the personal data contained therein is allowed under privacy law. Under the guidelines, employers must set up a policy to be communicated to all employees that clearly identifies how the e-mail and Internet systems are managed and, in particular, if employees may or may not use their email accounts for personal communication as well as the specific processing that will be carried out by the employer with particular regard to the possibility of searching and monitoring the data on Internet access and e-mail accounts, indicating which subjects will carry out the searching and/or monitoring and for which reasons. The policy also has to refer to the time frame in which the relevant data will be retained. In this respect, the guidelines provide that the software systems must be configured and programmed so as to regularly and automatically delete the personal data related to Internet access and network traffic, and in any event data should be retained for periods not in excess of the time required for achieving the specific and proven purposes for which they are retained.

It is further specified that once employees have been informed of the above-mentioned policy, the processing of the relevant data is allowed within the limits indicated in the policy, based on either freely given express consent or when one of the circumstances set out by Articles 24 (1) (f) and 24 (1) (g) apply (see section C above).

As a final note, it must be stressed that the rules of the Italian DPC as well as those of the above-mentioned Law Number 300/1970 are mandatory as they protect a public interest and employees are not in a position to forfeit their rights resulting therefrom vis-à-vis employers.

I.   ITALIAN PRIVACY LAW: SANCTIONS

Numerous administrative sanctions are contemplated in case of violation of rules of the DPC, the most noteworthy of which is the administrative sanction of up to Euros (EUR) 90,0000 in case of violation of the provisions on the notice of information on the processing of the data to be given to the data subject (Articles 161–166 DPC).

Specific violations of the DPC may also result in a criminal offence. For instance, the processing of data without having obtained prior consent, where required, for the purpose of gaining a profit or causing a harm, may punished, when the harm is caused, with a sentence of up to twenty-four months of imprisonment. Furthermore, violations of the provisions on data transfer abroad or on security measures may be punished, respectively, with a sentence of up to three years and up to two years (in the latter case, plus a fine up to EUR 50,000).

As regards civil sanctions, any subject alleging to have suffered a harm caused by an unlawful processing of personal data may file civil proceedings aimed at an award of damages. According to Article 15 of the DPC, a reversal of the burden of proof applies and the damage must be compensated 'if the person who has caused it does not prove that it had adopted all measures apt for avoiding the damage'. It is furthermore provided that moral damages must also be compensated in case of violation of Article 11 of the DPC, which includes the provision according to which data must not be retained longer than is necessary for the purposes for which the data were collected or subsequently processed.

As regards the effective application of the above-mentioned sanctions, the most recent available report on the activity of the Italian DPA notes that in 2008 the Italian DPA effected approximately 500 inspections, applied administrative sanctions in almost 350 cases, and collected over EUR 1 million in administrative sanctions. Based on this report, the Italian DPA is becoming more and more vigilant and the rules are applied in an increasing number of cases.

J.   PRETRIAL DISCOVERY VERSUS DATA PROTECTION IN ITALY

Paragraphs A to I above are relevant in determining whether and to what extent the exercise of a US pretrial discovery in Italy is or is not compliant with Italian privacy law. These paragraphs in substance illustrate the relevant Italian provisions of the Italian DPC, also having regard to Working Paper 158 on pretrial discovery for cross-border civil litigation issued on 11 February 2009 by the Article 29 Data Protection Working Party, which provides general guidance to data controllers subject to EU law in dealing with requests to transfer personal data to another jurisdiction for use in civil litigation, based on Directive 95/46/EC.

First, based on the above-illustrated rules on the scope of application of the Italian DPC, it is likely that Italian law will apply to all cases in which discovery must be carried out within the framework of US litigation on data that are collected or processed in Italy, that is: (i) if the party to the US litigation is an Italian entity; (ii) if the data are controlled by a subsidiary of the US company that is party to the US litigation, when the subsidiary is a company incorporated under the laws of Italy; and (iii) if the US company that is party to the US litigation otherwise controls plants/offices in Italy and therefore (even partially) uses equipment situated in Italy for the processing of the relevant data.

Furthermore, as stated, under Italian privacy law, 'personal data' include data relating to legal persons, which implies that the Italian provisions will have to be taken into consideration in effecting the discovery of all the data relevant for the US litigation, not only of those relating to natural persons. It is noteworthy, however, that according to the above-mentioned Article 24 (1) (d), consent of the data subject is not necessary in case the processing concerns data relating to economic activities, and is in accordance with the provisions on business and industrial secrets. Accordingly, as it is likely that the data referring to legal persons will in most cases only relate to the carrying out of business, the issue of consent, and in particular whether the exceptions provided for by Article 24 DPC (see below) apply, will only be relevant in respect to data of individuals.

The prerequisite of freely given express consent by the data subject may be avoided based on the exception of Article 24 (1) (f) of the DPC, which excludes the need of consent when processing is necessary to defend a legal claim in court. Some commentators have questioned whether this exception embraces foreign/international litigation or is limited to Italian litigation. No specific clarification has so far been issued by the Data Protection Authority. It is arguable that limiting this exception to application in Italian litigation would not be justified considering that the provision contains no express limitation to Italian litigation. It would further be discriminatory considering the general recognition granted by Italian law to the results of foreign judicial proceedings.[1] The fact that discovery would be 'pretrial' does not seem to be an obstacle for the application of Article 24 (1) (f) of the DPC, given the rather general language of the provision, which does not refer to the need that a specific phase in the lawsuit has been reached. In addition, Article 24 (1) (g) of the DPC could be invoked, which specifically mentions the legitimate

---

1. Law No. 218/1995 contemplates the general rule whereby judicial decisions issued in foreign jurisdictions are automatically recognized and given effect in Italy, only with the possibility to oppose recognition by instituting opposition proceedings based on exceptions mainly having to do with whether in the relevant judicial proceedings right of defence was granted to the defendant.

interests of the recipient or third parties having regard to the activity of a group of companies. Invoking the latter provision, however, would imply resorting to the Italian Data Protection Authority to obtain the 'green light' as well as to carefully balance the interests and rights of the data subjects, as specifically indicated in the provision.

As regards information of the data subject, in principle Article 13 (5) of the DPC allows avoidance of this requirement when the data are not collected from the data subject (which is a likely scenario when the data are collected by the US entity party to the US litigation from an Italian subsidiary that will provide the data they collected from data subjects in the first place) and the processing is necessary to defend a claim in court. However, the wording 'to defend a claim in court' may be construed as meaning 'to defend a claim in court by the data controller', which will not necessarily be the case when the data controller is the Italian subsidiary that is not directly involved in the US litigation. Additionally, the above-mentioned guidelines of the Italian Data Protection Authority on the use of Internet and e-mail systems by employers must be considered. It is therefore advisable, in case of a discovery exercise to be carried out involving e-mail accounts and other electronic files containing personal data of employers, to include in the policy a reference to the possibility of discovery under US law and, once the discovery exercise becomes necessary, provide for an addendum that gives more details of the processing that is being carried out on the data.

It must always be taken into account, however, that even in cases where it is possible to argue that consent is ruled out as indicated above, the data subjects (including employees) will retain the rights to require cancellation of their data or oppose the processing thereof for legitimate reasons under Article 7 of the DPC.

Based on Article 11 of the DPC, which provides that the data must be retained for no longer than is necessary for the specific treatment for the purposes of which they are collected, it is hard to argue that the personal data the processing of which is subject to Italian law must be retained, for instance, by the Italian subsidiary, for an unspecified period of time that may be necessary in view of potential future litigation in the United States. Furthermore, the above-mentioned guidelines on the use of Internet and e-mail systems expressly refer to the need for systems to periodically and automatically delete personal data that must not be retained for periods in excess of the time required for achieving the specific and proven purposes for which they are retained. If the US litigation has already been commenced or is imminent, however, there is room to argue that compliance with a pretrial discovery request represents a 'specific proven purpose' and that data may therefore be retained for longer with a view thereto.

As discussed, Italian law is rather strict on security measures. This deserves attention in combination with the rules on transfer of personal data abroad. In general, if the US recipient company has self-certified under the Safe Harbour scheme, the security measures provided therein and therefore adopted by the recipient should be considered sufficient. However, in case transfer is carried out based on contractual obligations or BCRs under Article 44 (1) (a) of the DPC, it must be considered that it is expressly provided that the data subject may enforce

Daniela Ampollini

the DPC rules in case the relevant contractual or BCR provisions are breached. The latter proposition may lead to the conclusion that the contractual provisions or BCRs must impose on the recipient of the data obligations responding to the minimum requirements for data protection established by the Italian DPC, which include appropriate security measures under the Italian DPC.

Again on transfer abroad, as mentioned, Article 43 (1) (e) allows transfer even without consent or the application of the above-described requirements (Safe Harbour, contractual obligations, or BCRs) for the purpose 'to defend a claim in court', which should (for the reasons set out above on the issue of consent in general) include for the purpose of the pretrial discovery in the framework of US litigation. It must be considered, however, that in Working Document 158 on pretrial discovery for cross-border civil litigation, it is expressly stated that the ground of Article 43 (1) (e) (which in substance corresponds to that foreseen by Article 26 [1] [d] of Directive 95/46/EC) may only be used to justify the transfer of a limited amount of data. Where the transfer of a vast amount of data is necessary, such as in case of pretrial discovery, however, other grounds should be used, that is, either consent of the data subjects, adoption of the Safe Harbour scheme, or contractual obligations or BCRs under Article 44 of the DPC.

IV.   CONCLUSION

The Italian legal system contemplates nothing comparable to US pretrial discovery, and added to this it has a comprehensive system of personal data protection rules that must be carefully considered when a pretrial discovery request is carried out in Italy. These rules do not prohibit the carrying out of pretrial discovery in Italy, but render it advisable to carefully design and adopt corporate policies taking into account the principles of Italian privacy legislation, with particular regard to the issue of information of the data subjects, management of corporate Internet and e-mail systems, and security measures and transfer abroad.

Chapter 5.12

Latvia

*Sarmis Spilbergs**

I. LATVIAN PERSONAL DATA PROTECTION LAW

A. BACKGROUND

The personal data protection regime in Latvia is closely based on Directive
95/46/EC.[1] It was implemented through the Personal Data Protection Law[2] (hereinafter PDPL) in 2000. Before the PDPL, unless protection was provided for in
certain specific laws (e.g., concerning medical data, criminal records, etc.), processing and protection of personal data was not regulated. The affected person
could only rely on the right to privacy under the general human rights statutes;
however, there was not sufficient guidance and certainty on how exactly the right
to privacy interrelated with personal data aspects – that is, the balance of legitimate
interests of others versus protection of personal data under the right to privacy.
Therefore, the PDPL introduced the definition of personal data, the requirements
for their legitimate processing, and rights of the data subjects.

   Within the last decade, the PDPL has been updated and supplemented constantly. Six amendments have been adopted and several supplementary regulations

---

*   Sarmis Spilbergs, LAWIN Klavins & Slaidins law offices, Riga, Latvia.
1. Council Directive 95/46 on protection of individuals with regard to the processing of personal
    data and on the free movement of such data, 1995 O.J. (L 281) 31 (EC).
2. Fizisko Personu Datu Aizsardzības likums [Personal Data Protection Law], adopted 23 Mar.
    2000. Published 'Latvijas Vestnesis', 123/124 (2034/2035), 06 Apr. 2000.

Catrien Noorda & Stefan Hanloser, *E-Discovery and Data Privacy*, pp. 143–150.
© 2011 Kluwer Law International BV, The Netherlands.

passed. It demonstrates that the competent authority is closely monitoring the efficiency of the regime and takes corrective actions if necessary. The substantive rights of data subjects, though, have not changed significantly. In that respect the PDPL is still similar to its initial wording, that is, the text of Directive 95/46/EC. The amendments mainly affect procedures that the data controllers and data processors have to observe – amongst others, procedures relating to registration of personal data processing, appointment of a data protection officer, exercise of data subjects' rights, procedures for export of personal data, and so forth.

The competent authority to ensure compliance with the PDPL is the Data State Inspectorate (DSI).[3] The DSI was set up in 2000 along with the coming into effect of the PDPL. The DSI is a specialized institution dealing exclusively with personal data protection matters. In case of violations, the DSI may impose administrative fines of up to Lats (LVL) 10,000 (Euros (EUR) 14,000). The decisions of the DSI are subject to review by administrative courts. In 2009 intentional illegal operations with personal data were criminalized. The criminal law now provides monetary penalties up to EUR 50,000, forced labour, and/or up to five years' imprisonment. Violations of a criminal nature are handled in accordance with criminal procedure law – that is, not by the DSI, but state prosecutors.

The annual reports of the DSI show that the number of alleged violation cases increases year by year. The latest published report notes that in 2009, the DSI received 158 complaints. Of the reviewed cases, the DSI found sufficient violations to impose sanctions on 52 occasions (26 administrative warnings and 26 monetary penalties up to LVL 1,000).

So far there have been approximately twenty-five administrative court cases where the PDPL has been cited. Only a few of those cases provide some new and/or relevant interpretation of the PDPL. In most cases the court assessed whether the person, relying on freedom of information laws, was entitled to obtain certain documents from a public institution where the institution had refused such disclosure based on the PDPL. Only a couple of these cases were appeals of a DSI decision by which violation of the PDPL was established and a fine imposed. There is no publicly available information regarding any criminal cases concerning illegitimate data processing; however, since criminal sanctions were introduced only in the end of year 2009, most likely there are either none or very few such cases up to the current date.

B. PERSONAL DATA

The PDPL provides a broad definition of personal data. The term 'personal data' is understood as any information relating to an identified or identifiable natural person.[4]

---

3. <www.dvi.gov.lv/eng/>.
4. Article 1.3, PDPL.

Data regarding a deceased person are not regarded as personal data.[5] Nevertheless data of a deceased person may allow identification of a living natural person and as such the data of the deceased are treated as personal data.

Data relating to legal entities – corporations, companies, state institutions, associations, or any other person that is not a natural person – are not personal data. Nevertheless, the documents of the aforesaid legal entities will often contain names of natural persons (i.e., persons signing the document, persons described in the document, persons referred to in the document, etc.), which will amount to personal data and therefore have to be processed in accordance with the PDPL.

In 2009, the DSI issued a recommendation 'Definition of personal data'.[6] The recommendation analyses the essential elements of the definition, such as, 'any information', 'relates to', 'identifiable person', and 'natural person'. The guidance demonstrates that not only the commonly perceived name and address of the person, but virtually anything attributable to a certain person (video footage, audio recording, items belonging to person, work e-mails, etc.) can qualify as personal data. In case of discovery requests, in most cases the request will relate to evidence that is attributable to a certain person and therefore will be allowed only if the PDPL permits such disclosure.

The PDPL also distinguishes special categories of personal data that enjoy further protection compared to regular personal data. Such data are sensitive personal data (data relating to race, ethnic origin, religious and political beliefs, participation in work unions, data relating to health and sexual life), identification codes, and records of criminal or administrative offences. Special categories of personal data may be processed only if the data controller can justify such processing based on one of the specific legal grounds laid down in the PDPL. In the context of discovery requests, the competent court will asses case by case whether a document containing sensitive personal data should be disclosed in full or with certain information concealed.

C.   EMPLOYEES' E-MAILS

No specific status has been assigned to employees' e-mails through legislation. The correspondence of an employee via work e-mail account is protected by the principle of secrecy (privacy) of correspondence, unless the employer has laid down rules regarding the use of the work e-mail account (i.e., for work-related purposes only) and has informed its employees about possible screening. The internal rules must respect a certain level of employee privacy at workplace,

---

5. 'Rukers M, "Fizisko personu datu aizsardzības likuma komentāri", SIA E-Sabiedrības Risinājumi', 2008, 16.
6. Recommendation of Data State Inspectorate, 'Personal Data Definition', 2008, available at <www.div.gov.lv/files/Personas%20datu%20/definicija%20rekomendacija.doc>, last accessed on 18 Oct. 2010.

and the employer has to refrain from inspecting correspondence that is clearly private and does not affect the employer's interests.

The employer may under no circumstances review private e-mail accounts (such as Gmail, Hotmail, Yahoo, etc.) even though such accounts could be accessed during the working hours and from a work computer.

Since the aspects of monitoring employee e-mails are not officially regulated in Latvia, some guidance regarding these issues can be sought from the 'Working document on the surveillance of electronic communications in the workplace'.[7]

In case of pretrial e-discovery requests, the employer might be prevented from disclosing its employee e-mails. To access such e-mail, the e-discovery request would have to be made against the employee in question, which in most cases would not be a party in the litigation.

D.   PROCESSING OF PERSONAL DATA

The processing of personal data is legitimate only if it is justified under the statutory grounds listed in the PDPL. The safest justification is the consent of the data subject; nevertheless the PDPL allows processing without a consent if it relates to fulfilment of contractual relations, the processing is legally mandated, it is performed to ensure the vital interests of data subject (life; health), to protect legitimate interests of the controller, and where there are some other grounds justifying processing of data by public bodies.

If processing is based on consent, the PDPL prescribes that the consent must be freely given. As regards formal requirements, the PDPL only requires that consent for processing of sensitive personal data must be expressed in writing. No specific formality requirements apply for consent for other categories of personal data. In practice, though, there are discussions of whether consent should be expressed as a separate document or clause. The DSI favours the view that the requirement of 'freely' given consent is satisfied when the consent clause does not impact the validity of the whole document. In adhesion contract situations, where the consent language is included among other terms and is not discussed separately, the consent could be considered as void. However, there is no jurisprudence on this issue at a national level yet. It is therefore recommended to add a separate signature line or thick boxes next to consent clauses in contracts.

The term 'processing' should be understood broadly. Processing involves any operation carried out in relation to personal data, including data collection, registration, recording, storage, arrangement, transformation, utilization, transfer, transmission and dissemination, blockage, or erasure.[8]

---

7. Article 29 Data Protection Working Party, 'Working document on the surveillance of electronic communications in the workplace', 5401/01/EN/Final WP 55, adopted 29 May 2002, available at <http://ec.europa.eu/justice_home/fsj/privacy/docs/wpdocs/2002/wp55_en.pdf>, last accessed on 25 May 2010.
8. Article 1.4, PDPL.

Unless exceptions apply, anybody who engages in data processing must register with the DSI. Registration is not required, for example, if processing is based on consent of the data subject, it arises out of contractual relations, it is performed for human resource management purposes or for journalistic purposes, if a data protection officer has been duly appointed, and so forth. Nevertheless, the PDPL also lists situations where the above-mentioned exceptions no longer apply – for example, if data would be exported outside the European Union/European Economic Area (EU/EEA). Thus, if the data controller intends to export data, for example, to the United States, the registration is mandatory. On the other hand, although the PDPL does not expressly provide so, the data controller should not be required to register data processing if disclosure of data to a country outside the EU/EEA is ordered via e-discovery request.

E.   TRANSFER ABROAD

If the data processor has satisfied the legitimacy requirements for data processing, the PDPL allows free data flow among EU/EEA countries. No specific consents from data subjects are needed to send data to another EU/EEA country; however, the data subject may request the data controller to inform regarding the possible data recipients. Data transfers outside the EU/EEA are permitted only if adequacy and additional legitimacy requirements are satisfied.

Adequacy relates to the level of data protection in force in the receiving country. The PDPL allows transfers to third countries only if the level of data protection is adequate to the level of data protection in force in Latvia. It is generally regarded that all EU/EEA countries have an adequate level of data protection on the basis of Directive 95/46/EC. With respect to non-EU/EEA countries, the DSI may make a specific assessment and recognize their data protection regimes as adequate. So far the DSI has recognized Argentina, Jersey, Faroe Islands, Guernsey, Canada, Isle of Man, Switzerland, and the US Department of Commerce's Safe Harbour Privacy Principles as having adequate level of protection.[9] The European Commission has also found adequate protection in transferring air passenger names to the US Bureau of Customs and Border Protection.[10] If the recipient is located in a country that is not among the recognized, the data exporter and data recipient may undertake to ensure the adequacy themselves by entering into a special contract. Although the PDPL provides that the national standards for essential terms to be included in such contracts will be passed by the Cabinet of Ministers,[11] to date such standards have not been passed and the parties are

---

9.   DSI decision No. 1-13/1559, dated 11 Mar. 2010, available at <www.dvi.gov.lv/files/Lemums_valstis_datu_aizsardzibas_pakape.pdf>, last accessed on 25 May 2010.
10. European Commission, Data Protection, Overview – Third countries, available at <http://ec.europa.eu/justice_home/fsj/privacy/thridcountries/index_en.htm>, last accessed on 8 Dec. 2009.
11. Article 28.4, PDPL.

requested to adhere to the EU Model Contracts.[12] The data controller would confirm the existence of the contract when registering data processing with the DSI. The registration would also require identifying the legal basis for data transfers abroad.

The PDPL provides that transfers of data to third countries are legitimate only if based on consent of the data subject (i.e., consent that expressly acknowledges data exports outside the EU/EEA) or if the transfer is necessary to fulfil contractual relations, if the data are public or publicly available, if the transfer is necessary to protect life and health of the data subject, and, finally, if the data have been requested in accordance with law and the transfer is necessary for litigation in a third country.

Accordingly, the PDPL foresees a special exception that allows exporting personal data to a non-EU/EEA country for litigation purposes. The request, however, would have to be made in accordance with law (please see section II – Discovery in Latvia). Since the obligation to export data would arise from a court order, in case of e-discovery requests the data controller would not need a specific consent from the data subject to send the data to a US entity. Nevertheless, the data controller would still have to be the legitimate owner of the data (i.e., the data must be legitimately obtained – for example, to disclose e-mails of employees, the employees must be informed that employer performs screening of e-mails).

Please note that in accordance with the judgment in the *Bodil Lindqvist*[13] case, publication of data on the Internet so that the data are made accessible to an indefinite number of people shall not be regarded as transfer of personal data to a third country. Hence, data acquired via public website will not require observing the aforementioned formalities; however, if data are sent to a particular recipient or made available only to particular group of recipients by other electronic means, it is regarded as transfer of data to a third country. In order for a data controller to be able to publish personal data on a public website, in most cases only consent of the data subject will justify such processing.

F.   THE APPLICABILITY OF THE PDPL

The PDPL applies to data processing if the data processor is established in Latvia, if data processing takes place outside Latvia in territories belonging to Latvia (Latvian embassies, ships and aircrafts registered in Latvia, Latvian military camps, etc.), or if the equipment used for data processing is located in Latvia (except if the equipment serves only for data transit though Latvia). Once the data have been legitimately exported to another country (including EU/EEA countries),

---

12. European Commission, Data Protction, Overview – Model Contracts, available at <http://ec.europa.eu/justice_home/fsj/privacy/modelcontracts/index_en.htm>, last accessed on 8 Dec. 2009.
13. Case C-101/01 Criminal proceedings against Bodil Lindqvist, available at <http://eur-lex.europa.eu/LexUriServ/LexUriServ.do?uri=CELEX:62001J0101:EN:HTML>.

the PDPL no longer applies and further processing is subject to the laws of the receiving country and/or contract entered into between the data exporter in Latvia and the data recipient in the third country. In case discovery is sought from a multinational company with several subsidiaries in various countries, it is vital to ascertain which entity is the data controller. If the Latvian entity is merely a data processor, the request for discovery should be made against the entity that acts as the data controller.

II.   DISCOVERY IN LATVIA

The principle of discovery and e-discovery, in the form as it known in the United States, is not known in the Latvian legal system. The ability to obtain evidence in possession of another party is ensured through civil procedure law in domestic cases, whereas cooperation between Latvian and foreign courts is governed either by Regulation 1206/2001[14] or the 1970 Hague Convention[15] on the Taking of Evidence Abroad in Civil or Commercial Matters. If court intervention is necessary to obtain evidence from a Latvian party, please note that in practice Latvian courts tend to order disclosure only of clearly identified documents. Latvian courts are reluctant to approve requests that are broadly formulated and therefore seek to access, for example, all documents of certain sort.

III.   BLOCKING STATUTES

Since the cooperation with foreign courts and public authorities is specifically regulated, it implies that such cooperation is expressly permitted. There are no 'blocking statues' in Latvia; nevertheless the legal framework on cooperation itself provides that on certain occasions the request may be refused. Pursuant to Article 23 of the 1970 Hague Convention, Latvia has not declared that it will not execute Letters of Request issued for the purpose of obtaining pretrial discovery of documents as known in common law countries.

IV.   CONCLUSION

Although personal data protection laws may encumber the pretrial discovery process, the PDPL expressly permits transfer of personal data abroad if such request is made pursuant to statutory requirements. Since Working Paper 158

---

14. Council Regulation (EC) No. 1206/2001 of 28 May 2001 on cooperation between the courts of the Member States in the taking of evidence in civil or commercial matters, OJ (L 174) 27 Jul. 2001, 1–24.
15. Convention on the Taking of Evidence Abroad in Civil or Commercial Matters, done at The Hague, on the 18th day of March, 1970.

Sarmis Spilbergs

on pretrial discoveries for cross-border civil litigation[16] permits disclosure of personal data and the DSI so far has closely followed documents adopted by the Article 29 Data Protection Working Party, it is unlikely that any Latvian authority would decline disclosure of evidence by arguing that the PDPL restricts them from doing so.

---

16. Working Document 1/2009 on pretrial discovery for cross-border civil litigation, adopted on 11 Feb. 2009, Working Paper 158 00339/09/EN, available at <http://ec.europa.eu/justice_home/fsj/privacy/docs/wpdocs/2009/wp158_en.pdf>, last accessed on 9 Dec. 2009.

Chapter 5.13

Liechtenstein

Vivien Gertsch and Markus H. Wanger[*]

I.   INTRODUCTION

In Liechtenstein, one of the smallest countries of Europe, data protection has not
been a big issue during the last century. Whereas there was a strict professional
secret for banks, lawyers, auditors, trustees, clerical persons, and officials. the
private collection of data was tolerated and the theme generally was of no importance. Still, as Liechtenstein became a member of the European Economic Area
(EEA) in 1995, most European Union (EU) Directives have to be implemented in
Liechtenstein as well. The European Data Protection Directive was implemented
in Liechtenstein by the Data Protection Act (DPA) dated 14 March 2002[1] and the
Data Protection Ordinance (DPO) dated 9 July 2002.[2] The DPA came into force on
1 August 2002.

   Pretrial discovery is practically unknown in Liechtenstein, at least in civil
matters. Most interesting, the various tax information exchange agreements
(TIEAs) provide for data exchange with a very low protection level for the persons
involved. Like in most other EU Member States, there is a tension between the
personal right to data protection and the possible economical right of companies or
states to data disclosure.

---

1. LGBl 55/2002, further referred to as DPA.
2. LGBl 102/2002, further referred to as DPO.

Catrien Noorda & Stefan Hanloser, *E-Discovery and Data Privacy*, pp. 151–162.
© 2011 Kluwer Law International BV, The Netherlands.

II.   THE DATA PROTECTION ACT

The DPA applies in cases where the processing of the data is performed in Liechtenstein, in areas where the Liechtenstein law is in force, or in cases where any means are used in Liechtenstein to assist in the processing.[3]

That the DPA applies inside Liechtenstein is rather obvious. The application in foreign areas subject to Liechtenstein law is without importance, as Liechtenstein never had colonies and currently has no ships and only eight aircraft under its flag; the reason for being of this rule is that it is a European standard and was simply copied.

However, the last case is of some importance. The DPA applies to all cases where means, whether automated or not, are used inside Liechtenstein to process data.[4] This means that as soon as visiting a website places a cookie on a user's computer, means of data gathering and/or processing are used in Liechtenstein. As a result, international giants such as Google are to abide by the DPA. As one might imagine, points of view on this specific rule differ very much depending on whether one sides for the companies exploiting information or on the supervisory authority's side.

Now that the geographical scope of application has been defined, we will discuss the contents of the DPA.

A.   MAIN PROVISIONS OF THE DPA

The DPA contains three principles for the use of data:[5]

   (i) Personal data must be collected in a lawful manner.
   (ii) Processing must not contravene the principle of good faith and must be adequate and not excessive in relation to the purpose for which the personal data are collected and/or further processed.
   (iii) Personal data may only be processed for the purpose for which they were collected, which is either evident from the circumstances or set down by law.

The DPA further provides that the information must be correct (basic principle of correctness) and that the personal data must be protected against unauthorized processing by appropriate organizational and technical means (basic principle of data security). In addition, anyone may ask a data controller if data relating to him or her are being processed.

---

3.   Article 2 II DPA.
4.   Article 2 II b DPA.
5.   Article 4 DPA.

B.   Personal Data

The DPA defines personal data as being all information relating to an identified or identifiable person (i.e., both natural and legal persons).[6]

Sensitive personal data include: (i) the standard types of sensitive personal data such as religion, race, health, political opinion (though this does not include trade union information); (ii) social security files; and (iii) criminal or administrative proceedings and penalties.

A processing for 'personality profiles' is a collection of data that allows the appraisal of fundamental characteristics of the personality of a natural person. Both sensitive personal data and data constituting a personality profile are subject to specific rules.

Personal data of employees are protected in the same way as other personal data. Usually personal e-mails may not be searched or transmitted without the consent of an employee. Most companies prohibit e-mails for private purposes but tolerate them if they are not hindering the work of an employee. Still, even if a company would not tolerate personal e-mails, the protecting laws may apply anyhow, because nobody can prevent an employee from receiving personal e-mails (he or she probably neither ordered nor wanted to receive), especially if the e-mail address is: name of the person @ firm where the person works. If the personal e-mails are not kept in a separate file the files of the employees usually may not be searched and data may not be transmitted without the consent of the employee. The same may apply to notices about meetings or to telephone logs, although in the absence of case law it is not certain that local courts would see it that way.

An exception to the prohibition of processing mixed e-mail accounts may be derived from the act stating that the processing of personal data shall be unlawful unless it is justified by the consent of the data subject.[7] As by the *argumentum ex contrario*, the employee's consent therefore provides a sufficient legal basis for the employer to search the employee's e-mail account. An aspect of the consent that will have to be further elaborated in case law is whether consent given in a standard clause of the employment contract can be deemed to be a free and true consent, as one may argue that the employee had a mental reservation that he or she did not express because of the relationship of authority/dependence.

Having designated custodians separating private files from business e-mails would be a variation of the above-mentioned situation. The system would still require the employee to give his or her consent, as the conditions set forth in Article 17 I a of the DPA would otherwise not be fulfilled. However, depending on how the custodians are chosen, it may increase the employee's comfort.

C.   Collection, Processing, and Use of Personal Data

The DPA distinguishes between data processing performed in the private and the public sector. In this context, the definition of 'processing' is meant to include any

6. Article 3 DPA.
7. Article 17 I a DPA.

operations relating to personal data, such as the collection, storage, use, modification, communication, archiving, or destruction of data.[8]

Processing data in the private sector is not allowed to unlawfully breach the privacy of the data subject.[9] In particular, this means that the data may not be processed against the express will of the data subject or for purposes other than those the data were collected for. As an exception to this rule, data made publically accessible by the data subject without expressly prohibiting their processing, for example, in social networks, may be processed without constituting a breach of privacy.[10]

Additionally, infringement of privacy is deemed as justified in cases of overriding public or private interest.[11] The DPA gives a non-exhaustive list of cases where such an overriding interest may be likely. The idea of having a public interest occurring in the private sector may at first be strange and shall therefore be illustrated with an example: An overriding private or public interest may be present where the processing of data is in direct connection with the conclusion or performance of a contract.[12] Insurance companies incur a high risk of being deceived by contract partners. If they would not have the right to process data about their customer, they would raise their premiums to account for the risk of being deceived. This would penalize honest customers and is therefore not in the public interest. The insurance's right to demand certain personal data on the contract partner may therefore be derived from the public interest.

All of the above regulations apply to data processing in the private sector; those relative to the public sector are stricter. Authorities are only allowed to process data if they are entitled by law to do so, or if it is the only way of achieving a task the authority has been charged with by law, or if the government authorized them, or if the data they process are publicly known, or if they have the data subject's consent.[13]

The processing of personal data may be entrusted to a third party if: (i) the data controller ensures that no processing occurs that he or she would not be permitted to carry out him- or herself; (ii) the processing is not prohibited by a legal or contractual duty of confidentiality; and (iii) said third party respects all duties that the data controller has. Some parts of the contract between the data processor and the data controller must be documented in written or another permanent form.

D.   DUTY TO INFORM AND RIGHTS OF DATA SUBJECT

Data controllers in Liechtenstein are subject to a set of informational requirements. These requirements can be of a general nature, such as the requirement to have files

---

8. Article 3 I g DPA.
9. Article 16 I DPA.
10. Article 16 III DPA.
11. Article 17 I b & Art. 17 II DPA.
12. Article 17 II a DPA.
13. Article 21 II DPA.

registered, or event-driven, such as the requirement to inform the Data Protection Commissioner before moving data outside the EEA.[14] Furthermore, the data controller is to make sure the data he or she processes are correct and the data subject may demand erroneous data to be corrected, and data controllers are to answer a request as to whether they process information on a certain data subject.[15]

1. Obligation to Register

The Data Protection Office keeps a publicly accessible register of files containing sensitive data.[16] Data controllers are under certain conditions required to register at the Data Protection Office, an act that will routinely trigger an inquiry by the Data Protection Commissioner[17] in order to make sure that the data controller is able to assure compliance with the DPA.

The public sector is to register any file containing sensitive data,[18] with the DPA foreseeing no exceptions to this rule.

The private sector is also subject to the registration requirement by default.[19] There is, however, a comprehensive list of exceptions that are exempt from this requirement.[20] Those exemptions are data collected for research, planning, and statistics purposes, provided the data are published in a way that does not permit to deduce the identity of the data subjects. Individuals who regularly process data or communicate data to third parties may not claim those exceptions if: (i) in doing so they are not subject to legal requirements; or if (ii) they do this without the data subject knowing about it.[21]

If there is the obligation to register, this must be done before the opening of the file.[22]

2. Event-Driven Information Requirements

Under the DPA, transfers of personal data to EU/EEA Member States are not subject to any additional restrictions.

The general rule under the DPA regarding notification is that the Commissioner must be informed in advance of any transfer of personal data to a foreign country, including to other EEA Member States, unless the transfer is required in order to comply with a legal obligation, and the data subject is aware of the transfer. However, under the DPA, the government may issue further regulations, particularly in order to simplify or create exemptions from the notification requirements

---

14. Article 7 II DPA.
15. Article 11 DPA.
16. Article 15 I DPA.
17. For additional information on this inquiry, see point 'E. Supervisory Authorities' below.
18. Article 15 II DPA.
19. Article 15 IIIa DPA.
20. Article 8 DPO.
21. Article 15 III DPA.
22. Article 15 IV DPA.

when the processing does not adversely affect the data subject, and to specify foreign countries that do not provide adequate protection for personal data. Under the DPO, notification of the transfer of personal data to countries that ensure adequate data protection is not required unless the data are sensitive data or data constituting a personality profile (see section B above). In addition, notification is not required for a transfer that is for personal purposes, in particular for research, planning, or statistical purposes if the data subject is not identified. The DPA does not mention any necessity for the Commissioner to approve the data transfers he or she is notified about; however, an inquiry in the Commissioner's initiative (see below) may be triggered.

Under Article 8 of the DPA, personal data may not be transferred to a foreign country other than an EU/EEA Member State if the transfer would infringe the privacy rights of the data subject, which means in particular if the recipient country does not ensure an adequate level of protection of personal data. The DPO, which specifies the foreign countries that ensure adequate protection for personal data, effectively implements the European Commission Decisions in regard to adequacy (see below), by including them in the list.

Note that there are no provisions of the DPA permitting transfers of personal data to non-EU/EEA countries that do not ensure adequate data protection if other conditions are met, such as protection of the data by contractual terms approved by the European Commission (see below). Accordingly, if the recipient country is not an EU/EEA Member State and does not ensure adequate data protection, the transfer is not permitted.

In particular, the government has to approve Model Contracts. The government, however, is bound to the opinion of the Data Protection Commissioner in this case.[23]

3.   Rights of the Data Subject

The data subject has a series of rights enforceable against the data controller. The data subject may object to the use of his or her data altogether on the basis that his or her overriding interests are violated.[24] The data subject may also block the disclosure of data relating to him or her.[25]

Liechtenstein guaranties a right of access that allows persons to check whether a specific individual or organization holds information on the person.[26] The file controller must, amongst other things, disclose what data he or she presently holds and where the data originated. Delegating data processing to a third party does not free from answering the above-mentioned inquiries: it is not just and reasonable to have the data subject run after files containing data on him or her.

---

23.   Article 8 III DPA.
24.   Article 14 DPA.
25.   Article 24 DPA.
26.   Article 11 DPA.

E. SUPERVISORY AUTHORITIES

Compliance with data protection standards in Liechtenstein is supervised by the Data Protection Commission, with the Data Protection Commissioner at its head.[27] The Commissioner is elected for a term of office of eight years by the parliament[28] and an independent authority not bound by instructions from any side.[29] The Commissioner supervises both state authorities[30] and the private sector.[31] No player in the private sector is exempt from supervision by the Commissioner; however, there is an exception concerning the authorities due to historical reasons: Until 2008, the Commissioner was appointed by the government, which was therefore not placed under the Commissioner's supervision to prevent the appearance of conflicts of interest. Since 2008, the Commissioner is elected by the parliament on the government's proposal;[32] however the government itself is still not subject to supervision by the Commissioner.[33]

Inquiries by the Commissioner can be launched either on the Commissioner's own initiative or as a reaction to some third party's report. In particular, inquiries on the Commissioners initiative are triggered if the methods of processing are capable of infringing one or more people's privacy rights or if the files involved have to be registered according to Article 15 of the DPA[34] or if data are to leave the EU/EEA.[35]

When inquiring in some case, the Commissioner may request the production of documents, obtain information, and have data processing activities demonstrated to him or her. State authorities are obligated to cooperate whilst this rule does not exist for the private sector, but for both public and private sector the Code of Criminal Procedure limits cooperation requirements.[36]

Where an investigation reveals that data protection provisions have been infringed, the Commissioner may recommend that the data processing activities should be modified or ceased. If the recommendation aims at some state authority, it is also to be forwarded to the government. Should the recommendation not be followed, the Commissioner may refer the case to the Data Protection Commission. While private-sector players may directly appeal against the Commission's decision, authorities have to do so through the Data Protection Office.[37]

---

27. Article 28 II DPA.
28. Article 28a I DPA.
29. Article 28 III DPA.
30. Article 29 DPA.
31. Article 30 DPA.
32. Article 28a I DPA.
33. Article 29 I DPA.
34. The point of this regulation is to trigger a precautionary inquiry into any new company that trades data, as well as in cases where data are brought out of the Commissioner's reach.
35. Article 30 DPA.
36. Article 29 DPA (state authorities) and Art. 30 DPA (private sector).
37. Article 29 DPA (state authorities) and Art. 30 DPA (private sector).

The Commissioner must submit an annual report to the parliament and to the government. These periodical reports are published.[38]

In cases of public interest, the Commissioner may inform the public of his or her findings and recommendations. Should data be subject to official secrecy, the consent of the competent authority is required. In the event such consent is withheld by the authority, the Data Protection Commission will make a decision, which will be final.[39] The purpose of this regulation is to prevent indirect violations of confidentiality: for instance, the tax authority is to maintain secrecy over data it receives, and having the Commissioner publish data that the tax authority had to give the Commissioner because of the obligation to cooperate could be a breach in confidentiality, thus the Commissioner has to ask the tax authority as competent authority for approval.

The Commissioner has the following additional duties:

(a) to support private individuals and authorities by giving a general introduction and providing individual consulting services;

(b) to submit opinions on questions of data protection laws in pending cases at the request of the decision-making bodies or appellate authorities;

(c) to certify the extent to which foreign data protection laws are equivalent to the data protection laws of Liechtenstein;

(d) to comment on bills and decrees of significance to data protection law and particularly to review their compliance with the provisions of EU Directive 95/46;

(e) to cooperate with data protection authorities both within and outside Liechtenstein; and

(f) to represent the Principality of Liechtenstein in the Working Party on the Protection of Individuals with Regard to the Processing of Personal Data pursuant to Article 29 of EU Directive 95/46.

F.   ENFORCEMENT

The DPA defines several criminal offences and their sanctions.[40] For the time being, legal persons usually cannot be charged for criminal behaviour; it is the persons acting for the company who are held responsible for either showing or instructing illegal behaviour:

(a) The unauthorized collection of sensitive personal data from a file that is not freely accessible may be punished by a fine up to 360 'daily rates' or imprisonment for a period of up to one year. A daily rate is a figure

---

38. Article 31 I DPA.
39. Article 31 II DPA.
40. Articles 39, 40, & 41 DPA.

calculated by reference to the income of the offender, which is to ensure that whatever the income is, the penalty will be badly felt.

(b) Breach by a data controller of the requirements in regard to notification, information, provision of access, and rectification (including wilful provision by a data controller to a data subject of incorrect or inadequate information, or wilful failure by a data controller to notify, when required, the Commissioner of the collection of personal data or the international transfer of personal data, or provision of incorrect information in such a notification) is punishable by imprisonment for a period of up to three months, or a fine of up to Swiss Francs (CHF) 20,000.

(c) Disclosure of personal data in breach of the DPA (which means wilful disclosure of confidential data, or sensitive data, or data that constitute a personality profile, without authorization) is punishable by imprisonment for a period of up to one year, or a fine up to 360 daily rates.

The following civil sanctions also apply under the DPA:

(i) under Article 37 of the DPA, in conjunction with Articles 39–41 of the Persons and Companies Act, infringement of the right of privacy under the Act provides a data subject with a right to pursue civil proceedings in court for rectification, destruction, or prevention of disclosure of personal data, and for compensation of damages suffered; and

(ii) the right of access to personal data may be pursued under a special non-contentious civil proceeding (*Rechtsfürsorgeverfahren*).

A request for information at the competent authority resulted in the information that during the last three years, no sanctions actually had to be imposed, as the Commissioner's recommendations and the threat of incurring a sanction proved sufficient to deter major and lasting wrongdoings.

Under Article 32(1) (b) of the DPA, the Commissioner may, at the request of a court or a government agency, be charged with making a decision in pending proceedings, and will give an opinion in respect of questions of data protection that arise in the course of court proceedings.

Under Articles 30–32 of the DPA, the Commissioner also has the power to require documents and information, and to make enquiries in order to establish the facts in regard to the processing of personal data. The Commissioner may recommend changes to or the cessation of processing, and if such a recommendation is not followed, may refer the case to the Data Protection Commission for a binding decision.

Other powers and functions of the Commissioner include making public his or her recommendations in regard to matters involving the public interest, issuing opinions in regard to the adequacy of data protection laws in other countries, and providing advice in regard to data protection regulations, and the extent to which they conform to the EU Data Protection Directive.

Vivien Gertsch and Markus H. Wanger

III.   PRETRIAL DISCOVERY IN LIECHTENSTEIN

A.   GENERAL OUTLINE

The mutual disclosure of documents and data is unknown in Liechtenstein. Each party has to bring in and mention the documents that support its position. During a trial that has already been started, a party may ask the other one to produce a document that is only in that party's hands. The judge may order the other party to hand out this document if it is needed.[41]

B.   INTERNATIONAL CONVENTIONS

Liechtenstein has not signed the Hague Convention on taking evidence in civil cases so far. However, concerning criminal cases, Liechtenstein signed the European Convention about legal cooperation in criminal cases in 1970[42] as well as a mutual legal aid treaty with the United States in 2002.[43] Thus in criminal cases a data exchange is possible.

C.   OTHER RELEVANT PROVISIONS

Though the cooperation with foreign courts or public authorities is not explicitly prohibited, there are several provisions that have to be respected. For instance, there are provisions in the Criminal Code for violation of the privacy of correspondence,[44] abuse of a computer system,[45] violation of the privacy of communication,[46] abuse through interception of data,[47] and violation of professional secrecies[48] of doctors, lawyers, persons working in the social aid service and the like, as well as their employees. Also the violation of trade secrets[49] has to be mentioned. Even trying to find out trade secrets is punished, and more so if the trade secret is being revealed for the purpose of transferring it abroad.[50] In addition, Liechtenstein has a very well-developed bank secrecy policy, which may cause problems in deciding which data may be revealed and which are protected.

---

41. § 303 Zivilprozessordnung (Civil Process Order) LGBl 9/1, 30 Dec. 1912.
42. Europäisches Übereinkommen über Rechtshilfe in Strafsachen LGBl 30/70, 15 Oct. 1970.
43. Vertrag zwischen dem Fürstentum Liechtenstein und den Vereinigten Staaten von Amerika betreffend die internationale Rechtshilfe in Strafsachen, LGBl 149/2003, 1 Aug. 2003.
44. § 118 Criminal Code, LGBl 37/1988, 22 Oct. 1988.
45. § 118a Criminal Code.
46. § 119 Criminal Code.
47. § 119a Criminal Code.
48. § 121 Criminal Code.
49. § 122 Criminal Code.
50. § 124 Criminal Code.

The Liechtenstein Electronic Communication Act (ECA)[51] creates the obligation to maintain secrecy on the provider's side[52] and states that the DPA is to be applied as a kind of catchall rule.[53] The ECA, however, also creates some loopholes in data protection that are specifically destined to law enforcement: people may be located through their cell phone in case of an immediate threat to their physical integrity[54] and personal communication may be passed along to the executive regardless of the risk of reading private e-mails that do not relate to the investigation that justifies the forwarding.[55] Finally, communication service providers are to keep records permitting the identification of the communicating parties until six months after the end of a contractual relationship.[56]

D.   CONCLUSION: RETENTION AND TRANSFER OF PERSONAL DATA

For any individual or company that can foresee a regulatory investigation or legal proceedings, it may be tactically advisable to secure data that are likely to be relevant in this context, on one hand in order to prove claims and on the other hand in order to show good faith by demonstrating that no attempts to hide something have occurred. Securing data, however, is 'data processing' as by the DPA's definition[57] and therefore the restrictions discussed in this article apply. In the case of communication service providers, a requirement to cooperate in an investigation can provide the legal justification to override privacy rights and collect and/or transfer data.

A conflict between the legitimate interest of the parties of the legal proceedings and the interests of the individuals whose data are affected cannot be denied. Whereas data could be given away with the consent of the persons involved, this consent may not be obtained easily. Concerning employees, there is also the question of whether consent in advance, for example, as part of their working contract, would be sufficient. As mentioned before, one could argue that such consent is not given in a free and unsolicited way and thus doubt whether the employee really gave his or her consent.

Another possibility to transfer data would be if legitimate interests necessitated the processing. It is very likely that an accusation in a foreign country would produce a legitimate interest for an entity to defend itself with everything that could be submitted for the defence. The same is the case if an entity starts legal proceedings in a foreign country. Also then it will need to have all proof it can get to legitimize its position. A possible guidance can be taken by the European Working Party on Protection of Individuals with Regard to the Processing of Personal Data

---

51. Gesetz über die elektronische Kommunikation (KomG) LGBl 91/2006, 6 Jun. 2006.
52. Article 48 KomG.
53. Article 49 KomG.
54. Article 51 KomG.
55. Article 52 KomG, for example, tapping of phones.
56. Article 53 KomG.
57. Article 3 I g DPA.

and its Working Paper 158 on pretrial discovery for cross-border civil litigation. The Liechtenstein Data Protection Commissioner is an observer in this Working Party, which means that he or she is aware of likely future developments in European standards, but may not actively participate in defining them. The recommendation that can be found is that the data are scanned by an external expert within the home country previously and only data that are of relevance are transmitted abroad afterward. This gives a clue but it is also a difficult solution because it adds another person to view the data, which possibly is not in the interest of the persons involved, either.

IV.   CONCLUSION

At the present time, pretrial discovery is not a big issue in Liechtenstein, nor are there cases pending or special legal provisions existing. This might increase because of the world-wide interdependence of entities and economic interests. Especially Liechtenstein entities that have a branch or activity in the United States or in another common law country will have to find answers to these questions. The European Data Protection Directive has been implemented in Liechtenstein; the implementation of special provisions concerning pretrial discovery is not scheduled at the moment.

Chapter 5.14

Lithuania

*Mindaugas Kiškis**

I. INTRODUCTION

The issue of transborder discovery, particularly in relation to data held in Lithuania but required in relation to legal proceedings, for example, in the United States, may become a really complicated one. As a great number of Lithuanian companies are related to US holdings or subsidiaries, they may become subject to significant pressure to produce documents and materials, including items stored electronically,[1] in relation to specific litigation and law enforcement investigations brought in the United States. The material that is required will frequently contain personal data relating to employees or third parties, for example, clients or customers.

Discovery proceedings are not subject to express regulation in Lithuania. Some basic rules, which imply rudimentary discovery proceedings, are set forth in the Bar Law of the Republic of Lithuania, as well as the Code of Civil Procedure of the Republic of Lithuania. There are no express statutory limitations on discovery of evidence. To the contrary, the basic principles of the Lithuanian civil procedure require the parties to disclose evidence upon the bona fide request of the other party. Unfortunately, there are no detailed rules to support this basic principle. Although the Republic of Lithuania is a member of the Hague

---

*   Mindaugas Kiškis, LAWIN Lideika, Petrauskas, Valiunas ir partneriai.
1. Such production of electronic evidence is called e-discovery in the common law countries.

Catrien Noorda & Stefan Hanloser, *E-Discovery and Data Privacy*, pp. 163–172.

Mindaugas Kiškis

Convention on the Taking of Evidence Abroad in Civil or Commercial Matters as of 21 April 2001, Lithuania has opted for the reservation under Article 23 thereof.

Being a Member State of the European Union (EU), Lithuania has implemented rather strict personal data protection requirements in the Data Protection Directive.[2] These requirements may materially restrict any data processing, including data transfers, due to protection of an individual's privacy; that is, they may become a real obstacle for discovery processes in the common law countries. Thus, a tension may arise between the disclosure obligations under US litigation or regulatory rules and the application of the data protection requirements of the EU. It is clearly recognized in the EU that the parties involved in litigation have a legitimate interest in accessing information that is necessary to make or defend a claim.[3] However, in any case this must be balanced with the rights of the individual whose personal data is processed.

II.   LITHUANIAN DATA PROTECTION LAWS

A.   BACKGROUND

It is sometimes forgotten in Lithuanian practice that the main purpose of personal data protection is the individual's privacy. The Lithuanian Constitution[4] provides that the private life of a human being is inviolable. The Lithuanian Civil Code[5] provides for protection of an individual's right to private life as well. Therefore, while balancing pretrial discovery and data protection requirements, the constitutional protection of an individual's private life should be taken into account.

The main Lithuanian act establishing protection of an individual's right to private life while processing personal data is the Data Protection Law,[6] fully implementing the Data Protection Directive. The most recent amendments to the Data Protection Law came into force on 1 January 2009. It should also be taken into account that some specific privacy requirements related to electronic communications are set forth in the Electronic Communications Law.[7]

It must be noted that neither the said legislation nor Lithuanian case law provides for exact guidance on balancing pretrial discovery and data protection requirements. Therefore, any potential conflict between these requirements in

---

2. Directive 95/46/EC of the European Parliament and of the Council of 24 Oct. 1995 on the protection of individuals with regard to the processing of personal data and on the free movement of such data.
3. Working Paper 158 of the Art. 29 Data Protection Working Party, 11 Feb. 2009, 7.
4. The Constitution of the Republic of Lithuania, adopted by Lithuanian citizens on 25 Oct. 1992, Art. 22.
5. The Civil Code of the Republic of Lithuania, 18 Jul. 2000, Art. 2.23.
6. The Law of the Republic of Lithuania on Legal Protection of Personal Data, 11 Jun. 1996.
7. The Law on Electronic Communications of the Republic of Lithuania, 15 Apr. 2004.

Lithuania should be resolved on a case-by-case basis and in accordance with general principles of privacy and personal data protection. Concerning current practice, Lithuanian authorities accurately follow the Working Paper 158 adopted by the Data Protection Working Party[8] as important guidance.

B.   SCOPE OF APPLICATION

The Data Protection Law applies to personal data only. The Data Protection Law defines personal data as any information relating to a natural person, the data subject, who is identified or who can be identified directly or indirectly by reference to such data as a personal identification number or one or more factors specific to his or her physical, physiological, mental, economic, cultural, or social identity. Thus, Lithuanian laws may restrict the pretrial discovery process only in respect of personal data rather than information on legal persons. Data concerning legal persons may be protected in Lithuanian jurisdiction as confidential information under contractual clauses.

The Data Protection Law applies to the processing of personal data where:

– personal data are processed by a data controller that is established and operates in the territory of Lithuania or a branch of a data controller of another European Economic Area (EEA) member state, established and operating in Lithuania;
– personal data are processed by a data controller that is established and operates in a non-member state of the EEA but that uses personal data processing equipment established in Lithuania, with the exception where such equipment is used only for transit of data through the territory of the EEA; and/or
– personal data are processed by a data controller that is established in a territory other than Lithuania but that is bound by the laws of Lithuania under international public law (including diplomatic missions and consular posts).

Following provisions of the Data Protection Law, the pretrial discovery process would be subject to Lithuanian data protection laws if any of the above conditions are met.

C.   FAIR DATA PROCESSING

As there are no specific provisions on processing personal data in respect of pretrial discovery, the general fair data processing rules should be followed.

---

8. The Article 29 Data Protection Working Party was set up under Art. 29 of the Personal Data Directive. It is an independent European advisory body on data protection and privacy. The Article 29 Working Party's opinions and guidelines expressed in its Working Papers are not binding on the national data protection authorities; however, they are persuasive authority in all Member States of the EU.

The Data Protection Law provides that personal data processing, including discovery-related processing, must be based on any of the following legitimate grounds, which very literally correspond with the ones set forth in the Data Protection Directive:

(1) consent of a data subject;
(2) processing necessary for the performance of a contract to which a data subject is party is being concluded or performed;
(3) processing is necessary for the performance of a legal obligation of a data controller to process personal data;
(4) processing is necessary in order to protect vital interests of a data subject;
(5) processing is necessary for the exercise of official authority vested by laws and other legal acts in state and municipal institutions, agencies, enterprises, or a third party to whom personal data are disclosed; and/or
(6) processing is necessary for the purposes of legitimate interests pursued by a data controller or by a third party to whom the personal data are disclosed, unless such interests are overridden by interests of a data subject.

The Data Protection Law provides that any personal data must be:

(1) collected for specified and legitimate purposes and later not processed for purposes incompatible with the purposes determined before the concerned personal data are collected;
(2) processed accurately, fairly, and lawfully;
(3) accurate and, where necessary, for purposes of personal data processing, kept up to date; inaccurate or incomplete data must be rectified, supplemented, erased, or their further processing must be suspended;
(4) appropriate, adequate, and not excessive in relation to the purposes for which they are collected and further processed; and
(5) kept in a form that permits identification of data subjects for no longer than is necessary for the purposes for which the data were collected and processed.

As a general rule, personal data may be processed in an automated way only when a data controller notifies and registers itself with the State Data Protection Inspectorate of Lithuania. However, the registration is not necessary where the personal data are processed:

(1) for the purposes of internal administration;
(2) for political, philosophical, religious, or trade-union-related purposes by a non-profit organization provided that the personal data relate only to the members of such organization or to other persons who regularly participate in activities thereof;
(3) by mass media; and
(4) in relation to state and official secrets.

D.   SURVEILLANCE OF ELECTRONIC COMMUNICATIONS IN
      THE WORKPLACE

In respect to accessing and searching employees' e-mail accounts and electronic files, there is no specific regulation or relevant case law. Therefore, the Working Party's Working Paper 55 on the surveillance of electronic communications in the workplace[9] is followed in Lithuania as important guidance while interpreting the general rules set forth in the Data Protection Law.

Thus, any surveillance of electronic communications in the workplace should comply with the principles for e-mail and Internet monitoring set forth in the Working Paper 55,[10] that is:

(1) Necessity principle – the employer must check if any form of monitoring is absolutely necessary for a specified purpose before proceeding to engage in any such activity. Traditional methods of supervision, less intrusive for the privacy of individuals, should be carefully considered and where appropriate implemented before engaging in any monitoring of electronic communications.

(2) Finality principle – the personal data must be collected for a specified, explicit, and legitimate purpose and not further processed in a way incompatible with those purposes.

(3) Transparency principle – no secret monitoring is allowed, except for the cases where it may be justified by legitimate employer interests, that is, specific criminal activity has been identified or infractions in the workplace have been detected, and so forth.

(4) Legitimacy principle – e-mail and Internet monitoring can only take place if it has a legitimate purpose; that is, it is carried out for the purposes of legitimate interests pursued by the employer and it must not disproportionally infringe upon the fundamental rights of employees. The need of the employer to protect his or her business from significant threats, such as to prevent transmission of confidential information to a competitor, can be such a legitimate interest.

(5) Proportionality principle – personal data including those involved in monitoring must be adequate, relevant, and not excessive with regard to achieving the purpose specified. The company policy should be tailor made according to the type and the degree of risk that the particular company faces.

E.   INTERNATIONAL DATA TRANSFERS

Lithuanian data protection laws do not restrict transfer of personal data to the EEA member states. However, personal data may be transferred to a third country

---

9. Working Paper 55 of the Art. 29 Data Protection Working Party, 29 May 2002.
10. Item 3.1 of Working Paper 55.

outside the EEA only with permission by the State Data Protection Inspectorate of Lithuania and provided that an adequate level of data protection is ensured. Permission is not necessary in the cases where:

(1) the data subject has given the consent for the transfer;
(2) the transfer is necessary for the conclusion or performance of an agreement between the data controller and a third party in the interests of the data subject;
(3) the transfer of personal data is necessary for the performance of an agreement between the data controller and the data subject or for the implementation of pre-contractual measures to be taken in response to the data subject's request;
(4) the transfer of personal data is necessary (or required by laws) for important public interests or for the purpose of legal proceedings;
(5) the transfer is necessary for the protection of vital interests of the data subject;
(6) the transfer is necessary for the prevention or investigation of criminal offences; and/or
(7) the personal data are transferred from a public data file in accordance with the procedure set forth in laws.

The European Commission has determined which third countries ensure an adequate level of data protection. Currently, Argentina, Canada, Guernsey, Isle of Man, Jersey, and Switzerland are on the list. Personal data may also be transferred to US data recipients that have subscribed to the Safe Harbour scheme or Binding Corporate Rules (BCRs); however, official permission for all data transfers outside of the EEA is required. Typically, obtaining of the permission takes up to sixty days. It is very rarely that permission is denied, and in most cases it is issued almost automatically. An alternative way to ensure sufficient data safeguards is using Standard Contractual Clauses (SCCs) approved by the European Commission;[11] however, this does not eliminate the need for the official permission for data transfer outside of the EEA.

F.   SUPERVISION AND LIABILITY

The institution responsible for supervision of personal data processing in Lithuania is the State Data Protection Inspectorate. The main functions of the inspectorate include examination of complaints and notifications of individuals, inspections on lawfulness of personal data processing, making decisions concerning violations

---

11. Commission Decision 2001/497/EC of 15 Jun. 2001 on Standard Contractual Clauses for the transfer of personal data to third countries, under Directive 95/46/EC, and Commission Decision 2002/16/EC on Standard Contractual Clauses for the transfer of personal data to processors established in third countries, under Directive 95/46/EC.

related to personal data processing, granting authorizations to transfer personal data to third countries, and so forth.

Under Lithuanian laws, infringement of personal data protection requirements may cause administrative (not criminal) or civil liability. The Code of Administrative Offences[12] establishes administrative liability for unlawful data processing, unlawful processing of data of state information systems, infringements of the data subject's rights, non-performance of the inspectorate's orders, and infringement of privacy protection related to electronic communications. The sanctions for such infringements are monetary penalties of up to Litas (LTL) 2,000 (Euros [EUR] 570). In certain circumstances, unlawful data processing may also cause civil liability for damages suffered by an individual. While being rather insignificant, the penalties are relatively frequent in practice – about a hundred penalties are imposed every year. It is noteworthy that in cases where infringement has affected multiple individuals, the single infringement is asserted and the penalty is imposed only once (i.e., no multiple penalties are imposed). So far there are no known civil liability claims.

Yet another peculiarity of liability for data protection infringements in Lithuania is that it is always imposed against the individual (against the data protection officer or if no data protection officer is appointed, against the chief executive officer [CEO]) and not the infringing entity. The infringement record lapses after one year; that is, infringements committed after twelve months of fulfilling the sanctions for the prior infringement are not deemed repeat infringements.

III.   PRETRIAL DISCOVERY

A.   BACKGROUND

The mutual disclosure of documents and data is unknown in Lithuania. Under the Code of Civil Procedure,[13] litigants provide evidence, including documents and electronic documents, that support their claims and objections. However, the court may, under request of litigants, order that a document or item be submitted to the court as evidence, no matter whether it is in the possession of a litigant or a third party. The litigant who is requesting such an order has to specify the circumstances that may be proved by the requested evidence.

B.   BLOCKING STATUTES

Some countries, mainly those in civil law jurisdictions, but also a few common law countries, have introduced laws (blocking statutes) in an attempt to restrict cross-border discovery of information intended for disclosure in foreign jurisdictions.

---

12. The Code of Administrative Offences of the Republic of Lithuania, 13 Dec. 1984.
13. The Code of Civil Procedure of the Republic of Lithuania, 28 Feb. 2002.

Mindaugas Kiškis

However, the cooperation with foreign courts or public authorities in litigation or regulatory investigations and proceedings is not restricted under Lithuanian law. In particular, there are no 'blocking statutes' that prohibit the transfer of information to foreign countries.

C. HAGUE CONVENTION ON THE TAKING OF EVIDENCE

As Lithuania is a party to the Hague Convention on the Taking of Evidence,[14] requests for information may also be made through a standard procedure for issuing 'Letters of Request' or 'Letters Rogatory', which are petitions from the court of one country to the designated central authority of another requesting assistance from that authority in obtaining relevant information located within its borders.

However, Lithuania, as well as many other parties to the Hague Convention, has declared under Article 23 of the Convention that it will not execute a Letter of Request issued for the purpose of obtaining pretrial discovery of documents. According to the Hague Convention, pretrial discovery is a procedure that covers requests for evidence submitted after the filing of a claim but before the final hearing on the merits. Thus, the said reservation virtually prevents pretrial discovery in Lithuanian jurisdiction under the Hague Convention.

IV. LITHUANIAN DATA PROTECTION VERSUS PRETRIAL DISCOVERY

A. BACKGROUND

The Working Party's Working Paper 158 clearly stipulates that the Data Protection Directive does not prevent data transfers for litigation purposes. However, where data controllers seek to transfer personal data for litigation purposes there must be compliance with certain data protection requirements. As there is no explicit regulation or case law on balancing e-discovery and data protection requirements in Lithuania, Working Paper 158 of the Data Protection Working Party is followed as the main guidance in Lithuania while interpreting general provisions of the Data Protection Law.

B. LAWFULNESS OF DATA PROCESSING

Both retention and transfer of personal data in the course of the pretrial discovery process are regarded as data processing. Thus, they require respective justification;

---

14. Hague Convention on the Taking of Evidence Abroad in Civil and Commercial Matters, 18 Mar. 1970.

that is, such processing has to satisfy one of the said legal grounds set forth in the Data Protection Law. There appear to be three relevant grounds, namely consent of the data subject, necessity for compliance with a legal obligation, or the legitimate interest pursued by the controller or by the third party to whom the data are disclosed.

Practically, the data subject's consent to data processing for litigation purposes can only be obtained in rare cases, while a pretrial discovery request would not be regarded as a legal obligation in the above meaning since Lithuania has made a reservation under Article 23 of the Hague Convention. Therefore, the most suitable ground would be that of legitimate interests pursued by the controller where such interests are not overridden by the interests of the data subject.

Clearly the interests of justice would be regarded as legitimate interests under the Personal Data Law. The interests of the data subject, who usually has no direct involvement in the litigation process, have to be balanced against these interests. Working Paper 158 provides for some guidance on balancing these interests. As a first step, data controllers should restrict disclosure if possible to anonymized or at least pseudonymized data. Then after filtering ('culling') the irrelevant data – possibly by a trusted third party in the EU – a much more limited set of personal data should be disclosed as a second step. Following these recommendations, data processing in the course of the pretrial discovery process would be regarded as lawful under Lithuanian data protection laws.

C.   LAWFULNESS OF DATA TRANSFER

Transfers of personal data in the course of the pretrial discovery process should satisfy the requirements set forth in the Data Protection Law as well. As mentioned, the Data Protection Law provides for the exception that personal data may be transferred outside the EEA without permit of the inspectorate even where an adequate data protection level is not ensured in cases where data are transferred for the purpose of legal proceedings. Thus, this provision may justify data transfers to third countries, for example, to the United States, in the course of pretrial discovery procedures.

The Data Protection Working Party suggests that the said provision should be applied in cases where the transfer of personal data for litigation purposes is likely to be a single transfer of all relevant information. In the cases where a significant amount of data is to be transferred, the use of BCRs or the Safe Harbour scheme should be considered.[15]

---

15. Working Paper 158, 13

V.   CONCLUSION

Lithuanian data protection laws do not prevent data transfers in the course of pretrial discovery procedures. In order to take place lawfully under Lithuanian laws, such procedures should comply with general data protection requirements, in particular those related to lawful data processing and data transfers.

Chapter 5.15
Luxembourg

Michel Molitor and Claire Leonelli*

I. INTRODUCTION

Luxembourg is a so-called civil law country where there is no real equivalent to pretrial discovery proceedings as known in common law countries. To this extent, one of the main principles of Luxembourg civil procedure consists of the fact that the burden of proof bears, as a rule, on the plaintiff, who has to offer evidence to support its case, and that the judge may reject as inadmissible the documents that have not been fairly and legally collected.

After a brief overview of the legal framework of civil pre-discovery proceedings in Luxembourg (section II), we will see how the specific requirements applying to the retention, processing, and transfer of data qualified as personal (section III) may impact foreign pre-e-discovery proceedings (section IV). Further conditions apply to the disclosure to third parties of data covered by banking secrecy, which may also fall within the definition of personal data, within the context of foreign pretrial proceedings (section V).

---

*   Michel Molitor, Partner, and Claire Leonelli, senior associate, MOLITOR, Avocats à la Cour.

Catrien Noorda & Stefan Hanloser, *E-Discovery and Data Privacy*, pp. 173–190.
© 2011 Kluwer Law International BV, The Netherlands.

II.   FOREIGN CIVIL PRE-DISCOVERY PROCEEDINGS:
           LEGAL FRAMEWORK

A.   BLOCKING STATUTE

Except EC Regulation Number 2271/96,[1] which is fully in force in Luxembourg, there is no express blocking statute in Luxembourg prohibiting the transfer of information abroad.

B.   CIVIL COOPERATION ON THE TAKING OF EVIDENCE WITHIN THE EU

Within the European Union (EU), the cooperation between the courts on the taking of evidence in civil or commercial matters is regulated by the Council Regulation (EC) Number 1206/2001 of 28 May 2001 (the 'Regulation 1206/2001').

This Regulation applies in civil or commercial matters where the court of a Member State, in accordance with the provisions of the law of that State, requests: (i) the competent court of another Member State to take evidence; or (ii) to take evidence directly in another Member State.

The execution of a request may be refused only for specific reasons listed by the Regulation. These specific reasons do not cover pretrial proceedings.

C.   CIVIL COOPERATION ON THE TAKING OF EVIDENCE OUTSIDE THE EU

1.   Hague Convention on the Taking of Evidence

Luxembourg is party to the Hague Convention on the Taking of Evidence Abroad in Civil or Commercial Matters of 18 March 1970 (the 'Hague Convention on the Taking of Evidence').

Luxembourg has made the reservation as meant in Article 23 of the Hague Convention in its ratification act of 26 July 1977.

2.   Other Cases

In the event that neither the Hague Convention on the Taking of Evidence nor other bilateral conventions are applicable, pretrial requests delivered by a court or a public officer from non-EU countries need to be submitted in Luxembourg to a exequatur procedure, that is, a court decision authorizing the enforcement of such requests.[2] Such exequatur proceeding would typically be applicable to US

---

1. Council Regulation (EC) No. 2271/96 of 22 Nov. 1996 protecting against the effects of the extra-territorial application of legislation adopted by a third country, and actions based thereon or resulting therefrom.
2. Article 678 of the Luxembourg New Code of Civil Procedure.

e-discovery proceedings considering the reservations filed by Luxembourg under the Hague Convention on the Taking of Evidence.

The exequatur of the pretrial request will only be granted if the following conditions are met:

- The request has the character of a writ of execution in the country where it is rendered.[3]
- The judge who issued the request has international jurisdiction over the case according to its applicable law as well as according to the Luxembourg international law.
- The request is rendered under the forms prescribed by the applicable foreign law and according to the law applicable to the merits of the case pursuant to Luxembourg law.
- The decision is not contrary to the Luxembourg public order.

III.   LUXEMBOURG DATA PROTECTION
           LAW: BACKGROUND

The Luxembourg law on the protection of individuals with regard to the processing of personal data dated 2 August 2002, as amended (the 'Luxembourg Data Protection Law') has implemented into local law Directive 95/46/EC. It has abrogated the previous law of 31 March 1979 regulating the use of personal data in the computing field.

The Luxembourg Data Protection Law applies to the processing of personal data (discussed under section A below) and states the conditions of lawfulness of such processing (section B); it also contains special provisions regulating more specifically the personal data of employees (section C) and cross-border transfers (section D).

A.   Luxembourg Data Protection Law: Material and
           Territorial Scope

1.   **Material Scope of the Luxembourg Data Protection Law**

The Luxembourg Data Protection Law applies to 'personal data', which is defined as '*any information of any type regardless of the type of medium, including sound and image, relating to an identified or identifiable natural person*' ('data subject').

Natural persons are considered to be identifiable if they can be identified, directly or indirectly, in particular by reference to an identification number or one or more factors specific to their physical, physiological, genetic, mental, cultural, social, or economic identity.

The notion of 'personal data' therefore covers a wide range of data, such as names, addresses, telephone numbers, e-mails, identification numbers, and also

---

3.   Luxembourg District Court ('*Tribunal d'arrondissement*'), 19 Oct. 1955, *Pas.* 17, 35.

banking account references. It does not include data related to a corporate body whose confidential data are not protected by the Luxembourg Data Protection Law.

It further applies to: (i) the processing of data wholly or partly by automatic means, and to the processing otherwise than by automatic means of personal data that form part of a filing system or are intended to form part of a filing system; (ii) any form of capture, processing, and dissemination of sounds and images allowing to identify natural persons; and (iii) the processing of data relating to public security, defence, investigating and prosecuting criminal offences, or the State security, even if those data are related to a major economic or financial interest of the State, without prejudice to the specific provisions of national or international law governing these areas.

2.   Territorial Scope of the Luxembourg Data Protection Law

The Luxembourg Data Protection Law applies to: (i) any processing carried out by a data controller established in the territory of Luxembourg; or (ii) any processing by a data controller that is not based in Luxembourg territory or the territory of any Member State of the EU but that uses processing resources situated in Luxembourg territory, with the exception of resources that are used only for the purposes of transit through the said territory or that of another EU Member State.

A 'data controller' is defined by Article 2 (n) of the Luxembourg Data Protection Law as a natural or legal person, public authority, agency, or any other body that solely or jointly with others determines the purposes and methods of processing personal data.

B.   LUXEMBOURG DATA PROTECTION LAW: LAWFULNESS OF PROCESSING

According to the Luxembourg Data Protection Law, any processing of personal data has to comply with the conditions discussed in the following subsections.

1.   Quality of the Personal Data Processed

According to Article 4, paragraph 1 of the Luxembourg Data Protection Law, the data controller must ensure that the personal data are processed fairly and lawfully and especially that these data are: (i) collected for specified, explicit, and legitimate purposes and not further processed in a way incompatible with those purposes; (ii) adequate, relevant, and not excessive in relation to the purposes for which they are collected and/or further processed; (iii) accurate and, where necessary, kept up to date; every reasonable step must be taken to ensure that data that are inaccurate or incomplete, having regard to the purposes for which they were collected or for which they are further processed, are erased or rectified; and (iv) kept in a form that permits identification of data subjects for no longer than is necessary for the purposes for which the data were collected or for which they are further processed.

2.   Legitimacy of Processing

According to Article 5 of the Luxembourg Data Protection Law, personal data may be processed only if:

(i) it is necessary for compliance with a legal obligation to which the controller is subject; or

(ii) it is necessary for the performance of a task carried out in the public interest or in the exercise of official authority vested in the controller or in a third party to whom the data are disclosed; or

(iii) it is necessary for the performance of a contract to which the data subject is party or in order to take steps at the request of the data subject prior to entering into a contract; or

(iv) it is necessary for the purposes of the legitimate interests pursued by the controller or by the third party or parties to whom the data are disclosed, except where such interests are overridden by the interests for fundamental rights and freedoms of the data subject; or

(v) it is necessary in order to protect the vital interests of the data subject; or

(vi) the data subject has given his or her consent.

Moreover, as a rule, processing of sensitive data, namely personal data that reveals, directly or indirectly, the racial and ethnic origins, the political, philosophical, religious opinions, or the trade union affiliation of persons, or which concern their health or sexual life, are prohibited pursuant to Article 6, paragraph 1 of the Luxembourg Data Protection Law.

By exception, processing of such data is possible in the main following cases:

(a) the data subject gave his or her express consent to such processing, subject to the inalienability of the human body and unless forbidden by law;

(b) the processing is necessary for the purposes of carrying out the obligations and specific rights of the data controller in the field of employment law insofar as it is authorized by law;

(c) the processing is necessary to protect the vital interests of the data subject or of another person where the data subject is physically or legally incapable of giving his or her consent;

(d) the processing is carried out with the consent of the data subject by a foundation, association, or any other non-profit-seeking body with a political, philosophical, religious, or trade union aim in the course of its legitimate activities and on condition that the processing relates to the necessary data solely of members of that body or to persons who have regular contact with it in connection with its purposes and that the data are not disclosed to third parties without the consent of the data subjects;

(e) the processing relates to data that have been clearly made public by the data subject;

(f) the processing is necessary to acknowledge, exercise, or defend a right at law; or

(g) the processing is necessary in the public interest for historical, statistical, or scientific reasons.

3. Security of the Personal Data Processed

According to Articles 22 and 23 of the Luxembourg Data Protection Law, the data controller must implement appropriate technical and organizational measures to protect personal data against accidental or unlawful destruction or accidental loss, alteration, and unauthorized disclosure or access, in particular, where the processing involves the transmission of data over a network, and against all other unlawful forms of processing.

4. Information of the Data Subject

According to Articles 26 and 28 of the Luxembourg Data Protection Law, data subjects have to be informed of: (i) the identity of the data controller and of his or her representative, if any; (ii) the purposes of the processing for which the data are intended; and (iii) when particular circumstances require that providing data subjects with such information is necessary to ensure them a fair processing of their data, any of the following further information: (a) the recipients or categories of recipients of the data; (b) the possible consequences for them of the absence of a reply; and (c) that they have the right to obtain communication, in an accessible form, of their personal data as well as the right to rectify them.

5. Formalities with the Luxembourg Data Protection Authority

As a rule, any processing of personal data has to be notified to the Luxembourg Data Protection Authority, that is, the *'Commission Nationale pour la Protection des Données'* (the 'CNPD'), beforehand. The notification procedure is a declaration procedure to the CNPD.

By exception, certain processing of personal data is exempt from any notification formalities, provided it complies with specific requirements, while other processing operations cannot be carried out before the prior authorization of the CNPD or of the Luxembourg government.

C.   LUXEMBOURG DATA PROTECTION LAW: EMPLOYEES' PERSONAL DATA

1. Legitimacy of the Processing of Employees' Personal Data

The processing of employees' personal data by their employers has to comply with the general principles described here above. In particular, the processing of employees' personal data has to be legitimated by one of the grounds listed by the Luxembourg Data Protection Law.

In this respect the consent of employees is not considered as a legitimate ground since it is considered that, due to the relationship of authority with the employer, such consent cannot be 'freely given'.

In practice, the processing of employees' personal data is considered as legitimate either when such processing is necessary for the employer to comply with a legal obligation or when it is necessary for the performance of the employment contract.

The processing of employees' personal data can only be carried out for the purposes for which they were collected and cannot infringe the privacy of employees.

Indeed, Luxembourg case law considers that employees benefit from a residual sphere of privacy at work and that they need to be protected from excessive monitoring by their employers.

More specifically, Luxembourg case law considers that employees have a right to the secrecy of correspondence, as enshrined by Article 28 of the Luxembourg Constitution, Article 460 of the Luxembourg Criminal Code, and Article 2 of the law relating to privacy of 11 August 1982.

According to this principle, it is not allowed to open private mails of employees without their prior consent, even if employees are not authorized to use the employer's information technologies for personal purposes.

E-mails and files received, sent, or stored on employees' computers are deemed to be professional, unless otherwise identified by their titles or the names of their folders. The employers therefore can review them unless they are marked 'private'.

2. Monitoring of Employees

In addition, any processing with the purpose of monitoring employees' activities has to comply with the provisions of Article L. 261-1 of the Luxembourg Labour Code.

Any investigation carried out by employers to discover e-documents with the purpose of checking the activities of their employees or with the effect of accessing private documents, files, or e-mails of employees would fall under these provisions.

The application of the Personal Data Protection Law and Article L. 261-1 of the Labour Code to processing with the purpose of monitoring employees, which may include e-discovery investigations, has the consequences discussed in the following subsections.

a. *Legitimacy of the Data Processed*

Article L. 261-1 of the Luxembourg Labour Code states that processing with the purpose of monitoring the employees' activities is only allowed if such is necessary:

- to ensure the safety and the health of the employees;
- to ensure the protection of the employer's assets;

- to supervise the production process relating exclusively to mechanical devices;
- to temporarily supervise the production or the performances of employees, when such a measure is the only way to determine their exact salaries; or
- for the purposes of a working time organization by flexible hours.

This list is limited and contains the only grounds that may be invoked to justify the processing of employees' personal data for monitoring purposes.

The CNPD clarified, in decision Number 73 dated 1 July 2005, that the term *'protection of the employer's goods'* justifies processing whose purpose is the monitoring of employees at work in order to protect the assets and the trade secrets of the employer against destruction, theft, vandalism, to prevent the disclosure of confidential information, and to guarantee the security and the functioning of the computer network.

However, according to the CNPD, the term 'protection of the employer's assets' does not enable the employer to monitor that its employees do not use their computing tools to commit acts likely to render the employer liable (such as sending defamatory e-mails, for instance). The 'protection of the employer's assets' also does not justify that the employer uses monitoring tools to verify that its employees do not breach the internal working rules (which may, for instance, prevent employees from using computing tools for personal reasons).

Consequently, in the above-mentioned decision, the CNPD considered as legitimate the two following purposes invoked by the claimant:

- the protection of economic, commercial, and financial interests of the company with a confidential character as well as the fight against prohibited practices (for instance, unfair competition, disclosure of files, violation of trade secrets or infringement of intellectual property rights owned by third parties, damage to the brand image of the company, etc.); and
- the security and/or the proper operation of computing systems, including the control of costs as well as the material protection of the company's facilities (for instance, overrun of the system, virus, etc.).

The CNPD also stated that the two following grounds could not justify the processing of personal data related to the employees for monitoring purposes:

- the prevention of unlawful acts, defamation, acts likely to be detrimental to human dignity (such as surfing on pornographic or pedophiliac websites or acts of racial, ethnical, or religious discrimination); and
- the compliance with principles and rules of use of the company's information technologies resources, especially those set forth in the internal working rules.

This decision does not prevent employers from enacting internal rules prohibiting employees from certain unlawful behaviours, such as downloading illegal content from the Internet, but forbids employers to control the use of the information technologies for these purposes.

Thus, what would be the conclusion in respect of US e-discovery investigation to substantiate or defend a legal claim? Please see section III below.

b.   *Proportionality of the Data Processing*

According to the CNPD, the employer must first carry out global controls of log files, hard disks, and e-mailboxes. It is only if such global controls reveal some irregularities (such as too-high use of the Internet passband, for instance) that the employer may perform individualized controls.

c.   *Information of the Employees*

Employees must be informed of the applicable working rules as well as any processing of their personal data and must be provided with information concerning, *inter alia,* the data controller, the purposes of the processing, and their rights to access and request correction of their personal data collected.

d.   *Information of the Employees' Representatives*

According to Article L. 261-1, paragraph 2 of the Labour Code, the Company Joint Committee,[4] or otherwise the employees' representatives, or otherwise the Inspectorate of Labour and Mines, has to be informed beforehand of any processing whose purpose is to monitor employees.

In addition, the Company Joint Committee, if any, has a power of deciding on whether or not processing for monitoring purposes is justified by one of the following motives:

- the employees' security and health;
- the temporary supervision of production or the performances of employees, when such a measure is the only way to determine their exact salaries; and
- the organization of working time by flexible hours.

The Company Joint Committee does not have a decision power when the data processing is necessary to ensure the protection of the employer's goods.

e.   *Prior Authorization of the CNPD*

According to Article 14, paragraph 1 b) of the Luxembourg Data Protection Law, any processing with the purpose of monitoring employees must be authorized by the CNPD in advance.

---

4. The Company Joint Committee ('*Comité mixte d'entreprise*') is a body of employees' representative that is mandatory in any company exceeding 150 employees over the three last years.

D. Luxembourg Data Protection Law – Cross-
Borders Transfers

1. Principles

As a rule, the transfer of personal data is free within the EU, provided that data subjects are duly informed of such transfer.

According to Article 18, paragraph 1 of the Luxembourg Data Protection Law, the data controller may not transfer personal data to a State that is not a Member State of the EU if this State does not offer a sufficient level of protection of individuals' privacy, liberties, and fundamental rights with regard to the actual or possible processing of their personal data.

The United States is considered as a non-safe country in this respect. By exception, US companies that have voluntarily adhered to the Safe Harbour scheme may freely receive personal data from Luxembourg. The question of what would apply to a US court order will be referred to under section IV below.

2. Exceptions

By exception, the data controller may transfer personal data to a non-safe country within the meaning set forth above if the data subject has expressly consented to the transfer or if the transfer is necessary for:

- the protection of the data subject's life;
- the protection of a public interest;
- the meeting of obligations ensuring the establishment, exercise, or defence of legal claims;
- the consultation, in accordance with legal conditions, of a public register that, according to legislative and regulatory provisions, is intended for public information and is open for public consultation or by any person demonstrating a legitimate interest;
- the performance of a contract between the data controller and the data subject, or of pre-contractual measures taken in response to the data subject's request; and
- the conclusion or performance of a contract, either concluded or to be concluded in the interest of the data subject between the data controller and a third party.

When the above-mentioned exceptions are not applicable, transfers of personal data to a State that does not offer a sufficient level of protection of individuals' privacy have to be authorized by the CNPD beforehand. The authorization of the CNPD in relation thereto is granted when the processing guarantees a sufficient level of protection of individuals' privacy as well as their liberties and fundamental rights, particularly on account of contractual clauses in accordance with Commission Decisions 2001/497 EC, or 2004/497 EC, or Binding Corporate Rules (BCRs) relating to the processing.

The signing of an agreement containing one of the relevant sets of clauses enacted by the European Commission for the transfer of personal data is strongly advisable (even if not compulsory), as the CNPD will be more likely to authorize the transfer.

Finally, the transfer of personal data outside the EU must be adequate, relevant, and non-excessive in relation to the purposes for which the data are transferred.

E.   LUXEMBOURG DATA PROTECTION LAW – SANCTIONS

1.   Criminal Sanctions

Anyone who infringes the requirements related to the confidentiality and security of the processed personal data as set by the Luxembourg Data Protection Law incurs eight days to six months of imprisonment and/or a Euros (EUR) 251 to EUR 125,000 fine.

Article 2 of the law of 11 August 1982 on privacy states that anyone who has voluntarily infringed someone's privacy by opening a message sent or forwarded in sealed envelope, taking knowledge of its content, or by deleting such a message incurs eight days to one year of imprisonment and/or a EUR 251 to EUR 5,000 fine.

Violations of the secrecy of correspondence are also published by Article 460 of the Luxembourg Criminal Code, according to which anyone who has deleted or opened a letter sent through postal services incurs eight days to one month of imprisonment and/or a EUR 251 to EUR 2,000 fine.

2.   Civil Sanctions

The non-compliance with the Luxembourg Data Protection Law may give rise to civil liability of the data controller in cases where such non-compliance causes or may cause damage to third parties.

Moreover, before civil courts, evidence obtained through processing that does not comply with the Luxembourg Data Protection Law is declared inadmissible and especially cannot be used to justify dismissal of employees.[5]

3.   Administrative Sanctions

Following a breach of the Luxembourg Data Protection Law, the CNPD may issue administrative sanctions, such as injunctions against the data controller to stop the data processing. The CNPD cannot, however, enact fines against the data controller who does not comply with the Luxembourg Data Protection Law.

---

5. Luxembourg Labour Court, 5 Mar. 2002, Laurent ./. Dyckerhof matériaux Achat S.A.

Michel Molitor and Claire Leonelli

IV.   FOREIGN CIVIL PRE-DISCOVERY PROCEEDINGS
           VERSUS LUXEMBOURG DATA PROTECTION LAW

According to Article 2(s) of the Luxembourg Data Protection Law, *'any operation or set of operations performed upon personal data, such as collection, recording, organisation, storage, retrieval, consultation, use, disclosure by transmission, dissemination or otherwise making available'*, operations that are usually required in the process of a pretrial discovery, are considered as processing of personal data.

With this respect, the data processing of information, within the frame of pretrial e-discovery, will have to comply with the above-mentioned provisions required under the Luxembourg Data Protection Law (see section B below).

The main issue consists of the determination of the grounds that may justify the transfer of personal data within the context of pre-discovery proceedings (see section A below).

A.   LEGITIMACY

The processing of personal data within the scope of pretrial discovery procedures needs to meet one of the legitimate grounds set out in Article 5 of the Luxembourg Data Protection Law.

1.   **Consent of the Data Subject**

The first ground that might be invoked by the data controller in order to justify the processing of personal data abroad in the context of a foreign pre-discovery trial could consist of the consent of the data subject.

Article 2(c) defines the consent of the data subject as *'any (. . .) free, specific and informed indication of his wishes by which the data subject or his legal, judicial or statutory representative signifies his agreement that the personal data may be processed'*.

Valid consent means that the data subject must have a real opportunity to withhold his or her consent without suffering any penalty, or to withdraw it subsequently if the data subject changes his or her mind.

In this respect, the Working Party set up under Article 29 of Directive 95/46/EC, an independent European advisory body on data protection and privacy that issued on 11 February 2009 the Working Document 1/2009 on pretrial discovery for cross-border civil litigation, considers that *'it is unlikely that in most cases consent would provide a good basis for processing'*.

Indeed, in most cases in practice, data subjects are employees whose consent is not considered as free due to their subordinate relationship with their employer.

As the Article 29 Working Party states in its paper, *'relying on consent may prove to be a "false good solution", simple at first glance but in reality complex and cumbersome'*.[6]

---

6.   Working Document 1/2009 on pretrial discovery for cross-border civil litigation, 9.

2.   Necessary for Compliance with a Legal Obligation

The processing of personal data in the context of foreign pretrial e-discovery might be legitimate if such processing is necessary for compliance with a legal obligation to which the controller is subject.

However, in this respect the Article 29 Working Party considers that an obligation imposed by a foreign legal statute or regulation may not qualify as a legal obligation by virtue of which data processing in the EU would be made legitimate, except if there exists a legal obligation in Member States of the EU to comply with an order of a court in another jurisdiction seeking discovery.

In Luxembourg, the CNPD has not ruled on this issue but it is very likely that the CNPD will rely on the opinion of the Article 29 Working Party. Consequently, it may be assumed that an order of an EU jurisdiction seeking discovery based on Regulation 1206/2001 could constitute a legitimate ground as regards the Luxembourg Data Protection Law, contrary to orders based on the Hague Convention on the Taking of Evidence, since Luxembourg has declared that Letters of Requests taking place in the context of pretrial proceedings will not be executed under this Convention.

3.   Compliance with a Legitimate Interest

Finally, compliance with the requirements of the pretrial e-discovery may be found to be necessary for the purposes of a legitimate interest pursued by the data controller or by the third party to whom the data are disclosed.

According to the Article 29 Working Party, this basis would only be acceptable where such legitimate interests are not *'overridden by the interests for fundamental rights and freedoms of the data subject'*. The Article 29 Working Party also invites to proceed with an *in concreto* assessment of the legitimate interest and data subjects' fundamental rights by carrying out a balance test taking into account issues of proportionality, the relevance of the personal data to the litigation, and the consequences for the data subject.

Once again, it is very likely that the CNPD will adopt a similar position in such cases.

B.   Conditions

Any data processing made within the scope of pretrial discovery that may be found legitimate will also have to comply with the above-mentioned requirements of the Luxembourg Data Protection Law, such as, among others, the formalities with the CNPD, which can take a significant period of time, especially when the prior authorization of the CNPD is required.

In the context of pretrial discovery, the requirements discussed in the following subsections need to be especially highlighted.

1.   Proportionality

According to Article 4, paragraph 1 of the Luxembourg Data Protection Law, personal data must be adequate, relevant, and not excessive in relation to the purposes for which they are collected and/or further processed.

The Article 29 Working Party notes that '*in relation to litigation there is a tension in the discovery process in seeking a balance between the perceived need of the parties to obtain all information prior to then determining its relevance to the issues within the litigation and the rights of the individuals where their personal data is included within the information sought as part of the litigation process*'. Moreover, it is a '*duty upon the data controllers involved in litigation to take such steps as are appropriate (...) to limit the discovery of personal data to that which is objectively relevant to the issues being litigated*'.

The Article 29 Working Party therefore invites the data controller to proceed with a 'filtering activity', which includes the possible anonymisation of data if need be, and to involve the data protection officers from the earliest stage.

2.   Transfers to Non-Safe Third Countries

As already mentioned, transfers of personal data to a non-EU country that does not provide a sufficient level of the protection of individuals' privacy, liberties, and fundamental rights are only possible if they are justified by one of the grounds listed by the Luxembourg Data Protection Law or authorized by the CNPD.

In this respect, it may be wondered whether such transfer of personal data may be justified as necessary to the meeting of obligations ensuring the establishment, exercise, or defence of legal claims.

The Article 29 Working Party considers that the transfer of personal data for litigation purposes can fall within the scope of the above-mentioned exception. It, however, notes that this exemption cannot be used to justify the transfer of all employee files to a group's parent company on the grounds of the possibility that legal proceedings may be brought one day in US courts. By rising such reserve, the Article 29 Working Party seems to imply that the transfer of personal data for litigation purposes can only be justified as necessary to the meeting of obligations ensuring the establishment, exercise, or defence of legal claims if such legal claims already exist and are not only hypothetical.

In addition, the Article 29 Working Party recognizes that compliance with a request made under the Hague Convention would provide a formal basis for a transfer of personal data but recognizes that not all Member States have signed the Hague Convention, and that even if a State has signed, it may be with reserva-tions, which is actually the case of Luxembourg. As already mentioned, pretrial e-discovery US requests need to comply with the exequatur procedure mentioned under section II above in order to be enforceable in Luxembourg.

Consequently, it is likely that the transfer of personal data to the United States within the context of pretrial investigations will be considered as necessary to the meeting of obligations ensuring the establishment, exercise, or defence of legal claims if and only if the Luxembourg court accepts to declare enforceable in Luxembourg the pretrial e-discovery United States request. In the absence of such declaration of enforceability from the Luxembourg Courts, it is likely that the transfer of personal data to the United States within the context of a pretrial discovery US requests will be subject to the prior authorization of the CNPD.

V. LUXEMBOURG BANKING SECRECY – OVERVIEW

A. LUXEMBOURG BANKING SECRECY

1. Principles

According to Article 41, paragraph 1 of the Luxembourg law of 5 April 1993 on the financial sector, as amended (the 'Banking Law'), directors, members of management and supervisory bodies, managers, employees, and all other persons employed by credit institutions, other professionals of the financial sector, settlement agents, central counterparties, clearing houses, and foreign operators of systems authorized in Luxembourg are obliged to keep secret all information entrusted to them in the course of their professional activities.

The disclosure of such information shall be punished pursuant to Article 458 of the Luxembourg Criminal Code (see point 2 below on the sanctions).

In application of these provisions, any professional of the financial sector is in principle prohibited from disclosing to third parties data covered by banking secrecy.

Data protected by banking secrecy include any information concerning the relationship between a client and a professional of the financial sector established in Luxembourg, such as the client's financial situation and investment profile, his or her bank statements or asset portfolio, and also the simple fact to be client or not of such establishment.[7]

Banking secrecy is thus considered as *'the obligation for the bank to keep secret the information that it has received within the scope of its activities'*.[8]

2. Exceptions

Article 41, paragraph 2 of the Banking Law states that the obligation to secrecy ceases when the disclosure of information is authorized or imposed by or under the terms of a legal provision, even if the implementation of such legal provisions has preceded the Banking Law.

---

7. Haiko Heymer, 'La gestion internationale du risque bancaire face au secret professionnel au Luxembourg', ALJB, Bulletin Droit et Banque n°41, 19.
8. Alain Steichen, 'Le secret bancaire face aux autorités nationales et étrangères', Bulletin droit et banque, novembre 1995, n°24, 24 à 57; Luxembourg Court of Appeal, 28 Nov. 2000, N° 19224.

Michel Molitor and Claire Leonelli

Moreover, pursuant to Article 41, paragraph 3 of the Banking Law, the obligation to secrecy does not apply vis-à-vis national and foreign authorities in charge of prudential supervision acting within their powers and for the purpose of such supervision, and provided the information communicated is covered by the professional secrecy of the supervisory authority receiving it. The transmission of necessary information to a foreign authority for the purposes of prudential supervision must be made through the parent company or the shareholder or the member itself subject to such supervision.

Article 5 of the Luxembourg law dated 12 November 2004 on anti-money laundering, as amended, states that professionals of the financial sector have to cooperate with the Luxembourg authorities in charge of the fight against money laundering and the financing of terrorism.

Article 458 of the Luxembourg Criminal Code discharges the banks of any criminal liability when they are called to testify with the courts and when the disclosure of data covered by banking secrecy is imposed by law.

In the same way, Article 41, section 7 of the Banking Law discharges professionals of the financial sector of any civil or criminal liability when acting in the context of the above-mentioned legal exceptions.

Finally, it is worth mentioning that in addition to those legal exceptions to banking secrecy, Luxembourg case law has confirmed that banking secrecy is not absolute, notably by a decision of the Luxembourg Court of Appeal dated 5 November 2003.[9]

In this decision, the Luxembourg Court of Appeal has stated that banking secrecy 'ceases in front of the protection of the rights recognized by law or acknowledged by Courts' and that 'it is necessary that the enforced production of a document be indispensable to the manifestation of the truth and that the claimant do not have any other means to obtain the document'.

This case law might legitimate the disclosure of banking secrecy within the context of US e-discovery investigations. However, there is currently no published court decision that has decided upon this issue.

B.	SANCTIONS IN CASE OF NON-AUTHORIZED DISCLOSURE

1.	**Criminal Sanctions**

According to Article 458 of the Luxembourg Criminal Code, the disclosure of information covered by banking secrecy is punishable by eight days to six months of imprisonment and a EUR 500 to EUR 5,000 fine.

---

9. Luxembourg Court of Appeal dated 5 Nov. 2003 No. 26588, BIJ 2004, 8, as construed by Luxembourg Court of Appeal dated 24 Mar. 2004.

2.   Civil Sanctions

The obligation of confidence is also a civil law obligation. Disclosure of a secret may undoubtedly be detrimental to a client. Such may give rise to a liability action against the investment firm. According to Luxembourg case law, the obligation of banking secrecy is an obligation to achieve a result (*'obligation de résultat'*). The victim consequently has to prove the material breach of the bank as regards banking secrecy and that such a breach has caused him or her damage.[10]

3.   Disciplinary Sanctions

Following any breach of banking secrecy, the Luxembourg Supervisory Commission of the Financial Sector (the *'Commission de Surveillance de Surveillance Financier'* – the 'CSSF') may issue injunctions against the bank on the basis of Article 59 of the Banking Law, independently or on a complaint of a third party. To the extent that the bank does not follow any such injunction, its managers may be subject to suspension from the exercise of their functions.

Moreover, Article 7 of the Banking Law provides that the approval of the credit institution in Luxembourg is subject to the professional reputation of its management. Consequently, if the managers have committed criminal offences, they would no longer qualify for the purposes of such condition of reputation and one of the conditions for approval of the credit institution no longer exists. Such bank could therefore be subject to withdrawal of its banking license.

VI.   FOREIGN PRE-E-DISCOVERY PROCEEDINGS VERSUS LUXEMBOURG BANKING SECRECY

As mentioned above, Article 41, paragraph 2 of the Banking Law states that the obligation to secrecy ceases when the disclosure of information is authorized or imposed by or under the terms of a legal provision, even if the implementation of such legal provisions has preceded the Banking Law.

The first exception to banking secrecy is contained in Article 458 of the Luxembourg Criminal Code and provides that the banking secrecy is not applicable in cases of testimony before courts.

Luxembourg case law considers that the bank has the possibility to accept to disclose, at the occasion of a judicial testimony, information covered by banking secrecy but that it cannot be forced to do it.[11] However, the bank cannot spontaneously provide the court with documents.

Article 11 of the Hague Convention on the Taking of Evidence and Article 14, section 1 of Regulation 1206/2001 states that a request for the hearing of a person is

---

10. Luxembourg Court of Appeal, 2 Apr. 2003; Luxembourg Court of Appeal, 11 May 2005, No. 26434.
11. Luxembourg Supreme Court (*'Cour Supérieure de Justice'*), 21 Mar. 1957, *Pasicrisie* 17, 43.

not executed when the person concerned claims the right to refuse to give evidence or to be prohibited from giving evidence, notably under the law of the state of the requested court.

These Articles only cover testimonies and not the other measure of inquiry that may be ordered. Luxembourg authors, however, uphold that, insofar as banking secrecy may be opposed in civil proceedings and as the bank may refuse to produce documents, the same is applicable in the context of international legal assistance in civil matters.[12]

When banking secrecy covers data that refer to natural persons and not to companies, such data will also fall under the scope of the Luxembourg Data Protection Law.

---

12. Chapter 'Luxembourg', Pit Reckinger, in Neate: *Bank confidentiality*, 4ème ed., September 2006, IBA, 460.

Chapter 5.16

The Netherlands

*Catrien Noorda**

I.   RESTRICTIONS ON US PRETRIAL DISCOVERY IN
         THE NETHERLANDS

In the Netherlands, it is possible to file a request with a court to order the other party
to a legal relation to provide documents in respect of such relation. However, the
documents should to a certain extent be specified. 'Fishing expeditions' are not
allowed. The Netherlands also has made a reservation pursuant to Article 23 of the
the Hague Convention on the Taking of Evidence Abroad[1] treaty, providing that
requests for pretrial discovery will not be carried out.

        On the other hand, the Netherlands does not provide for a blocking statute
prohibiting a party to comply with requests for pretrial discovery as part of foreign
legal proceedings. If the potential evidence involves personal data, such pretrial
discovery requests will, however, have to comply with Dutch data protection law.

II.   DUTCH DATA PROTECTION LAW

Dutch data protection law is laid down in the Personal Data Protection Act (PDPA)
and general administrative regulations on the basis thereof. The PDPA is an

---

*   Catrien Noorda, Howrey LLP, Amsterdam, the Netherlands.
1.   The Hague Convention on the Taking of Evidence Abroad in Civil or Commercial Matters of 18
     Mar. 1970.

Catrien Noorda & Stefan Hanloser, *E-Discovery and Data Privacy*, pp. 191–199.
© 2011 Kluwer Law International BV, The Netherlands.

implementation of Directive 95/46 EC[2] (the 'Directive'). In addition to the PDPA, data protection rules may follow from sector-specific legislation such as the Social Securities Act or the Telecommunications Act. As this book is intended as a general guide, this contribution will be limited to the general rules following from the PDPA.

The supervisory authority monitoring compliance with the PDPA is the Data Protection Commission ('*College Bescherming Persoonsgegevens*'). In interpreting the PDPA in the light of the Directive, the Data Protection Commission generally follows the opinions of the Article 29 Working Party.

A.   SCOPE

The PDPA applies to the fully or partly automated processing of personal data and the non-automated processing of personal data entered into a file or intended to be entered therein.

1.   Processing of Personal Data

The definitions of processing and personal data are identical to the definitions in the Directive. The Dutch Data Protection Commission generally interprets the definitions broadly, thereby following the opinions of the Article 29 Working Party.

2.   Geographical Scope

The PDPA applies to the processing carried out in the context of the activities of an establishment of the controller in the Netherlands. According to the Data Protection Commission, this means that the PDPA does not apply in the event the controller has a branch office in the Netherlands but is established in another European country.[3] This seems contrary to the Directive, which provides that when the same controller is established in several Member States, it has to comply with the laws of each separate Member State. The opinion has been much critized in legal literature and it is uncertain whethera court would follow this opinion.[4]

B.   RULES FOR LEGITIMATE PROCESSING

1.   Legitimate Ground

Article 8 of the PDPA (which is virtually identical to Article 7 of the Directive) provides that a processing is only legitimate if one of the grounds enumerated in

---

2.   Directive 95/46 EC on the protection of individuals with record to the processing of personal data and on the free movement of such data.
3.   This opinion of the Data Protection Commission was put at issue by E.M.L. Moerel in Computerrecht 2008, 61, and was confirmed by the Commission in Computerrecht 2008, 108.
4.   See Moerel above and G-J Zwenne and P.C. Knol, Privacy & Informatie 2009, 173–179.

Article 8 applies. Under Dutch data protection law, in practice, of the grounds enumerated in Article 8 PDPA, the following may serve as a basis for compliance with e-discovery requests:

(a) the data subject has unambiguously provided his or her consent for the processing (Article 8 under a); or

(b) the processing is necessary for the purposes of the legitimate interests pursued by the controller or by the third party or parties to whom the data are disclosed, except where such interests are overridden by the interests or fundamental rights and freedoms of the data subject, in particular his or her right to privacy (Article 8 under f).

Article 8 also provides that a processing may be based on 'compliance with a legal obligation' (Article 8 under c), but from the explanatory notes to the PDPA, it follows that this ground only applies to processing necessary for compliance with a Dutch national legal obligation.[5]

a.   *Concerning a Consent*

Under Dutch data protection law, consent has to comply with the requirements set out above (Chapter 3.E.1). This means that under Dutch law, employee consent would likely be considered invalid because of the requirement of Article 1 under i of the PDPA that consent should be 'freely given' (Article 2(h) of the Directive). Concerning b – Legitimate Interests

Because of the problems connected with consent as a basis for processing, most processing as part of e-discovery will have to be based on the legitimate-interest basis as provided in Article 8 of the PDPA. In this respect, in the Netherlands, the same applies as set out above (Chapter 3.E.2): the processing must be proportionate to the purposes thereof and the privacy interests of the data subject must be observed as much as possible. In the Dutch legal situation, this also means that correspondence that is marked private and correspondence by works council members has to be disregarded unless unlawful behaviour is specifically suspected.

2.   Special Categories of Data

In implementation of Article 8 of the Directive, the processing of the special categories of data mentioned therein is prohibited under the PDPA (Article 16 PDPA). The PDPA provides for several exemptions to this prohibition, none of which is likely to apply in the event of e-discovery investigations (Articles 17–22 PDPA). Therefore, special categories of data should be either disregarded or one of the general exemptions should be relied on. In this respect the same applies as set out above (re Chapter 3.E.2).

---

5. Even though this is not expressly mentioned, it follows from the terminology used, which is very specific for Dutch legislation (see Tweede Kamer, vergaderjaar 1997–1998, 25 892, No. 3, 83)

C.   TRANSPARENCY

1.   Informing Data Subjects

Pursuant to Article 34 of the PDPA, and in implementation of Articles 10 and 11 of the Directive, the data subject has to be informed of the identity of the controller, the purposes of the processing, and all other information necessary to guarantee a proper and careful processing, ultimately at the time of the recording of the data or, in the event data are to be transferred to a third party, no later than at the moment of transfer. In the event of processing of data for e-discovery purposes, 'other information' would include:

   (a) recipients or categories of recipients of personal data;
   (b) the existence of the right of access to and the right to rectify the data;
   (c) whether or not data are transferred to a country not offering an adequate protection level and the safeguards offered to nevertheless protect the data processing; and
   (d) whether or not the processing has been notified to the Data Protection Commission and if so under which notification number.

In implementation of the Directive, the PDPA provides that the obligations to provide information do not apply in the event such would prove an impossible or a disproportionate effort. Under Dutch law, it is defendable that it is a disproportionate effort to inform all of the individuals to which e-mail files may relate, that is, not only the sender and recipients of the emails but also persons put in 'cc' or who are just mentioned in the e-mails. Even though no case law is available about this issue, it seems sufficient to only inform the owners of e-mail accounts that are provided by the controller. In view of the explanatory notes to the PDPA, it is not likely that the disproportional effort exemption will apply in the event it is objectionable to at all inform the individuals because of a sensitive nature of the litigation or the risk that evidence is destroyed. However, in this event it could be argued that informing the individuals is contrary to the rights and freedoms of others (Article 13, section 1(g) of the Directive and 43(e) of the PDPA), arguing that 'others' would include the controller itself. Again no case law is available about this issue, but chances of success are increased if a controller has anticipated possible future e-discovery investigations and has implemented a general e-mail monitoring policy informing employees of possible future investigations (including the mandatory information set out above) in its organization.

2.   Notification of the Data Protection Commission

In accordance with Article 18 of the Directive, the PDPA (Article 27) provides that an automated processing that serves a single purpose or several related purposes has to be notified to the Data Protection Commission. The Exemption Regulation on the basis of the PDPA provides that certain categories of processing that are often present in organizations are exempt from the obligation to notify under specific conditions that are provided for each exemption. Amongst others, exemptions apply to employee and salary administrations, and to computer and communication systems. E-discovery investigations could fall within the scope of these exemptions as they do allow processing for the purposes of internal control and dispute handling. However, pursuant to Article 44 of the Exemption Regulation, the exemptions do not apply if data are transferred to a country outside of the European Economic Area (EEA) that is not considered by the Dutch Ministry to provide an adequate level of protection of personal data and the transfer is not necessary for vital interests or based on the consent of the individual. As US e-discovery will mostly involve a transfer to the United States, this means that US e-discovery processing will have to be notified to the Data Protection Commission.

A proposal to amend the Exemption Regulation is expected to enter into force during the course of 2010. Amongst others the proposal provides that transfers outside of the EEA under the Safe Harbour regime or on the basis of a license granted by the Dutch Ministry will no longer lead to inapplicability of an exemption. However, transfers for the defence of legal claims that are not taking place on the basis of Safe Harbour or a license will still fall outside the scope of the Exemption Regulation, which means that network systems eligible for US e-discovery searches will most likely remain subject to the notification obligation of the PDPA.

D.   RIGHTS OF THE DATA SUBJECT

The PDPA contains a detailed elaboration of the right of access provided in Article 12 of the Directive. Pursuant to Article 35 of the PDPA, the data subject has the right to request the controller to inform him or her of whether or not his or her personal data are processed. If such is the case, the controller has to provide the data subject with a complete overview of the data processed about him her, including a description of the purposes of the processing, the categories of data processed, and the recipients and categories of recipients of the data. Upon receipt of this overview, the data subject has the right to request correction, addition, removal, or shielding off of the data in case they are incorrect, incomplete, unlawful, or irrelevant for the purposes. If the controller refuses to comply with this request, the refusal has to be motivated in writing. Otherwise the controller has to comply with the request as soon as possible.

It will be clear that compliance with a request for rectification can be problematic in view of the US discovery rules. As in respect of the information obligation, it could be argued that compliance with a request for rectification is contrary to the rights and freedoms of others (which would include the controller; Article 13, section 1(g) of Directive and 43(e) of the PDPA). However, in the absence of case law in respect of this specific issue, it is not certain that the argument will succeed. An alternative could be to keep records of the rectification together with the original processing.

Catrien Noorda

E.   CONTROLLER/PROCESSOR

The responsibility to comply with obligations pursuant to the PDPA lies with the controller. The controller is defined in Article 1, section d of the PDPA as the party that, alone or with others, determines the purposes of and the means for the processing of personal data. The controller should be distinguished from the processor, which is defined by Article 1, under section f, as the party that processes personal data on behalf of the controller without being subject to its direct authority. The latter part of this definition, which is not included in the definition as provided in the Directive, has been added to distinguish the processor from employees working within the organization of the controller. If third parties such as law firms or forensic accountants are involved in performing e-discovery investigations, they will in most instances qualify as processors. Also, if an e-discovery investigation in respect of a group of companies takes place centrally within one group company, such company will likely qualify as processor on behalf of the other group companies. Pursuant to Article 14 of the PDPA, the controller has to enter into processing agreements with the processors, which should contain at least the following mandatory provisions:

(1) the processor may only process personal data on the instructions of the controller;
(2) the processor has to guarantee appropriate technical and organizational measures in accordance with Article 13 of the PDPA (or of the data privacy act applicable in the Member State where the processor is established) to safeguard the data processing; and, as the controller, is obliged to make sure the measures are in place; and
(3) the controller has to be allowed to verify these measures.

F.   RULES FOR THE TRANSFER OF PERSONAL DATA

In implementation of Article 25 of the Directive, the PDPA provides that transfer of personal data to countries outside of the EEA is prohibited, unless the country concerned provides an adequate level of protection of personal data. The controller has to determine him- or herself whether or not the protection in a certain country can be considered adequate. In practice, the controller can, however, only assess this with reasonable certainty if the European Commission has designated the protection level in a certain country as adequate. As set out above, this is the case in respect of the United States if the recipient is certified to adhere to the Safe Harbour Privacy Principles. Otherwise, the transfer is permitted if one of the exemptions of Article 77, subsection 1 applies or if the Dutch Minister has granted a license for the transfer. As the exemptions are identical to Article 25 of the Directive and the Data Protection Commission follows the Article 29 Working Party opinions, in this respect reference is made to Chapter 3.H.

The Dutch Minister will grant a license for transfer if in his opinion the controller offers sufficient safeguards to protect the data. This will in any event be the case if the controller has entered into one of the EU Model Contracts with the recipient of the data or if Binding Corporate Rules (BCRs) are implemented within the controller's organization. As set out above in Chapter 3.H, these safeguards do not, however, provide a solution for onward transfers to counterparties in litigation or government institutions as part of the e-discovery or associated litigation. Nevertheless, they do provide a solution if transfers take place within a group or to a third-party processor as part of internal investigations in anticipation of e-discovery. In this respect it is important to be aware of the time involved in obtaining a license of the Dutch Ministry. At present, the lead time is two to four weeks for a simple transfer on the basis of Standard Contractual Clauses (SCCs). Obtaining a license on the basis of BCRs may take at least three months. In view hereof, it is advisable for multinational companies to have the desired structures and licenses to freely transfer data within the group in place before an e-discovery investigation ever takes place.

G. Sanctions/Enforcement

The PDPA does not provide for severe punitive sanctions. In the event a processing is not notified to the Data Protection Commission, an administrative or criminal fine of Euros (EUR) 4,500 may be imposed. The Data Protection Commission is not authorized to impose fines in the event the material provisions of the PDPA are violated.

In addition to the possibility to impose administrative fines, the Data Protection Commission has the power to exercise administrative force. This means that the Commission can start investigations as to the compliance of a company or an organization with the PDPA as part of which it can enter the premises with police force. If compliance is not sufficient, the Commission can issue an order under penalty sum to comply with the PDPA. Probably also as a result of the limited authority of the Data Protection Commission to impose punitive fines, this enforcement tool has been proven the most effective and has been exercised the most in recent years. In 2006–2009, the Data Protection Commission only imposed an administrative fine in three cases. Administrative force has been applied 135 times during these years (of which 68 took place in 2008).[6]

Finally, an individual may file a civil claim for an injunction or an order to provide access or rectification under penalty sum or claim damages in civil proceedings. As the monetary interests in starting litigation in relation to privacy are generally low, the amount of case law in respect thereof is limited.

---

6. Jaarverslag Cbp 2009.

H.   SPECIFIC RULES APPLICABLE TO E-MAIL AND INTERNET USAGE
      BY EMPLOYEES

The Data Protection Commission has published a report on the monitoring of
e-mail and Internet use by employees.[7] Even though the rules do not specifically
relate to search of e-mail files for the purposes of e-discovery, they do relate to
internal investigations regarding non-observance of company policy rules and
other possible misconduct. As such investigations will be conducted in a way
similar to e-discovery searches for evidence, the conditions under which those are
permitted provide guidance for e-discovery investigations as well. According to
the report, the provisions of the PDPA lead to the following rules of thumb to be
observed when investigating e-mail and other electronic files of employees:

(1) a clear policy on monitoring and searching e-mail and other electronic
    files has to be in place, setting out the purposes for which searching may
    be done, the categories of persons performing the search and having
    access to the search results, the way in which the interests of the data
    subjects will be safeguarded, and the way in which the rights of the data
    subjects can be exercised;
(2) the policy has to be published in a way easily accessible for the employee
    (for instance, a hard copy to be provided to the employee upon employ-
    ment and an electronic version permanently accessible through the
    intranet);
(3) the investigation has to be carried out using keywords as much as possible;
(4) reports on the investigation have to be anonymized as much as possible;
(5) the integrity of the persons conducting the investigations and having
    access to the reports has to be guaranteed by confidentiality obligations;
(6) private and business correspondence has to be separated as much as
    possible;
(7) the investigation has to be limited to the prior-defined purposes; and
(8) private correspondence, correspondence of works council members, and
    correspondence of a medical nature have to be disregarded as much as
    possible.

I.   EVALUATION OF THE PDPA

The effectiveness of the PDPA has recently been evaluated.[8] In its opinion on this
evaluation, the Dutch cabinet of ministers has announced that it will submit a
proposal to change the PDPA during the course of 2010.[9] The proposal will,

---

7. Goed werken in netwerken-Regels voor controle op e-mail en internet gebruik van werknemers,
    tweede herziene druk, College beschermng persoonsgegevens, April 2002.
8. Evaluatie Wbp 1e fase, Zwenne, G-J e.a. 2007 en Evaluatie Wbp 2e fase Winter, H.B. 2008,
    <www.wodc.nl>.
9. TK 2009–2010, 31051, No. 5.

amongst others, contain provisions to encourage self-regulation and to improve the authority of the Data Protection Commission to impose administrative fines (see below). Further changes of the PDPA are envisaged at a later stage as part of the general evaluation of the Directive.

III.   CONCLUSION

The conclusion is that in the Netherlands, processing of e-mails and other digital files containing personal data for e-discovery purposes is permitted, provided:

(1) the rules of thumb of the Data Protection Commission for e-mail monitoring are followed;
(2) only a limited set of personal data strictly necessary for the litigation is transferred to recipients outside of the EEA;
(3) data subjects are priory informed of the e-discovery process;
(4) processing agreements are entered into with possible processors and if processors are located outside of the EEA a permit is obtained on the basis of either BCRs or Model Contracts or, if the processor is located in the United States, Safe Harbour certification is in place; and
(5) the processing is notified to the Data Protection Commission.

Given the time involved with compliance, it is advisable to have a framework of measures (policy, notification, permit, Safe Harbour) in place before actual e-discovery ever takes place.

Chapter 5.17

Norway

*Attorney Line Coll and Rune Opdahl**

I.   INTRODUCTION

The main aim of data protection regulations is to provide a person with a certain
degree of control relating to the processing of personal data. Prevention of
unknown or unwanted disclosure of personal data is essential in meeting this.

E-discovery is, on the contrary, about ensuring and promoting disclosure of
data. Thus, there is an inherent conflict between these two legal conventions, which
may in some cases raise complex legal questions and be the source of possible
tension between parties involved.

Compared to data protection, pretrial discovery in general and e-discovery in
particular are rather recent acquaintances in Norway. Until now, this jurisdiction
has barely seen the beginning of the implications of e-discovery.

II.   NORWEGIAN DATA PROTECTION
            LAW: BACKGROUND

Norway has had general data protection and privacy legislation since the 1970s.
The Personal Register Act was passed in 1978. The European Data Protection
Directive was implemented in Norwegian law by passing of the Personal Data

*   Attorney Line Coll and Attorney Rune Opdahl, Wiersholm, Mellbye & Bech, Oslo, Norway.

Catrien Noorda & Stefan Hanloser, *E-Discovery and Data Privacy*, pp. 201–208.
© 2011 Kluwer Law International BV, The Netherlands.

Act (PDA, or Act) in April 2000, which entered into force on 1 January 2001.[1] Simultaneously, the subordinate Personal Data Regulations (PDR, or Regulations) of December 2000, which supplinent the PDA, entered into force.[2] The Act and the Regulations shall ensure that personal data are processed in accordance with fundamental respect for the right to privacy, including the need to protect personal integrity and private life and ensure that personal data are of adequate quality. The most recent amendments of the PDA came into effect on 1 September 2009, whereas the relevant amendments of the PDR – relating to e-mail access – came into effect 1 March 2009. The PDA is under revision. The expected finalization is some time during 2011.

In addition to the specific data protection laws, privacy and data protection are regarded as fundamental rights and are protected under the Norwegian Human Rights Act of 1999[3] with reference to Article 8 of the European Convention of Human Rights (ECH).

Recently, a few cases relating to the use of e-mails as legal evidence have created quite a stir in Norway. These cases were a starting point of a growing public awareness on the value of and privacy risks related to electronic documentation and e-mails in particular. The latest case of particular relevance is a decision by Asker og Bærum tingrett, regarding retention and discovery of employee e-mail communication.[4]

A.   Norwegian Data Protection Law: Personal Data

The PDA regulates all processing of personal data carried out wholly or partly by automatic means, and other processing of personal data that forms part of or is intended to form part of a personal data filing system. The Act applies to 'personal data', defined as any information and assessments that may be linked to a natural person. The term 'personal data' is defined and interpreted broadly. Hence, most kinds of data relating directly or indirectly to an identifiable natural person will be deemed as 'personal data' under the PDA. The PDA does not, as a main rule, apply to information relating to legal entities such as corporate data, business information, and so forth. However, information relating to legal entities may, in certain limited cases, be subject to the regulations set out in the PDA. This relates to processing of information about sole proprietorships and the processing of credit information relating to persons other than natural persons (see section 4-1, second paragraph of the PDR).

---

1. Lov om behandling av personopplysninger (personopplysingsloven), 14 Apr. 2000 No. 31.
2. Forskrift om behandling av personopplysninger (personopplysningsforkriften), 15 Dec. 2000 No. 1265.
3. Lov om styrking av menneskerettighetenes stilling i norsk rett (menneskerettsloven), 21 May 1999 No. 30.
4. Case 09-160051TVI-AHER/1 from 13 Nov. 2009. The decision may still be appealed, and thus the decision is not yet legally binding.

It is important to note that employees are subject to the same rights and obligations as any third party under the PDA. The parties in a discovery process may not rely on any privilege when it comes to the transfer and disclosure of information relating to employees that conflicts with the privacy rights of the employees.

B.   NORWEGIAN DATA PROTECTION LAW: EMPLOYEES' E-MAILS

E-mails are under Norwegian law defined as personal data. This applies regardless of their content (work related or private). The PDA and PDR regulate discovery of employees' e-mail correspondence. In addition, the Norwegian Employment Protection Act regulates control of employees, such as monitoring of their use of the information technology system.[5]

Discovery of employees' e-mails and other electronically stored information (ESI) on an employer's information technology system is in particular regulated in Chapter 9 of the Regulations. These provisions apply to existing and previous employees, as well as others (consultants) who have been or are engaged to work for the employer. It may under the circumstances also apply to students of schools and universities and for individuals engaged in work for organizations.

Pursuant to Chapter 9 of the PDR, accessing of employees' ESI is legal provided that: (i) access is necessary in order to safeguard daily business operations or other justified interests on the hand of the employer; or (ii) if there are strong reasons to believe that an employee through misuse of, for example, his or her e-mail account, is coarsely in breach of his or her work-related obligations. If one of these two conditions is fulfilled, employee consents are not required. This is an important aspect since it is questioned whether such consents may be deemed valid. Private communication through the employees' business e-mail accounts is not as such exempted from the scope of access. However, accessing such private communication will rarely fulfil the condition mentioned above. Thus, in practice, e-discovery processes conducted in Norway tend to handle ESI labelled 'private' or found in private folders more carefully than ESI with content that is presumably work related.

Discovery of employees' ESI is subject to certain procedural requirements, providing safeguards for the employees' privacy interests. Such procedural requirements, *inter alia,* relate to prior or subsequent notification and information to be provided to the employee(s).

Pursuant to section 9–5 of the PDR, the employer is not allowed through agreement, regulations, or by other means to derogate from the provisions of Chapter 9 of the PDR to the disadvantage of the employees.

---

5.   Lov om arbeidsmiljø, arbeidstid og stillingsvern mv. (arbeidsmiljøloven), 17 Jun. 2005 No. 62.

C.   NORWEGIAN DATA PROTECTION LAW: COLLECTION, PROCESSING, AND USE

Processing of personal data is regulated in accordance with the European Data Protection Directive. 'Processing' is defined broadly, and comprises a wide range of use of data – collection, storing, use, transfer, and so forth. Personal data may be processed only if requirements set out in section 11 of the PDA are met (which in all material aspects corresponds with Article 6 of the European Data Protection Directive). Subject to sections 8 and 11 of the PDA, personal data may only be processed if the data subject has consented thereto, if there is statutory authority for such processing, or if the processing is necessary in order to fulfil certain criteria set out in section 8 of the PDA.

For processing of sensitive personal data, comprising data such as information relating to health, sex life, racial or ethnic origin, or information about trade union membership, additional criteria are set out in section 9 of the PDA.

Pursuant to Chapter 6 of the PDA, processing of non-sensitive data is subject to a notification requirement, whereas processing of sensitive personal data is subject to a license requirement. However, the PDR sets out various exceptions to these requirements, relating, *inter alia,* to processing of employee, customer, and supplier data, which may be applicable in a pretrial discovery process.

D.   NORWEGIAN DATA PROTECTION LAW: DATA CONTROLLER; DATA PROCESSOR

The data controller is defined as the person who determines the purpose of the processing of personal data and which means are to be used. 'Person' should in this respect be interpreted as the legal entity in charge of the processing. The data controller is responsible for ensuring that all processing of personal data is in accordance with the PDA. This applies to both processing of personal data carried out by the controller itself and to processing done by a data processor on behalf of the controller.

A data processor is a person who processes personal data on behalf of the controller. Also here, the word 'person' must be interpreted as a legal entity taking on a processing assignment from the controller. The use of data processors may only take place subject to a specific data processing agreement (see section 15 of the PDA).

In an e-discovery process, the responding party in Norway would normally be considered a controller (similar to the foreign requesting party), whereas vendors engaged for the technical processing normally would be considered data processors.

E.   NORWEGIAN DATA PROTECTION LAW: TRANSFER ABROAD

Restrictions on transborder dataflow set out in sections 29 and 30 of the PDA are in accordance with the European Data Protection Directive. Transfer of personal data to controllers and processors in other EU Member States or member states of the European Economic Area (EEA) is not restricted, provided always that the general principles and criteria for data processing are met. If personal data are to be transferred to countries outside the EEA, that is, to third countries, this is only permitted if an equivalent level of data protection is ensured. Transfer of personal data to the United States is, as a starting point, deemed a transfer to a country without a satisfying level of data protection. The controller must assess this before transferring data.

Consent may establish a basis for transfer. However, it may be questioned whether consent for transfer of personal data in relation to e-discovery should be considered valid.

A legal basis for transfer of personal data to third countries may be established if the transfer is necessary for the establishment, exercise, or defence of legal claims. The Norwegian Data Inspectorate has in previous matters by informal channels of communication expressed reluctance to recognizing foreign pretrial regulations, such as the US discovery regime, in this context.

An adequate level of data protection may normally be obtained through a data transfer agreement between the requesting and responding party based on the EU model clauses. Use of such agreements as a basis for transfer of data to non-EU/EEA countries is subject to approval by the Norwegian Data Inspectorate. Transfer to US-based recipients may also take place if the recipient is certified under the Safe Harbour Programme.

F.　　　　NORWEGIAN DATA PROTECTION LAW: CONFLICTS OF LAWS

The territorial extent of the PDA and the PDR is set out in section 4 of the PDA. The Act and the Regulation will apply to controllers who are established in Norway. The legislator refers to preamble number 19 of the European Data Protection Directive with regards to the assessment of 'established'.[6] Multinational companies that have a subsidiary or branch offices in Norway are considered 'established' in Norway and thus subject to Norwegian law in respect to the processing relating to Norway. In addition, the PDA and the PDR apply to controllers who are established in states outside the territory of the EEA if the controller makes use of equipment in Norway, unless the equipment is only used for transfer of personal data through Norway.

Since multinational companies tend to store their data at various locations worldwide, even data relating to Norwegian employees, and tend to use equipment in various jurisdictions, determining whether Norwegian data protection laws apply for an e-discovery project is a challenge. ESI stored with a corporate company located abroad does not exclude the application of Norwegian data protection laws if the data in question relate to employees, customers, or suppliers of a subsidiary/associated company established in Norway.

---

6. Ot.prp. No. 42 (1998–1999), 105–106.

Issues relating to conflict of laws are also triggered when the general principles and criteria for processing and transfer of personal data in a pretrial discovery process are assessed, as mentioned in sections E above and IV below.

G. NORWEGIAN DATA PROTECTION LAW: SUPERVISORY
    AUTHORITIES; ENFORCEMENT

The Norwegian Data Protection Inspectorate is the supervising authority for the PDA and the PDR. Anyone who wilfully or through gross negligence does not comply with certain provisions of the PDA may be liable for fines or a coercive fine, which is an administrative sanction, imposed by the Norwegian Data Inspectorate. In severe cases, imprisonment for a term not exceeding one year may be imposed. In particularly aggravating circumstances, a sentence of imprisonment for a term not exceeding three years may be imposed. However, imprisonment has not been seen awarded so far.

III. PRETRIAL DISCOVERY IN NORWAY: BACKGROUND

The mutual disclosure of documents and data, which is seen in discovery processes, is unknown in Norway. The litigants in civil cases are obliged to provide information about important documents or other evidence of which they are aware of and of which they cannot expect the opposite party to be aware of, irrespective of whether such evidence supports their position or the position of the opposite party.[7] In addition, the opposite party may require disclosure by the other party of documents in the other party's or in a third party's possession, provided that the request is fairly specified. This means that pretrial discovery, in the US sense, is not seen in Norwegian litigations.

A. PRETRIAL DISCOVERY IN NORWAY: BLOCKING STATUTES

There are no particular blocking statutes under Norwegian law applicable to e-discovery that expressly prohibit transfer of information to foreign courts or authorities. Neither are there any special provisions obstructing application of pretrial discovery law enacted in another jurisdiction.

B. PRETRIAL DISCOVERY IN NORWAY: HAGUE CONVENTION ON THE
    TAKING OF EVIDENCE

Norway is signatory to the Hague Convention on the Taking of Evidence Abroad in Civil or Commercial Matters (Hague Convention). Thus, it may create a

---

7. Lov om mekling og rettergang i sivile tvister (tvisteloven), 17 Jun. 2005 No. 90 Ch. 5.

mechanism for gathering evidence stored in Norway. However, there are no prominent pretrial discovery processes in which a Norwegian judicial authority was requested in accordance with the Hague Convention by an international judicial authority to obtain evidence and to disclose and transfer such evidence to the requesting authority. Norwegian law does not designate the Hague Convention as an exclusive or first resort for discovery sought from a foreign litigant.

IV.   PRETRIAL DISCOVERY VERSUS DATA PROTECTION
             IN NORWAY

Any use of personal data as part of a pretrial discovery is considered 'processing'. Hence the PDA and PDR apply. If the pretrial discovery concerns employees, labour legislation must also be complied with.

A presumption for a successful e-discovery is that relevant data are available or not deleted. There are no particular provisions under Norwegian laws allowing storage of personal data for potential future discovery processes. Retention of personal data is governed by the general principle of section 11 of the PDA: Personal data shall be retained no longer than what is necessary for the purposes for which the data were collected or for which they are further processed. This implies that extraordinary retention for potential discovery processes will normally not be allowed if the data should be erased with regard to the ordinary course of business. Certain transaction-related data – not only personal data – are subject to retention requirements set out in the Accounting Act, regardless of whether such data are electronically or non-electronically stored.[8]

Section 9–4 of the PDR may cause a challenge for pretrial discovery as it requires e-mail accounts of employees, including all e-mail, to be deleted upon termination of the employment, unless the e-mail is necessary for the daily operation of the business.

In the above-mentioned 2009 case (Case 09-160051TVI-AHER), the Court considered, in accordance with section 9–4 of the PRD, the duty to delete e-mail accounts and correspondence upon termination of employment. It follows from the preparatory works of the PDR that a period of six months after termination should be sufficient in order for the employer to evaluate the need for further retention of ESI. The Court found that the provision must be interpreted broadly. Retention of ESI for a period longer than six months is not automatically illegal, and the right to retention is not limited to only information that is needed in the daily operation of the business. In the particular case, retention was done in order to safeguard and document a possible case of liability. The Court held that retention of necessary documentation in this respect was not in conflict with the PDR.

Pretrial discovery pursuant to foreign law triggers the question of whether such law shall be recognized under Norwegian data protection law as a legal basis for processing and transfer of personal data. Pursuant to sections 8 and 9 of the

---

8. Lov om bokføring (bokføringsloven), 19 Nov. 2004 No. 73.

PDA, accordingly, 'legal obligations' or 'necessity in order to establish, exercise or defence of legal claim' may establish a legal basis for processing – including searching in and accessing of ESI. However, the Data Inspectorate has in previous matters by informal channels of communication expressed reluctance to recognizing foreign pretrial regulations, such as the US discovery regime, as a legal basis for processing of personal data subject to Norwegian data protection laws. The issue of whether foreign laws/legal obligations may establish a legal basis for transfer to third countries is discussed above in section E.

V.   CONCLUSION

As introductorily discussed, data protection has been part of the Norwegian legal tradition for some considerable time, whereas pretrial discovery still is regarded as alien. Still, experience has shown that approximately worded Norwegian data protection laws normally provide for sufficient flexibility to accommodate pretrial discovery initiated pursuant to foreign – typically US – legislation. Recent provisions have been enacted that particularly deal with processing and accessing of employee e-mails, which is highly relevant in a discovery process. At present there is limited case law on how to interpret and apply these provisions. The Norwegian legal framework for pretrial discovery is still in motion.

Chapter 5.18

Poland

Przemyslaw Pietrzak and Magdalena Nilsson *

I.   INTRODUCTION

Under the Act on Personal Data Protection (the 'Personal Data Protection Act')[1] of 29 August 1997, which complies in its current version with the European Data Protection Directive 95/46/EC, the term 'personal data' encompasses any information relating to an identified or identifiable natural person. Polish law restricts the transfer of personal data to any country outside the European Economic Area (EEA) that does not guarantee the same level of privacy protection as Poland. These regulations are of particular relevance to the Polish affiliates of US-based companies that are under pressure to produce documents and material in relation to litigation and law enforcement investigation brought against them in the United States since the documents and material that are required will often contain personal data relating to clients or other third parties, as well as employees.

II.   PRETRIAL DISCOVERY IN POLAND: BACKGROUND

The mutual disclosure of documents and data is unknown in Poland. There is no formal discovery process. The Polish Code on Civil Procedure imposes on the

---

*   Przemyslaw Pietrzak, Partner, and Magdalena Nilsson, Attorney at Law at Schönherr Pietrzak Siekierzyński Bogen Sp.K., Warsaw, Poland.
1.   Dz.U. of 2002, No. 101, item 926.

Catrien Noorda & Stefan Hanloser, *E-Discovery and Data Privacy*, pp. 209–216.
© 2011 Kluwer Law International BV, The Netherlands.

parties an obligation to indicate only the evidence that supports facts to which the parties attribute legal consequences.[2] It is also possible for the court to admit evidence not indicated by the parties. However, the legal literature and judicial decisions maintain that admitting the evidence by the court *ex officio* should always be treated as a last resort measure, as this is a significant exception to the obligation to present evidence by the parties.[3] Polish law provides for some specific exceptions to the above rule, for example, in civil procedure in labour law or family law matters.

A.   PRETRIAL DISCOVERY IN POLAND: BLOCKING STATUTES

Polish law does not provide for any restrictions for cooperation with foreign courts or public authorities in litigation or regulatory investigations and proceedings. There are no 'blocking statutes' that prohibit the transfer of information abroad. However, some restrictions are imposed by the general regulation regarding data protection. Further, specific regulations, for example, regarding national security, banking law, telecommunication law, and so forth, apply.

B.   PRETRIAL DISCOVERY IN POLAND: HAGUE CONVENTION ON THE
           TAKING OF EVIDENCE

The Hague Convention on the Taking of Evidence Abroad in Civil or Commercial Matters of 18 March 1970[4] (the 'Hague Convention') enables taking evidence in Poland for the purpose of proceedings pending abroad. Pursuant to the Hague Convention, foreign courts may file applications for assistance in conducting the taking of evidence in Poland through the Polish Ministry of Justice, which transfers the application to the relevant district court. Poland made a reservation under Article 23 of the Hague Convention and stated that it would not consider applications regarding the proceedings known under common law as 'pre-trial discovery of documents'.[5]

In addition, the procedure of the taking of evidence abroad is governed by Council Regulation (EC) Number 1206/2001 of 28 May 2001 on cooperation

---

2. Article 232 of the Polish Code on Civil Procedure.
3. Kodeks Postępowania Cywilnego. Komentarz pod redakcją T.Erecińskiego, LexisNexis 2009 678.
4. The Hague Convention on the Taking of Evidence Abroad in Civil or Commercial Matters of 18 Mar. 1970.
5. Article 23 of the Hague Convention; Government Declaration as of 11 Apr. 2000 on acceding by the Republic of Poland to the Convention on the Taking of Evidence Abroad in Civil or Commercial Matters, drawn up in the Hague on 18 Mar. 1970 (Journal of Laws of 21 Jun. 2000).

between the courts of the Member States in the taking of evidence in civil or commercial matters.[6]

III. DATA PROTECTION PRINCIPLES IN POLAND: BACKGROUND

The Personal Data Protection Act determines the principles of personal data processing. The term 'personal data' refers to any information relating to an identified or identifiable natural person, that is, the data subject. An identifiable person is one who can be identified, directly or indirectly, in particular by reference to an identification number or to one or more factors specific to his or her physical, physiological, mental, economic, cultural, or social identity. Within the above meaning, personal data are both data that enable determining the identity of a given person (for example, the name, surname, address, personal identification number, tax identification number, etc.) and data that do not enable an immediate identification, but that enable determining the person's identity, without unusual effort or outlays, especially by means of easily available and commonly accessible sources.

A. POLISH DATA PROTECTION LAW: FORMAL REQUIREMENTS FOR LAWFUL DATA PROCESSING

'Personal data processing' means any operation that is performed upon personal data, such as collection, recording, storage, organization, alteration, disclosure, and erasure, and in particular those performed in computer systems.

According to the Personal Data Protection Act, processing of personal data is permitted only if:

(i) the data subject has given his or her consent, unless the processing consists in the erasure of personal data;
(ii) the processing is necessary for the purpose of exercise of rights and duties resulting from a legal provision;
(iii) the processing is necessary for the performance of a contract to which the data subject is a party or in order to take steps at the request of the data subject prior to entering into a contract;
(iv) the processing is necessary for the performance of tasks provided for by law and carried out in the public interest; or
(v) the processing is necessary for the purpose of the legitimate interests pursued by the controllers or data recipients, provided that the processing does not violate the rights and freedoms of the data subject.

---

6. Council Regulation (EC) No. 1206/2001 of 28 May 2001 on cooperation between the courts of the Member States in the taking of evidence in civil or commercial matters.

According to the interpretation issued by the Polish Inspector General for Personal Data Protection (the 'Inspector General'), the wording of the consent should clearly state for which purpose and to what extent and by whom the data will be processed. In addition, such consent should be included in a separate document.

In reference to the processing of personal data of employees, according to the opinion of the Inspector General, as well as jurisprudence of the Polish Supreme Administrative Court,[7] the employees' consent cannot be generally considered as sufficient to legalize the processing of the employees' personal data. This is because of the unequal position of the employer and the employee. The employee is dependent on, and subordinated to, the employer. These circumstances may prevent the employee from granting free consent.

B.   POLISH DATA PROTECTION LAW: DATA CONTROLLER

The entity that is responsible for deciding on the purposes and means of processing personal data is treated as a data controller and therefore is entrusted with certain obligations. In particular, the controller is obliged to implement technical and organizational measures to protect the personal data against unauthorized disclosure, takeover by an unauthorized person, processing in violation of the regulations, or any change, loss, damage, or destruction. Moreover, the controller is required to keep the documentation describing the manner of data processing and measures referred to in the preceding sentence. The data controller is obliged to notify the Inspector General of its 'data filing system', which means any structured set of personal data. According to the information obtained from the Inspector General, the personal data relating to more than two customers is considered as a data filling system by the Inspector General. Such notification has to be filed on an official form. In addition, the data controller is obliged to notify the Inspector General of any changes that affect the information on the official notification form within thirty days following the date of such change.

C.   POLISH DATA PROTECTION LAW: ACCESSING EMPLOYEES'
           E-MAIL ACCOUNTS

The right of the employer to monitor the correspondence of its employees when using their business e-mail addresses is not expressly regulated under Polish law.

According to the opinion of the Inspector General, the employer should first inform the employee about its intention to monitor the employee's business e-mails. The employer who provides the employee with an Internet account and business e-mail address is, in principle, entitled to check how the employee uses it and fulfils his or her duties, as well as whether no company secrets are revealed. The employer may check how many business and private e-mails were received

---

7.   Ruling of the Supreme Administrative Court of 1 Dec. 2009, I OSK 249/09.

and sent within working hours. However, the employer may not read private messages. The Inspector General emphasizes that the employer has to adjust the rules for using a business e-mail account so that the control does not infringe the rights of the employees.[8] Due to the fact that the monitoring of employees' e-mails and transfer of the e-mails to the United States for discovery purposes is a form of personal data processing, the employees' consent cannot be deemed as sufficient to legalize such actions (see section III.A. above).

D.	POLISH DATA PROTECTION LAW: TRANSFER OF PERSONAL DATA ABROAD

Under Polish data protection law, the transfer of personal data to member states of the EEA is not restricted. Only the transfer to countries that do not belong to the EEA is subject to certain restrictions described in the Personal Data Protection Act. The transfer of personal data to these countries may only take place if the country of destination ensures at least a level of data protection in its territory that equals the level of protection in Poland.

Taking the differences between the data protection regimes of the European Union (EU) and of the United States into account, the latter is not regarded as a country safeguarding an appropriate level of data protection. Since such a situation hampers the economic exchange between the EU Member States and the United States, the US Department of Commerce, in consultation with the European Commission, developed a 'Safe Harbour' framework allowing US entities to meet the requirements of the European Data Protection Directive 95/46/EC. The certification of the participating entities to the Safe Harbour Programme ensures that they provide an adequate level of personal data protection specified by the provisions of Directive 95/46/EC.

Further, the data may be transferred to the United States on the following grounds:

(i) where the recipient has entered into a transfer contract with the Polish company transferring the data by which the latter adduces adequate safe-guards, for example, based on the standard contract clauses issued by the European Commission in its Decisions of 15 June 2001 or 27 December 2004; or

(ii) where the recipient has a set of binding corporate rules in place, which have been approved by the Inspector General.

---

8. These principles were confirmed by the European Court of Human Rights in its judgment of 3 Apr. 2007 in the matter of *Copland v. United Kingdom* (application no. 62617/00). The Court ruled that the employer may monitor its employees. However, the control may not infringe Art. 8 of the European Convention on Human Rights, which states that everyone has the right of respect for his or her private and family life, and his or her home and correspondence.

213

The transfer of the personal data to third countries is also permitted if it is required by legal provisions or by the provisions of any ratified international agreement.

In addition, the controller may transfer the personal data to a third country provided that:

   (i) the data subject has given his or her written consent (with respect to the requirements of the consent, please refer to our comments in point III.A. above);

   (ii) the transfer is necessary for the performance of a contract between the data subject and the controller or takes place in response to the data subject's request;

   (iii) the transfer is necessary for the performance of a contract concluded in the interests of the data subject between the controller and another subject;

   (iv) the transfer is necessary or required by reasons of public interests or for the establishment of legal claims;

   (v) the transfer is necessary in order to protect the vital interests of the data subject; or

   (vi) the transfer relates to data that are publicly available.

In any other cases, the transfer of personal data to a third country that does not ensure an adequate level of personal data protection may take place subject to prior consent of the Inspector General, provided that the foreign data controller ensures adequate safeguards with respect to the protection of the privacy, rights, and freedoms of the data subject.

E.   POLISH DATA PROTECTION LAW: STORAGE OF PERSONAL DATA

Pursuant to the Working Paper 158 on pretrial discovery for cross-border civil litigation, which was adopted on 11 February 2009 by the European 'Working Party on the Protection of Individuals with Regard to the Processing of Personal Data', data controllers in the EU have no legal grounds to store personal data at random for an unlimited period of time because of the possibility of litigation in the United States.[9] However, if the personal data are relevant and to be used in a specific or imminent litigation process, they should be retained until the conclusion of the proceedings and any period allowed for an appeal in the particular case.

F.   POLISH DATA PROTECTION LAW: SANCTIONS AND ENFORCEMENT

Data protection breaches such as processing data without authorization, not registering the data filing system, or making the data accessible to unauthorized parties are penalized with: fine (from New Zloty (PLN) 100 up to PLN

---

9.   Working Paper 158 of 11 Feb. 2009.

720,000), limitation of freedom (from one month up to twelve months), or imprisonment (from one month up to three years). The limitation of freedom includes: not being allowed to change the place of stay without the court's consent, unpaid work for public purposes (twenty to forty hours per month), and providing the court with explanations regarding the course of the penalty. Instead of working for public purposes, the court may order that 10%–25% of the remuneration shall be deducted and transferred for public purposes.

The sanctions are imposed by a state court (not by the Inspector General) as a result of a proceeding commenced on the basis of indictment brought to the court by the public prosecutor. The public prosecutor commences with the investigation *ex officio* or upon notification of a suspected data protection crime (submitted by any person).

The Inspector General (him- or herself or via the subordinated inspectors) can conduct controls in terms of conformity of the personal data processing with respective legal provisions. In the event that a violation of the provisions of law has been determined, the Inspector General can issue an administrative decision ordering the restoration of the conformity with the legal provisions (e.g., removing of the infringements, application of additional measures to secure that personal data, erasure of the personal data). The Inspector General cannot impose any fines if the decisions are not executed. On the basis of information gathered during the control, the Inspector General can request commencement of disciplinary proceedings against persons responsible for the breaches, information on the results of such proceedings, and measures that have been taken. In the event the control reveals violations that may constitute a crime, the Inspector General is obliged to file a respective notification with the office of public prosecutions in order to commence a criminal investigation and court proceedings.

IV.   PRETRIAL DISCOVERY: EXPORT OF PERSONAL
        DATA TO THE UNITED STATES

A transfer of personal data to the United States must satisfy the grounds for processing personal data (see section III.A. above). In addition, the requirements regarding the transfer of personal data to third countries must be met (see section III.D. above).

Under Polish law, there are two potential grounds for transferring personal data to the United States for litigation purposes: a consent given by the data subject or a legitimate interest pursued by the Polish data controller or the data recipient abroad. Obtaining consent from the data subject to process his or her personal data may be difficult or even impossible. Therefore, often the right legal basis for a data transfer for discovery purposes is a legitimate interest. However, this basis will only be acceptable if the processing does not violate the rights and freedoms of the data subjects.[10] As an alternative to consent or legitimate interests, the Polish data

---

10. Article 23.1, point 5 of the PDPA.

controller could at first sight resort to the provision allowing the transfer of data abroad for the exercice of rights and duties resulting from a legal provision. However, since Poland made a reservation under Article 23 of the Hague Convention, the request of a foreign court does not constitute such a prerequisite to process the data.

As far as grounds of transfer of personal data to the United States are concerned, and where the transfer of personal data for litigation purposes is likely to be a single transfer of all relevant information, the most pertinent ground is the establishment of legal claims. The data subject's consent is a valid basis for a transborder transfer of personal data, but can hardly be obtained in practice.

V.   CONCLUSION

Polish law does not prohibit the transfer of personal data for litigation purposes. However, such transfer must be in compliance with the Polish data protection regulations.

Chapter 5.19
Portugal

*Carlos de Almeida Sampaio**

I.   INTRODUCTION

The Portuguese legislator has been confronted with the tension between mandatory
pretrial discovery requirements and data protection laws since the 1990s. Although
Portugal is one of the parties to the Hague Convention, Portuguese law has dealt
primarily with data protection[1] and only after the approval of EC Regulation
Number 1206/2001 of the European Council of 28 May 2001, the legislator has
approached the cooperation between European Union (EU) Member States' courts
in discovery requirements, namely in civil and commercial matters.

The conflict mentioned above may become an issue for companies doing
business with the United States or that have an affiliated company there, since the
Portuguese State declared that it will not comply with any Letter Rogatory whose
purpose is a pretrial discovery of documents pursuant to the Hague Convention on
the Taking of Evidence Abroad in Civil or Commercial Matters of 18 March 1970
(approved by Decree Number 764/74, of 30 December).[2]

---

*   Carlos de Almeida Sampaio is partner in Cuatrecasas, Gonçalves Pereira and professor of
     Intellectual Property and IT Law in the University of Lisbon (Lusíada) Law School.
1.   Law No. 67/98 of 26 Oct. 1998.
2.   The Hague Convention on the Taking of Evidence Abroad in Civil or Commercial Matters of 18
     Mar. 1970 (approved by the Decree 764/74 of 30 December).

Catrien Noorda & Stefan Hanloser, *E-Discovery and Data Privacy*, pp. 217–229.
© 2011 Kluwer Law International BV, The Netherlands.

Carlos de Almeida Sampaio

II.   PORTUGUESE PERSONAL DATA PROTECTION
        LAW: BACKGROUND

The Portuguese Personal Data Protection Law (PDPL) was approved by Law
Number 67/98 and entered into force on 26 October 1998. The law harmonized
the Portuguese legal systems with Directive 95/46/EC of the European Parliament
and Council regarding the protection of individuals with regard to the processing of
personal data and the free movement of such data, and it has not been revised since
then.

However, the authority established under the PDPL (*'Comissão Nacional de
Protecção de Dados'* – hereinafter CNPD) has produced significant jurisprudence
about a number of issues that could collide with the pretrial discovery requirements, namely in commercial matters, access to employees' data by the employer,
and transfer of data to foreign jurisdictions, usually at foreign courts' requests.[3]

The electronic communications have been more recently dealt with by the
Portuguese legislator under Law Number 41/2004 of 18 August (applicable to
personal data processing and to privacy protection in the electronic communications area, detailing and complementing the PDPL) and Law Number 32/2008 of
17 July partially harmonizing the Portuguese law with Directive 2006/24/CE of the
European Parliament and Council of 15 March regarding data processing in the
framework of electronic communication services and electronic communications
public networks.

A.   PORTUGUESE PERSONAL DATA PROTECTION LAW: PERSONAL DATA

The PDPL applies to information of an individual exclusively. Information about
companies and other business or corporate entities is therefore excluded.
The PDPL deals with individuals as a whole and does not distinguish between
economic, business, or professional groups (such as employees, services providers,
clients, and others). All of them are for the purpose and up to the extension of the
law considered 'data subjects'.

The CNPD also interprets 'personal data' very broadly. Therefore names,
e-mail addresses, bank details, or any information that may identify or turn the
person identifiable, even if the identification is only possible after the intervention
of a third party, as in the case of Internet protocol (IP) addresses, are protected by
the PDPL. The same applies to all categories of information generated by employees at work, such as any kind of e-mail content, calls from the company, websites
visited, and work results. Under the data protection legal regime, any disclosure of
such information that identifies or turns identifiable a natural person must comply
with the PDPL.

Law No. 32/2008 of 17 July regulates the storage and transmission of
certain data that are required to identify the user or subscriber of an electronic

---
3.   See the CNPD's Decision of 29 Oct. 2002 and the CNPD's Decision of 29 Oct. 2004.

communication service for purposes of investigation, detection, and punishment of serious crimes. It is important to note that the maintenance of data disclosing the content of the messages is prohibited without prejudice of the regulation included in Law No. 41/2004 and in the Portuguese Criminal Procedure Code regarding communications monitoring and recording.

B.   PORTUGUESE DATA PROTECTION LAW: EMPLOYEES' DATA

Regarding the protection of employees as data subjects, the Portuguese Labour Code follows the principles of the PDPL and adopts a strict regulation regarding an employee's right to privacy and personal data. For example, in matters of personal messages, it is recognized that employees are entitled to confidentiality regarding any content of such personal messages. Access to any information considered not professional that the employee sends, receives, or consults, namely via e-mail, is restricted accordingly.

In its decision of 29 October 2002, the CNPD developed the principles to align the employer's power to rule at its will the use of the company's means of communication under the Labour Code with the limits provided by the PDPL. The decision is applicable to any data processed in telephone central systems, e-mails, or access to the Internet. The CNPD concluded that any control of such data and any processing require a previous legalization by the CNPD and that the admissible use of the e-mail, telephone, and Internet by the employees shall be included in an internal regulation that is familiar to the employees. The access to communications or the use of any listening or storage device and interception or surveillance of communications by the employer is prohibited. Exceptions apply if the call recording is admissible to prove commercial or contractual statements, when the data subjects involved expressly consented to it, or to prove compliance with the recent regulation on call centres.[4]

C.   PORTUGUESE DATA PROTECTION LAW: PRIVACY AND
            DATA PROTECTION PRINCIPLES

The processing of personal data is generally prohibited. Exceptionally, personal data may be processed (used, consulted, stored, collected, among other ways of processing) if at least one of the legal conditions set out in Article 6 of the PDPL is fulfilled. The principal legal condition is that the data subject has given his or her unambiguous consent. The processing may happen for the performance of a contract entered into by the data subject, for the compliance with a legal obligation of the controller, to protect vital interests of the data subject, and for the performance of a task carried out in public interest or to accomplish legitimate interests of the controller or of a third party to which the data are communicated, unless such

---

4. Decree-law No. 134/2009 of 2 June.

interests are overridden by the interests or fundamental rights and freedoms of the data subject.

The personal data shall be processed for determined, legal, and clear purposes. The data may not be processed for purposes different from those that determined its collection and shall be adequate and not excessive for the processing purpose. In addition, the personal data processed shall be accurate, updated, and maintained only during the period of time required for the processing or collection purpose.

The PDPL assigns several rights to the data subject; these are the right to be informed of the controller's identity, of the processing purposes, of the categories of people to whom the data may be communicated, the right of access and rectification of the data, and the right of opposition to the processing.

D.   PORTUGUESE DATA PROTECTION LAW: FORMAL REQUIREMENTS
          FOR A LAWFUL DATA COLLECTION, PROCESSING, AND USE

Personal data processing must be legalized by the CNPD in advance. A notification is necessary for 'ordinary' data processing; that is, the controller notifies the processing and may process immediately, whereas a prior authorization is required if sensitive data are processed. In the latter case, the controller must wait for the CNPD's decision on the prerequisites processing of the personal data. Under the PDPL, sensitive data are, *inter alia*, data regarding political opinions, religion, race, private life, health, sexual life, and also data suspicious of illegal activities, criminal or administrative infringements, decisions that apply penalties, security measures, administrative fines, and others.

E.   PORTUGUESE PERSONAL DATA PROTECTION LAW: DATA
          CONTROLLER AND DATA PROCESSOR

The data controller is the entity that determines the purposes of data processing and the processing means. If the controller conveys the performance of certain tasks to a third party, such entity is considered a data processor. The data processor processes personal data on behalf of the data controller.

It is mandatory for any data controller to adopt technical and organizational security measures to protect the personal data against any kind of destruction, loss, modification, non-authorized access, and so forth. That scope of these measures is different depending on the nature of the personal data involved. Whenever the data controller retains a data processor, the data controller must select a data processor that gives adequate warranties regarding the technical security measures for the processing. Any relation between the data processor and the data controller shall be regulated by a written agreement where the data processor assumes the obligations to act only on behalf of the data controller, according to its instructions, and to respect the security measures legally imposed on the data controller. Under the

PDPL the data controller and the data processor have confidentiality obligations, which remain effective even after the termination of their cooperation.

F.   PORTUGUESE PERSONAL DATA PROTECTION LAW: TRANSFER OF
          PERSONAL DATA ABROAD

The transfer of personal data to any Member State of the European Union (EU) is unrestricted under Portuguese data protection law. In contrast, personal data may only be transferred to countries outside the EU if the PDPL is respected and if the country to which the data are being transferred assures an adequate level of protection of the personal data. The CNPD will analyse the terms of the intended transfer as well as the law of the country of destination in order to decide whether the country of destination assures an adequate protection level. The transfer to a country that does not assure such an adequate level of protection may exceptionally be permitted by the CNPD if the data subject consents to the transfer or if, for example, the transfer is required for the execution of an agreement entered into by the data subject or for the recognition or defence of specific rights in a legal action. As an alternative, the data controller can assume the obligation to protect the privacy as well as the rights and liberties of the data subjects involved, namely by entering into adequate Standard Contractual Clauses (SCCs). If the transfer is made pursuant to SCCs preapproved by the Commission,[5] the transfer will not require previous authorization of the CNPD; but even if the transfer is permitted, the CNPD has to be notified of the transfer.

Pursuant to Article 14 of Law Number 67/98, the controller must implement appropriate technical and organizational measures to protect personal data against accidental or unlawful destruction or accidental loss, alteration, unauthorized disclosure, or access, especially where the processing involves the transmission of data over a network, and against all other unlawful forms of processing. Such measures shall ensure a level of security appropriate to the risks resulting from the processing and the nature of the data that shall be protected. This provision also establishes that in cases where processing is carried out on behalf of the controller, he or she must choose a processor providing sufficient guarantees in respect of the technical security measures and organizational measures governing the processing to be carried out. Furthermore the controller has to ensure compliance with those measures.

Article 15 of Law No. 67/98 provides more specified measures to be taken by the controller when the processing refers to sensitive data, that is, personal data revealing philosophical or political beliefs, political party or trade union membership, religion, and racial or ethnic origin, or the processing itself concerns data refering to health or sex life, including genetic data. These measures have to be

---

5. Cf. the SCCs approved in the Decision of 27 Dec. 2001 on Standard Contractual Clauses for the transfer of personal data to processors established in third countries.

fulfilled in order to: (a) prevent unauthorized persons from entering the premises used for processing such data (control of entry to the premises); (b) prevent data media from being read, copied, altered, or removed by unauthorized persons (control of data media); (c) prevent unauthorized input and unauthorized obtaining of knowledge, alteration, or elimination of personal data input (control of input); (d) prevent automatic data processing systems from being used by unauthorized persons by means of data transmission premises (control of transmission); (e) guarantee that authorized persons may only access data covered by the authorization (control of access); (f) guarantee the checking of the bodies to whom personal data may be transmitted by means of data transmission premises (control of transmission); (g) guarantee that it is possible to check *a posteriori*, in a period appropriate to the nature of processing, the establishment of the regulations applicable to each sector in which personal data are input, when, and by whom (control of input); (h) prevent unauthorized reading, copying, alteration, or elimination of data when transmitting personal data and in transporting the respective data (control of transport).

G.   PORTUGUESE DATA PROTECTION LAW: SUPERVISORY AUTHORITIES AND ENFORCEMENT

The CNPD is the Portuguese data protection authority. The CNPD is an independent supervisory body with powers of authority throughout the national territory. It is endowed with the power to supervise and monitor compliance with the laws and regulations in the area of personal data protection with strict respect for human rights, fundamental freedoms, and guarantees enshrined in the Portuguese Constitution and the law.

The offences concerning the violation of data protection rules laid down below may give rise to administrative offences or to criminal liability.

1.   Administrative Offences

– Law Number 67/98, of 26 October, Portuguese Data Protection Law

According to Article 37 of the PDPL, any entity that, as result of a negligent behaviour, fails to comply with the obligation to notify the CNPD about personal data processing, provides inaccurate information, or complies with the obligation to notify without following all necessary requirements, or, having been notified by the CNPD, continues to allow access to data to controllers who fail to comply with the provisions of the PDPL, are committing an offence to be punished as follows:

(a) in the case of an individual, a minimum of Euros (EUR) 249.40 and a maximum of EUR 2,493.90; and

(b) in the case of a legal person, a minimum of EUR 1,4964.00 and a maximum of EUR 14,964.00.

The penalties referred to above will be increased to the double in cases where the processing of personal data is subject to prior authorization of the CNPD, such as: (a) the processing of sensitive data, (b) the processing of personal data relating to a suspect of illegal activities, (c) the processing of personal data related to credit and/or the solvency of the data subjects, (d) the combination of personal data not provided for in a legal provision, and (e) the use of personal data for different purposes than the ones intended at their collection.

Article 38 of the PDPL states that entities that fail to comply with any of the following provisions of the PDPL are committing an administrative offence punishable with a minimum fine of EUR 498.80 and a maximum of EUR 4,987.98;

  (a) appointment made by a controller who is not established in the EU territory of a representative established in Portugal, in order to replace him or her in all of its rights and obligations without prejudice to its own liability; and
  (b) fulfilment of the obligations foreseen in Articles 5, 10, 11, 12, 13, 15, 16, and 31 paragraph 3 of the PDPL.

Negligence, as well as any attempt to commit the administrative offences aforementioned, will always be punished.

According to the PDPL, the CNPD is responsible for the application of the fines provided in the referred Law. After being approved by the CNPD's chairman, the deliberation of the CNPD shall be enforceable if it is not challenged within the statutory period. The amount collected as a result of the application of fines shall be shared with the Portuguese State.

  – Law Number 32/2008, of 17 July, which implements the Portuguese jurisdiction Directive 2006/24/EC of the European Parliament and of the Council, on the retention of data generated or processed in connection with the provision of publicly available electronic communications services or of public communications networks

Without prejudice to the application of the PDPL and according to Article 12 of Law Number 32/2008 of 17 July, the following issues shall be deemed to be an administrative offence and be amerced with penalties ranging between EUR 1,500.00 and EUR 50,000.00 or between EUR 5,000.00 and EUR 10,000 000.00, according to whether an individual or legal entity is concerned:

  (a) failure to retain categories of data provided for in Article 4;
  (b) non-compliance with the period of retention as in Article 6;
  (c) failure to provide data to competent authorities under Article 9; and
  (d) failure to send data necessary to identify authorized personnel, pursuant to Article 8, paragraph 2.

2.   Criminal Liability

– Portuguese Data Protection Law

According to Article 43 of the PDPL, any person who intentionally:

(a) fails to notify the application for authorization of the CNPD regarding the processing of personal data;

(b) provides false information in the notification or in applications for authorization for the processing of personal data or makes alterations in the latter that are not permitted by the legalization instrument;

(c) misappropriates or uses personal data in a way incompatible with the purpose of the collection;

(d) promotes or carries out an illegal combination of personal data;

(e) fails to comply with the obligations provided for in this Act or in other data protection legislation when the time limit fixed by the CNPD for complying with them has expired; or

(f) continues to allow access to open data transmission networks to controllers who fail to comply with the provisions of this Act after notification by the CNPD not to do so, shall be liable to up to one year's imprisonment.

Article 44 of the PDPL provides that any person who without due authorization gains access by any means to personal data prohibited to him or her shall be liable to up to one year's imprisonment or a fine of up to 120 days between EUR 100.00 and EUR 10,000.00 daily. Criminal proceedings are dependent upon a complaint. The penalty shall be increased to double when access:

(a) is achieved by means of violating technical security rules;

(b) allows the agent or third parties to obtain knowledge of the personal data; or

(c) provides the agent or third parties with a benefit or material advantage.

According to Article 45 of the PDPL, any person who without due authorization erases, destroys, damages, deletes, or changes personal data, making them unusable or affecting their capacity for use, shall be liable to up to two years of imprisonment or a fine of up to 240 days. The penalty shall be increased to double if a severe damage is caused. In the negligence framework the penalty in both cases shall be up to one year's imprisonment.

Moreover, according to Article 46 of the PDPL, any person who, after being ordered to do so, does not interrupt, cease, or block the processing of personal data shall be subject to a penalty corresponding to the crime of qualified non-compliance. The same penalty shall apply to any person who, after being notified:

(a) refuses to provide the cooperation specifically required of him or her by the CNPD without just cause;

(b) does not erase or totally or partially destroy the personal data; or

(c) does not destroy the personal data after the period for keeping them provided for in Article 5 above has elapsed.

According to Article 47 of the PDPL, any person bound by professional secrecy according to the law, who reveals or discloses personal data, totally or in part without just cause and without due consent, shall be liable to up to two years' imprisonment or a fine of up to 240 days. Criminal proceedings are dependent upon a complaint. The penalty shall be increased by half the maxima if the agent:

(a) is a civil servant or equivalent according to penal law;
(b) acts with the intention of obtaining a material advantage or other unlawful gain; or
(c) adversely affects the reputation, honour and esteem, or the privacy of another person.

A person guilty of negligence shall be liable to up to six months' imprisonment or a fine of up to 120 days.

Please also note that any attempt to commit the crimes set forth above shall always be punishable.

– Law Number 32/2008, of 17, July, which transposes to the Portuguese jurisdiction Directive 2006/24/EC of the European Parliament and of the Council of 15 March on the retention of data generated or processed in connection with the provision of publicly available electronic communications services or of public communications networks

Without prejudice to the application of the PDPL, according to Article 13 of Law Number 32/2008 of 17 July, the following actions shall be deemed as crimes punished by imprisonment of up to two years or a fine up to 240 days:

(a) failure to comply with any of the provisions on data protection or security provided in Article 7;
(b) failure to block data under paragraph 2 of Article 7 (data protection and security); or
(c) access to data by an unauthorized person under paragraph 1 of Article 8 above.

Penalties shall be doubled where the crime:

(a) is committed through infringement of safety technical standards;
(b) has made personal data available to the infringer or third parties; or
(c) has provided the infringer or third parties with material benefits or advantages.

Attempt and negligence are punishable.

Material enforcement actions brought by the CNPD include the following:

(i) On 3 April 2006, the Portuguese Criminal Court rendered its judgment in a case involving the CNPD and Presselivre – Imprensa Livre S.A. (a media company hereinafter designated 'Presselivre'). The CNPD claimed that Presselivre violated Articles 10, 38 paragraph 1, b), 27, and 37 paragraph 1, b) of the PDPL. Subsequently, in exercising the powers conferred on it by the same Law, the CNPD adopted a decision imposing two fines of EUR 1,500 each. Presselivre argued that after being aware of its legal obligations, Presselivre had rectified the situation by notifying the CNPD of the processing of personal data. In those circumstances, the Portuguese Criminal Court ruled that the fines above referred would be replaced by a private reprimand since the situation had been corrected.

(ii) On 24 February 2006, the Portuguese Judicial Court of Lisbon issued a decision in a case involving the CNPD and Lisboagás GDL – Sociedade Distribuidora de Gás Natural de Lisboa S.A. (a main Portuguese natural gas company hereinafter designated 'Lisboagás'). The CNPD claimed that Lisboagás violated Articles 27, paragraph 1 and 37 paragraphs 1, b) and 2 of the PDPL. Subsequently, in exercising the powers conferred on it by the same Law, the CNPD adopted a decision imposing one fine of EUR 6,000. Lisboagás argued that the processing of personal data occurred before the respective authorization by the CNPD because Lisboagás was only processing personal data in an experimental phase but afterwards Lisboagás was going to, and actually did, notify the CNPD. In those circumstances, the Portuguese Criminal Court confirmed the application of the fine above referred.

(iii) On 19 May 2005, the Portuguese Judicial Court rendered its judgment in a case involving the CNPD and Pedras D'el Rei – Gestão de Turismo S.A. (a large resort developer in the south of Portugal hereinafter designated 'Pedras D'el Rei'). The CNPD claimed that Pedras D'el Rei violated Articles 27 and 37 paragraphs 1, a) and 2 of the PDPL. Subsequently, in exercising the powers conferred on it by the same Law, the CNPD adopted a decision imposing one fine of EUR 6,000. Pedras D'el Rei argued its ignorance of the obligation to notify the CNPD. In those circumstances, the Portuguese Criminal Court ruled that the fine above referred would be replaced by a fine of EUR 2,500 since the situation had been corrected.

(iv) On 20 May 2004, the Portuguese Judicial Court decided in a case involving the CNPD and PT Comunicações S.A. (a Portuguese state-owned telecommunications operator hereinafter designated 'PT'). The CNPD claimed that PT violated Articles 10 and 12.

Paragraph b) of the PDPL. Subsequently, in exercising the powers conferred on it by the same Law, the CNPD adopted a decision imposing one fine of EUR 500. PT denied the occurrence of the facts for which it was accused. In those circumstances, the Portuguese Criminal Court confirmed the application of the fine above referred.

The PDPL also demands that the systems used guarantee logical separation between data relating to health and sex life, including genetic data, and the other personal data.

III.   PRETRIAL DISCOVERY IN PORTUGAL: BACKGROUND

Pretrial e-discovery is mainly understood by the Portuguese legislation in the framework of an investigation procedure about a potential illicit act, namely but without limitation, criminal matters. For instance, Portuguese law permits the transfer of stored personal data both by electronic communications services suppliers or communications public networks providers, as well as personal data stored by the CNPD under Law Number 32/2008 of 17 July. The disclosure and transfer of personal data always require a judicial order.[6]

Apart from these specific statutory provisions, there is no jurisprudence regarding the pretrial discovery of evidence or potential evidence. However, two lines of orientation can be identified: First, the requirement to inform the data subject; second, the limitation of the disclosure in accordance with the judge's ruling in a judicial order.

A.   PRETRIAL DISCOVERY IN PORTUGAL: BLOCKING STATUTES

Portuguese procedure codes have no specific provisions with the purpose to restrict cross-border discovery of information intended for disclosure in foreign jurisdictions. Nonetheless, blocking statutes may be found in specific legislation.

One significant illustration of the existence of blocking statutes in Portuguese legislation is enclosed in Law Number 109/2009 of 15 September (hereinafter the Cybercrime Law), which operated the transposition of the Council Framework Decision 2005/222/JHA of 24 February 2005 on attacks against information systems into the Portuguese legal system. Pursuant to Article 22 of the Cybercrime Law, Portuguese authorities may be required by the authorities of any other foreign state, for the purpose of a subsequent judicial cooperation request, to preserve any information technology (IT) data related to cybercrime, to crimes committed by means of IT system, or to crimes for which the collection of electronic stored evidences is necessary, when located within its borders. However, this request may be refused by the Portuguese authorities, under Article 23 of the Cybercrime Law, in four situations: (a) whenever the IT data are of political nature or are a political offence according to the Portuguese legislation definitions; (b) whenever the IT data may violate the sovereignty, the security, the public order, or any other constitutional interests of the Portuguese Republic; (c) whenever the foreign State does not assure an adequate level of protection of the personal data; (d) whenever there are reasons to believe that the subsequent judicial cooperation request will be refused due to the lack of verification of the dual criminality rule.

B.   PRETRIAL DISCOVERY IN PORTUGAL: HAGUE CONVENTION ON THE
          TAKING OF EVIDENCE

The Hague Convention on the Taking of Evidence Abroad in Civil or Commercial Matters of 18 March 1970 was approved by the Portuguese State by Decree Number 764/74, of 30 December. This Convention establishes a standard

---

6. Similarly, a new law against cybercrime of 15 Sep. 2009 (Law No. 109/2009) has been adopted, which regulates the disclosure of information.

procedure of petitions that may be used by a court of one country to the designated authority of another in order to obtain relevant information located within the latter.

In spite of its approval, the Portuguese State, as previously referred, declared under Article 23 that it will not comply with any Letter Rogatory whose purpose is a pretrial discovery of documents. Therefore, a Letter of Request or a Letter Rogatory addressed to the Portuguese designated authority will not be accepted if it aims at the discovery of any document in relation to a foreign pretrial legal proceeding.

Issues may arise on the interpretation of the expression 'pretrial discovery of documents'. A literal interpretation appears to restrict the scope to 'documents', whereas the designated authority may interpret it in a more extensive way, including electronically stored information (ESI). There is, however, no published case law regarding this subject.

IV.	PRETRIAL DISCOVERY VERSUS DATA PROTECTION IN PORTUGAL: RETENTION AND TRANSFER OF PERSONAL DATA

Pursuant to the PDPL, personal data may only be maintained during the period of time required for the processing or collection purpose. The data controller determines the period of time when notifying the CNPD of the data processing. The ultimate decision is, however, always taken by the CNPD. The CNPD may define the retention period for specific categories of data processing, which then become binding to any data controller. As an alternative, the period of time of the retention may also be stipulated by law. In this case, the CNPD must be previously heard by the legislator.

The mere possibility of a litigation in the United States does not constitute a legal ground, pursuant to Portuguese legislation, to allow controllers to store personal data for an unlimited period of time.

Considering the disclosure obligations under US litigation, the United States does not assure an adequate level of protection of the personal data. Consequently, the transfer of personal data may only be done under the conditions set forth above under section II.F. With the United States, it has to be emphasized that an adequate level of protection of the personal data is in place if the transfer is made to an entity that complies with the Safe Harbour Privacy Principles for the personal data transferred from a Member State to the United States expressed in the Commission Decision of 26 July 2000.

V.	CONCLUSION

Portuguese law establishes thoroughly the regime of the transfer of personal data to foreign states, but it is sufficiently extensive and wide to allow in some cases the transfer of personal data to countries that do not assure an adequate level of protection of the personal data and, in particular, to the United States.

Nonetheless, although cooperation with foreign courts and public authorities in litigation, including the transfer of personal data regarding litigation proceedings, is generally permitted, the reservation made by the Portuguese State under Article 23 of the Hague Convention excludes the possibility of cooperation aiming at the pretrial discovery of documents that should be understood in the most extensive way.

Chapter 5.20

Romania

*Silvia Popa**

I. INTRODUCTION

While the relevant legislation has been passed rather recently, public authorities, private persons, as well as legal entities express a growing concern for personal data protection. Such concern may impact on their response to a pretrial discovery request, a procedure that is not available in the domestic civil procedure. At this point, the assessment of the compatibility of a pretrial discovery request with the Romanian data protection legislation is somewhat hindered by the limited domestic courts' case law in the area of data protection and by the absence of specific legislation in some key areas.

II. PRETRIAL DISCOVERY IN ROMANIA: BACKGROUND

Exhaustive disclosure of case-related facts and documents is not required under Romanian law. The parties are only required to produce before the courts the documents referred to in their submissions, which are notified to the other party. However, if throughout the proceedings it appears that the parties to trial or third parties hold in their possession documents that are relevant to the case and

---

*   Silvia Popa, LL.M., attorney at law with Schoenherr si Asociatii SCA in Bucharest, Romania, and Laura Ielciu, associate with Schoenherr si Asociatii SCA in Bucharest, Romania, former assistant lawyer at the Registry of the European Court of Human Rights.

Catrien Noorda & Stefan Hanloser, *E-Discovery and Data Privacy*, pp. 231–240.
© 2011 Kluwer Law International BV, The Netherlands.

necessary for the adjudication of the case, the courts may order on their own motion that such documents be produced. A court order to the same effect can be granted upon request of one of the parties to the trial. Failure of a party to the trial to produce documents thus requested entitles the court to assume that the other parties' allegations in respect of the content of such documents are correct.[1]

A.   PRETRIAL DISCOVERY IN ROMANIA: BLOCKING STATUTES

Cooperation of private persons or private legal entities with foreign courts or public authorities in litigation or regulatory investigations and proceedings is not restricted under Romanian law.

A statute[2] regulating international cooperation in civil and commercial matters was passed in 2003. The provisions of this statute complement those of the international conventions ratified by Romania, including the Hague Convention on the Taking of Evidence. This statute provides for some restrictions on the transfer of information and documents to foreign authorities. However, such restrictions only apply in respect of the Romanian authorities; they do not concern private persons or legal entities. Romanian authorities may refuse to give effect to a request of transfer of information or documents made by foreign authorities when such transfer is likely to endanger national sovereignty or national security. It should be noted that similar restrictions are provided for by the Hague Convention on the Taking of Evidence.

In addition, the Romanian statute prohibits the transfer of documents that cannot be 'circulated'. The scope of this latter restriction is not very clear. According to an opinion expressed in academic literature,[3] this provision should be read in conjunction with Article 173 of the Code of Civil Procedure, which restricts the courts from ordering a party to produce documents when: (i) such documents contain strictly private issues; (ii) the holder of the information and documents in question is under a statutory duty of confidentiality, unless the case qualifies as an exception under the relevant Romanian statute;[4] and (iii) producing the document exposes its holder or a third party to criminal pursuits or public contempt.

---

1. Codul de procedura civila (Code of Civil Procedure) as currently in force, Arts 112, 116, 129 para. 5, 172 para. 1, and 175 para. 1.
2. Law No. 189/2003 of 13.05.2003 on civil and commercial international judicial cooperation, republished in the Official Gazette., Part I, No. 543 of 05/08/2009.
3. Sergiu-Leon RUS, 'Comisiile rogatorii internationale efectuate in sistemul Legii nr. 189/2003', *Revista Romana de Drept al Afacerilor*, 1/2006, 90.
4. For instance, Government Emergency Ordinance No. 99/2006 on credit institutions provides for some exceptions to the duty of confidentiality the banks are subject to. Thus, the banks can disclose confidential information when such disclosure is justified by a legitimate interest of the bank or when disclosure is ordered in court proceedings.

B.   PRETRIAL DISCOVERY IN ROMANIA: HAGUE CONVENTION ON THE
       TAKING OF EVIDENCE

Romanian courts are likely to require resort to the procedure set forth by the Hague Convention on the Taking of Evidence for obtaining documents and information located in Romanian territory. While there is no explicit ruling to that effect, such position can be assumed since the courts are required to provide legal basis for their decisions. Therefore, acceding to a request that is not based on the said Convention, when the requesting authority is based in a Contracting State, would lack legal basis. Such position could furthermore be supported by the fact that the legal provisions regulating international cooperation are regarded as mandatory.

Romania has issued a declaration under Article 23 of the Hague Convention on the Taking of Evidence whereby Romanian authorities shall execute a Letter of Request issued within a pretrial discovery procedure to the extent that the 'pretrial discovery procedure' is construed as securing of evidence (investigation *in futurum*). Under the Romanian Code of Civil Procedure, the securing of evidence is an adversarial procedure that can be resorted to by the parties to a future or ongoing litigation when there is a pressing need for evidence to be collected immediately. A request for securing of evidence is admissible only when there is a risk that such evidence will disappear or might be difficult to obtain in the future. However, such restrictions do not apply if the other party adheres to the securing of evidence request. Hence, while Romanian law does not rule out the execution of a Letter of Request issued for pretrial discovery, it very much limits the scope of such a request, which might dissuade the US courts from resorting to the Hague Convention on the Taking of Evidence in relation to litigants located in Romania.

III.   DATA PROTECTION IN ROMANIA: BACKGROUND

While protection of private life is a constitutional principle since 1991, specific legislation on data protection was not passed until 2001. The European Court of Human Rights held in its judgment *Rotaru v. Romania*, given in 2000,[5] that the legislative framework existing at that time failed to ensure adequate and effective personal data protection. In that case, the European Court of Human Rights held, *inter alia*, that no case law indicating that a person alleging illegal collection of personal data and disposal thereof could seek relief before courts was available to it.

Specific legislation in this area was passed in Romania with a view to implementing the *acquis communautaire* as a requirement for Romania's accession to the European Union (EU). Thus, the European Data Protection Directive[6] was

---

5. Judgment of 4 May 2000 [GC], *Reports of judgments and decisions* 2000-V. Also available at
    <www.echr.coe.int>.
6. Council Directive 95/46 regarding the protection of individuals with regard to the processing of
    personal data and on the free movement of such data, O.J. (L 281) 23 Nov. 1995, 31–50.

implemented in November 2001 by Law Number 677/2001 ('Data Protection Act'),[7] further amended in 2005.

Against this background, several decisions given by the Constitutional Court since 2000 reveal that the Constitutional Court has become increasingly sensitive to data-protection-related issues. Thus, the constitutional scrutiny of data protection legislation recently led the Constitutional Court to declare unconstitutional a statutory provision passed in the area of public communication networks and electronic communication services,[8] on grounds that such provision was ambiguous and that it did not provide sufficient safeguards against misuse of personal data collected by virtue of the statute.[9]

Protection of personal data shall be further enhanced by the new Criminal Code, expected to come into force in 2010 or soon thereafter. Under the new Criminal Code, unauthorized transfer of electronic data or alteration of such data shall constitute offences punishable by imprisonment.[10]

A. ROMANIAN DATA PROTECTION LAW: PERSONAL DATA

Any information related to an identified or identifiable private person falls under the scope of the Data Protection Act. The National Supervisory Authority for Personal Data Processing (the 'Supervisory Authority'[11]) interprets the concept of 'personal data' in line with the principles set out in the European Court of Justice's case law and the guidelines issued by various EU organs.[12] Romanian courts tend to adhere to the position expressed by the Supervisory Authority when adjudicating under the Data Protection Act.[13]

The Data Protection Act is applicable to both public authorities and private individuals or bodies, irrespective of the context in which personal data are processed. The term 'personal data' refers not only to information revealing aspects of a person's private life and activities carried out, but also to information providing

---

7. Law No. 677/2001 of 21/11/2001 on protection of individuals with regard to the processing of personal data and on free movement of such data, published in the Official Journal, Part I, No. 790 of 12 Dec. 2001.
8. Law No. 298/2008 of 18 Nov. 2008, which implemented Directive 2006/24/EC of the EU Parliament and Council on retention of data generated or processed in connection with the provision of publicly available electronic communications services or public communication networks and amending Directive 2002/58/EC, O.J. (L 105) 13 Apr. 2006 54–63.
9. Constitutional Court, decision no. 1258 of 8 Oct. 2009, published in the Official Journal, Part I, No. 798 of 23 Nov. 2009.
10. Article 364 and 362 of the new Criminal Code.
11. The National Supervisory Authority for Personal Data Processing monitors and controls data processing falling within the scope of the Data Protection Act.
12. For instance, the European Working Party on the Protection of Individuals with Regard to Processing of Personal Data ('Article 29 Working Party'), an EU advisory board issuing opinions and guidelines on data-protection-related issues. In its Working Paper 136 of 20 Jun. 2007, the Art. 29 Working Party explains that an extensive concept of 'personal data' is an underlying purpose of the European Data Protection Directive.
13. Supervisory Authority's Yearly Activity Report for 2008, 67–69, available at <www.dataprotection.ro>.

details related to his or her professional life. Thus, employees can rely on the protection offered by this Act in relation to their employers to the same extent as any third party.

It follows from the above that work-related documents revealing a person's position within a company or information on their wage, appraisals, trade union membership, and so forth fall within the scope of the Data Protection Act and their processing, including disclosure to third parties, must comply with the requirements set out thereby.

B.   ROMANIAN DATA PROTECTION LAW: EMPLOYEES' E-MAILS

The Constitution recognizes the inviolability of correspondence as a fundamental right placed under the protection of criminal law. Thus, e-mails qualify as 'correspondence' under Article 195 of the Criminal Code, which renders violation of correspondence secrecy a criminal offence. Furthermore, employees' correspondence by e-mail is protected under the Data Protection Act, since e-mails (whether private or professional) are likely to contain personal data. However, there are no specific legal provisions regulating employers' screening, storage, and disclosure of employees' e-mails.

Under Article 195, paragraphs 1 and 2 of the Criminal Code, 'violation of correspondence secrecy' is to be construed as covering unauthorized access to or interception, destruction, or disclosure of any correspondence or communication. In the absence of specific rules, constitutional and criminal law protection applies to private and professional correspondence alike. Hence, only a waiver of the protection granted under the Constitution and the Criminal Code could authorize the employers' surveillance of employees' e-mails. To that end, the employers must seek unambiguous consent of the employees.

In practice, internal regulations regarding the use of professional e-mail and information technology (IT) resources by the employees are sometimes issued and the employees are instructed to use business e-mail only for professional purposes and are warned of possible e-mail screening, storage, and disclosure. Such regulations serve to determine the limits of employees' privacy expectations as well as those of employers' interference with employees' correspondence. However, in the absence of a specific legal framework and relevant case law, it is difficult to assess whether such regulations are of any consequence with regard to the requirement to seek employees' consent for surveillance of their e-mail correspondence.

C.   ROMANIAN DATA PROTECTION LAW: COLLECTION, PROCESSING, AND USE

Any operation that could virtually be performed upon personal data represents 'processing' of such data[14] within the meaning of the Data Protection Act and

---

14. That is, collection, record, storage, modification, extraction, use, disclosure to third parties, blocking access, erasure, destruction, etc.

hence falls within the scope of this Act. As a matter of principle, personal data processing is allowed only if the individual whose data are subject to processing has given an unambiguous consent to that end. The Data Protection Act sets forth some statutory exceptions to the consent requirement, which vary depending on the nature of the personal data in question; however, such exceptions are to be narrowly construed.

Whenever the above requirements for processing of personal data are fulfilled, such actions are to be carried out for clearly defined, explicit, and legitimate purposes. Processing is further submitted to a proportionality requirement: only relevant data can be processed, to the extent and throughout the time required by the purpose justifying their processing. Finally, incorrect or outdated personal data should be either erased or rectified.

D.   ROMANIA DATA PROTECTION LAW: DATA CONTROLLER, DATA PROCESSOR

The data controller is the natural or legal person who sets the purpose and the means of personal data processing. The data controller may process personal data either directly or through a data processor (namely, a natural or legal person acting on the data controller's behalf).

The data processor acts exclusively under the instructions and the supervision of the data controller. Thus, only the data controller can make the decision to disclose such data to third parties. Both are under a statutory obligation to ensure the confidentiality and the security of the data processing.

Personal data once collected may be transferred to third parties, if the data subject consented to such transfer or if the transfer is authorized under an exception to the consent requirement. Upon transfer, the third party – the recipient of such data – becomes the data controller and, as such, is liable for all obligations imposed by the Data Protection Act on data controllers.

E.   ROMANIAN DATA PROTECTION LAW: NOTIFICATION TO THE SUPERVISORY AUTHORITY

Data controllers are under a statutory duty to notify any processing to the Supervisory Authority before carrying out any operation or set of operations of processing of personal data that pursue the identical or related purposes. The notification shall specify, *inter alia,* the purposes of the data processing, the data subject to the processing, and the category of persons to whom the processed data relates. Furthermore, when disclosure of such data is contemplated by the data controller, the recipient must also be specified. Where the recipient is located abroad, the notification must also specify the categories of data subject to transfer and the country of destination.

F.   ROMANIAN DATA PROTECTION LAW: TRANSFER ABROAD

Transfer of personal data to recipients based in Member States of the EU or the European Economic Area (EEA) is unrestricted, subject to compliance with the Data Protection Act. When the recipient is based in a country outside the EU or the EEA, the transfer is allowed only if an equivalent data protection standard is ensured in the country of destination.

The Supervisory Authority may nevertheless authorize personal data transfer to a country even though its domestic law was found not to provide an equivalent level of data protection. To this effect, the data controller must ensure that the recipient shall provide the required data protection – for instance, by executing an agreement containing appropriate data protection clauses.

The Safe Harbour Privacy Principles for the protection of personal data transferred from EU Member States to the United States and the Frequently Asked Questions (FAQs) issued by the government of the United States on 21 July 2000 have been recognized as providing an equivalent level of protection by the EC Commission.[15] Hence, transfer of personal data to a recipient located in the United States is allowed if the recipient self-certifies its adherence to the Safe Harbour Privacy Principles.

G.   ROMANIA DATA PROTECTION LAW: CONFLICT OF LAWS

The Data Protection Act is applicable to the processing of personal data performed by data controllers based in Romania and to the processing of personal data by means located in Romanian territory irrespective of the data controllers' location. Given the rather extended scope of application of the Data Protection Act, resort to conflict of law rules might be necessary in cases when the data controller is not based in Romania.

H.   ROMANIAN DATA PROTECTION LAW: ENFORCEMENT

The Supervisory Authority ensures data controllers' and data processors' compliance with the obligations set out by the Data Protection Act. Under this Act, breaches of such obligations qualify as administrative offences (*Rom. contraventii*) and are punishable by fines of up to Romanian Lei (RON) 50,000,[16] unless such

---

15. Decision 520/2000/EC of 26 Jul. 2000 pursuant to Directive 95/46/EC of the European Parliament and of the Council on the adequacy of the protection provided by the Safe Harbour Privacy Principles and related Frequently Asked Questions issued by the US Department of Commerce, 2000 O.J. (L 215/7) 25 Aug. 4–47.
16. Around EUR 12,000.

breaches occur in such circumstances that they are incriminated as criminal offences under a different statute.[17]

Resort to investigative powers by the Supervisory Authority is subject to the scrutiny of both the courts and the public. Thus, information about the investigations carried out and fines applied in case of breach of the Data Protection Act is periodically released on the Authority's website.[18] According to a press release dated 10 May 2010,[19] the Supervisory Authority carried out an investigation on an alleged illegal processing of consumers' personal data by the national telecommunication provider Romtelecom. The investigation revealed that Romtelecom had disclosed personal data of its customers to an insurance company, without the written prior consent of the customers. The company was fined an aggregate RON 5,000[20] for processing personal data without consent and for use of such data for a different purpose than providing communication services.

In a different case, following an investigation carried out in March 2003, the Supervisory Authority fined the oil and gas producer SC Petrom SA for processing personal data without prior notification to the Authority. The investigation revealed that SC Petrom SA had installed video cameras for surveillance of the access to its precincts and that it failed to notify the Supervisory Authority thereof. The fine applied was RON 2,700.[21]

Finally, it should be noted that persons alleging breaches of the Data Protection Act may additionally rely on the general provisions of the Civil Code regarding tortuous liability in order to claim moral damages for illegal processing of their personal data. Thus, in a judgment given on 16 March 2009,[22] the First District Bucharest Court of First Instance awarded moral damages in amount of Euros (EUR) 10,000[23] for illegal disclosure of personal data. The claimant alleged a breach of, *inter alia,* the Data Protection Act following the release by the Bucharest First District's City Hall on its website of a list disclosing the personal identification data of all the persons benefitting from free city transportation subscriptions due to severe handicap.

---

17. The new Criminal Code, scheduled to enter into force in 2011, qualifies as criminal offences punishable by up to five years of imprisonment the unauthorized transfer of electronic data, the unauthorized alteration of electronic data, as well as unauthorized restriction of access to electronic data.
18. Available at <www.dataprotection.ro>.
19. Available at <www.dataprotection.ro>.
20. Around EUR 1,205.
21. Around EUR 630.
22. Available at <www.juridice.ro/100724/judecatoria-sectorului-1-daune-morale-pentru-publicarea-pe-internet-a-datelor-personale.html>. According to the information released on the website, the judgment became final upon dismissal of the appeal brought against it.
23. RON 42,670.

IV. PRETRIAL DISCOVERY VERSUS DATA PROTECTION
     IN ROMANIA: BACKGROUND

Under Romanian law, no blocking statute prevents private persons and legal entities from complying with a pretrial discovery request issued by a US court. However, the data protection requirements set forth by the Data Protection Act might limit the scope of the disclosure of case-related facts and documents to the US-based party.

A. PRETRIAL DISCOVERY VERSUS DATA PROTECTION IN
    ROMANIA: RETENTION AND TRANSFER OF DATA

Under the Data Protection Act, processing of personal data must pursue a clearly defined purpose and such data can be stored only for as long as justified by the purpose of their processing. When, without prior anticipation, previously collected data appear to be relevant to a future litigation and are likely to be transferred to a third party, the purpose of the retention of such data changes. Hence, a new notification must be filed with the Supervisory Authority.

A change in purpose of the data processing requires as a rule the consent of the data subject for further processing. However, the Data Protection Act authorizes data controllers to bypass such requirement when the processing is justified by legitimate interests of the data controller, if such interest overrides the data subject's interests or fundamental rights. Such exception from the consent requirement applies when the data controller faces litigation and data processing is necessary for the purpose of the making or defending of a claim before courts. In assessing the scope of such exception, a fair balance needs to be stricken between the data controller's interest in the litigation and the data subject's right to protection of personal data. To this end, the data controller may resort to the guidelines issued by the Article 29 Working Party,[24] knowing that the Supervisory Authority regards such guidelines as persuasive authority. Thus, processing of personal data for the purpose of disclosure in a pretrial discovery procedure must meet a requirement of proportionality, meaning that the data processing must be both relevant and not excessive in relation to such purpose. Furthermore, the actual consequences of processing such data for the data subject must be given weight.

In practice, such assessment is to be made by the data controller, which should filter the data so as to determine those that are relevant and proceed, to the extent possible, to anonymizing the documents that shall be disclosed. When the data controller is not EU-based, the filtering should be performed, if possible, by an EU-based trusted third person.

---

24. Working Document 1/2009 on pretrial discovery for cross-border litigation (WP 158) adopted on 11 Feb. 2009.

Silvia Popa

B.   Pretrial Discovery versus Data Protection in Romania:
                         Export of Personal Data to the United States

Under the Romanian Data Protection Act, the transfer of personal data to a recipient located in the United States is exceptionally allowed, notwithstanding non-existence of the recipient's self-certification under the Safe Harbour Privacy Principles, when the transfer is deemed necessary for supporting a legal claim. However, such permission is limited since personal data in such context must be processed only in relation to and only as long as justified by the above-mentioned purpose.

V.   CONCLUSION

Although a US pretrial discovery is not regulated under Romanian law, its scope may be limited by the personal data protection requirements set forth by the Data Protection Act.

240

Chapter 5.21
Serbia

*Aleksa Anđelković**

I. INTRODUCTION

E-discovery is still a fairly unknown phenomenon in Serbia, where so far not even a commonly accepted definition of e-discovery exists. According to Keteltas and Rosenthal, e-discovery involves 'the preservation, collection, processing and production of electronically stored documents'.[1] In absence of a commonly accepted definition of e-discovery in Serbia, the term 'e-discovery' is used within the meaning of the definition of Keteltas and Rosenthal within the context of this contribution.

However, when taking a look at the early beginnings of the implementation of frameworks for the processing and producing of electronic documents, it was not Serbia but rather the Federal Republic of Yugoslavia (where Serbia has been part of) that first dealt with the use of electronic systems for preserving, collecting, processing, and producing electronic documents in 1986 through the 'Concept of juridical information system in Yugoslavia' (PRIS).[2]

---

* Aleksa Anđelković LL.M, is an attorney at law at Moravčević Vojnović Zdravković oad, Belgrade, Serbia, in cooperation with Schönherr Rechtsanwälte GmbH, Vienna, Austria.
1. Keteltas Gill & Rosenthal John, 'Discovery of Electronic Evidence', in *Electronic Evidence: Law and Practice*, ed. Paul R. Rice (2008), 2.
2. Koncepcija Pravosudnog informacionog sistema Jugoslavije (PRIS).

Catrien Noorda & Stefan Hanloser, *E-Discovery and Data Privacy*, pp. 241–246.

In the following years the Serbian industry sector experienced a strong process of privatization where the level of usage of electronic systems for processing and storing electronic documents significantly increased.

However, e-discovery within the meaning of the definition given by Keteltas and Rosenthal still is a new and unknown legal term in Serbian statutory law. Thus, it is rather realistic that Serbian legal professionals' ambitions with respect to e-discovery will in the medium term be fairly limited to monitoring the respective developments in other countries. Accordingly, Serbian involvement in e-discovery can best be described as a 'view from the gallery'. Nevertheless, from today's perspective, e-discovery requests will frequently involve data transfer and data disclosure issues. Therefore, whenever it comes to processing, storing, or producing electronically stored documents within the definition of e-discovery given by Keteltas and Rosenthal, the respective Serbian legal provisions dealing with disclosure and transfer of personal data will have to be considered accordingly. Having said this, the present contribution gives a guideline on applicable regulations that will have to be considered under Serbian law in the context of e-discovery.

II.   PRIVACY AND DATA PROTECTION IN SERBIA

A.   LEGAL FRAMEWORK

On a constitutional level, the protection of personal data in Serbia is determined by the Constitution of the Republic of Sebia.[3] Article 42 of the Constitution states:

> Protection of personal data shall be guaranteed. Collecting, keeping, processing and using of personal data shall be regulated by the law. Use of personal data for any the purpose other the one were collected for shall be prohibited and punishable in accordance with the law, unless this is necessary to conduct criminal proceedings or protect safety of the Republic of Serbia, in a manner stipulated by the law.
>
> Everyone shall have the right to be informed about personal data collected about him, in accordance with the law, and the right to court protection in case of their abuse.

On a federal level, personal data is protected in Serbia by the 'Act on protection of data on persons'[4] (the 'Act 2008'), which determines 'the conditions for personal data collection and processing, the rights and protection of the rights of persons whose data are collected and processed, limitations to personal data protection, proceedings before an authority responsible for data protection, data security, data

---

3.   Ustav Republike Srbije, Official Gazette of the Republic of Serbia, 98/06.
4.   Zakon o zaštiti podataka o ličnosti, Official Gazette of the Republic of Serbia, 97/2008; <www.poverenik.org.rs/images/stories/dokumentacija-nova/zakon-o-zastiti-podataka-o-licnosti_en.pdf>, 1 Dec. 2009.

filing, data transfers outside the Republic of Serbia and enforcement of this Act' (Article 1).

B.   HISTORY OF DATA PROTECTION IN SERBIA

However, when the Act 2008 was adopted in the year of 2008 it was not the first step in data protection in Serbia. It was rather in 1998 when the Federal Republic of Yugoslavia implemented the 'Act on the protection of data on persons'[5] (the 'Act 1998'). The Act 1998 protected for the first time the secrecy of personal data, including privacy data, data on the integrity of persons, data on personal and family life, and other personal data related to identified or identifiable persons.

Under the Act 1998, data transfers including the transfer of personal data outside of Serbia were subject to the principle of reciprocity. According to this principle, the transfer of data was only permitted if the country the personal data was to be transferred to provided for (a) protection of personal data of people not being citizens of this country and (b) a level of protection not being lower than the data protection level of the Act 1998.

The Act 1998 also provided for the setup of a national data protection authority, which, however, was not established until 2008. This absence of a data protection regulator until 2008 caused some legal uncertainty in Serbian data protection law, especially with respect to transfers of data abroad.

C.   CURRENT STATUS OF DATA PROTECTION

Given this background of data protection law in Serbia, it was not before the adoption of the Act 2008 in the year of 2008 that Serbia made a significant step toward shaping the legal framework for protection of personal data in Serbia in a much more sophisticated way.

Under the Act 2008, personal data are now defined more broadly as 'any information relating to a natural person, regardless of the form of its presentation or the medium used (paper, tape, film, electronic media etc.), regardless on whose order, on whose behalf or for whose account such information is stored, regardless of the date of its creation or the place of its storage, regardless of the way in which such information is learned (directly, by listening, watching etc., or indirectly, by accessing a document containing the information etc.) and regardless of any other characteristic of such information' (Article 2 of the Act 2008).

In the wake of the implementation of the Act 2008, finally a national data protection authority was established. Since then data protection agendas are within the competency of the Commissioner for Information of Public Importance and Personal Data Protection[6] (the 'Commissioner').

---

5. Zakon o zaštiti podataka o ličnosti, Official Gazette of the Federal Republic of Yugoslavia, 24/98 and 26/98.
6. Official presentation of the Commissioner, <www.poverenik.org.rs/>, 1 Dec. 2009.

After the Commissioner was established he released in almost one year more than thirty opinions regarding the application of the Act 2008 on various issues ranging from publishing persons' identification numbers in the media in the course of privatization processes to personal data disclosure in the course of World Bank projects being implemented in Serbia (the latter coming close to the e-discovery definition of Keteltas and Rosenthal).[7]

D.   DATA TRANSFERS IN THE LIGHT OF E-DISCOVERY

As said, from a Serbian data protection perspective, e-discovery deals to a large extent with the disclosure and transfer of personal data. Whenever it comes to transferring personal data, Serbian data protection law distinguishes between data transfers to states that are parties to the Council of Europe Convention for the Protection of Individuals with Regard to Automatic Processing of Personal Data (the 'Convention') and those that are not. While data transfers to countries being parties to the Convention do not require formal approval of the Commissioner, data must only be transferred to countries not being parties of the Convention 'if such state or international organization has a regulation or a data transfer agreement in force which provides a level of data protection equivalent to that envisaged by the Convention'. However, in each case the Commissioner is entitled to assess 'whether the requirements are met and safeguards put in place for the transfer of data from the Republic of Serbia and is authorized to approve such transfer'. In other words: Data transfers to countries not being parties to the Convention, such as the United States, will always be subject to approval from the Commissioner. However, also data transfers to countries being parties to the Convention might be scrutinized by the Commissioner on a case-by-case basis. With this it can be stated that e-discovery requests will frequently touch the Commissioner's competencies.

III.   ADDITIONAL REGULATIONS TO BE CONSIDERED
            WITH RESPECT TO E-DISCOVERY

A.   TELECOMMUNICATIONS ACT

In Serbia specific categories of personal data are protected by the Serbian Tele-communications Act.[8]
    The Telecommunications Act sets out obligations on telecommunications operators regarding their customer data and limits the use of such data. Beside this, Serbian telecommunications law also limits the storage and processing of traffic data. Such data storage is limited to the principles of

---

7. Report of the Commissioner, November 2009, <www.poverenik.org.rs/images/stories/informator-o-radu/2009/novembar2009/novembar-09-informator.pdf>, 1 Dec. 2009.
8. Zakon o telekomunikacijama, Official Gazette of the Republic of Serbia, 44/03, 36/2006, 50/09.

(a) proportionality, where traffic data must only be stored and processed to the extent necessary for customer billing purposes;

(b) retention, where traffic data must only be stored as long as potential claims may be contested from the customer; and

(c) privacy, where any activity or use of equipment threatening or interfering with the privacy and confidentiality of messages transmitted via telecommunications networks is prohibited unless valid consent has been obtained from the affected customer or in cases where these activities are performed in compliance with the law or a valid court order.

So whenever an e-discovery request relates to traffic data, the respective restrictions under Serbian telecommunications law will have to be considered accordingly.

B.　　　　LABOUR ACT

The Labour Act of the Republic of Serbia[9] sets out restrictions regarding the collecting, processing, and use of employee data.

As a general rule any employee has the right to not only access all of his or her data being kept with his or her employer but also to ask for deletion of this data if they are not or not any more relevant for his or her employee relationship and therefore must not be kept any longer with the employer.

Further restrictions to the collecting and use of personal employee data are set out in Article 83, which prohibits the disclosure of personal employee data to third parties 'except in cases and under conditions stipulated under the law, or if it is necessary for substantiating rights and duties resulting from the labour relationship or in relation with the labour'.

Given the cited legal framework it can be concluded that Serbian labour law limits the legitimacy of collecting and disclosing personal employee data only to such kind of data that are relevant for the employee relationship. Although the exact scope of data being relevant for the employee relationship in terms of the Serbian Labour Act always depends on the factual case, it can be generally expected that the Commissioner will interpret the 'relevance' of such data and, with this, the scope of their protection, in a rather extensive manner.

C.　　　　CIVIL PROCEDURE ACT

The Serbian Civil Procedure Act[10] is far from providing statues that even come close to e-discovery-related provisions. Generally, the parties to the trial are obliged to present all facts that are relevant to their request or might give evidence

---

9. Zakon o radu, Official Gazette of the Republic of Serbia, 24/05, 61/05, 54/09.
10. Zakon o parnicnom postupku, Official Gazette of the Republic of Serbia, 125/04.

or support their position. However, the Civil Procedure Act does not provide for respective procedural provisions on the enforced disclosure of documents or information supporting the parties' procedural positions. Instead, the parties to the civil proceedings are only required to produce documents that support their own position.

IV.   NO BLOCKING STATUTES

There are no restrictions under Serbian law for cooperation with foreign courts or public authorities in the course of civil/or criminal procedures or other regulatory investigations.

V.   FUTURE TRENDS

How will e-discovery develop in Serbia? Possible changes in data protection law might be anticipated by (a) activities of the Commissioner and/or by (b) changes of the legislative framework. It can be anticipated that the Commissioner will gradually expand notions of personal data and protection of personal data. This trend can already be seen through opinions of the Commissioner. Regarding the anticipated changes in the legislative framework, there are currently two proposals discussed at the National Assembly of Serbia: the Proposal of the Act on confirming the Convention on taking evidence abroad in civil and commercial matters and the Proposal of the Act on confirming the Convention on the service abroad of judicial and extra-judicial documents in civil or commercial matters. Both legislative proposals deal with the legitimacy of the disclosure of documents (including electronically stored documents). However, the date of enactment of these laws is still open and must not be expected before the end of 2010.

VI.   CONCLUSION

With respect to e-discovery in Serbia, it can be stated that things are yet rather underdeveloped. Anyway, the transfer of data to countries that are not party to the Convention is subjected to the authorization procedure of the Commissioner, where the level of data protection in the receiving country will be assessed accordingly. Additionally, the disclosure of employee data is subjected to the Commissioner's assessment as well, where the Commissioner will scrutinize whether the data disclosure is relevant for the employee relationship. Finally, an eye has to be kept on the pending Proposal of the Act confirming the Convention on taking evidence abroad in civil and commercial matters, which, upon becoming effective, might form a sufficient legal basis for validly dealing with e-discovery requests.

Chapter 5.22
Slovakia

*Jana Habánová and Michal Lučivjanský**

I.   INTRODUCTION

In a globalized world it is quite common that businesses are conducted internationally. Accordingly, complex legal implications may arise. One of these issues is
the tension between discovery obligations under US law and the data protection
rules applying in European countries. Data protection legislation of the Slovak
Republic (similarly to most European Union (EU) Member States) provides for a
broad scope of data protection that may be in conflict with an e-discovery request.
The situation is complicated also due to the fact that pretrial discovery is a common
law institution that is not present in the Slovak Republic with its civil law tradition.

II.   DISCOVERY IN SLOVAK LAW: INTRODUCTION

In Slovak law the legal institution known in the Anglo-American system as discovery, that is, pre-trial mutual disclosure of documents and evidences, is
unknown. Nevertheless, the Slovak Code of Civil Procedure[1] allows a litigant

---

*   Jana Habánová and Michal Lučivjanský, Schönherr Rechtsanwälte GmbH, organizačná zložka,
     Bratislava, Slovak Republic.
1.   Section 78–78h of the Act No. 99/1963 Coll. Code of Civil Procedure, as amended (*Občiansky
     súdny poriadok*).

Catrien Noorda & Stefan Hanloser, *E-Discovery and Data Privacy*, pp. 247–255.

to lodge a petition for the production of evidence should there be doubts in the ability of producing evidence, that is, a risk that such evidence could not be produced at all or only with great difficulties. Such petition can be lodged only prior to the main proceedings; the competent court shall be the court trying the case on its merits or the court in which jurisdiction the evidence in question is found. The Code of Civil Procedure also contains a specific regulation for situations where the evidence in question is requested as evidence for special proceedings conducted pursuant to the applicable rules on the protection of competition.[2] Also, there are specific provisions regarding the preservation of the relevant evidence in case of infringement of intellectual property rights.

A.   DISCOVERY IN SLOVAK LAW: BLOCKING STATUTES

A general blocking statute or provisions concerning restrictions or prohibitions of transfer of information to foreign courts or public authorities do not exist in Slovak law. Nevertheless, the Electronic Communication Act contains a provision[3] stipulating that traffic data, location data, and data of the communicating parties stored by a telecommunication company or by an Internet provider may be provided only to Slovak courts and administrative bodies. Therefore, the transfer of these data to authorities and courts outside of the Slovak Republic is not allowed.

B.   DISCOVERY IN SLOVAK LAW: THE HAGUE CONVENTION ON THE TAKING OF EVIDENCE

The Hague Convention on the Taking of Evidence Abroad in Civil or Commercial Matters[4] can be used in a standard procedure when there is a request for the production of specific information and evidence in civil and commercial litigations. The Slovak Republic, a member of the Hague Conference on Private International Law (a regular member since 1968 as part of Czechoslovakia) is bound by this Convention and has ratified it[5] with two procedural modifications.

This Convention contains a provision[6] that in 'civil or commercial matters a judicial authority of a Contracting State may, in accordance with the provisions of the law of that State, request the competent authority of another Contracting State, by means of a Letter of Request, to obtain evidence, or to perform some other

---

2.   Act No. 136/2001 Coll. on the protection of competition, as amended (*Zákon o ochrane hospodárskej súťaže*).
3.   Section 59a of the Act 610/2003 Coll. on electronic communication, as amended (*Zákon o elektronických komunikáciách*)
4.   Convention of 18 Mar. 1970 on the Taking of Evidence Abroad in Civil or Commercial Matters (Hague Conference on Private International Law).
5.   The Ministry of Foreign Affairs Regulation No. 129/1976 (*Vyhláška ministra zahraničných vecí 129/1976 Zb. o Dohovore o vykonávaní dôkazov v cudzine v občianskych a obchodných veciach*).
6.   Article 1 of the Hague Convention on the Taking of Evidence.

judicial act'. The Convention also includes a specific provision in its Article 23 that gives the right to the Contracting State at the time of signature, ratification, or accession to declare that it will not execute Letters of Request issued for the purpose of obtaining pretrial discovery of documents as known in common law countries. Some of the Contracting States of this Convention (e.g., Germany, France, and Spain) made such a declaration. The Slovak Republic has not taken advantage of Article 23; therefore a Letter of Request issued for a common law discovery can be executed by the Central Authority, which is in the Slovak Republic the Ministry of Justice.

Notwithstanding the above, the Hague Convention on the Taking of Evidence has not been used very often as an instrument to obtain evidence for common law discovery since the US Supreme Court handed down its landmark decision in the *Aérospatiale* case.[7] In this decision, the US Supreme Court held that the Hague Evidence Convention is an optional but not mandatory procedure for obtaining documents and information located in the territory of a Convention Contracting State, and US parties are free to use procedures set out in the US Federal Rules of Civil Procedure.

The European legislation provides yet another instrument – Council Regulation (EC) Number 1206/2001[8] – for the request to obtain evidence. This regulation, however, only governs relationships between Member States of the EU and therefore is out of the scope of this country report.

III.   SLOVAK DATA PROTECTION LAW: INTRODUCTION

The right to protection against unauthorized collection, publication, or other misuse of personal data and the right to protection of personal data are two of the basic rights and freedoms granted by the Constitution of the Slovak Republic[9] and the Civil Code.[10] These rights had not been protected in the Slovak Republic in a codified form until 2002, and the two existing regulations for their protection[11] were often criticized as insufficient. Therefore, with 1 September 2002 a new, comprehensive piece of legislation, the Act on the Protection of Personal Data[12] (hereinafter referred to as the 'PDPA') entered into effect, which is now the general statute for data protection in the Slovak Republic and which has also established

7. *Société Nationale Industrielle Aerospatiale v. United States District Court*, 482 U.S. 522 (1987).
8. Council Regulation (EC) No. 1206/2001 of 28 May 2001 on cooperation between the courts of the Member States in the taking of evidence in civil or commercial matters.
9. Article 19(3) and Art. 22(1) of the Act No. 460/1992 Coll. Constitution of the Slovak Republic *(Ústava Slovenskej republiky)*.
10. Section 11, 12, 13, 15, and 16 of the Act No. 40/1964 Coll. Civil Code, as amended *(Občiansky zákonník)*.
11. Act No. 256/1992 Coll. and then Act No. 52/1998 Coll. on data protection in information systems.
12. Act No. 428/2002 Coll. on protection of personal data, as amended *(Zákon o ochrane osobných údajov)*.

Jana Habánová and Michal Lučivjanský

a new public authority for supervising this area – the Office for Personal Data Protection of the Slovak Republic (hereinafter referred to as the 'Office'). The PDPA has been amended four times – the last time with effect from 1 January 2009. The PDPA has implemented the relevant European legislation[13] in this area.

A.   Slovak Data Protection Law: Protection of Personal Data

The PDPA provides protection only for personal data. The PDPA defines personal data as any information relating to an identified or identifiable natural person. This definition is an implementation of Directive 95/46/EC and can be considered as quite broad. The interpretation of the term 'personal data' is within the discretion of courts and public authorities; however, the so-called Article 29 Working Party[14] provides guidelines[15] to the interpretation of this definition, which extends the scope of the term 'personal data' also to data such as call logs for a telephone, video surveillance, drug prescriptions, and so forth.

The PDPA distinguishes a sub-category of a personal data – special categories of personal data. Processing of these data is prohibited (however, there are some exceptions under specific circumstances). Within this category fall certain personal data stipulated in the EU legislation,[16] though the PDPA extends this protection to even more data categories – data relating to breaches of administrative and penal provisions of law and biometrical data.

From the above-mentioned provisions it follows (in the context and the scope of this country report) that the majority of e-discovery requests will most probably deal with the PDPA's provisions on the protection of personal data.

B.   Slovak Data Protection Law: Processing of Personal Data

The definition of processing personal data in the PDPA provides that this term covers any operation or set of operations that are performed on personal data, such as obtaining, collecting, recording, organizing, and so forth. Only the controller

---

13. Directive 95/46/EC of the European Parliament and of the Council of 24 Oct. 1995 on the protection of individuals with regard to the processing of personal data and on the free movement of such data as amended by the Regulation (EC) No. 1882/2003 of the European Parliament and of the Council of 29 Sep. 2003 (Ú.v. EÚ L 284, 31 Oct. 2003)
14. Working Party on the protection of individuals with regard to the processing of personal data established on the basis of Art. 29 of the Directive 95/46/EC.
15. Opinion 4/2007 on the concept of personal data, Working Paper 136 of 20 Jun. 2007. The Article 29 Working Party is the independent EU Advisory Body on Data Protection and Privacy established by Art. 29 of Directive 95/46/EC.
16. Article 8(1) of the Directive 95/46/EC of the European Parliament and of the Council of 24 Oct. 1995 on the protection of individuals with regard to the processing of personal data and on the free movement of such data – 'Member States shall prohibit the processing of personal data revealing racial or ethnic origin, political opinions, religious or philosophical beliefs, trade-union membership, and the processing of data concerning health or sex life'.

and processor are authorized to process personal data of a data subject (a natural person whose personal data are processed). A controller is a public authority or a natural or legal person who determines the purposes and the means of processing personal data or, in cases where the purpose and means are stipulated by the special act, the controller is the person determined by law or the person fulfilling the terms stipulated by law. If the controller does not process personal data itself, such data processing must be conducted by the processor, that is, a public authority or a natural or a legal person processing personal data on behalf of the controller and only to the extent and under conditions agreed upon with the controller in a written contract or a written authorization.

An important part of the PDPA provisions deals with the principles of processing personal data. The first and most important provision is that personal data may only be processed upon the consent of the data subject, or without this consent if the purpose of the processing of personal data is stipulated by a special act.[17] The PDPA also contains some further exceptions from the requirement of obtaining the data subject's consent.[18] Other important principles of processing personal data are the unambiguous and concrete determination of the purpose of processing, trustworthiness of personal data, and accuracy of personal data.

C.   SLOVAK DATA PROTECTION LAW: PROTECTION OF
      EMPLOYEES' E-MAILS

In the context of an e-discovery request, an important legal issue is the protection of employees' private e-mails, which is affected by the personal data protection provisions stipulated in the PDPA and also by the protection of the secrecy of mail messages. The secrecy of mail messages (as one of the basic human rights) in connection with e-mails is stipulated in the Labour Code[19] and applies to situations where a business e-mail address is used by the employee also for private communication. The Labour Code[20] stipulates that the employer may not encroach upon employees' privacy at workplaces by monitoring the employees without them being informed or by checking their personal mails. By an extensive interpretation of this provision, not only personal mails but also personal e-mails are protected. Therefore, screening and discovery of such employee e-mails, without a prior notice, could be considered as a violation of law. However, there are no judgments or administrative decisions available in this respect.

---

17. For example, Act No. 595/2003 Coll. on income tax, as amended *(Zákon o dani z príjmov)* or Act 610/2003 Coll. on electronic communication, as amended *(Zákon o elektronických komunikáciách)*. Such an act must stipulate a list of processed personal data, the purpose of their processing, and the group of data subjects.
18. Section 7(4) of the Act No. 428/2002 Coll. on the protection of personal data, as amended *(Zákon o ochrane osobných údajov)*, for example, for the purpose of artistic or literary expression, for the purpose of informing the public by means of the mass media, etc.
19. Article 11 of the Act No. 311/2001 Coll. Labour Code, as amended *(Zákonník práce)*.
20. Article 11 of the Act No. 311/2001 Coll. Labour Code, as amended *(Zákonník práce)*.

To prevent the above scenario, there are two options. The first one is that before screening of business e-mails the employer obtains prior consents of its employees for such screening. Or, a special clause in individual employment contracts can provide for e-mail screening. The second option is to conclude a separate agreement between the employer and the employees regarding the use of business e-mail accounts only for performing work. This option, however, raises several issues; for example, if such agreement is concluded and the employee has used his or her business e-mail account for personal communication, any of the e-mails in his or her mailbox can be considered both as personal and as business e-mails, which may lead to disputes and litigation.

D.   SLOVAK DATA PROTECTION LAW: INTERNATIONAL ASPECTS

Very important provisions of the PDPA in relation to e-discovery requests are those governing the international aspects of data protection, mainly the part bearing the title 'Trans-border personal data flow'.[21]

Regulation of the international personal data flow depends on the country that will be the final destination of the respective personal data. The flow of personal data between the Slovak Republic and the other Member States of the EU is not restricted. If the country of destination is not an EU Member State, namely the United States, an adequate level of protection of personal data must be ensured for the transfer of personal data. The level of protection is assessed mainly upon legal regulations on data protection in the country of destination and upon other circumstances surrounding the transfer. Assessment is carried out by the European Commission. Due to the fact that the United States has not adopted any universal data protection legislation in the private sphere, it is not considered as a country with an adequate level of protection of personal data. Therefore, for the transfer of personal data to the United States, the method of so-called 'Safe Harbour' may be used. This term refers to the summary of certain technical and administrative measures ensuring the privacy of such transfer. A list of US corporations and organizations that observe the Safe Harbour Privacy Principles is kept by the US Department of Commerce. Other possibilities for data transfers to the United States are transfers with prior written consent of data subjects together with the use of Standard Contractual Clauses (SCCs)[22] or the use of Binding Corporate Rules (BCRs), that is, an internal document of transnational corporations containing a global privacy policy (BCRs shall be approved by the data protection authority in every country where the respective transnational corporation is doing business).

---

21. Section 23–23a of the Act No. 428/2002 Coll. on the protection of personal data, as amended (*Zákon o ochrane osobných údajov*).
22. These SCCs are regulated by the legislation of the EU, mainly by the 2002/16/EC: Commission Decision of 27 Dec. 2001 on Standard Contractual Clauses for the transfer of personal data to processors established in third countries, under Directive 95/46/EC, and by the 2001/497/EC: Commission Decision of 15 Jun. 2001 on Standard Contractual Clauses for the transfer of personal data to third countries, under Directive 95/46/EC.

E. SLOVAK DATA PROTECTION LAW: PUBLIC AUTHORITY

The public authority responsible for the field of data protection in the Slovak Republic is the Office for Personal Data Protection of the Slovak Republic. This Office was established pursuant to the PDPA as a state administration authority with competence over the entire territory of the Slovak Republic. The Office independently carries out various tasks, for example, the inspection of the level of personal data protection, registration of filing systems, issuing of binding decisions (in case of ambiguous situations), recommendation of taking certain measures for ensuring the protection of personal data, imposing of sanctions, and so forth.

F. SLOVAK DATA PROTECTION LAW: ENFORCEMENT

The PDPA grants the Office the power to enforce the respective regulations for personal data protection. The available sanctions for the violation of provisions of the PDPA are: (i) disclosure of details of a legal person and of its violating the law; (ii) ordering the breaching party to perform certain actions or to refrain from performing certain actions; and (iii) a fine up to approximately Euros (EUR) 331,939, depending on the circumstances. Further, the data subject whose rights have been violated is entitled to claim damages under the provisions of the Civil Code.[23] According to the Office's report,[24] during the period from January 2007 to December 2008 the Office investigated 525 notifications by natural and legal persons. The fines levied for this period amounted to Slovak Koruna (SKK) 1,153,000 (EUR 39,272.65).

The Criminal Code also contains provisions[25] relating to the protection of personal data. The first one is causing damage to and misuse of the information recorded on a medium. Unauthorized manipulation of personal data is the second one.

IV. DISCOVERY REQUEST AND SLOVAK DATA PROTECTION LAW

In the event of an e-discovery request, the responding party doing business in the Slovak Republic will be in most of the cases confronted with the provisions of the PDPA. The reason is that e-discovery requirements (such as retention and transfer of personal data) fall under the term 'processing of personal data' if the requested data contain personal data, which is highly probable. Therefore, such an e-discovery request must be made in compliance with the PDPA requirements for

---

23. Sections 420–450 of the Act No. 40/1964 Coll. Civil Code, as amended *(Občiansky zákonník)*.
24. Personal Data Protection Report 2007 – 2008, 33.
25. Section 247 and s. 374 of the Act No. 300/2005 Coll. Criminal Code, as amended *(Trestný zákon)*.

processing. A guide for e-discovery requests in connection with data protection can be found in the Working Document 1/2009[26] adopted by the Article 29 Working Party.

The proceedings required for the transfer of personal data to the United States, which is deemed to be a country with an inadequate level of protection of personal data, depends on the method selected for such a transfer:

– Safe Harbour – in case of using this method, a written request for the consent to the transfer of personal data (with specific requirements) must be submitted to the Office by regular mail. It is not required to incorporate the SCCs into the transfer contract pursuant to EU law. The Office has a statutory period of thirty days for issuing its decision should the form and contents of the request qualify for granting such consent.
– Prior written consent together with SCCs – this is the most commonly used method of transferring personal data. Slovak law provides for double protection: besides a prior written consent of the data subject, also SCCs (pursuant to EU law) must be incorporated (this kind of protection is not common in all of the Member States of the EU). The consent of the Office for the use of SCCs must be obtained only in a case where the transfer of personal data is conducted by the controller-processor method.[27]
– Binding Corporate Rules – this internal data protection policy shall be first approved by a so-called leading authority in the country, where the corporation has the majority of its assets. Subsequently, this document shall be approved by the data protection authority in all the countries where the transnational corporation is doing business. The use of BCRs yields numerous advantages for transnational corporations, but the process of obtaining approval from all of the countries can be quite time consuming, and every data protection authority has a veto right for any provision of the BCRs. Therefore, this method is not used very often. The Article 29 Working Party provides guidelines[28] also for the use of this method.

---

26. Working Document 1/2009 on pretrial discovery for cross-border civil litigation, Working Paper 158 adopted on 11 Feb. 2009.
27. Section 23(7) of Act No. 428/2002 Coll. on protection of personal data, as amended (*Zákon o ochrane osobných údajov*).
28. Working Document on transfers of personal data to third countries: Applying Art. 26 (2) of the EU Data Protection Directive to Binding Corporate Rules for International Data Transfers, Working Paper 74 adopted on 3 Jun. 2003; Working Document Setting Forth a Co-Operation Procedure for Issuing Common Opinions on Adequate Safeguards Resulting from 'Binding Corporate Rules', Working Paper 107 adopted on 14 Apr. 2005; Recommendation 1/2007 on the Standard Application for Approval of Binding Corporate Rules for the Transfer of Personal Data, Working Paper 133 adopted on 10 Jan. 2007.

V.   CONCLUSION

Although Slovak law regulates personal data protection in a complex and strict way, processing of an e-discovery request in compliance with the personal data protection rules is possible via the three methods described above. Nevertheless, the responding party has to process this request with special care and diligence, observing the provisions of the PDPA and respective EU law.

Chapter 5.23
Slovenia

*Tomaz Petrovic**

I.   INTRODUCTION

The common law pretrial discovery is unknown to the Slovenian law system. In some cases, pretrial discovery could confer even more rights to the litigants than they could claim under Slovenian procedural law.[1] Therefore, the risk of conflict with Slovenian procedural rules is imminent when common law requests for evidence in pretrial discovery procedures are lodged. Furthermore, alarms are wailing for the protection of personal or even sensitive data, which are protected by the Slovenian Constitution.

---

*   Tomaz Petrovic, Attorney at Law, and Peter Zorin, Associate, at Law Firm Filipov Petrovic, Jeraj in Partnerji, D.O.O. in cooperation with Schönherr Rechtsanwälte GmbH, Ljubljana, Slovenia.
1.   Zakon o pravdnem postopku (Civil Procedure Act, hereinafter: ZPP), Slovenian Official Gazette 73/2007, and Zakon o kazenskem postopku (Criminal Procedure Act, hereinafter: ZKP), Slovenian Official Gazette 116/2003, provides in general that the litigants produce only those documents in court that support their case and are not obliged to produce any other requested documents unless they are specifically asked by the court.

Catrien Noorda & Stefan Hanloser, *E-Discovery and Data Privacy*, pp. 257–262.

II. SLOVENIAN DATA PROTECTION
     LAW: BACKGROUND

The protection of data is among the human rights that are guaranteed by the Slovenian Constitution.[2] The first law on data protection was passed in the last days of the Socialist Republic of Slovenia,[3] which was later assumed by the Republic of Slovenia and was later changed during the process of harmonization and alignment with the legal framework of the European Union (EU) in 1999 and 2001.[4] In Slovenia, data protection has been fully implicated in the legislation (mainly with the Personal Data Protection Act (ZVOP)) and is also sustained with some jurisprudence.[5] The valid ZVOP therefore incorporates the principles of legality and fairness, proportionality, and non-discrimination in the legally determined cases of retention and processing of data.

A. SLOVENIAN DATA PROTECTION LAW: NOTIFICATION OF
    THE AUTHORITY

Under Slovenian law, any person who or establishment that intends to collect or process personal data is obliged to set up a catalogue regarding the collection of personal data including determination – for example, the title, the data controller, the legal grounds, the purpose, and the duration of the retention and processing – and has to notify the competent authority at least fifteen days prior to the outset of this data collection and has to inform the same authority within eight days in case of any changes to the respective collection.

B. SLOVENIAN DATA PROTECTION LAW: EXPORT OF PERSONAL DATA

The transfer of personal data abroad is allowed only under the conditions set out in the ZVOP or respectively in Regulation 1206/2001 for inter-EU personal data exchange for processing. According to Article 63 of the ZVOP, personal data can be exported to a non-EU Member State upon the competent authority's decision that the country of data import ensures an adequate level of personal data protection. If the country is on a special list held by the competent authority, which states which countries do have the adequate level of personal data protection, no such decision is needed. Anyway, the data can always be exported upon the personal

---

2. Ustava Republike Slovenije (Constitution of the Republic of Slovenia, hereinfter: Constitution), Slovenian Official Gazette 33I/1991-I.
3. The ZVOP entered into force on 24 Mar. 1990.
4. The ZVOP was amended a few times since then; the valid ZVOP was published in the Ul RS 94/07.
5. Nataša Pric Musar, Zakon o varstvu osebnih podatkov s komentarjem, GV Založba, Ljubljana 2006, 19–24.

consent of the data subject or upon a special provision of an international treaty such as the Hague Convention.

C.   SLOVENIAN DATA PROTECTION LAW: LEGAL REQUIREMENTS FOR THE RETENTION OF DATA

Personal data can only be processed if such processing is allowed by the law or upon personal consent of the data subject.[6] The data controller that collects the personal data can subcontract the maintenance of the data collection to a registered data processor.[7] The processing of sensitive personal data underlies even stricter rules imposed by the ZVOP and can be carried out only under these conditions (e.g., explicit personal consent, in case of life emergency, for scientific purposes). Special protection measures such as special labelling or special cryptographic techniques for transmission of these data apply as well. For cases where no adequate level of data protection can be established, the European Commission issued a decision[8] on Standard Contractual Clauses (SCCs) for the transfer of personal data to processors established in third countries under Directive 95/46/EC. Eventually the data subject has to be informed about the fact that data regarding the data subject have been collected and about the purpose of this data collection.

D.   SLOVENIAN DATA PROTECTION LAW: SEARCHING OF EMPLOYEES' E-MAILS

The employees' written correspondence, e-mails, and other communication is regulated through strict provisions of the Employment Relationship Act (ZDR),[9] which do not allow the search of employees' private communication by the employer, regardless of the type of communication. An employee may, however, give his or her consent to a measure of surveillance. But generally, these searches of the employee's correspondence are prohibited unless they are based upon valid internal regulations. Such regulations are required in the light of a recent judgment[10] of the European Court of Human Rights, which is binding for Slovenia as member of the Council of Europe, where the Court stated that: 'the collection and storage of personal information relating to the [employees] use of the telephone, e-mail and internet, without her knowledge, therefore amounted to an interference with her right to respect for her private life and correspondence'.

---

6. According to Art. 8 of the ZVOP, also the purpose of the data retention/processing has to be defined by law.
7. The data processor has to fulfil the requirements of the ZVOP regarding the data protection mechanism and has to be registered in a public evidence.
8. Commission Decision of 27 Dec. 2001 on standard contractual clauses for the transfer of personal data to processors established in third countries, under Directive 95/46/EC.
9. Zakon o delovnih razmerjih, Slovenian Official Gazette 42/02.
10. COPLAND *v.* THE UNITED KINGDOM, 62617/00 [2007] ECHR 253 (3 Apr. 2007).

Thus the employer must always obtain explicit consent from the employee prior to any data collection or search, or an internal regulation governing the searches has to be adopted. In practice we advise that the employer drafts an internal regulation in which it defines which specific searches are to be conducted concerning the employees' e-mails, specifies the purposes for which the searches may be conducted, and makes the internal regulation available to the employees so that they are properly informed about the possible searches in advance. Notably, all searches must have a specific purpose and must be proportionate, that is, even if the internal regulation prescribes daily searches, this would still be considered too invasive and thus illegal.

III. PRETRIAL DISCOVERY IN SLOVENIA: BACKGROUND

Mutual disclosure of case-related facts by the parties as known in the United States[11] is not known in Slovenian jurisdiction.[12] The litigants only produce those documents in court that support their case. Only if one party refers to a specific document in its pleadings can the court order that the document be lodged with court, no matter whether it is in the possession of a litigant or a third party.

The court can enforce the respective documents from a party only through a special action, whereas a third party can be summoned by court to deliver a document by a mere court decision. However, if a party denies the possession of such evidence, although later proven that this is untrue, the court cannot compel the party to provide such evidence, but can consider this fact to the prejudice of the party.

A. PRETRIAL DISCOVERY IN SLOVENIA: BLOCKING STATUTES

The Slovenian legislation does not prohibit any disclosure of information to a foreign court, a public authority, or a third party, if the disclosure meets the provisions of the ZDOP.

B. PRETRIAL DISCOVERY IN SLOVENIA: HAGUE CONVENTION ON THE TAKING OF EVIDENCE

In Slovenia, the rules of the Hague Convention[13] are applied to those countries that either are not a Member State of the EU or that have not yet concluded a bilateral

---

11. *Black's Law Dictionary*, 1999, West Group, Minnesota: 'Compulsory disclosure, at a party's request of information that relates to the litigation'.
12. Darko Trajanov, Predhodno razkritje dokazov, Diplomska naloga, 2002, Ljubljana.
13. Zakon o ratifikaciji konvencije o pridobivanju dokazov *v.* civilnih in gospodarskih zadevah *v.* tujini (Convention on the Taking of Evidence Abroad in Civil or Commercial Matters, hereinafter: Hague Convention), Slovenian Official Gazette 19/2000.

agreement on this subject with Slovenia.[14] For the exchange of evidence between EU countries, Regulation Number 1206/2001 applies. Therefore, the taking of evidence in Slovenia under the Hague Convention will apply to, *inter alia*, the United States, Canada, and China.

Slovenia did not issue any declaration under Article 23 of the Hague Convention; therefore Slovenia will have to execute Letters of Request issued for the purpose of obtaining pretrial discovery of documents as known in the United States, without further restrictions.

IV.   PRETRIAL DISCOVERY VERSUS DATA PROTECTION LAWS IN SLOVENIA – BACKGROUND

There are two important facets of the pretrial discovery process that collide with the data protection provisions. The first is that pretrial discovery can include not just discovery within the context of legal proceedings but also the preservation of data in relation to prospective legal proceedings. The second is that within the common law countries the disclosure requirements are not limited to personal data or only electronic documents. The sought information may include special sensitive personal data or data of third parties. Moreover, the term 'document' includes also electronic documents such as e-mails, other electronic communications, word-processed documents, documents stored on servers or back-up systems, and electronic documents that have been 'deleted'.[15] As to the preservation of evidence or data for prospective legal proceedings, the ZVOP,[16] the Civil Procedure Act (ZPP),[17] or, respectively, the Criminal Procedure Act (ZKP)[18] ask for the fulfilment of some special requirements. The ZVOP is also very strict on the preservation and processing of sensitive personal data.[19]

A.   PRETRIAL DISCOVERY VERSUS DATA PROTECTION IN SLOVENIA: LEGAL REQUIREMENTS FOR THE COLLECTION, PROCESSING, AND USE OF DATA FOR THE PURPOSES OF E-DISCOVERY

Although the Slovenian legal system is flexible enough to accept e-discovery requests, some requirements will have to be fulfilled prior to fulfilment of such

---

14. Štebal Špela, Pridobivanje dokazov *v.* cicilnih in gospodarskih zadevah *v.* tujini, Pravna praksa, 2005, No. 40, GV Založba, Ljubljana.
15. Working Document 1/2009 on pretrial discovery for cross-border civil litigation, Brussels, 2009.
16. Zakon o varstvu osebnih podatkov (Personal Data Protection Act, hereinafter: ZVOP), Slovenian Official Gazette 86/2004.
17. See fn. 1.
18. See fn. 1.
19. According to the ZVOP, these data have to be labelled appropriately for the purpose of identification and if transmitted electronically, they must be transmitted using the appropriate cryptographic methods. These data can only be processed under the legally defined circumstances (consent of the data subject, necessary for protection of life, already publicized data by the subject, etc.).

requests. First, the data subject will have to be informed about the data collection and in some cases he or she will have to give his or her consent. The competent authorities will have to be notified as well in due time on the fact of the data collection, purpose, subject, and so forth. Second, if the requesting subject or, respectively, data processor fulfils all the requirements on export of personal data abroad, the processor will have to guarantee the appropriate data protection. Also, the guidelines of the EU Working Party will have to be considered in the handling of these documents.[20]

B.   PRETRIAL DISCOVERY VERSUS DATA PROTECTION IN SLOVENIA:
        RETENTION OF PERSONAL DATA FOR E-DISCOVERY PURPOSES

According to the Data Protection Act, personal data can be stored only as long as needed for the purpose for which they were collected. If the data had to be erased in the ordinary course of business earlier, consent of the data subject is required due to the following reasons: First, the retention would have no legal grounds and would therefore be regarded as an infringement of the ZVOP. Second, such retention would open issues on the use of this illegally retained evidence similar to the 'fruit of the poisonous tree doctrine'[21] and therefore refrain the Slovenian courts from using such evidence.

V.   CONCLUSION

Although pretrial discovery is not known to Slovenian law, a pretrial discovery request can be accommodated by the Slovenian courts and other authorities upon fulfilling the legal requirements for the collection of personal data and preservation of evidence under Slovenian law.

---

20. See Working Document 1/2009.
21. This doctrine known in the United States (*Silverthorne Lumber Co. v. United States*, 251 U.S. 385, 40 S. Ct. 182, 64 L. Ed. 319 [1920]) was incorporated into the Slovenian jurisprudence and legal theory as a guideline for not considering illegally acquired evidence.

Chapter 5.24

Spain

Álvaro Velázquez and Laura Cantero*

I.   INTRODUCTION

The confrontation between the right of individuals to obtain safeguards ensuring
the privacy of their personal data and the mandatory disclosure thereof derived
from judicial requests in the framework of litigation is one of the numerous examples of collision of rights and interests that modern legal systems must face and
solve through intermediate solutions.

    This issue becomes particularly problematic if those requests bring cause of
legal proceedings being heard outside the Spanish jurisdiction. Even more, several
questions rise particularly on how to attend to requests for information received
from the United States as a part of pretrial discovery proceedings, as a necessary
step to gather all the evidence that mandatorily must be compiled in the context of
those proceedings.

    This chapter provides a general description of the data privacy and discovery
(or assimilated) systems in Spain, as an overview to finally reach a conclusion on
how these confronted institutions may merge, specially with an eye on discovery
requests received from foreign jurisdictions.

---

*   Álvaro Velázquez and Laura Cantero, Howrey Martínez Lage S.L., Madrid, Spain.

Catrien Noorda & Stefan Hanloser, *E-Discovery and Data Privacy*, pp. 263–276.
© 2011 Kluwer Law International BV, The Netherlands.

II.   SPANISH DATA PROTECTION LAW

A.   Spanish Data Protection Law: Framework

Protection of personal data is mainly governed in Spain by Organic Law Number 15/1999, dated 13 December 1999 (the 'LOPD'), by means of which the European Data Protection Directive 95/46/EC was transposed into the Spanish legal system, with the aim of harmonizing the level of protection acknowledged in the European Union (EU) context for individuals' personal data.

The entry into force of the LOPD, in January 2000, entailed the abrogation of the former regime represented by Organic Law Number 5/1992 of 29 October 1992, on the Automated Processing of Personal Data (the 'LORTAD'). The LORTAD was issued to develop and under the inspiration of Article 18.4 of the Spanish Constitution of 1978, which, in the framework of the more general fundamental right to personal and family privacy, established the need to defend individuals' privacy from any risks linked to computing and information technology (IT).[1] That is why the LORTAD only applied to automated processing of personal data, whereas the LOPD currently in force broke the existing link between data protection and computing, being applicable to any processing of personal data, irrespective of being automated or manual.

Despite of being previous to the European Data Protection Directive, the LORTAD already represented a large advance in the data protection field in Spain, as it was deemed as a huge opportunity to bring our legal system closer to the rest of the EU Member States in this area of law. Consequently, no substantial breaks were required when the LOPD was drafted to implement Directive 95/46/EC, as Spain was already in line with most of the principles set out in that European law.

After the entry into force of the LOPD, a landmark decision of the Constitutional Court came to proclaim the autonomy of the protection of personal data as fundamental right separate from the right to personal and family privacy, being worthy of independent protection.[2]

Even though the LOPD has been enforceable in Spain since 2000, it was only in 2007 that the necessary Development Regulation for said law was passed by the Spanish government, by means of Royal Decree Number 1720/2007 dated 21 December 2007, which entered into force in April 2008,[3] establishing, amongst other issues, several transitional deadlines for data controllers to implement the safety measures per protection level for files containing personal data set out by the Royal Decree.

---

1. Cf. Art. 18.4 Sp. Constitution.
2. Decision of the Constitutional Court No. 292/2000 of 30 Nov. 2000, resolving an unconstitutionality appeal against Arts 2, 21.1, and 24.1 of the LOPD.
3. Up to that date, the LOPD of 1999 coexisted jointly with and was interpreted where necessary under the light of the regulations that had developed the already abrogated LORTAD, mainly Royal Decrees 1332/1994 of 20 Jun. 1994, and 994/1999 of 11 Jun. 1999.

Apart from these general-scope regulations, some autonomous regions have passed their own data privacy laws,[4] within the framework of their competencies, to govern files containing personal data created or managed by public bodies or entities within their jurisdictions and, depending on their respective autonomous governments, also with their own control authorities.

In this chapter, however, only the general regime set forth by the LOPD and its Development Regulation will be assessed.

B.   SPANISH DATA PROTECTION LAW: PERSONAL DATA

The LOPD applies to individuals' personal data, defined as any information relating to an identified or identifiable natural person.[5] The Development Regulation of 2007 adds that this information may be numerical, alphabetical, graphical, photographical, acoustic, or of any other kind.

Apart from not being applicable to legal persons, the Development Regulation has clarified that the data protection system also does not apply to those files maintained by these legal persons referred to the individuals rendering their services within the organization, provided that they only contain the names and surnames, the functions performed or the positions held, and the professional e-mail, postal address, telephone, and fax numbers.

Only these employees' data, as being excluded from the application of the LOPD, could freely flow in the framework of cross-border discovery proceedings with no implications from the perspective of data privacy regulations. Any other kind of data related to employees will need to be processed and transferred abroad, if appropriate, in accordance with the instructions set forth by the LOPD. Not only employees' data, but also client's data in contact databases would not be deemed as personal data on the same grounds as above, provided that the data strictly refer to the specific features listed.

Besides, the Development Regulation determines that data related to sole traders, when referred to in their condition as traders, industrialists, or ship-owners, also do not fall within the scope of the LOPD. On the contrary, this exception does not apply to self-employed or freelance professionals (e.g., lawyers, architects, etc.), as they would not render their services under the shape of company and their activity is not ruled by the Commerce Code. Accordingly, the data of these professionals are deemed as 'personal' for the purposes of the application of the LOPD in any case.[6]

---

4. Madrid: Law No. 8/2001, dated 13 Jul. 2001; Catalonia: Law No. 5/2002, dated 19 Apr. 2002; Basque Country: Law No. 2/2004, dated 25 Feb. 2004.
5. Article 2.a) of Directive 95/46/EC and Art. 3.a) of the LOPD.
6. Decision of the Supreme Court (Contentious-Administrative Chamber, 6th Section) of 20 Feb. 2007 and Decisions of the National Court (Audiencia Nacional) (Contentious-Administrative Chamber, 1st Section) of 11 Feb. 2004 and 21 Nov. 2002, amongst others.

C. SPANISH DATA PROTECTION LAW: DATA COLLECTION
    AND PROCESSING

The general rule governing any processing of personal data is that said processing must be supported by the unambiguous consent of the data subject,[7] unless otherwise established by any applicable laws or regulations. Broadly speaking, the consent of the data subject is the key that allows, ensures, and opens the door to any processing of his or her data (including disclosures to third parties and even the international transfer of the data) in lawful conditions.

Assuming this general premise, the LOPD itself excludes the need to secure consent of the data subject to process his or her data in several scenarios,[8] for instance, where the data refer to the parties to a business, employment, or administrative relationship and their processing is necessary in its context, or where the processing of data contained in sources accessible to the public is necessary to satisfy a legitimate interest of the controller or of a third party to whom the data are disclosed, unless the fundamental rights of the data subject are jeopardized.

In any case, personal data may only be collected for their processing, and actually be processed, under a proportionality criterion, which means that they must be adequate, relevant, and not excessive in relation to the scope and the purposes for which they were collected. Besides, the LOPD prohibits using personal data for purposes incompatible with those for which they were collected (historical, statistical, or scientific purposes excluded), and establishes a duty of information toward the data subject when his or her data are collected. In short, an 'informed consent' of the data subject for the processing of his or her data is required.

D. SPANISH DATA PROTECTION LAW: RETENTION OF PERSONAL DATA

When the personal data are no longer necessary for the purpose that originally justified their collection, the LOPD obliges the data controller to cancel them.

In any case, the data must be retained for the time necessary as statutorily established in each relevant case (e.g., medical histories must be conserved by health centres for five years), if appropriate, or as agreed in the framework of the relationship between the data controller and the data subject.[9] In this regard, attention must be paid to the deadlines for bringing the relevant legal actions that may assist the parties in each case, depending on the nature of the relationship

---

7. Unambiguous consent (that may be tacit) is not enough when processing especially sensitive data: data referring to racial origin, health, and sexual life require the express consent of the data subject, and data revealing the ideology, membership in trade unions, and religious beliefs can only be processed with the data subject's express and written consent.
8. Cf. Art. 6.2 LOPD.
9. Cf. Art. 16.5 LOPD.

established between them. Once the statutory deadlines have expired, the data must be cancelled.

However, cancellation of the data does not imply their complete physical deletion, but merely their temporary blockade.[10] This means that personal data must be preserved and retained by the controller only for the purposes of meeting any eventual requests from the public authorities (administration or courts) with regard to any liabilities that may have arisen for the data processing and until the expiration of the deadline to seek said liabilities under the LOPD,[11] with any other use, access, or processing of the data while blocked being prohibited. On expiry of such liability, the personal data shall be permanently deleted.

Accordingly, for personal data to be definitely erased, it is necessary that both the corresponding statutory deadlines, if appropriate, and the periods for seeking liability under the LOPD have lapsed.

E.   SPANISH DATA PROTECTION LAW: TRANSFER OF PERSONAL DATA

As for any other kind of processing, the unambiguous (and informed) consent of the data subject is the essential key for any communication of his or her personal data to be lawful under the LOPD. Communication of personal data to any third parties other than the data controller is only legitimate if the data subject consents to the communication or in case that any of the exceptions[12] to said consent set forth by the LOPD is applicable.

Amongst the cases where the subject's consent is not necessary to communicate his or her data, the LOPD allows the communication where data are disclosed to judicial administration bodies (courts, judges, public prosecutor, etc.) in the exercise of their functions. It is important to remark that this unconsented communication of data will only be lawful if the data are directly disclosed to the pertinent body; it is not possible to appeal to this exception if the data are disclosed to any third party for this latter to submit them with the corresponding court.[13]

Notwithstanding this particular exception in the LOPD, expressly referred to data disclosure for judicial purposes, in many cases the communication of data in

---

10. Cf. Art. 16.3 LOPD and Art. 5.1.b) of the Development Regulation.
11. Cf. Art. 47.1-2 LOPD.
12. Cf. Article 11.2 LOPD.
13. Decision of the Supreme Court (Contentious-Administrative Chamber, 6th Section) of 12 Apr. 2005: '(. . .) when the provision exempts from obtaining the consent of the data subject, is only, in accordance with the provisions of paragraph d) above, when the recipient are the Courts in the exercise of the functions that they are assigned. And the expression "recipient" is simple and unambiguous, i.e. the person who is sent a letter, a document or any other thing, and certainly this is not the case, as the recipient of the census data was not the Court of Benavente, but the president of the hunting society "Los Jarales", holder of the hunting preserve "Santa Cristina de la Polvorosa", who arranged of his own free will a confidential data involving two people that, unilaterally, filed as evidence in a civil proceedings being heard before First Instance and Prosecution Court No. 2 of Benavente, so it is clear that the recipient of the data obtained without consent of the owners was not the Court to which they were finally provided'.

the context of legal proceedings, will find legal support in sector-specific laws authorizing said communication for the sake of the fundamental right to effective judicial protection (Article 24 of the Spanish Constitution). In these cases, the duty of secrecy binding data controllers[14] yields in view of the superior value of this fundamental right.

In any case, the LOPD excludes from the consideration of communication of data the access to personal data by a third party (data processor) with the purpose of providing a service to the data controller. Accordingly, the disclosure of data to the data processor does not require the consent of the data subject. However, the LOPD imposes a strict regime, obliging the data controller and the data processor to sign a specific written contract to regulate the data processing on behalf of third parties. Besides, where a data processor exists, the data controller must notify this circumstance and the identity of that processor to the Spanish Data Protection Agency.

This rigid system makes the processing on behalf of third parties a non-attractive resource for the flow of data within companies of the same group. In practice, companies will try to obtain the consent of their employees to allow the movement of their data within the group members, or just try to find legal support in another exception of the LOPD, according to which consent is not required when the processing brings cause of a legal relationship whose course, performance, and monitoring necessarily involves the connection between such processing and files of third parties (e.g., legal relationship represented by the contract of employment).

F.   SPANISH DATA PROTECTION LAW: INTERNATIONAL TRANSFERS OF PERSONAL DATA

As a direct consequence of the implementation of Directive 95/46/EC, the transfer of personal data abroad is not restricted when the recipient country is a Member State of the European Economic Area (EEA) or a country ensuring an adequate level of protection as declared by the European Commission (EC).

Apart from this general premise, again, the basic rule to transfer personal data outside of the European Union (EU) in perfect agreement with the LOPD is obtaining the unambiguous consent of the data subject to do so.

In the absence of consent, the LOPD provides several situations in which the transfer outside of the EU will still be lawful, amongst them, when the transfer is necessary for the recognition, exercise, or defence of a right in legal proceedings.

Beyond all of these cases, the authorization of the Director of the Spanish Data Protection Agency will be necessary to transfer data abroad. For authorization to be granted, it is necessary to justify that the destination country provides an adequate level of protection, and the Agency will also assess the circumstances surrounding the intended transfer and subsequent processing (e.g., purpose, nature of the data, governing laws and regulations in the destination country, etc.).

---

14.   Cf. Art. 10 LOPD.

It must be remarked that the United States has been classified by the EC within the catalogue of countries not providing an equivalent level of protection as that in the EU, except for those companies and institutions adhering to the Safe Harbour Programme. Accordingly, transfers to the United States not consented to by the data subject, not falling within any one of the exceptions of the LOPD, and addressed to a recipient not adhered to the aforementioned programme, must obtain the authorization of the Director of the Spanish Data Agency. The existence of a contract between the transferring company in Spain and the recipient in the United States, including clauses imposing on the recipient the establishment of adequate safeguards, may help to solve this obstacle, notwithstanding any other considerations that the Agency may appreciate in each particular transfer of data.

In any case, whatever the scenario for the data transfer may be from all the options described above, the transfer must be made in full compliance with the rules and principles established by the LOPD.

G.   SPANISH DATA PROTECTION LAW: LABOUR CONTEXT; EMPLOYEES' E-MAILS

The use of employees' e-mails by the employer in any discovery proceedings or related process requires clarifying first the conditions in Spain that rule the access of employers to said e-mails that make use of the business electronic address assigned to the employee.

The e-mail address, even if provided by the employer in the context of an employment relationship, is deemed as personal data subject to the regime of the LOPD. However, the employer is entitled to access, monitor, and process the information contained in e-mails exchanged using the business e-address without the employee's consent pursuant to Article 6.2 of the LOPD, allowing the unconsented processing where the data refer to a contract for an employment relationship, and the processing is necessary for its maintenance or fulfilment.

Besides, the Labour Act[15] acknowledges the right of the employer to adopt any appropriate surveillance measures to verify the accomplishment by the employee of his or her labour duties and obligations.

Conflicts in this regard have traditionally arisen in the field of labour law in connection with employees' dismissals for undue use of the company resources made available, much more than from the perspective of data privacy. In order to properly combine all of the three fundamental interests involved in these conflicts (protection of personal data, business interest, and secrecy of communications), a doctrinal and case-law line is gradually acquiring more and more relevance, according to which the employer is entitled to access the content of employees' e-mails on condition that they make use of an e-mail address provided by the employer for the exercise of the employment functions, and that the employees had been previously informed on that possible access and the means through which

---

15.   Royal Legislative Decree No. 1/1995 of 24 Mar. 1995 (Estatuto de los Trabajadores).

it will be carried out. Accordingly, the previous information to the employees is the key for the employer to be allowed to access and screen any e-mail sent or received using a business e-mail address.[16]

H. SPANISH DATA PROTECTION LAW: SANCTIONS AND ENFORCEMENT

Breaches to the LOPD are classified as minor, serious, and very serious infringements, depending on the specific nature of the illicit act committed.[17] These infringements may be sanctioned with economic penalties that are amongst the highest fines applied in the EU framework, compared to other countries having also transposed Directive 95/46/EC. Penalties that may be imposed for each different category of infringement are as follows:[18]

– Minor infringements: Fine of Euros (EUR) 601.01 up to EUR 60,101.21.
– Serious infringements: Fine of EUR 60,101.21 up to EUR 300,506.05.
– Very serious infringements: Fine of EUR 300,506.05 up to EUR 601,012.10.

The time limits for seeking liabilities derived for any breach of the LOPD are three years for very serious infringements, two years for serious infringements, and one year for minor infringements, all of them starting from the day when the infringement was committed.

The Spanish Data Protection Agency ('the Agency') is the public body entitled to watch over compliance with data privacy regulations in Spain (except for the competencies assumed by the regional data privacy authorities in the autonomous regions where they have been established; see section II.A. of this chapter). Accordingly, the Agency holds legal authority to inspect data files and impose the penalties set out in the LOPD. Its decisions are subject to appeal before the National Court (*'Audiencia Nacional'*) and afterward before the Supreme Court (*'Tribunal Supremo'*).

The Agency is subject to the principle of proportionality at the time of graduating the fines to be imposed. A common practice of the Agency derived from this binding principle is imposing low penalties within the allowed range

---

16. Decision of the Supreme Court (Labour Chamber, 1st Section) of 26 Sep. 2007: '(. . .) what the employer must do in accordance with the requirements of good faith is setting out in advance the rules of use of those means – applying absolute or partial prohibitions –, and inform employees that control will exist and of the means to be applied in order to verify the correctness of the uses, as well as the measures to be taken where necessary to ensure the effective labour use of the mean work when necessary, without prejudice to the possible application of other preventive measures such as exclusion of certain routes. Thus, if the mean is used for private use against these prohibitions and with knowledge of controls and applicable measures, it could not be understood that, during the inspection, "a reasonable expectation of privacy" has been violated'.
17. Cf. Art. 44 LOPD.
18. Cf. Art. 45 LOPD.

corresponding to the category of the infringement at issue. This way to proceed ensures that in most cases the amount of the fine will be confirmed in the appeal stage before the National Court (provided that the characterization of the offence is also confirmed), minimizing the risks that the sanction is revoked on the grounds of lack of proportionality.

Besides, the Agency may apply a penalty corresponding to the category immediately below if deemed appropriate in the light of the circumstances, from which a qualified reduction of the offender's culpability should be deduced.

Serious infringements are the most frequent subject matter of administrative sanctioning proceedings brought before the Agency (around 75% of the cases), followed by minor infringements, and with very serious infringements being the rarest case.

This preponderance of serious infringements, together with the 'lowest fine' principle commented above, is the cause that the amount of a high percentage of the fines imposed by the Agency is EUR 60,101.21.

Besides, from the data made available by the Agency, it may be inferred that companies from the IT and banking sectors accumulate a large number of these serious infringement fines.

From the perspective of the LOPD provisions that are breached, rules governing the subject's consent (Article 6) are those most frequently infringed, followed by the relevant provisions of the quality of data (Article 4).

It must be remarked that this liability regime is not applicable in respect of any infringements committed in relation to personal data files controlled by public bodies or entities, which are subject to different (and much softer) rules.[19] Indeed, the LOPD does not establish economic penalties in these cases, but the Agency's decision resolving the sanctioning proceedings will merely state the measures to be adopted by the responsible body or entity to correct or cease the effects derived from the infringement.

III.   PRETRIAL DISCOVERY IN SPAIN

A.   PRETRIAL DISCOVERY IN SPAIN – FRAMEWORK

The Spanish legal system does not have any formal pretrial discovery process. The parties to the litigation have to build their own case by offering all of the evidence they have in support of their arguments. The Spanish legislation has, however, recognized in some cases the need to provide some type of formal instrument in order to facilitate the obtaining of evidence to support a litigation when such evidence is not available to the parties involved. It is, however, known that such evidence does indeed exist and is possessed by the other party. Thus, the Spanish Civil Procedure Act (the 'CPA') contains two different sets of processes to obtain disclosure of specific documents.

---

19. Cf. Art. 46 LOPD.

The first is limited to the request for exhibition, in the framework of an already initiated litigation, of a specific original document relating to the subject matter of the proceedings or to the effectiveness of any other means of evidence of which the party has knowledge as to its contents and scope, and is capable of providing a simple copy of such document or of describing the document at length (Article 328 of the CPA). Thus, this limited discovery is restricted to the cases where the document itself is already known and the aim of the request is rather to verify some presumption or fact already alleged and *prima facie* established by the applicant or any secondary implications of such fact. The judge shall consider the request, evaluating the relevance of the fact that is being proved for the merits of the case before ruling on the admissibility. This request shall be made upfront by the applicant together with its main complaint, or as soon as the need to verify such document arises in the framework of the litigation.

The second procedure is the rather new catalogue of permitted preliminary requests aimed to the obtaining of evidence in order to prepare a subsequent litigation. These were first introduced in the Spanish legal system after the thorough reform of the CPA undertaken in 2000, although precedents existed in some specific fields of the law. Examples of such pretrial discovery procedures are the requests for verification of facts under the 1986 Patents Act, which is an inquisitive confidential procedure that patentees may prompt in order to verify whether a patent is being infringed by requesting the competent judge to investigate, via dawn raids, the premises and processes of a party that is presumably infringing a patent and there is no other way to obtain such evidence (convenience and necessity requirements). Under the Patents Act, however, the requesting party does not obtain direct evidence of the infringement, but a report by an independently appointed expert examining the potential infringing devices and only when the judge considers that there is indeed a presumption of infringement. If not, the applicant does not receive any type of information, and the judge shall declare the secrecy of the proceedings. Use of the disclosed information is restricted to the preparation of a subsequent mandatory patent infringement complaint to be filed within a period of time, and is forbidden for any other type of use. Confidentiality shall always be preserved. The 1990 Unfair Competition Act provided for the possibility of requesting this type of preliminary request by referring to the procedure set out by the Patents Act.

Under the 2000 CPA, the catalogue of further preliminary requests for the preparation of a subsequent action in Articles 256.1.1 to 256.1.6 of the CPA was widened, to comprise some specific examples such as requests for interrogation of potential defendants or disclosure of the relevant documents to show their capacity, requests for the exhibition of the thing whose property is being claimed, and requests for determination of the people affected in class actions for the defence of the interests of consumers.

A basic underlying principle that inspires the whole system of limited discovery in the Spanish civil proceedings is that requests for discovery must be, in any case, weighed by the competent judge, and shall be of a nature that may allow the judge, if the disclosure is rejected by the requested party, to apply a presumption establishing the fact alleged by the requesting party (*ficta confessio*, as foreseen by Article 329 of the CPA). Thus, the limited discovery always refers to the verification or confirmation of a factual situation that has been already established with sufficient indicia by the applicant; it is not possible to admit any investigative or inquisitive measure aimed only to 'fish' data on facts that have not been sufficiently indicated. The requested party would then be obliged to cooperate with the judiciary, as provided by Article 118 of the Spanish Constitution, which has been interpreted by the Spanish Constitutional Court within that context as comprising also an obligation to disclose the information that is relevant for the proceedings when it is requested by the courts, because it would not be fair to benefit from any obstacles or hindrances put by such party prejudicing the position of the counterparty, since nobody must benefit from their own faults.[20]

An exception to that rule would be the specific preliminary requests aimed to provide protection to the owners of intellectual property rights, which were introduced in Articles 256.1.7 and 256.1.8 of the CPA further to Enforcement Directive 44/2004, which now allow for the investigation of the extent and scope of the fraud by ascertaining the identity of the people involved in the distribution and importation of the infringing goods, as well as the economic relevance, by accessing financial information possessed by the party that may be presumably responsible for the *prima facie* established infringement. The specific laws on industrial property rights already provided for similar duties of disclosure for the defendants in actions for infringement already initiated, at least in the financial part, since they permitted requests by the industrial property owner to obtain disclosure of financial and economic data of the potential infringer in order to establish the amount of damages caused, although in the framework of proceedings already initiated (Article 65 of the Spanish Patents Act, Article 43.4 of the Trademarks Act, and Article 55.4 of the Industrial Designs Act).

In practice, requests for disclosure of information generally referring to facts would be normally rejected by Spanish judges, unless those facts for which such information would provide supportive evidence have been at least *prima facie* established by sufficient indicia by the applicant. Spanish courts would commonly ground such rejection on the lack of substantiation of the specific necessity for the gathering of such disclosure of evidence, in contrast with the necessary preservation of confidentiality. However, it is noted also that the mechanisms provided by the Spanish civil procedure rules have evolved and been renewed in these last years, and there exists a tendency, found in the courts of appeals that are reviewing decisions rejecting requests for disclosure adopted by first-instance courts, to be more open to the granting of such preliminary requests, as they are seen as a filter that may help to prevent unnecessary and inappropriate suits from proceeding further and a useful tool to provide litigants with sufficient evidence to build proper claims.

---

20. Decisions of the Constitutional Court of 28 Nov. 1991, 17 Jan. 1994, and 17 Jul. 1995, a principle that has also been affirmed by the Supreme Court in Decisions of 28 Feb. 1997, 26 Jul. 1999, and 5 Oct. 2006.

B.   PRETRIAL DISCOVERY IN SPAIN – BLOCKING STATUTES

Spain has not adopted any specific law or statute prohibiting persons from providing or requesting evidence that may ultimately be used by foreign authorities. Accordingly, there is no specific restriction, justified by state interests such as sovereignty, trade activities, or bank and secrecy policies, that may be alleged to deny any disclosure by Spanish nationals.

However, there is specific EU legislation that was cited by the Spanish National Authority in charge of the implementation of the Hague Convention on the Taking of Evidence as blocking statutes, that could be referred to to prevent compliance with specific requests for evidence received from foreign authorities. These are:

(a) Article 5(1) of Council Regulation (EC) No. 2271/96 of 22 November 1996 protecting against the effects of the extra-territorial application of legislation adopted by a third country, and actions based thereon or resulting therefrom, according to which EU residents shall not comply, 'whether directly or through a subsidiary or other intermediary person, actively or by deliberate omission, with any requirement or prohibition, including requests of foreign courts, based on or resulting, directly or indirectly', from the specific provisions of the US laws cited in the Annex (the National Defense Authorization Act for Fiscal Year 1993, Title XVII 'Cuban Democracy Act 1992', the Cuban Liberty and Democratic Solidarity Act of 1996 and the Iran and Libya Sanctions Act of 1996) 'or from actions based thereon or resulting therefrom'; although the Regulation provides for a procedure to authorize full or partial compliance 'to the extent that non-compliance would seriously damage their interests or those of the Community'.

(b) A general reference to the general principle guiding the international transfer of personal data already mentioned above, as established by Article 25(1) of Directive 95/46/EC, allowing Member States to permit such transfer only 'the third country in question ensures an adequate level of protection'.

C.   PRETRIAL DISCOVERY IN SPAIN – HAGUE CONVENTION ON THE
          TAKING OF EVIDENCE

According to the Spanish authority in charge of the application of the Hague Convention on the Taking of Evidence Abroad, which was ratified in 1987 (entered into force on 21 July 1987), the application of the Convention is mandatory. Thus, it must be understood that Spanish authorities would only be obliged to process requests for taking of evidence received under the Hague Convention, and Spanish nationals may only be compelled to cooperate and disclose evidence if the request has followed the procedure set out by the Hague Convention.

In practice, there is no case law by Spanish courts on decisions rejecting the recognition in Spain of a foreign judgment rendered on the basis of evidence taken by a foreign court in Spain outside the channels provided by the Hague Convention, which would be ultimately the problem that may arise if the foreign court considers that it can actually proceed under those different procedures provided by its own domestic legislation.

Further, Spain made a declaration under Article 23 clarifying that 'Spain does not accept Letters of Request derived from the "pretrial discovery of documents" procedure known in common law countries'. Accordingly, requests for US-style pretrial discovery made through the Hague Convention would be rejected in Spain and, according to the Central Competent Authority, they would be rejected in their entirety, despite the fact that some portions of them may be more restricted, if the portion that seeks document is too general and therefore cannot be honoured. However, it is also noted that the Spanish authorities did consider the amendment of such generic declaration, as suggested by the 2003 Special Commission, to file a more specific declaration based on either the United Kingdom's declaration or Article 16 of the Additional Protocol of 1984 to the Inter-American Convention on the Taking of Evidence Abroad.

IV.   PRETRIAL DISCOVERY VERSUS PROTECTION OF
           PERSONAL DATA IN SPAIN

If the request for evidence under the Hague Convention is made to the Spanish authorities after the pretrial stage, the transfer of personal data to the United States (or any other country that is a party to said Convention) will be in agreement with the LOPD, as Article 34.a) authorizes the international movement of personal data when it is 'the result of applying treaties or agreements to which Spain is a party'.

During the pretrial stage, however, the reservation under Article 23 of the Hague Convention prevents Spanish authorities from answering judicial orders from the United States requesting the compilation and transfer of the relevant information to prepare litigation. As there is no legal obligation in Spain to attend to those pretrial discovery requests, no controversy will arise from the perspective of data protection.

If, however, the affiliate company (and data controller) in Spain decided to provide the partner company in the United States with the relevant information voluntarily and assuming that the company in Spain did not have its employees' consents, it is unsure whether the 'preparation of trial' would be deemed as a valid argument to justify the application of Article 34.f) of the LOPD, allowing the international transfer of personal data when it is 'necessary for the recognition, exercise or defence of a right in legal proceedings'.

In any case, any communication or international transfer of data by a data controller subject to Spanish law, even those justified by reason of the defence of rights in legal proceedings, must be done in full compliance with the rest of rules and principles set out in the LOPD. In this regard, proportionality must be strictly observed; a communication or transfer of data for litigation purposes, even if justified under the legal provisions governing these two figures, if it affects more personal data than those necessary for the purported aim of the data disclosure, is not admissible. If the request for information involving personal data is received by the Spanish authorities under the provisions of the Hague Convention (requests for pretrial discovery excluded, as said in section III.C.), the Spanish authorities will watch over the adequacy of the data requested for the relevant purpose.

If it is the data controller in Spain who will voluntarily transfer personal data to the partner company in the United States involved in litigation (for pretrial discovery purposes), even if the transfer may be legally supported (e.g., because he or she obtained the consent from the data subjects), the data controller shall also ensure that the personal data transferred are not excessive in view of the purpose pursued, previously filtering any documents and personal data that exceed the real necessity grounding the disclosure. Otherwise, the data controller could incur several infringements of the LOPD.

Chapter 5.25

Switzerland

Jürg Schneider, Ueli Sommer and
*Michael Cartier**

I. INTRODUCTION

At first glance, the purposes of the law governing data protection appear to conflict
with those of the law governing production of evidence. The focus of the former is
on limiting the collection and flow of data, while the latter seeks to facilitate the
flow of data from one party to the other.

However, if the data being sought are required for legitimate purposes and if
the proper procedures are applied, Swiss data protection law does not hinder the
exchange of information. In addition, proceedings pending before Swiss civil
courts as well as those proceedings under mutual legal assistance are excluded
from the scope of data protection law in Switzerland.

Observation of the proper procedures is also important in order to avoid
running afoul of Switzerland's 'blocking statute'. A party collecting evidence for
a foreign court proceeding without first obtaining authorization, that is, proceeding
other than by way of mutual legal assistance proceedings, will face criminal
liability.

'E-discovery', a term originating in the United States, is making inroads into
(continental) Europe. However, in the absence of pretrial discovery in Switzerland

---

*   Dr Jürg Schneider, Dr Ueli Sommer and Dr Michael Cartier are lawyers of Walder Wyss Ltd.,
     Attorneys at Law, Zurich, Switzerland.

Catrien Noorda & Stefan Hanloser, *E-Discovery and Data Privacy*, pp. 277–293.
© 2011 Kluwer Law International BV, The Netherlands.

that is comparable to common law discovery proceedings, in this chapter we will use the term 'e-disclosure' to describe the provision of electronic evidence in Swiss (civil law) courts and/or administrative proceedings.

II.   SWISS DATA PROTECTION LAWS: BACKGROUND

Under Swiss law, the processing of personal data by private persons is essentially governed by the Swiss Federal Act on Data Protection of 19 June 1992 (FADP) and the Swiss Federal Ordinance to the Federal Act on Data Protection of 14 June 1993 (OFADP).[1] The latest revisions of the FADP and the OFADP came into effect on 1 December 2010.[2]

As Switzerland is neither a member of the European Union (EU) nor the European Economic Area (EEA), Directive 95/46/EC (Directive)[3] is not applicable in Switzerland and Swiss data protection legislation is not fully in line with the requirements of the Directive. Nevertheless, the European Commission has decided that Swiss law provides adequate protection of personal data.[4] For this reason, transfers of personal data from an EU Member State to Switzerland are, in principle, permitted under Article 25(1) of the Directive.

Finally, it should be noted that Switzerland has ratified the Council of Europe Convention on the Protection of Individuals with Regard to Automatic Processing of Personal Data (Convention No. 108) and its Additional Protocol.

A.   SWISS DATA PROTECTION LAWS: EXCLUSION OF CERTAIN PENDING
                   PROCEEDINGS FROM THE SCOPE OF THE FADP

According to its Article 2 paragraph 2 lit. c, the FADP does not apply to pending civil proceedings, criminal proceedings, international mutual assistance proceedings in civil and criminal matters, and proceedings under constitutional or under administrative law, with the exception of administrative proceedings of first instance.[5]

---

1. The FADP and the OFADP also apply to the processing of personal data by federal bodies. The processing of personal data by cantonal bodies is governed by twenty-six cantonal data protection laws.
2. The official German, French, and Italian versions of the FADP and the OFADP as well as unofficial English translations are available online on the Federal Authorities of the Swiss Confederation's website: <www.admin.ch/ch/d/sr/c235_1.html> (FADP in German); <www. admin.ch/ch/d/sr/c235_11.html> (OFADP in German); <www.admin.ch/ch/e/rs/c235_1.html> (FADP in English); <www.admin.ch/ch/e/rs/c235_11.html> (OFADP in English).
3. Directive 95/46/EC of the European Parliament and of the Council of 24 Oct. 1995 on the protection of individuals with regard to the processing of personal data and on the free movement of such data (O.J. [L 281] 23 Nov. 1995).
4. Commission Decision 2000/518/EC (O.J. [L 251/1] 25 Aug. 2000).
5. Other exceptions to the application of the FADP concern personal data that are processed by a natural person exclusively for personal use and that are not disclosed to outsiders, deliberations of

This exception was introduced into the FADP because, in the opinion of the legislature, the specific procedural rules applicable to the types of pending proceedings mentioned above sufficiently protect the personality rights of the persons concerned.[6] Certain legal scholars hold that these exceptions only apply if the relevant procedural rules provide for a protection of the personality that is equivalent to that provided by the FADP.[7] This is also the opinion of the former Federal Commission on Data Protection in respect to internal and international mutual assistance proceedings.[8] In the absence of an explicit legal requirement, however, we are of the opinion that the exception provided for in Article 2 paragraph 2 lit. c of the FADP applies even if the relevant procedural rules do not provide for equivalent protection.[9]

As mentioned above, these exceptions apply only to pending proceedings. Therefore, the processing of personal data before the opening of the proceedings, after the closing of the proceedings (including possible recourses), and outside of the proceedings remains subject to the FADP. This applies in particular to the processing of personal data in preparation for civil proceedings. It should also be mentioned that the exceptions provided for in Article 2 paragraph 2 lit. c of the FADP only apply to pending proceedings before Swiss authorities, including Swiss national arbitral tribunals and international arbitral tribunals based on Chapter 12 of the Swiss Federal Act on Private International Law (FAPIL), provided that such tribunals have their seat in Switzerland. With regard to e-disclosure, the aforementioned exceptions will only apply in very restrictive circumstances, and it is important to check for each case whether those circumstances are present or not.

B.   SWISS DATA PROTECTION LAWS: PERSONAL DATA

Except for the exceptions discussed previously (see A. above), the FADP applies to the processing of personal data by private persons. The term 'personal data' is broadly defined as all information relating to an identified or identifiable natural person or legal entity (Article 3 lit. a and b FADP).

Unlike the Directive and the national data protection legislation of most EU Member States, the FADP applies not only to the processing of personal data

---

the Swiss Federal Assembly and parliamentary committees, public registers based on private law, as well as personal data processed by the International Committee of the Red Cross (see Art. 2 para. 2 lit a, b, d and e FADP).

6. Botschaft zum Bundesgesetz über den Datenschutz vom 23. März 1988 (Message of the Swiss Federal Council regarding the draft Federal Act on Data Protection of 23 Mar. 1988) (BBl 1988 II 442 to 444).

7. Urs Maurer-Lambrou/Simon Kunz in Basler Kommentar zum Datenschutzgesetz, 2nd edn Basle/Geneva/Munich, 2006, ad Art. 2 FADP, N 27.

8. Decision 10 Jan. 1997 of the Federal Data Protection Commission (published in: Verwaltungspraxis der Bundesbehörden (VPB), 62.40, 3c/ee).

9. See also David Rosenthal/Yvonne Jöhri in Handkommentar zum Datenschutzgesetz, Zurich/Basle/Geneva 2008, ad Art. 2 para. 2 FADP, N 30.

regarding natural persons but also to the processing of personal data regarding legal entities, such as corporations, companies, and foundations. As a result, the application of the FADP is much broader in scope than equivalent legislation in most other countries.

A person is 'identified' in the sense of Article 3 lit. a of the FADP if, based on the information available, it is already evident which person the data concern. A person is 'identifiable' in the sense of Article 3 lit. a of the FADP if the information available does not directly identify the person concerned but if there is a possibility to do so in combination with other information. However, the mere theoretical possibility of identifying the person concerned is not sufficient to make a person 'identifiable' in the sense of the aforementioned provision. In fact, if the effort to identify the person concerned is such that based on general experience one would not expect that an interested party would undertake such effort, then a person is not considered 'identifiable'.[10] This needs to be checked in each individual case. However, it should be noted that in practice the Federal Data Protection and Information Commissioner (FDPIC) tends, in close cases, to consider that a person is 'identifiable' in the sense of the FADP.

Due to the broad statutory definition of personal data, which even includes data concerning legal entities, most if not all e-disclosure proceedings will involve personal data: electronic copies of contracts mentioning the name of the contracting parties as well as third parties; e-mails sent by employees; files regarding employee phone calls; electronic files containing information about corporations; other electronic business correspondence; electronic financial information on companies or natural persons; and so forth. For this reason, it is important that the respondent to an information request in disclosure proceedings carefully assesses whether, to what extent, and under which conditions the provision of such information is permitted under the FADP.

For the sake of completeness, it must also be noted that the FADP provides more specific and stronger legal protection for sensitive personal data[11] and personality profiles.[12] The processing of such data imposes specific duties such as providing information (Article 14 FADP), special formal requirements with respect to the consent of the persons concerned (Article 4 paragraph 5 FADP), and justification in case of disclosure to third parties – including companies within the same group – for processing data to be used for such third parties' own purposes (Article 12 paragraph 2 lit. c FADP). To the extent that e-disclosure proceedings include sensitive personal data and personality profiles and to the extent the FADP applies, these additional requirements need to be carefully observed.

---

10. Botschaft zum Bundesgesetz über den Datenschutz vom 23. März 1988 (Message of the Swiss Federal Council regarding the draft Federal Act on Data Protection of 23 Mar. 1988) (BBl 1988 II 444 and 445).
11. Sensitive personal data include data on: (i) religious, ideological, political, or trade-union-related views or activities; (ii) health, the intimate sphere, or racial origin; (iii) social security measures; and, (iv) administrative or criminal proceedings and sanctions (Art. 3 lit. c FADP).
12. A personality profile is a collection of data that permits an assessment of essential characteristics of the personality of a natural person (Art. 3 lit. d FADP).

C.   SWISS DATA PROTECTION LAWS: PROCESSING

According to Article 3 lit. e of the FADP, and with the exceptions mentioned
previously (see A. above), any operation involving personal data, in particular the
collection, storage, use, revision, disclosure, archiving, or destruction of data,
irrespective of the means applied and the procedure used, falls under the FADP.
As a result, and with the exceptions mentioned previously (see A. above), the
collection, use, and disclosure of personal data in relation to e-disclosure fall under
the FADP.

Unlike other data protection legislation, the FADP does not *per se* require a
justification for the processing of personal data. Justification is only required if the
processing would constitute an unlawful breach of the data subject's privacy.
According to Article 12 paragraph 2 of the FADP, any violation of the principles
set out in Article 4,[13] Article 5 paragraph 1,[14] or Article 7 paragraph 1[15] of the
FADP, any processing that takes place against the express wishes of the data
subject, as well as disclosing sensitive personal data or personality profiles to third
parties, qualifies by law as an unlawful breach of the privacy of the data subject and
therefore requires a justification.[16]

Since, in most cases, the respondent will not have anticipated information
requests related to e-disclosure, the release of information to the requesting litigant
would frequently amount to a violation of one or more of the aforementioned
principles. Therefore, disclosure of information to the requesting litigant requires
a justification in the majority of cases: either the valid consent of the data subject
concerned, an overriding private or public interest, or the law (Article 13 FADP).
As a requirement to disclose personal data based on foreign law is not sufficient,[17]
disclosure of personal data in the context of an e-disclosure abroad requires the
prior valid consent of the data subjects concerned or the existence of an overriding
private interest. In many cases and depending on the circumstances and the respective interests, the litigant receiving a request might have an overriding private
interest to disclose personal data concerning third parties (such as data on employees, co-contractors, etc.), if required to do so by foreign law. However, this is not
always the case. In order to be on the 'safe side', it is therefore recommended to
obtain the consent of the individuals and legal entities whose personal data are
affected.

---

13. In particular, principles of good faith, proportionality, and transparency as well as the require-
    ment to limit the processing to the purpose indicated at the time of collection that is evident from
    the circumstances or that is provided for by law.
14. Requirement to make certain that the personal data processed are correct.
15. Requirement to protect personal data against unauthorized processing through adequate tech-
    nical and organizational measures.
16. The list contained in Art. 12, para. 2 of the FADP is not exhaustive and there are other cases or
    circumstances in which the processing may constitutes an unlawful breach of privacy.
17. According to the majority of legal scholars, a 'law' in the sense of Art. 13 of the FADP includes
    only Swiss federal, cantonal, and communal law.

Jürg Schneider et al.

For the sake of completeness, however, we would like to point out that due to other restrictions imposed by Swiss law (see section III below) the provision of personal data in the context of an e-disclosure in proceedings abroad is only permissible under very restrictive circumstances. Thus, even if the litigant receiving a request to disclose such information has an overriding private interest or even if the individuals and legal entities whose personal data are affected have given their valid consent, this will not impact the other restrictions, which must still be observed and in many cases prohibit such disclosure outside of international mutual assistance proceedings. However, as we have seen before (see section A above), the FADP does not apply to international mutual assistance proceedings pending before Swiss authorities. Thus, in many cases in which a disclosure is lawful under such proceedings, the FADP will not apply to the particular disclosure and may be disregarded.

D.   Swiss Data Protection Laws: Employee E-mails

Employee e-mails regularly contain personal data regarding the employee, his or her correspondents, the employer, and third parties. Thus, the processing of employee e-mails by the employer (or third parties) is generally subject to the FADP. This applies to e-mails containing only business-related content as well as e-mails that have a private character.

It is also important to mention that according to Article 328b of the Swiss Code of Obligations (SCO), an employer may only process personal data pertaining to its employee to the extent that such personal data concern the employee's qualification for employment or are required for the execution of the employment agreement. Pursuant to Article 362, paragraph 1 of the SCO, no deviation shall be made from Article 328b of the SCO to the detriment of employees by agreements, standard employment contracts, or collective employment contracts.

While many legal scholars are of the opinion that Article 362, paragraph 1 of the SCO prohibits any processing to the detriment of employees, others estimate that employees may still unilaterally (but not in the employment contract) consent to a processing to their detriment and that even an overriding private or public interest or the law could justify a violation of Article 362, paragraph 1 of the SCO.[18] In our opinion, it can reasonably be argued that a unilaterally informed consent by an employee could justify the processing of employee personal data even if it is to the employee's detriment. However, the Swiss Federal Supreme Court has not rendered any decision on this question and therefore the legal situation remains unclear.

Based on the foregoing, it appears that the ability to process employee e-mails in relation to an e-disclosure depends on the circumstances of the individual case. If the e-mails only contain business-related information and if the provision is not

---

18.   David Rosenthal in Handkommentar zum Datenschutzgesetz, Zurich/Basle/Geneva 2008, ad Art. 4 para. 5 FADP, N 100 et seq. and ad art. 328b SCO, N 64 et seq.

to the detriment of the employee, consent of the employee is not necessary if the other general requirements of the FADP have been met (see in particular footnotes 13, 14, and 15) or if the employer has an overriding private interest to provide the information. If the e-mails contain private information of the employee or if the provision is to the employee's detriment, prior informed consent of the employee is required.

Even if the use of employee e-mails is admissible under the FADP in relation with the personal data regarding employees, personal data relating to other persons (correspondents, third parties, etc.), which is contained in such e-mails, must still be processed in accordance with the FADP. Depending on the circumstances, this may imply the necessity of obtaining prior approval from the other persons involved. Finally, it should be noted that the provision of e-mails in relation with an e-disclosure is always subject to the general limitations, which will be set out in section III below.

E.   SWISS DATA PROTECTION LAWS: CONTROLLER OF THE
           DATA FILE; PROCESSOR

The FADP draws a distinction between the controller of the data file and the mere processor. The controller of the data file is the private person or federal body that decides on the purpose and content of a set of personal data that is structured in such a way that the data are accessible by data subject (Article 3 lit. i in relation with Article 3 lit. g FADP). A processor is any other person processing personal data, in particular a person processing data on behalf of another person (either a controller of the data file or another processor).

Both the controller and the processor need to comply with the requirements of the FADP.[19] However, special requirements apply to the controller of the data file, such as:

– the controller of a data file is obliged to inform the data subject of the collection of sensitive personal data or personality profiles (Article 14 paragraph 1 FADP);
– the private controller of a data file shall maintain a record of the automated processing of sensitive personal data or personality profiles if preventive measures cannot ensure data protection (Article 10 paragraph 1 OFADP);
– the controller of a data file has the obligation to notify certain data files for registration with the FDPIC (Article 11a paragraph 3 FADP); and
– the controller of a data file has the obligation to inform the FDPIC in relation to certain transborder disclosures in respect of the safeguards taken

---

19.   The meaning of 'controller of a data file' under the FADP is not exactly the same as the meaning of 'controller' under Art. 2 lit. d of the Directive. Under the FADP, this results in the person entrusting a third party with the processing of personal data not necessarily being the controller of the data file and a person processing personal data on behalf of a third party also needing to comply with the data processing principles (and not only the controller of a data file).

> or in respect of the applicable data protection rules (Article 6 FADP in
> relation with Article 6 OFADP).

For this reason, the respondent in the context of an e-disclosure needs to carefully analyse whether it qualifies as a controller of the data file in relation to the information requested or as a mere processor (in particular on behalf of another party).[20] For example, since the requesting litigant in an e-disclosure will use the personal data provided by the respondent for its own purposes and not for the purposes of the respondent, the disclosure by the respondent could trigger an obligation to register the data file, provided that such disclosure takes place regularly[21] and unless certain others exceptions apply (see Article 11a paragraph 3 and 5 FADP in relation with Article 4 OFADP). Additionally, a disclosure abroad could trigger an obligation to enter into a data transfer agreement and, for the controller of the data file, an obligation to notify the FDPIC prior to disclosure (see F below), and so forth.

F.   SWISS DATA PROTECTION LAWS: TRANSFER ABROAD

Like legislation in EU Member States, the FADP restricts the disclosure of personal data abroad if the legislation of the recipient's country does not provide for an adequate level of data protection with respect to the personal data concerned (Article 6 paragraph 1 FADP). This restriction applies to disclosures to recipients that process the data on behalf of the transferor and to disclosures to recipients that process the data on their own behalf.

Before disclosing any personal data abroad in the context of an e-disclosure, the respondent therefore needs to determine if the legislation in the recipient's country provides for an adequate level of data protection compared to the Swiss legislation.[22] With respect to recipients located in an EU or EEA Member State, adequate statutory protection generally exists for personal data regarding natural persons. For personal data regarding legal entities, adequate protection only exists in those EU and EEA Member States that by law extend protection to legal entities as well. With respect to a recipient located in the United States, adequate protection does not exist, regardless of the type of personal data, unless disclosure is made to a

---

20. As a general rule, a person processing personal data on behalf of another party may only process the data if and to the extent that the assigning party is itself permitted to process the personal data (see Art. 10a para. 1 lit. a FADP) and in accordance with the instructions of the assigning party.
21. In most cases, however, the disclosure in the context of an e-disclosure will not be made 'regularly', but rather only in exceptional and unplanned situations so that the disclosure as such will not trigger an obligation to notify the data file for registration.
22. The FDPIC publishes a list of countries that are deemed to provide an adequate level of data protection: <www.edoeb.admin.ch/themen/00794/00827/index.html?lang=en>. Unless the list explicitly provides otherwise, it only covers the processing of personal data regarding natural persons and no equivalent protection exists for the processing of personal data regarding legal entities.

recipient that has self-certified under the US-Swiss Safe Harbour Agreement (self-certification under the US-EU Safe Harbour Agreement is not sufficient). In addition, since the US-Swiss Safe Harbour Agreement only covers personal data relating to natural persons, adequate protection does not exist for the disclosure of personal data regarding legal entities to a recipient in the United States.

A transfer abroad to a recipient in a country without legislation providing for an adequate level of data protection is only permitted if one of the specific conditions of Article 6 paragraph 2 of the FADP is met, such as if:

(i) sufficient safeguards, in particular agreements, ensure adequate protection; or
(ii) the data subjects have consented in the specific case; or
(iii) disclosure is essential in the specific case for the establishment, exercise, or enforcement of legal claims before the courts.

According to the FDPIC, the exception under (iii) applies to claims before state courts and arbitral tribunals alike. However, the disclosure of personal data under this exception needs to be both essential and necessary (*'unerlässlich'*) and may only occur in a specific case. This implies that if a claim may be lodged without transferring personal data, no such data may be disclosed under this exception. Additionally, if there is a risk that the state court or the arbitral tribunal may use the personal data for purposes other than the proceedings, the personal data may not be disclosed under this exception unless the court or tribunal has agreed in writing to refrain from using the personal data for other purposes. The exception under (iii) also applies to a disclosure to a person abroad preparing court filings (such as a legal adviser, etc.). In addition, it is not necessary that the individual or legal entity disclosing the personal data is a party to the court proceedings. In particular, the disclosing entity may be an expert, a witness, or even a third party with no particular function in the court proceedings, provided that the disclosure is essential and necessary for the proceedings.

It is questionable whether the provision of personal data in disclosure proceedings is covered by the exception under (iii) above. This must be specifically verified in each individual case, as it is not possible to make a general statement in this respect.

If the disclosure is not covered by the exception under (iii) above, and no other exception applies, a specific data transfer agreement providing for adequate data protection needs to be entered into and the controller of the data file needs to inform the FDPIC prior to the transfer (Article 6 paragraph 3 FADP and Article 6 OFADP). Since it will often be quite difficult to obtain the prior written consent for a disclosure from all data subjects concerned in a particular case, the exception under (ii) above will be unavailable in most cases in the context of an e-disclosure.

Finally, it must be kept in mind that the FADP does not apply to international mutual assistance proceedings in civil and criminal matters pending before Swiss authorities (see section A. above). Therefore, disclosure of personal data abroad under and in accordance with either the applicable cantonal or federal rules regarding mutual assistance or the applicable conventions regarding mutual international assistance in civil and criminal matters is not subject to the FADP.

G. SWISS DATA PROTECTION LAWS: CONFLICT OF LAWS

The FADP covers all types of processing of personal data in Switzerland by private persons and federal bodies.

In addition, certain provisions of the FADP that are not subject to the principle of territoriality[23] may also apply to the processing of personal data outside of Switzerland. In fact, even if processing takes place outside of Switzerland, a data subject may have the option to file an action in a Swiss court for violation of his or her privacy rights (based on an international convention or based on Article 129, paragraph 1 and Article 130, paragraph 3 FAPIL). In such a case, the data subject will often be entitled to ask the competent court to apply Swiss law (cf. Article 139 FAPIL).

Based on the foregoing, even if no processing takes place in Switzerland, the processing of personal data in relation with an e-disclosure might still be subject to the FADP. This possibility must be taken into account in the context of an international e-disclosure.

H. SWISS DATA PROTECTION LAWS: SUPERVISORY AUTHORITIES
AND SANCTIONS

The FDPIC supervises compliance by federal bodies with the FADP (Article 27 FADP). In the private sector, the FDPIC investigates cases of data processing in more detail on its own initiative or at the request of a third party if: the methods of processing are capable of breaching the privacy of a larger number of persons (system errors), data files must be registered, or there is a duty to provide information in relation with a disclosure of personal data abroad (Article 29, paragraph 1 FADP). On the basis of such investigations, the FDPIC may recommend that the processing methods be changed or abandoned (Article 29, paragraph 3 FADP). If a recommendation is not complied with or rejected, the FDPIC may refer the matter to the Swiss Federal Administrative Court for a decision and, if necessary, appeal that court's decision to the Swiss Federal Supreme Court.

Data subjects whose privacy rights have been violated may lodge civil claims based on Article 28 though 28f of the Swiss Civil Code. In particular, the data subjects may request an injunction against an imminent injury, the removal of an existing injury, claim for damages, and, under certain circumstances, seek the disgorgement of profits, and so forth.

---

23. The public law provisions of the FADP, such as the obligation to register a data file (see Art. 11*a* FADP), are subject to the principle of territoriality. The public law provisions of the FADP only apply to facts that occur in Switzerland.

Violations of certain provisions of the FADP are subject to criminal sanctions: a person who wilfully and in an unlawful manner procures sensitive personal data or personality profiles, which are not publicly available from a data file, is subject to a penalty of imprisonment of up to three years or a fine of up to Swiss Francs (CHF) 1,080,000 (Article 179[novies] of the Swiss Penal Code (SPC) in relation with Article 34 SPC). If this provision is violated in conjunction with business-related activities falling within the purpose of a corporation, and if, due to an insufficient organization within the corporation, these violations cannot be ascribed to a specific natural person, the violation is ascribed to the corporation itself, which is then subject to a fine of up to CHF 5,000,000 (Article 102, paragraph 1 SPC).

Private persons who wilfully provide inaccurate or incomplete information, or wilfully breach their obligation to provide the minimum information about the collection of sensitive data or personality profiles required by law, may be punished by a fine of up to CHF 10,000, and face up to three months' imprisonment if the fine is not paid (Article 34 FADP in relation with Article 106 SPC). The same sanction applies in cases of: wilful failure to notify a data file for registration, wilful failure to notify the FDPIC of a cross-border transfer, or, when notifying a data file for registration, wilfully providing false information, or if a person provides the FDPIC with false information or refuses to cooperate in the course of an investigation (Article 34 FADP in relation with Article 106 SPC).

Finally, the FADP prohibits the disclosure of sensitive personal data or personality profiles to third parties for processing for their own purposes without lawful justification. Breach of this prohibition constitutes a sanctionable offence if knowledge of the sensitive data or the personality profiles has been gathered in the course of a professional activity requiring knowledge of such data. The offending party faces a fine of up to CHF 10,000, which, if the fine is not paid, may be replaced by imprisonment for up to three months (Article 35 FADP in relation with Article 106 SPC).

Until now, no judgments on fines and/or sanctions for breach of the FADP have been published. However, according to the Swiss Federal Office of Statistics, in 1996 there was one conditional sentence of imprisonment of five days with a fine of CHF 750 for violation of the FADP. It is unknown whether the violation related to Article 34 or 35 of the FADP. Further, four criminal offences for violation of the FADP were registered with the police in 2009 (no statistics on sentences available) and ten sentences for violation of Article 179[novies] of the SPC have been pronounced between 1984 and 2007.

II.   PRETRIAL DISCLOSURE IN
              SWITZERLAND: BACKGROUND

Pretrial discovery comparable to common law discovery proceedings does not exist in Switzerland. However, there are legislative developments that in the future will allow earlier access to (electronic) evidence in Switzerland.

Jürg Schneider et al.

In Switzerland, civil procedure and thus rules on the taking of evidence are currently still governed by twenty-six cantonal codes of civil procedure. A federal code of civil procedure, that is, the Swiss Code of Civil Procedure (SCCP), will enter into force in 2011.

Currently, evidence will generally only be taken by a judge after the proceedings have been initiated and the parties have pled their cases and indicated which evidence they deem relevant. In other words, proceedings may be divided into a pleading stage and an evidentiary stage. A party may request the court to order the opposing party or any third parties that are in possession of relevant evidence to submit it to the court. However, such a request requires the moving party to sufficiently describe the evidence and to make detailed comments as to its contents and relevance. Merely describing a class of potentially interesting documents is not sufficient. Thus, open-ended and wide-scale discovery is not possible.

There are only limited possibilities available to have evidence taken by a judge prior to the filing of a suit. Currently, most cantons have limited this to preservation of evidence, that is, if evidence necessary for a claim is in danger of being destroyed. However, certain cantons – as well as the new SCCP – permit a pretrial request for the taking of evidence for purposes of a future suit absent any need for that evidence to be preserved.[24] The purpose of this provision is not to enable a 'fishing expedition' but to avoid unnecessary proceedings by allowing a party to evaluate its chances of proving its claim.

The SCCP will thus allow 'pretrial' disclosure in that parties will be able to seek the disclosure of specific evidence from either the opposing party or a third party even absent a pending proceeding. However, the party requesting disclosure will still need to narrowly describe the evidence it seeks and the interest it has in such evidence.

A.   PRETRIAL DISCLOSURE IN SWITZERLAND: BLOCKING STATUTE

In Switzerland the taking of evidence is a judicial, and thus sovereign, function executed by domestic courts rather than the parties. Accordingly, Switzerland views the taking of evidence for foreign proceedings – regardless of whether the foreign procedural code puts the collection of evidence into the hands of the parties – as constituting acts of a foreign state. Such acts, if they occur within the territory of Switzerland, violate Swiss sovereignty unless they are undertaken by a competent Swiss court or authorized by the appropriate Swiss authorities by way of judicial assistance.

Article 271 of the SPC thus specifically prohibits the taking of evidence by foreign officials and attorneys for a foreign proceeding, or any action taken by a person located in Switzerland to comply with an order issued by a foreign court by

---

24.   Article 158, para. 1 SCCP: *'The court takes evidence at any time, if: (a) the law provides such a right; or (b) the party making the application credibly evidences that the means of proof are endangered or that it has a justifiable interest'*.

producing documents or electronic archives located in Switzerland, without involving the appropriate Swiss authorities. Any individual who is found taking evidence without the necessary authorization is subject to imprisonment of up to three years or a fine of up to CHF 1,080,000. If this provision is violated in conjunction with business-related activities falling within the purpose of a corporation, and if, due to an insufficient organization within the corporation, these violations cannot be ascribed to a specific natural person, the violation is ascribed to the corporation itself, which is then subject to a fine of up to CHF 5,000,000 (Article 102, paragraph 1 SPC).

Further, Article 271 of the SPC cannot be avoided by, for example, transferring evidence located in Switzerland outside Swiss borders for purposes of complying with a foreign country's order since there are also penalties for aiding and abetting a violation of the article.

Switzerland does not recognize any 'voluntary' production of documents even if there is a duty to provide such documents under a foreign procedural law, and the documents are intended for use in foreign proceedings.[25] To avoid any risk, the party asked to produce documents should insist on the documents being requested by way of mutual legal assistance.

At the same time, Article 271 of the SPC generally does not prohibit a party from voluntarily submitting pre-existing documents in foreign proceedings in support of its own case. This is considered a permissible party act that does not require the intervention of a Swiss authority.[26] However, where documents are prepared on the basis of investigations, questioning, and so forth, this can nevertheless be considered the taking of evidence, which falls solely within the competence of the Swiss authorities.

B.   PRETRIAL DISCLOSURE IN SWITZERLAND: HAGUE CONVENTION

Switzerland has ratified the Hague Convention on the Taking of Evidence Abroad in Civil or Commercial Matters, dated 18 March 1970 (Hague Convention), which permits the taking of evidence by means of 'Letters of Request', which seek the taking of evidence and are submitted by a judicial authority in one treaty country to the relevant central authority in another treaty country.

While Switzerland accepts Letters of Request from other treaty countries issued in connection with pretrial discovery proceedings, it has exercised its right under Article 23 of the Hague Convention to limit the circumstances in which it will execute such requests.[27] In particular, Letters of Request will not be executed if the request: has no direct and necessary link with the underlying proceedings in question; requires a person to indicate what documents are in his or her possession;

---

25. See Decision of the Swiss Federal Supreme Court, DFSC 65 I 39, para. 4.
26. See Decision of the Swiss Federal Supreme Court, DFSC 114 IV 128, para. 2c.
27. See reservation No. 6 of Switzerland to the Hague Convention: <www.admin.ch/ch/d/sr/i2/0.274.132.de.pdf> (Hague Convention including Switzerland's reservations in German).

requires a person to produce documents other than those specifically mentioned in the request; or if there is a risk to the legitimate interests of a party. The purpose of these limitations is to exclude requests for a general search for documents ('fishing expedition').[28]

Essentially, Switzerland will only grant assistance to foreign pretrial discovery proceedings if a request meets standards similar to those applicable to Swiss court proceedings with regard to a court order for the production of documents. Accordingly, the Letter of Request must clearly establish, in sufficient detail, the link between the evidence requested and the issues in dispute. If the Letter of Request is overly broad or seeks disclosure of information or documents specifically covered by Switzerland's reservation to the Hague Convention, the Letter of Request will only be partially executed ('blue pencil approach') unless the Letter of Request as a whole is defective and the admissible parts cannot be identified.[29]

C.   PRETRIAL DISCLOSURE IN SWITZERLAND: RETENTION AND PRESERVATION OF EVIDENCE

Apart from a general good faith duty in proceedings, parties do not have a duty to preserve potentially relevant data whenever litigation or regulatory investigations and proceedings are reasonably anticipated. Exceptions exist where the law specifically provides for the retention of documents or where the competent authority has ordered the preservation of evidence.

The main instance where the law specifically requires the retention of documents is with regard to business files. Firms that are registered in the Commercial Registry are subject to a statutory retention period of ten years, during which they must retain their annual financial reports, books, and business correspondence (Article 962 SCO). The failure to observe statutory retention periods can result in criminal sanctions (Article 325 SPC).

The Swiss legislature has acknowledged that such business documents are an important source of information for both civil claimants and administrative bodies. Accordingly, a court or administrative authority can order such documents to be provided in a form readable without any aids (i.e., in paper form) or in their native electronic format with the company providing the necessary hardware, software, and even personnel to make the data readable (Article 963 SCO).

III.   PRETRIAL DISCLOSURE VERSUS DATA PROTECTION IN SWITZERLAND: BACKGROUND

As mentioned at the outset of this chapter, the FADP does not apply to civil proceedings, criminal proceedings, international mutual assistance proceedings in civil and

---

28. See Decision of the Swiss Federal Supreme Court, DFSC 132 III 291, para. 2.1.
29. See Decision of the Swiss Federal Supreme Court, DFSC 132 III 291, paras 3.2 and 4.6.

criminal matters, or proceedings under constitutional or under administrative law, with the exception of administrative proceedings of first instance, provided that such proceedings are pending before Swiss authorities (see section II.A. above).

Since there is no equivalent to a mutual pretrial discovery proceeding, evidence will be disclosed in Swiss proceedings on the basis of a court order either in the course of a main proceeding or as a matter of 'provisional taking of evidence', which is also a court proceeding.

To the extent that a party is preparing its case and collecting its documents internally for a proceeding that is not yet pending before Swiss authorities, the exclusion from the FADP does not apply. Accordingly, if data covered by the FADP are encompassed by such actions, the FADP will apply to such data collection.

IV.   ARBITRATION, DISCLOSURE AND
        DATA PROTECTION

As a neutral and stable country Switzerland has a long tradition of dispute resolution by means of arbitration, and with its modern and flexible arbitration law is often chosen as the place of arbitration proceedings. Thus, the question arises as to whether documents to be produced in arbitration proceedings in Switzerland also fall under the same restrictions as mentioned above.

The parties to an arbitration with its seat in Switzerland are largely free to regulate the proceedings, including the production of documents, amongst themselves (Article 182 FAPIL). Often in arbitration cases involving parties that hail from civil and common law countries, the flexibility of arbitration allows the parties to agree on a procedure (e.g., International Bar Association (IBA) Rules on the Taking of Evidence in International Commercial Arbitration) that permits a more extensive production, while still requiring a narrow identification of the requested evidence.

From a Swiss legal point of view, arbitral tribunals are generally considered private rather than official proceedings, and thus the blocking statute (Article 271 SPC) will not apply (see section II.A. above). Furthermore, if the seat of the arbitration is in Switzerland, the proceedings could in any case not be considered foreign. Should the parties fail to voluntarily comply with an order of the arbitral tribunal, the tribunal can request the assistance of the court at its seat (Article 184 paragraph 2 FAPIL), which will apply its own procedural rules.

If the production of documents is sought from parties in Switzerland engaged in 'foreign' arbitration proceedings, the blocking statute also does not apply by virtue of the private nature of arbitration. However, if the arbitral tribunal is not independent and essentially acts as a mere instrument of a foreign country, the private nature is nullified and the blocking statute will still apply.[30]

---

30. Dorothee Schramm, Entwicklungen bei der Strafbarkeit von privaten Zeugenbefragungen in der Schweiz durch Anwälte für ausländische Verfahren, in: AJP/PJA 2006, 492.

Furthermore, if the documents are not voluntarily produced in a foreign arbitration proceeding, thus necessitating enforcement by a court order, such intervention is no longer private in nature and must be enforced by means of mutual legal assistance.

In other words, in a pending arbitration proceeding with its seat in Switzerland, information and evidence can generally be collected, taken, and exchanged in such form as agreed by the parties. In particular, the blocking statute does not apply and such proceedings will be considered as a pending civil proceeding before Swiss authorities, thus excluding the application of Swiss data protection laws, that is, the FADP (see section II.A.).

With regard to arbitration proceedings taking place outside Switzerland, the blocking statute does not – as a general principle – apply to the voluntary production of documents sought from parties in Switzerland. However, such foreign arbitration proceedings are not considered to be 'pending civil proceedings before Swiss authorities'. Accordingly, the provisions of the Swiss data protection laws are applicable and must be respected (see section II.A.). Also, if documents are not voluntarily produced and the intervention of courts or authorities is required, the blocking statute does apply and mutual legal assistance must be requested.

V.   *PRO MEMORIA*: PROTECTION OF MANUFACTURING
         AND BUSINESS SECRETS AGAINST
         INDUSTRIAL ESPIONAGE

The SPC provides general protection for manufacturing and business secrets, making it a crime to divulge or abuse secrets that a party is bound to keep secret due to statutory or contractual duty (Article 162 SPC).

Additionally, the SPC protects manufacturing and business secrets against industrial espionage by foreign official agencies, foreign organizations, private enterprises, or their agents (Article 273 SPC). A violation of Article 273 of the SPC is sanctioned with imprisonment of up to three years (in severe cases up to twenty years) or a fine of up to CHF 1,080,000. If this provision is violated in conjunction with business-related activities falling within the purpose of a corporation, and if, due to an insufficient organization within the corporation, these violations cannot be ascribed to a specific natural person, the violation is ascribed to the corporation itself, which is then subject to a fine of up to CHF 5,000,000 (Article 102, paragraph 1 SPC).

A secret in the sense of Article 273 SPC is every fact : (1) that is not evident to the recipients or publicly accessible outside of Switzerland; (2) that the owner of the secret wishes to keep confidential; (3) for which there is an objective interest in keeping the secret; and for which (4) there is a sufficient connection ('*Binnenbeziehung*') to Switzerland. As a result of Article 273 of the SPC, manufacturing and business secrets can only be released or communicated abroad when the owner of the secret relinquishes its intent to keep the information secret, implicitly or explicitly agrees to disclose this information or permits its disclosure, and all concerned third parties consent. However, if Switzerland has an immediate, sovereign interest in keeping the information secret, Article 273 of the SPC applies regardless of whether the owner of the secret or concerned third parties consent to its disclosure. Furthermore, Article 273 of the SPC also applies to instances where a party travels outside of Switzerland, for example, to give testimony, if such testimony would disclose manufacturing and business secrets.

Article 273 of the SPC does not apply in cases in which Swiss authorities have granted judicial assistance and the information disclosed to foreign authorities is in accordance with judicial assistance proceedings.

VI.   CONCLUSION

In proceedings pending before Swiss authorities (including if data are requested by means of mutual legal assistance or if data are requested in an arbitration proceeding with its seat in Switzerland), Swiss data protection laws do not apply. The role of 'gatekeeper of the data' is then played by the Swiss authorities, who have the authority to either order the evidence to be exchanged or grant the legal assistance request.

Apart from pending proceedings before Swiss authorities, such as situations where a request for mutual legal assistance is absent, disclosure would be made on the basis of an order made by a foreign court or arbitral tribunal, or even when data subjects are willing to disclose the data voluntarily, the provisions of the Swiss data protection laws apply to the processing of personal data and need to be considered.

Furthermore, failure to abide by proper procedures – in particular the mutual legal assistance procedures where required – and/or failure to apply to the appropriate Swiss authorities, where required, could lead to criminal sanctions for the parties involved.

Chapter 5.26

United Kingdom

Hazel Grant*

I.   INTRODUCTION

By way of introduction, the Data Protection Act of 1998 (DPA) applies throughout
the United Kingdom (UK). Comments in this chapter on data protection issues
therefore apply throughout the UK. However, the court system in Scotland is
different to that in England and Wales. Consequently, commentary in this
chapter on litigation and discovery considers only the position in England and
Wales.

In England and Wales there is a discovery process in litigation called disclosure. The disclosure process has two main steps: (1) providing disclosure itself, that
is, stating that a document exists or has existed and (2) inspection, that is, allowing
an opponent to view the original document or providing the opponent with a copy
of the document disclosed. There is also a duty to preserve relevant documents,
once litigation is in contemplation. Certain documents are exempted from disclosure, for example, legally privileged documents. The rules on disclosure are
contained in Part 31 of the Civil Procedure Rules (CPR).[1]

Disclosure usually takes place during the litigation, after statements of case
have been served, but disclosure may be ordered before an action has commenced.
Pre-action disclosure can be ordered between likely parties to an action and in

---

*   Hazel Grant Bristows, London, UK.
1.   Civil Procedure Rules Part 31.

Catrien Noorda & Stefan Hanloser, *E-Discovery and Data Privacy*, pp. 295–306.
© 2011 Kluwer Law International BV, The Netherlands.

certain situations against third parties, for example, under *Norwich Pharmacal*[2] or *Bankers Trust*[3] orders.

II.   BLOCKING STATUTES AND THE
HAGUE CONVENTION

If parties are willing to organize the gathering of evidence in England and Wales without the intervention of the courts, there is no restriction against this. Subject to data protection law and general law compliance (e.g., confidentiality), an organization can choose to provide disclosure of evidence outside England and Wales. There are no blocking statutes that would prevent voluntary disclosure in this way.

If the intervention of the courts is required, there are several ways to obtain disclosure, including obtaining an order for discovery in aid of foreign proceedings under the Evidence (Proceedings in Other Jurisdictions) Act of 1975, which was passed to give effect to the Hague Convention on the Taking of Evidence Abroad in Civil or Commercial Matters of 1970. There are a number of limitations, such as the requirement for individual documents to be specified in the request (thus ruling out 'fishing expeditions'). The procedure for making an application is governed by Part 34 of the CPR. In addition, a *Norwich Pharmacal* order may be made for discovery in aid of foreign proceedings.

Article 23 permits a Hague Convention Contracting State to 'declare that it will not execute Letters of Request issued for the purpose of obtaining pretrial discovery of documents as known in Common Law countries'. The UK made such a declaration in 2003. The UK declaration states that the UK will not execute Letters of Request for pretrial discovery, where such requests require a person to state what documents are or have been in his or her possession, custody, or power or to produce any documents other than a particular document specified in the Letter of Request. Essentially this declaration states that the UK courts will not allow a fishing expedition.

III.   DATA PROTECTION LAW IN ENGLAND AND WALES

Data protection law in England and Wales is set out in the DPA. The DPA implements Directive 95/46 EC (the 'Directive'). The Data Protection Authority with competence to enforce the DPA is the Information Commissioner's Office (ICO).

---

2. *Norwich Pharmacal v. Commissioners of Customs and Excise* [1974] AC133.
3. *Bankers Trust v. Shapira* [1980]1 WLR 1274 (CA).

A.   SCOPE

1.   The Definition of Personal Data and Processing

The DPA applies to computerized processing of personal data, and so will apply to electronically stored information (ESI). Although the definition of personal data is based on that in the Directive, case law in the UK has led to some inconsistencies of approach between UK courts and the opinions of the Article 29 Working Party.

The ICO as supervisory authority has issued guidance[4] on its interpretation of the definition of personal data, which attempts to align UK case law and the Article 29 Working Party Opinion on this definition (see Chapter 3 page 16, footnote 10).

Broadly, UK courts have interpreted the definition of personal data in a more restrictive fashion than would data protection regulators (and the Article 29 Working Party). UK court decisions state that, to be personal data, information must be biographical in a significant sense and have a focus on the individual (rather than some transaction or event in which he or she may have figured).

Thus, organizations can find it difficult to decide on what constitutes personal data, since if an organization were to make a decision on how to handle certain information and that were to lead to a court hearing, the court would follow previous judgments and have a restrictive view of personal data. However, if a decision on what constitutes personal data led to a complaint to the ICO, the regulator is likely to take a more expansive view on what constitutes personal data, and so there might be a different outcome.

In the case of ESI, this may be relevant, since there may be an argument that, for example, emails written by employees contain only limited personal data. (This would be on the basis that the emails do not contain significant biographical information and do not focus on an individual. An email is likely to contain personal data of the sender, but may not be considered to include personal data of recipients or even those named in the email. Consequently, there may be only a reduced number of individuals whose personal data are affected by the e-discovery.)

'Processing' is very widely defined to include obtaining, recording, holding, using, or disclosing the information. In practice, any action with respect to, or use of, personal data will be included in the definition of processing.

2.   Geographical Scope

The DPA applies to processing carried out by a UK established entity, such as a registered company, partnership, or branch or agency. Processing of ESI carried out by a UK company, for example, would be governed by the DPA.

In addition, if processing is carried in the UK on behalf of an entity that does not have a UK or other European Economic Area (EEA) presence, then the DPA will apply to that processing. This would apply if, for example, a US entity

---

4. Technical Guidance Note – determining what is personal data, dated 21 Aug. 2007, available at: <www.ico.gov.uk>.

used a UK service provider or agency to process ESI for the purpose of US litigation (see section III.B below for further information on the use of service providers and agents).

B.   CONTROLLERS AND PROCESSORS

Under the DPA, data controllers are responsible for compliance with the DPA and make decisions on the purpose and essential means of processing. Data processors are agents acting on behalf of the controller (other than employees of the controller). Under UK data protection law it is possible for there to be joint data controllers in respect of the same information.

Professional advisors involved in performing or assisting in e-discovery investigations could be seen as processors or controllers. There is some limited UK data protection case law indicating that a professional advisor would be seen as a controller, due to the discretion that the advisor has in handling information.

E-discovery investigations could be outsourced within a group of companies or to a service provider, in which case, again, the service provider/group company could act as a processor or controller, depending on the discretion given to it.

The distinction is important since under UK data protection law it is not necessary to inform an individual if there is an outsourcing to a data processor. However, if there is outsourcing to a data processor there needs to be a written agreement with the processor that specifies the following:

(a) the processor will process the personal data on the instructions of the controller; and

(b) the processor will put in place appropriate technical and organizational measures to protect the personal data against unauthorized disclosure or loss (i.e., security measures).

If there is a transfer of data to another data controller, then there is a need to inform the individual of the transfer (see section III.D below on transparency) and to comply with one of the preconditions for processing (see section III.E below). In addition, although an agreement is not strictly necessary for compliance with the DPA, it is advisable to put in place an agreement limiting the use of the data by the new data controller.

C.   RULES FOR LEGITIMATE PROCESSING

The DPA sets out eight data protection principles in relation to the processing of personal information, the first of which requires that processing must be fair and lawful. Processing is only held to be fair if:

(a) The individual has been provided with sufficient information (i.e., the processing is transparent (see section III.D below)); and

(b) One of the pre-specified grounds for processing has been met (see section III.E below).

D.   TRANSPARENCY

Under the first data protection principle, when personal data are collected a data controller should inform the individual what processing will be carried out in respect of his or her personal data. In addition, other information should be provided such as the name of the data controller and any other information that may be necessary to ensure the processing is fair (e.g., transfers to third parties). This is an inherent issue with discovery, since it is unlikely that litigation will have been notified by the data controller to the individual whose data may be revealed during a pre-action discovery request.

There is an exemption to this requirement where:

(a) the obligation of transparency is inconsistent with the disclosure; and
(b) the disclosure is required by a court; or
(c) the disclosure is necessary for the purpose of or in connection with any legal proceedings (including prospective legal proceedings) or for the purpose of obtaining legal advice or is otherwise necessary for the purpose of establishing, exercising, or defending legal rights.

Where the data controller can argue that the obligation to notify employees would be inconsistent with the e-discovery, then this exemption may be available. However, this would normally only be relevant where there was some risk that the employees might hide or delete evidence or warn potential defendants. (This legal proceedings exemption also applies to other obligations under the DPA. See sections 2.7, 2.8, and 2.11 below).

Where information is received by a new data controller, then that data con-troller should also inform the individual of the processing that it will carry out in respect of his or her data. This notification may be carried out by the new data controller or the original data controller. This would be relevant where a new data controller is appointed, for example, to carry out analysis of ESI or provide legal advice on the ESI.

There are two possible exemptions to this requirement to notify the processing by a new controller:

(1) If the obligation to notify is disproportionate, then it can be avoided. There is no case law on this disproportionate efforts exemption and limited guidance. In an environment where all of the relevant affected individuals are employees of one business and it would be possible to contact them all with one email, it would seem very difficult to argue that such efforts would be disproportionate. (If this disproportionate efforts exemption is being used, the new data controller is also required to keep a record of the reasons why it applies).

(2) If the disclosure of the data is necessary for compliance with a legal obligation other than a contractual obligation (e.g., a court order imposed on the controller). This would allow the disclosure under court order to an opposing party, without the need for the opposing party to notify the individuals.

E.   PRE-CONDITIONS FOR PROCESSING

Of the pre-conditions for processing under the DPA, the most likely grounds would be:

(a) the consent of the individual;
(b) disclosure is necessary for compliance with a legal obligation other than a contractual obligation; or
(c) the processing is necessary for the purposes of legitimate interests pursued by the data controller or by a third party or parties to whom the data are disclosed, except where the processing is unwarranted in any particular case by reason of prejudice to the rights and freedoms or legitimate interests of the individual.

Turning to consent first, the ICO's guidance on UK data protection law is that, as with the Directive, consent must be specific, informed, and freely given. It is generally understood that employees would be very unlikely to be in a position to give freely given consent in respect of their own personal information. This is certainly the view of the ICO in its guidance on employment-related information.

The pre-condition that disclosure is necessary for compliance with a legal obligation would apply where a competent court ordered the disclosure of the information.

In respect of the final pre-condition (legitimate interests), the ICO takes a very broad view. It is one of the most frequently used grounds for the justification of processing of personal information. It would certainly be within the contemplation of the ICO that carrying out litigation or complying with litigation requirements would be in the legitimate interests of a data controller. The only question would be the extent to which the interference with the individual's rights was unwarranted. If this ground were to be used it would therefore be sensible for the disclosing party to carry out some steps to be able to show that there is no unwarranted interference – for example, minimizing the information disclosure (by searching by author/topic/dates); redacting irrelevant information; redacting personal information of the employees, such as private comments or conversations; and/or limiting the individuals or organizations that will have access to the information.

If it is possible to anonymize the information that is to be disclosed, then this would avoid data protection issues in the disclosure of the information (as the information would no longer refer to a living individual). However, it is likely that this would reduce the evidential value of the ESI and therefore not be appropriate. (Note that even if ESI is anonymized, other rights such as confidentiality may still apply. Also the analysis of the original, non-anonymized ESI would still need to comply with the DPA.)

F.   SPECIAL CATEGORIES OF DATA

The DPA includes a definition for sensitive personal data, which covers the special categories of data listed in Article 8 of the Directive and additionally information concerning the commission or alleged commission of any offence, together with any proceedings for offences.

The DPA includes several grounds for the processing of sensitive personal data, including one where the disclosure is:

(a) necessary for the purpose of or in connection with any legal proceedings (including prospective legal proceedings);
(b) necessary for the purpose of obtaining legal advice; or
(c) otherwise necessary for the purpose of establishing, exercising, or defending legal rights.

It is likely therefore that this ground would apply to the disclosure and processing of any sensitive personal data in an e-discovery procedure (see section III.K for further discussion of this wording), provided that the disclosure was necessary. (The ICO in guidance emphasises the need to show necessity to meet this ground.)

G.   NEW PURPOSES

Under the DPA the second data protection principle requires that personal data should be processed for a legitimate purpose notified to the individual (and to the ICO, on which see section III.I below). There should no processing for a new purpose without recollection or obtaining the consent of the individual or some other justification for the processing.

It is quite possible the data were originally collected for a non-litigation purpose and therefore to provide the information for litigation would be seen as a secondary or new purpose in breach of the DPA. That said, there is little by way of case law or guidance on this issue and, in practice, any enforcement that the ICO has carried out on change of purpose tends to focus on the first data protection principle (transparency and the pre-condition for processing) rather than this point.

This principle is also subject to the legal proceedings exemption discussed in section III.D above.

H.   DATA MINIMIZATION AND DATA RETENTION

Again, under the DPA data protection principles, the third principle requires that the amount of personal data processed should be minimized. Compliance with this principle, that personal data should be adequate, relevant, and not excessive in relation to the purpose for which they are processed, is inherently in conflict with e-discovery since e-discovery maximizes the disclosure of data.

Similarly, the fifth data protection principle requires that personal data be kept for no longer than is necessary for the purpose for which they are processed. The duty to preserve evidence will require the extended retention of personal data for periods in excess of the normal retention periods. Unless the purposes of processing have been extended to include litigation, there will be a breach of the fifth data protection principle.

These third and fifth principles are also subject to the legal proceedings exemption discussed in section III.D above.

I.   NOTIFICATION TO THE ICO

Organizations subject to the DPA need, in most cases, to notify their processing with the ICO. The notification includes details of the data processed, the purposes of processing, and whether any international transfers take place. Therefore, if the controller is based in the UK and is providing information for the purpose of pre-action discovery in the United States, this should be added to the UK entity's notification with the ICO. This is a relatively simple administrative action. However, the updating should be carried out since failure to ensure that the ICO notification is accurate and up to date involves the commission of a criminal offence.

There is no requirement to notify with the ICO (or obtain the ICO's prior approval) when there are any transfers of personal data outside the UK, unlike some other EU jurisdictions (see section III.K below on transfers).

J.   RIGHTS OF THE DATA SUBJECT

Under the DPA, individuals have a right of access to information held about them. This includes a right to be informed of whether or not any information about the individual is processed and, if it is processed, to provide details of the purpose of processing, categories of information processed, recipients and sources of the information, together with a copy of the information or access to it.

Consequently, employees whose data are being transferred as part of an e-discovery process would have the right find out about the transfer and know what information was being transferred. This right is subject to some exemptions, which are unlikely to apply in the case of e-discovery.

An individual also has the right to request correction or blocking of his or her information if this should be incorrect or incomplete.

In addition, an individual has the right to require a data controller to cease processing that causes the individual substantial and unwarranted damage or distress. Litigants have attempted to use this right to prevent opponents from processing their personal data in litigation, but this has been rejected by the courts. Therefore, although it is possible that an employee might use this right to prevent the analysis or transfer of his or her personal data, it is quite likely that the court would reject such a claim.

K.   Rules for the Transfer of Personal Data outside the EEA

1.   Introduction

Under the DPA, the transfer of personal data to countries outside the EEA is prohibited unless the recipient country provides an adequate level of protection for personal data. This is set out in the eighth data protection principle. The determination of whether or not an adequate level of protection exists is an obligation on the data controller. The ICO has stated that it will not provide any informal or ad hoc approvals of transfers. Therefore in the UK a data controller, generally, follows the following steps:

(a) consults the list of 'white' countries (i.e., those countries approved by the European Commission as having an adequate level of protection); in the case of the United States this applies if the recipient is Safe Harbor registered;
(b) considers whether any of the exemptions apply (see below);
(c) makes the transfer in accordance with the EC-approved model clauses; and, as a last resort
(d) makes an independent assessment of whether or not adequate protection exists in respect of the transfer (see below).

2.   Exemptions

Under the DPA, there is an exemption for a transfer that is necessary:

(a) for the purpose of, or in connection with, any legal proceedings (including prospective legal proceedings);
(b) for the purpose of obtaining legal advice; or
(c) for the purposes of establishing, exercising, or defending legal rights.

In ICO guidance,[5] it is confirmed that any legal proceedings are relevant, including legal proceedings outside the UK (e.g., in a third country). In addition, the ICO in its guidance draws attention to the Article 29 Working Party's example, where the Working Party stated that this derogation may apply in the case where a parent company based in a third country is sued by an employee of the group based in one of the European subsidiaries, and the parent company requests the European

---

5. The Eighth Data Protection Principle and International Data Transfers, version 4, 29 Apr. 2010, available at <www.ico.gov.uk>.

subsidiary to transfer certain data relating to the employee where the data are necessary for the defence.

In other guidance,[6] the ICO states:

the legal proceedings do not have to involve you or the individual as a party and the legal rights do not have to be yours or the individual's. Although this exemption could apply widely, transfers are only likely to fall under this category if they are connected with legal proceedings or getting legal advice.

Consequently, if a data controller in the UK chooses to participate in e-discovery in the United States, it is likely that it will be able to rely upon this exemption for the transfer of personal data.

3. Assessments of Adequacy

It remains possible in the UK for a data controller to make its own assessment of adequate protection. In this case the responsibility for the transfer falls on the shoulders of the data controller. It is not necessary for the data controller to notify the ICO of the transfer or obtain prior authorization for the transfer. In fact, the ICO has stated that it does not intend to provide ad hoc approvals in this way.

Therefore, for example, it may be possible for a UK data controller to decide that a transfer to the United States should be protected by an adequate level of protection due to the parties involved, the technical measures taken to protect the information, and/or contractual or commercial measures put in place.

L. SANCTIONS/ENFORCEMENT

The ICO has the power to levy a fine for a breach of one of the data protection principles (which would include the first principle, requirement for fair and lawful processing, and the eighth principle requiring adequate level of protection of personal data when outside the EEA). The maximum level of a fine is UK Pounds (GBP) 500,000. At the time of writing, no fines have yet been levied (although the power to fine has been in force for less than six months).

In addition to the power to levy fines, the ICO has various powers to require the disclosure of information (via an information order) and to require changes to processing or prohibit processing (via an enforcement order). In practice, information orders and enforcement orders are rarely used. Instead the ICO has an informal process of obtaining a written undertaking from a data controller, usually signed at the chief executive level within the data controller's organization. The written undertaking is then published on the ICO's website. Undertakings are unlimited in time and require the data controller to remedy certain aspects of its

---

6. The Guide to Data Protection, available at <www.ico.gov.uk/for_organisations/data_protection_guide.aspx>.

data protection compliance practices. It is therefore a highly public and very cost-effective method of ensuring data protection compliance, in the view of the ICO.

To date, most enforcement action in the UK has focused on data losses or security breaches, with no enforcement in relation to data transfers or use of data in e-discovery.

M.   EMPLOYEE MONITORING

The ICO has published detailed guidance[7] on the handling of employment-related information. This includes a section on monitoring employees and in particular their electronic communications.

In principle, the monitoring of employees' emails is permitted provided that the employer has been clear that monitoring will occur (i.e., to negate any expectation of privacy in relation to emails) and the investigation or monitoring is carried out in a proportionate fashion. This would require that, for example, not every email is reviewed, clearly private emails are not reviewed, and the review is carried out (if possible) either automatically, without human intervention, or by a distinct group of individuals who are not close working colleagues of the employee under observation.

IV.   CONCLUSION

In the context of pre-action discovery involving a number of EU jurisdictions, it is likely that, in comparison with other EU jurisdictions, the UK will pose fewer data protection problems.

The UK regulator, the ICO, has had traditionally a very reasonable and pragmatic approach to data protection compliance. Assuming this continues, taking the following steps would be likely to mitigate the risk of data protection breaches in the UK to an acceptable level:

(a) Minimizing the scope of UK personal data collected, for example, by location, teams involved, roles of employees, authors or recipients of known documents, categories of documents, time of creation, and/or redaction of relevant personal data.
(b) Where possible, using anonymized information, although this is likely to reduce the evidential weight of the document.
(c) Being clear on the purposes for which the information will be used, where the information will be transferred (i.e., to which jurisdictions), to whom the information will be disclosed (e.g., to legal advisors, witnesses, and the

---

7.   The Employment Practices Code and Supplemental Guidance, both dated June 2005 and available at <www.ico.gov.uk>.

adverse party), and also the possible disclosure of the documents to the court and contents entering the public domain.

(d) Where possible, avoiding the collection of employees' private information and in all cases complying with the UK data controller's employee monitoring policy.

(e) Where possible, conducting a preliminary review in the UK to assess what information is relevant and making that available in response to the pre-action discovery request.

(f) Where using another legal entity to carry out a preliminary review (e.g., another group company or a hosted solution), consider whether the other legal entity is a data controller or processor. If the other legal entity is a processor, put in place a controller-processor agreement. If the other legal entity is a controller, put in place limitations on how the data will be used.

(g) Incorporating UK data protection concerns into the protective order, for example, limiting the other party to use the documents containing UK personal data only for the purpose of litigation, to require the other party to apply appropriate security measures and not to disclose the UK personal data other than as necessary for the litigation, and, finally, to return all UK personal data documents at the conclusion of the litigation.

Chapter 6.1

Israel

Liad Whatstein[*]

I.   INTRODUCTION

Pretrial discovery is available under Israeli law. The guiding principle is that all relevant documents must be discovered by the litigants in the interest of serving justice. The courts have the necessary powers to compel discovery and production of documents.

When discovery is burdensome or involves a large number of documents, courts are likely to limit its scope. Therefore, in practice, discovery in Israel is substantially narrower in scope than US-style discovery. This is likely to remain the case with regard to discovery of electronic data.

Israeli courts impose additional restraints on discovery of confidential information and may require *prima facie* proof of the plaintiff's case as a prerequisite for discovery of the defendant's trade secrets. On the other hand, it seems that privacy issues are given little deference as a ban to discovery.

There are no blocking statutes in Israel preventing the transfer of information or data to other jurisdictions. Israeli courts will endeavour to implement discovery requests by foreign judicial instances to the fullest possible extent.

II.   THE PROCEDURAL FRAMEWORK OF PRETRIAL DISCOVERY

Discovery proceedings are an important part of the pretrial proceedings in litigation conducted in Israel. Under the Civil Procedure Regulations of 1984, each party

Catrien Noorda & Stefan Hanloser, *E-Discovery and Data Privacy*, pp. 307–317.

may require the other party to discover 'all the documents which are related to the subject matter of the proceedings and which are, or have been, under its control or custody, and which it found after diligent investigation and inquiry'.[1] In addition to requiring the opposing party to discover all pertinent documents, the parties are entitled to demand specific discovery of particular documents or categories of documents.[2]

In response to a demand for discovery of documents, the responding party must submit an affidavit listing all documents that it found and all documents that are no longer under its control or custody. In addition, the responding party must confirm in an affidavit that 'to the best of its knowledge and belief, and after conducting diligent investigation and inquiry, it does not have, and has never had, under its control or custody, or under the control or custody of anyone on its behalf, any document that relates to the subject matter of the proceedings other than the documents listed in the affidavit'.[3]

After the parties exchange the discovery affidavits, they may review and obtain copies of the documents listed in the affidavits. In practice, parties to complex litigation routinely negotiate mutually agreeable procedures and time-lines with respect to the production of the documents and the costs of copying.

In addition to discovery demands, the parties can (and normally do) exchange interrogatories. Answers to the interrogatories are given in an affidavit. There are no 'live' depositions or cross-examinations at the pretrial stage.

A.   SANCTIONS FOR BREACH OF DISCOVERY OBLIGATIONS

If a party to the litigation does not respond to the discovery demands or provides partial information, it is possible to petition the court to order further discovery. Such petitions are commonly submitted. Regulation 122 provides that if the plain-tiff is in breach of a court order requiring further discovery, production of docu-ments, or response to interrogatories, the court is entitled to strike out the statement of claim. If the party in breach is the defendant, the court is entitled to strike out the statement of defence and to enter judgment by default against the defendant.[4]

In practice, and in view of the dire consequences, courts rarely exercise their powers to strike out the pleadings when a party is in breach of its discovery obligations. In most cases, the court will extend the deadline to comply with the court order and the party in breach will get a second or even a third opportunity to comply. However, when the court is convinced that the party in breach acted

---

1. Regulation 112 of the Civil Procedure Regulations.
2. Regulation 113 of the Civil Procedure Regulations.
3. This is the mandatory text of the affidavit in response to a demand for discovery in accordance with Form 11 of the Civil Procedure Regulations.
4. Another sanction is provided in Regulation 114A. According to this Regulation, a party will not be entitled to submit in trial a document that was not listed in its discovery affidavit. The court may nevertheless grant leave to submit the document subject to an award of costs if the omission to discover the document can be 'reasonably justified'.

'maliciously' or that its conduct amounts to a 'contempt' of the order, it will strike out the claim or the statement of defence.[5]

In some instances, parties have tried to invoke 'ordinary' contempt of court proceedings to address breach of court orders requiring further discovery. However, the courts held that discovery orders can only be enforced via Regulation 122 and that contempt of court proceedings are not available in such matters.[6]

B.   Scope of Discovery

As stated, the Civil Procedure Regulations require that the litigants discover all documents that are 'related to' the litigation and have been found after 'diligent investigation and inquiry'. The Supreme Court held that any document that could assist the party seeking discovery to support its case or undermine its opponents' case is subject to discovery.[7] The Court further held that litigation should be conducted with 'open cards' and that any 'reasonable connection' between the documents and the parties' assertions suffices in order to make them subject to discovery.[8] At the same time, and not necessarily in line with the rhetoric about conducting litigation with 'open cards', the Supreme Court noted that the court's power to order discovery must be used 'with caution' and that burdensome discovery or discovery aimed at 'fishing for evidence' should not be allowed.[9]

In a recent decision, the Supreme Court attempted to clarify the prevailing guidelines with respect to the scope of discovery.[10] As stated by the Court, the basic principle remains that relevant documents must be discovered. However, a court can narrow down the scope of discovery of relevant documents if the burden of producing the documents is 'unreasonable under the circumstances'.

The test is flexible and depends on the 'degree of relevance' of the particular document or class of documents to the proceedings. If a document or a class of documents is essential to the proceedings, or if a party's case depends on the production of a particular document or class of documents, discovery will be ordered even if it is burdensome. On the other hand, if the documents are only indirectly relevant to the proceedings, they will not be subject to discovery if searching the documents and producing them involves an unreasonable burden.

---

5. C.A. 2271/90 *Jumbo Company for Trade and Construction v. Mordechai*, PD 46(3) 793; C.A. 43/76 *Sde Eliezer Community v. Savir*, PD 31(1) 656.
6. HCP 490/82 *Bank Leumi v. The National Labour Court*, PD 37(4) 578.
7. C.A. 40/49 *Chiat v. Chiat*, PD 3 159.
8. MLA 6649/07 *Local Municipality of Shlomi v. Shectman & Co. Construction and Development Company*, tk-el, 2007(4) 4761; MLA 7956/08 *Ma'danyot Ha'achim Becavod (94) Ltd. v. Gan Zvi*, tk-el 2009(2) 484.
9. C.A. 40/49 *Chiat v. Chiat* PD 3 159, 162; MLA 6297/97 *Rkach v. Teva Pharmaceutical Industries Ltd.*, tk-el 98(1) 410.
10. MLA 9322/07 *Gerber Products Company v. Randi Co. Ltd.*, tk-el 2008(4) 586.

C.   Discovery of Trade Secrets and Confidential Information

Israeli courts have a wide discretion to order the discovery of documents containing trade secrets or confidential information. Under the Commercial Wrongs Act of 1999, the court may enter any appropriate order to protect a party's trade secret or ensure that it will not be published. Accordingly, the court can order that particular classes of documents will only be discovered to a limited number of employees of the party seeking discovery or only to the party's in-house or external counsel or even only to external experts.

The Supreme Court held that the scope of discovery of the defendant's trade secrets will be 'directly proportional' to the *prima facie* evidence that was presented by the plaintiff. If the plaintiff can present strong *prima facie* evidence in support of the claim, the plaintiff's interests to obtain wide scope of discovery will outweigh the defendant's interests in safeguarding its trade secrets.[11] In a subsequent case the Supreme Court cautioned against the abuse of discovery, in particular by the plaintiff, for the purpose of obtaining access to a party's trade secrets. The Court held that discovery of trade secrets should not be allowed in the absence of some 'minimal evidentiary basis' supporting the allegations of the party seeking discovery. Even when such evidentiary basis has been presented, only relevant documents that are 'essential' for the hearing will be discovered.[12]

The approach requiring *prima facie* proof of the plaintiff's case as a prerequisite for discovery of trade secrets, or limiting discovery only to 'essential' documents, may seem overly restrictive. It does not confer sufficient weight to the court's powers to formulate the protective order in a manner that will prevent abuse of discovery. It may also be inconsistent with the rhetoric of the Supreme Court about conducting litigation with 'open cards'. For instance, the Supreme Court emphasized that 'the law stands on the truth. The essence of the judicial process is the unveiling of the truth . . . the judge's role is to do everything in its power to unveil the truth . . . the law of evidence is based on the unveiling of the truth which serves the private interest and the public interest'.[13] Wide scope of discovery seems to be the natural result of this perception of the court's judicial role. It can therefore be expected that the judicial approach with regard to discovery of trade secrets will continue to develop and that courts will find ways to permit discovery while preventing its abuse by formulating appropriate protective orders.

D.   Discovery of Electronic Data and Evidence

The Civil Procedure Regulations do not specifically relate to electronic data or evidence. It is, however, apparent that discovery obligations are not limited to paper evidence and also cover electronic data and digitally stored documents or

---

11. MLA 918/02 *Vitalzon v. Pentacom*, PD 56(4) 865.
12. MLA *Bitom Petrochemical Industries Ltd. v. Chemifern – Israel Ltd.*, PD 58(1) 97.
13. MLA 1412/94 *Medicinal Union Hadassah Ein KArem v. Gilaad*, PD 49(2) 516, 522.

information. Such interpretation is also in line with older case law holding that the term 'documents' should not be narrowly interpreted and, for instance, requiring the discovery of video cassette and taped recordings.[14]

In practice, parties to litigation demand, and obtain, discovery of digitally stored documents and evidence, e-mail correspondence, and the like. For instance, in MLA 6823/05 *Abraham Ruimi v. Bank Leumi LeIsrael*, the bank brought a monetary claim against Ruimi to collect an outstanding loan. Ruimi alleged that he was not personally liable to pay this amount. In support of his assertions, Ruimi petitioned the Court to obtain discovery of all internal e-mail communications of the bank's employees in connection with the loan. The Supreme Court ordered the bank to discover the e-mail correspondence. However, the Court sought to limit the burden of searching for e-mail correspondence in the bank's computer systems and servers. It therefore instructed that the bank would only be required to discover e-mail messages that contain the name of the defendant or the serial number of the defendant's account. In addition, only computers of bank employees who were directly handling the loan were to be searched for such e-mail correspondence.[15]

Electronic discovery can of course raise complex questions. The volume of electronically stored information is much larger than that in traditional paper discovery. Searching across computerized systems to identify relevant digitally stored information can be costly and time consuming. In addition to digitally stored documents, parties can seek discovery of additional types of electronically stored information such as backup and archival files, system logs, storage systems, web-site information, information on databases, historical files, database programs, and much more. Israeli courts have not yet wrestled with these issues but will probably apply the current discovery rules to electronic discovery. Accordingly, extensive and burdensome discovery demands, exceeding 'straightforward' discovery of electronically stored documents and requiring substantial effort and cost, are likely to be permitted only if it can be shown that the discovery requests are directly relevant and essential to support the litigant's case.

III.   DATA PROTECTION AND PRIVACY

The Privacy Protection Act of 1981 is the main statutory mechanism in Israel for the protection of an individual's right to privacy. The Act provides that violation of a person's privacy constitutes an actionable civil wrong. If done maliciously, it can also constitute a criminal offence. The Act further provides a limited list of acts that amount to violation of privacy. These include, among others, the unauthorized use of a person's name, image, likeness, or voice for a commercial purpose; breach of confidentiality obligations stipulated by law or under an express or implied agreement regarding a person's private affairs; publication of matters relating to a person's private life, including matters relating to a person's sexual conduct or

---

14.   C.F. 487/90 *Ezra Aharoni v. Yosef Menashe*, PM 1993(2) 397.
15.   MLA 6823/05 *Abraham Ruimi v. Bank Leumi LeIsrael*, tk-el 2006(1) 337.

health; publication of a person's photograph in circumstances where such publication could humiliate or denigrate that person; and so forth.[16]

The Act also sets out the legal prerequisites for holding and registering databases used for commercial purposes. The following databases must be registered with the Registrar of Data Bases: databases that contain information on more than 10,000 individuals; databases that contain 'sensitive information' on a person's character, privacy, health, economic situation, and beliefs; databases that contain information on individuals when the information was not provided by the individuals or with their consent; databases operated by public bodies and government agencies; databases used for direct mailing purposes.

A petition to record the database must specify the identity of the owner of the database, the type of information to be included in the database, the purpose of the database and of the data collection, and details on whether the data will be transferred outside of Israel. The Registrar will accept the registration of the database unless the Registrar deems that the database may be used as a disguise for illegal acts or that the data were collected illegally. The database may only be used for the purposes that were declared upon registration.

The Registrar must examine the application for registering the database within a period of ninety days. In the absence of a response from the Registrar within this time frame, the applicant will be entitled to start using the database. According to the most recent statistics of the Israeli Law, Information & Technology Authority, in recent years about 450 applications to record databases were filed each year. There is a backlog of about 1,500 applications that have not yet been examined although the period of ninety days has already elapsed. The Authority is now undertaking substantial efforts to cut the backlog and speed up examination. In 2008, the Authority also set up an enforcement unit for the purpose of investigating violations of the Privacy Protection Act. The unit recently investigated leakage of personal information in databases owned by government agencies, credit card companies, and banks. Generally, the enforcement resources of the Authority are limited and the main sanctions are the revocation of the registration and the imposing of administrative fines.[17]

A.   DISCOVERY OF PERSONAL DATA

Attempts to limit the scope of discovery on the grounds of privacy were not favourably regarded by the courts. As a matter of principle, it was held that the Privacy Protection Act of 1981 does not necessarily ban discovery. The general guidelines applicable to discovery are also applicable to documents containing private information, and the scope of discovery will primarily be determined on the basis of the degree of relevancy of the information to the proceedings.

---

16. Sections 1–5 of the Privacy Protection Act, 1981.
17. For more information, see the Report of the Israeli Law, Information & Technology Authority, 2008, published 20 Jul. 2009.

Moreover, with respect to plaintiffs, courts were even less tolerant to attempts to ban discovery on privacy grounds, holding that plaintiffs will normally be estopped from asserting that their right to maintain their privacy is stronger than their obligation to discover relevant documents. As the Court stated rather blatantly in a 2009 case, if the plaintiff prefers to protect its privacy it has the option of striking out the claim.[18]

For instance, in MLA 8019/06 *Yediot Achronot Ltd. v. Merav Levin*, the defendant newspaper published a story about a famous TV presenter who was allegedly found wandering in the streets in a 'state of delusion' and described her as a 'lunatic and delusional woman'. The TV presenter filed a libel suit. In discovery proceedings, the newspaper demanded that the TV presenter discover her medical history. The Supreme Court permitted discovery under protective order of all documents pertaining to the presenter's medical situation on the day she was found wandering in the streets and a few days thereafter. The Supreme Court also permitted the newspaper to seek a review of the scope of the order and potentially obtain further discovery of the entire medical history of the presenter if it were to later transpire that such information would become necessary for the proceedings.[19]

Rather surprisingly, privacy considerations enjoyed an unexpected support in a recent judgment of the Supreme Court in MLA 4447/07 *Rami Mor v. Barak*. In a majority holding, the Supreme Court held that courts cannot force Internet service providers to reveal the identities of anonymous talk backers posting libelous comments on the Internet. The majority held that there is no legal framework that authorizes the court to enter such orders. In addition, the majority commented that anonymity is an important part of the right of privacy and must be protected in order to enhance free exchange of ideas on the Internet. It seems that the attempt to protect the individual's right to remain anonymous was a key consideration in the Court's ruling. This is a controversial ruling that is unlikely to influence discovery outside the context of the Internet. It is also reasonable to assume that either the Supreme Court or the legislator will reconsider the issues relating to the discovery of the identity of surfers and will come up with a more balanced approach, at least permitting some limited discovery in cases of libelous or otherwise infringing comments posted on the Internet.[20]

B.   DISCOVERY OF EMPLOYEE'S E-MAIL CORRESPONDENCE

The Labour Courts permitted employers to search the employee's computer and submit as evidence private e-mail correspondence of the employee.

---

18.   MLA 88551/00 *Apropim Ltd. v. The State of Israel – Ministry of Construction*, PD 55(2) 102; MLA 8019/06 *Yediot Achronot Ltd. v. Merav Levin*, tk-el 2009(4) 333.
19.   MLA 8019/06 *Yediot Achronot Ltd. v. Merav Levin*, tk-el 2009(4) 333.
20.   MLA 4447/07 *Rami Mor v. Barak* (as yet unpublished, 25 Mar. 2010).

In LF (T.A.) 10121/06 *Tali Isakov-Inbar v. The Controller of Women's Employment*, the employee sued the employer for unlawfully terminating her employment while she was pregnant. As part of its evidence, the employer submitted files containing private e-mail correspondence of the employee in which she was apparently circulating her CV to potential employers. The employee petitioned the Labour Court to strike out this evidence, which was allegedly obtained in violation of her right to privacy. The Court held that, in the absence of express or implied consent by the employee, the employer is not entitled to open private e-mail correspondence or review its contents. However, the Court found that the circumstances of the matter justify an inference of implied consent by the employee. Among others, the employee did not have a personal password to her e-mail account and was notified by the employer that e-mail servers are monitored by the employer. This sufficed for the Court to hold that the employee waived her right for privacy and the employer was therefore entitled to review and use the private e-mail correspondence.[21]

Based on the decision in LF (T.A.) 10121/06 *Tali Isakov-Inbar v. The Comptroller of Women's Employment,* it seems that artificially inferring an implied consent by the employee to the violation of its privacy can be pretty straightforward even in circumstances that are applicable in most workplaces. In a subsequent decision, the Labour Court was not even looking for an implied consent to the breach of the employee's privacy. It simply held that the employee's right of privacy must be balanced against the employer's interests to obtain and submit relevant evidence to defend against the employee's claim. It therefore permitted the employer to search the employee's laptop computer and submit private e-mail correspondence sent by the employee as part of the evidence in trial.[22]

On the other hand, in LF (Naz.) 1158/06 *Afikei Maim v. Rani Fisher*, the Labour Court did not permit the employer to submit as evidence private e-mail correspondence of the employee although this correspondence allegedly demonstrated that the employee was setting up a competing business while still in employment. Interestingly, the Court emphasized that in the absence of an explicit consent by the employee, it will be exceptionally difficult to conclude that there is an implied waiver of the employee's right to privacy. The mere fact that the employee knew that his e-mails were saved on the employer's server does not in itself suffice to determine that there was an implied consent to breach of privacy. This decision is inconsistent with the previous Labour Court decisions and it is yet to be seen which judicial approach will eventually prevail.[23]

In a Collective Labour Agreement entered in June 2008 between the Histadrut (Israel's largest labour union) and numerous employers' associations, an attempt was made to regulate the protection of the privacy of e-mail correspondence. This

---

21. LF (T.A.) 10121/06 *Tali Isakov-Inbar v. The Comptroller of Women's Employment,* tk-av 2007(3), 2594.
22. Req. (T.A.) 3951/08 *Segev v. WizMagic,* tk-av 2008(3) 5439.
23. LF (Naz.) 1158/06 *Afikei Maim v. Rani Fisher,* tk-av 2008(2) 586.

agreement recognized the employee's rights to use the computer provided to him or her by the employer 'for personal purposes that are subject to the employee's right to privacy' to the extent that such use is 'at a reasonable scope' and is not illegal. Under the agreement, the employer is entitled to undertake routine monitoring and maintenance activities to protect data security and integrity, safeguard confidentiality of business information, and prevent hacking or leakage of information.

The key provision of the Collective Labour Agreement is in Section 3(d). It permits the employer 'to take actions to monitor the employee's use of the computer, internet or email' only if it has reasonable grounds to assume in good faith that the employee is using the computer in an unlawful manner, uses the computer in a manner exposing the employer to claims by third parties, or uses the computer 'in a manner that could harm the business'. Otherwise, the employer is not entitled to enter the employee's private e-mail account and the employee's personal files without an express consent by the employee. The Collective Labour Agreement therefore seems to provide more deference to the employee's privacy rights than at least some of the case law of the Labour Court.

The case law discussed above addresses the discovery of the employee's e-mail correspondence in litigation between the employer and the employee. The courts have not yet addressed issues relating to the discovery of employee's e-mail accounts as part of litigation between the employer and third parties. In such circumstances, when discovery is required for proceedings against a third party, the employee's interests are normally not at stake. It is therefore speculated that courts will permit the employer to search and discover the employee's e-mail accounts, subject to devising appropriate safeguards and restrictions to ascertain that the employee is notified of the potential discovery and no personal e-mail correspondence of the employee is disclosed in the process.

C.   TRANSFER OF DATA, DISCOVERY, AND EVIDENCE TO OTHER JURISDICTIONS

Israel is a party to the Hague Convention on the Taking of Evidence Abroad in Civil or Commercial Matters. Generally, the Hague Convention provides a system for cooperation between Member States for the taking of evidence outside the jurisdiction. The system is well known and involves the sending of a Letter of Request from a judicial authority in one Member State to the competent authority in another Member State. The Hague Convention Regulations of 1970 were enacted in order to set out the required procedural framework for the implementation and interpretation of the Hague Convention. In addition to the Hague Convention, the Act for Mutual Legal Assistance of 1998 further regulates the legal cooperation between Israel and other states. The Act is wider in scope than the Hague Convention and also regulates legal assistance in criminal matters, transfer of individuals to other jurisdictions for testimony, confiscation of assets within Israeli jurisdiction, and so forth.

Liad Whatstein

Article 23 of the Hague Convention provides that a Contracting State may declare that it will not execute Letters of Request issued for the purpose of obtaining pretrial discovery. Israel did not declare under Article 23 of the Hague Convention and the provisions of the Hague Convention can also be invoked to obtain pretrial discovery in Israel.

There are no blocking statutes in Israel preventing the transfer of information or documents to judicial authorities abroad. Under section 5 of the Act for Mutual Legal Assistance of 1998, the Minister of Justice may decline a request for cooperation by another judicial authority on grounds relating to public policy or the safeguarding of the interests of the state. This provision is likely to be exercised only in the most extreme of circumstances.

In addition, section 8 of the Act for Mutual Legal Assistance of 1998, provides that any act conducted in Israel pursuant to a request for legal assistance by another state will be subject to the laws prevailing in Israel over similar acts. Section 18(a) further provides that a person summoned for testimony or to provide evidence in accordance with a request by a foreign judicial authority will be subject to all rights and obligations of a witness who was summoned to testify before an Israeli court.

Accordingly, a party required to provide discovery of documents under the Hague Convention and the Act for Mutual Legal Assistance of 1998 will be entitled to object to discovery on all grounds discussed above and that are available to a party to litigation conducted in Israel. Among others, such party will be entitled to object to discovery on the grounds that the information is privileged, constitutes trade secrets, that its production will violate its right to privacy, and so forth. As indicated above, it is also possible to object to discovery on the grounds that its scope is excessively burdensome. One can, however, assume that the court will take into consideration the scope of discovery that is customary in the jurisdiction that initiated the request for legal assistance in Israel. Accordingly, the scope of discovery that will be permitted for requests originating from the United States is likely to be wider than the scope that would have been otherwise approved for 'local' Israeli litigation.

For instance, in the *Warner Bros.* decision, Warner Bros. sought to enforce an order by the District Court of California ordering an Israeli bank to discover eleven categories of documents. The Israeli Court held that its obligation is to implement the decision of the foreign court to the fullest extent. However, the bank is entitled to object to discovery in accordance with the grounds available under Israeli law. Accordingly, the Court did not compel discovery of one of the categories of documents because it involved excessive discovery of confidential information of the bank.[24]

In addition to pretrial discovery, Israeli courts will also implement decisions of foreign courts relating to procedures that are not available under Israeli law. In CA 9785/02 *Yarkoni v. Boston Scientific Corporation*, the Court held that it is authorized to order that the applicant be deposed in Israel pursuant to the request

---

24. Petition 113/03 *Warner Bros. v. Bank Leumi*, tk-shalom *2004(1), 5279*. See also Petition 42/04 *The Judicial Authority v. Mira Nakash*, tk-shalom *2005(1)1621*.

of the US District Court for the Southern District of New York. As described above, 'live' pretrial depositions are not available under Israeli law (the parties can only exchange written interrogatories). However, this does not preclude the court's authority to assist the foreign court and order that the deposition be conducted in Israel.[25]

In line with their flexible approach, it also seems that Israeli courts will follow the *Aerospatiale* judgment given by the Supreme Court of the United States.[26] Thus, in MLA 3810/06 *Dori v. Shamai Goldstein*, one of the Supreme Court judges cited the *Aerospatiale* judgment with approval, held that the Hague Convention is not exhaustive, and that alternative arrangements that are not regulated by the Hague Convention, such as the taking of testimony via video conference, can also be available in appropriate circumstances.[27]

IV.   CONCLUSION

Israeli case law with respect to most, if not all, of the issues discussed in this chapter is still developing. The hallmark of the Israeli legal system is its flexibility and practical approach. It is therefore expected that the discovery rules will be further developed to permit discovery of all pertinent information and evidence without allowing an abuse of the system or creating excessive costs to the litigants. At the same time, Israeli courts will continue to cooperate with foreign judicial instances seeking to obtain pretrial discovery in Israel to the fullest extent permitted by law.

---

25. C.A. 9785/02 *Yarkoni v. Boston Scientific Corporation,* tk-el 2003(1) 1266.
26. *Société Nationale Industrielle Aerospatiale v. United States District Court,* 482 U.S. 522 (1987).
27. MLA 3810/06 *Dori v. Shamai Goldstein, tk-el 2007(3) 4667.* The case revolved around the question as to whether the defendant, an Israeli citizen, must come to Israel to be cross-examined or may instead be cross-examined via video conference in the United States. The majority of the judges declined to permit video conference in the circumstances of the matter. The minority judge, among others, cited the *Aerospatiale* judgment in support of his opinion that the courts should openly consider means of taking evidence that are not specifically regulated in statute. The majority judges did not consider that video conference was appropriate under the circumstances but did not appear to dispute the principle enunciated in the *Aerospatiale* judgment. Hence, even if this judgment cannot be regarded as a binding precedent adopting *Aerospatiale,* it clearly is a step in the *Aerospatiale* direction.

Chapter 6.2

Macau

*Gonçalo Mendes da Maia**

I.   INTRODUCTION

The differences between common and civil law systems are bound to yield difficulties in the harmonization of pretrial procedures and disclosures. In the Macau
Special Administrative Region ('Macau'), due to its clear civil law background,
with a strong influence and legacy of the Portuguese administration, these differences are quite clear and have definitive reflexes in the way that common law
concepts such as discovery are treated.

II.   MACAU DATA PROTECTION LAW: BACKGROUND

Until 2005, data protection was not given an extensive legal treatment in Macau,
and was only marginally regulated in the Macau Civil and Penal Codes as a general
obligation of respect for privacy of persons, correspondence, and communications.
     However, the increased gaming, hospitality, and commercial activities in the
region created a marked increase in the circulation of personal information that, if
left unregulated, could lead to abusive usage by economic agents and undue intru-
sions in the personal privacy of residents or persons disclosing their personal data
in Macau.

---

*   Member of the Portuguese and Macau Bar Associations.

Catrien Noorda & Stefan Hanloser, *E-Discovery and Data Privacy*, pp. 319–324.
© 2011 Kluwer Law International BV, The Netherlands.

Thus, in 2005, the Macau Legislative Assembly passed the Data Protection Law (DPL), which entered into force on 4 January 2006[1] and sought to regulate the conditions for treatment, conservation, and transfer of personal data in Macau.[2] In addition to the DPO, and in order to enforce the DPO's criteria and provisions, the Office for Personal Data Protection (OPDP) was created in 2007.[3]

A.   MACAU DATA PROTECTION LAW: PERSONAL DATA

The DPO applies solely to 'personal data', construed as any information of any type, irrespective of the type of medium involved, including sound and image, relating to an identified or identifiable natural person; an identifiable person is one who can be identified, directly or indirectly, in particular by reference to an indication number or to one or more factors specific to his or her physical, physiological, mental, economic, cultural, or social identity.[4] This scope of application excludes the protection of corporate data, business information, know-how, or any other information that is not directly associated with a determined single person.

B.   MACAU DATA PROTECTION LAW: COLLECTION, PROCESSING,
                    AND USE

Pursuant to the DPL, personal data must be processed in a transparent way and with strict respect for the privacy of private life as well as the personal rights, liberties, and guarantees established in the Basic Law of Macau, in the international laws in force in Macau, and in local regulations.[5] Personal data must be: processed lawfully; obtained for specific, legitimate, and predetermined purposes directly related to the data processor's activity to abide by such purposes; adequate and not excessive in relation to their purpose; exact and, if necessary, updated; and maintained in such a way as to enable identification of the data holders only during the necessary period required for its relevant purpose.[6] The processing of personal data can only be carried out if the data holder has expressly consented to it, except in the specific cases of: (i) treatment for the purposes of pre-contractual diligences to be taken at the request of the data holder in respect of contracts where the data holder is a party (e.g., online purchases or automated contracting of goods or services); (ii) compliance with a legal obligation to which the data holder is subject under Macau law; (iii) protection of vital

---

1. Law No. 8/2005, dated 4 Aug. 2005.
2. Although there is no express reference, the DPL has a strong influence in terms of its basic principles and solutions of Directive 95/46/EC.
3. Chief Executive's Notice No. 83/2007, dated 7 Mar. 2007, which creates the DPO.
4. Section 4 (1) 1 of the DPL.
5. Section 2 of the DPL.
6. Section 5 of the DPL.

interests of the data holder, if he or she is physically unable to provide his or her consent; (iv) public interest matters or in the discharge of public authority powers by the entity treating the data; and (v) for the protection of the legitimate interests and rights of the entity treating the data, provided that the interests or rights of the data holder should not prevail.[7] The processing of personal data relating to philosophical or political beliefs, participation in any labour union or political union, religious beliefs, private life, and racial or ethnical origin, as well as information relating to health and sexual life, including genetic information, is prohibited,[8] except under express legal or regulatory authorization or upon authorization of the public authority when required by public interest or when the data holder grants its express consent.

C.   MACAU DATA PROTECTION LAW: DATA CONTROLLER, DATA PROCESSOR

The data controller must use adequate technical and organizational measures to safeguard personal data against destruction, accidental or incidental loss, change, diffusion, and/or unauthorized access, especially when the processing is made online, taking into account the risk of the data processing and the nature of the data.[9]

When the processing is subcontracted to a data processor, the controller's safeguard shall ensure that the subcontracted party has the conditions required to guarantee protection of the data and shall also ensure compliance with these measures.[10] The subcontracting of data processing must be set out in a written contract, or other written enforceable document, that binds the subcontractor and that restricts the subcontractor to act solely upon instructions of the contracting entity, imposing the security measures and technical means adequate to safeguard the data.[11]

The controller shall take the special security measures required for adequate control of the integrity of the data,[12] namely to control:

- entry in the premises where data are processed;
- access to data supporting materials;
- insertion and/or manipulation of data;
- adequate use of data;
- authorized recipients of data;
- the identity and timing of all data insertion, modification, and deletion operations; and
- access to and integrity of data upon their transmission.

---

7. All in s. 6 of the DPL.
8. Section 7 of the DPL.
9. Section 15 (1) of the DPL.
10. Section 15 (2) of the DPL.
11. Section 15 (3) of the DPL.
12. Section 16 of the DPL.

Any and all entities responsible for processing and/or that have professional access to personal data are subject to professional secrecy in relation to the personal data to which they have access.[13]

D. MACAU DATA PROTECTION LAW: TRANSFER ABROAD

The transfer of personal data to a place located outside Macau shall be made with full respect of the requirements and limitations established in the Personal Data Protection Law and shall be transferred only if the recipient jurisdiction guarantees adequate data protection.

The adequacy of the level of protection shall be determined in view of the means and circumstances of the transfer and/or the sensitivity and nature of the data to be transferred, the purpose and duration of the processing of the data, and the legal framework in the origin and destination countries – in particular on the effectiveness and enforceability of the security and integrity controls in relation to personal data.

Such determination (if a certain jurisdiction offers adequate protection level) pertains to a public authority specifically created for these purposes, namely the OPDP, as defined in section II above and detailed in section F below.

However, transfer of personal data to a jurisdiction that does not offer adequate protection can only take place if the data subject has expressly consented to it or if the processing is necessary for:

– execution of a contract to which the data holder is part or pre-contractual diligence at its request;
– execution of a contract in the interest of the data holder, between the data processor and a third party;
– compliance of a legal obligation to protect a relevant public interest or to the declaration, exercise, or defence of a right in court proceedings;[14]
– protection of the data holder's vital interests when he or she is physically unable to give consent; and
– when the processing is made through a public record that is legally or statutorily destined to public information and is accessible by the public or by a person that proves to have a legitimate interest, as long as the consulting conditions established are fulfilled.

E. MACAU DATA PROTECTION LAW: CONFLICT OF LAWS

The DPL governs the collection, treatment, and usage of personal data retrieved in Macau, regardless of the nationality of the data holder.

---

13. Section 18 of the DPL.
14. This exception, set forth in para. 3 of s. 20 of the DPL, has specific relevance in the field of e-discovery, whereas it facilitates the transfer of data to other jurisdictions, when said data have judicial relevance in the context of court proceedings.

F.   MACAU DATA PROTECTION LAW: SUPERVISORY
       AUTHORITIES, ENFORCEMENT

The OPDP is the supervisory public body charged with the supervision and enforcement of the provisions set out in the DPL. In the discharge of these powers, the DPL may apply to transgressors a number of administrative offences with fines ranging from 1,000 to 100,000 Macau Patacas[15] and also criminal offences that can lead to imprisonment up to 240 days and aggregated fines.[16]

Although there isn't abundant case law regarding the actions of the OPDP due to its recent inception, there are approximately thirty public cases of rulings made by the OPDP, including a noticeable case in 2008 where the OPDP fined a public body, *in casu* the Macau Consumer Council, for undue disclosure to third parties of personal data of one of its constituents.[17]

III.   PRETRIAL DISCOVERY IN MACAU: BACKGROUND

Pretrial discovery is a non-existent concept in Macau procedural law. As a civil matrix jurisdiction, the disclosure of documents and evidence in Macau court proceedings is made at the trial stage. The provision of documents can be made during the stage of written submissions that precedes the court hearings, but the disclosed documents are provided at the discretion of each party and are not subject to compulsory disclosure or discovery.

A.   PRETRIAL DISCOVERY IN MACAU: BLOCKING STATUTES

Cooperation with foreign regulatory and judicial entities is not restricted in Macau. Indeed, Macau is a party to a number of bi- and multilateral judiciary cooperation agreements with other jurisdictions that foresee the disclosure and transmission of information for prosecution and/or defence in criminal or civil litigation.

B.   PRETRIAL DISCOVERY IN MACAU: HAGUE CONVENTION ON THE
       TAKING OF EVIDENCE

Macau is a party to the Hague Convention on the Taking of Evidence,[18] through an extension decree passed during Portuguese administration.[19] Subsequently, with the resuming of the People's Republic of China's sovereignty, certain restrictions to the applicability of the Hague Convention in Macau were introduced, namely the

---

15.   Sections 30 et seq. of the DPL.
16.   Sections 37 et seq. of the DPL.
17.   Case No. 24/2008 settled by the OPDP.
18.   Hague Convention on the Taking of Evidence Abroad in Civil or Commercial Matters of 18 Mar. 1970.
19.   Presidential Decree No. 196/99, dated 22 Oct. 1999.

opting out of the acknowledgement, compliance, and execution of Letters of Request issued for the purposes of obtaining pretrial discovery documents.[20] Under this Notice, Macau shall not accept any such Letters of Request, which positively excludes the possibility of foreign counsel seeking discovery documents in Macau through the application of the Hague Convention.

IV.   PRETRIAL DISCOVERY VERSUS DATA PROTECTION IN MACAU: BACKGROUND

The DPL accepts and sets out the transfer of personal data – regardless of the adequateness of the levels of protection in the target jurisdiction – to the extent that such disclosure is *'necessary or legally required on important public interest grounds, or for the establishment, exercise of defence of legal claims'*.[21] However, said transfer must observe certain requirements, set out in the DPL, in order to be validly authorized by the OPDP. Specifically, the transfer must be firstly requested and validated by the OPDP.[22]

A.   PRETRIAL DISCOVERY VERSUS DATA PROTECTION IN MACAU: EXPORT OF PERSONAL DATA TO THE UNITED STATES

Under the aforementioned section 20 of the DPL, personal data can be transferred to the United States, even if the OPDP deems that the protection levels granted by the US data protection laws are inadequate. To that end, a request must be filed with the OPDP, under the terms of section 21 of the DPL. Moreover, the OPDP must expressly authorize the transfer.

V.   CONCLUSION

Although Macau has only recently begun thoroughly regulating the protection of personal data, said protection has grown in strides through the inception of the DPL and the OPDP, which provide supervision and control over the processing, usage, and transfer of personal data. From a procedural standpoint, although Macau law and the DPL itself allow for cooperation with foreign jurisdictions in the provision of personal data for the purposes of judicial claims and procedures (even if the protection levels of said foreign jurisdictions are deemed inadequate), Macau will not honour Letters of Request for the provision of any documents for pretrial discovery issued under the Hague Convention, which significantly increases the difficulty of obtaining cross-border disclosure of personal data for the purposes of discovery.

---

20. § 2 of the Notice of the Minister of Foreign Affairs of the People's Republic of China, dated 16 Dec. 1999.
21. Section 20 1 (3) of the DPL.
22. Sections 21 et seq. of the DPL.

Chapter 6.3

Malaysia

*Sukumar Karuppiah and Jasdev Singh Gill**

I.   INTRODUCTION

Whilst the rules relating to discovery and inspection of documents in Malaysia do not restrict the scope of discovery to merely paper-based documents, the rules have yet to evolve to include specific procedures in respect of electronically stored information ('ESI'). As such, there does not exist any specific framework by which litigants can engage in discovery of ESI. It is left to the parties concerned to seek discovery of ESI either through a mutually acceptable framework drawn up by the parties or for the litigants to seek a court order for the other party to produce ESI.

The privacy of individual data has only recently become the focus of legislators with the introduction of the Personal Data Protection Bill 2009,[1] which has not, at the time of writing this chapter, been passed into law. As such, the conflict between the discovery process and the rights of an individual to the privacy of his or her personal data has yet to be tested in the Malaysian courts.

---

*   Sukumar Karuppiah and Jasdev Singh Gill are partners in the firm of Jasdev Chambers in Kuala Lumpur, Malaysia.
1.   Personal Data Bill 2009.

Catrien Noorda & Stefan Hanloser, *E-Discovery and Data Privacy*, pp. 325–332.
© 2011 Kluwer Law International BV, The Netherlands.

Sukumar Karuppiah and Jasdev Singh Gill

II. RULES RELATING TO DISCOVERY: BACKGROUND

The procedures relating to the process of discovery and inspection of documents in Malaysia are contained in the Rules of the High Court 1980[2] ('RHC').

The RHC provides for mutual discovery of documents after the close of pleadings in civil or commercial actions begun by writ. In a writ action, discovery is a matter of right, and is automatic. There is no necessity at all for an order of the court.[3] For all other originating processes, an order of the court is required. The discovery is in respect of documents that are or have been in the possession, custody, or power of the parties and that relate to the matters in question in the action.[4] In writ actions where discovery is automatic, the parties are, however, free to dispense with or limit the scope of discovery that they may otherwise be required to make to each other.[5]

A. SCOPE OF THE DISCOVERY RULES

The discovery of documents takes effect within a short specified period upon close of pleadings. There is no necessity for the parties to seek an order from the court to begin the process of discovery unless the other party refuses to disclose certain documents, in which case a court order compelling the party to produce the documents may be obtained.[6] The RHC also provides for the right of a litigant to request for inspection and copies of documents mentioned in the pleadings or affidavits filed between the parties in an action.[7] Non-production or refusal may subject the party to a court order to produce the same.[8]

B. DEFINITION OF 'DOCUMENTS'

The term 'documents' is not defined in the RHC. The Evidence Act[9] ('EA'), however, defines 'document' to mean:

> any matter expressed, described or howsoever represented, upon any substance, material, thing or article, including any matter embodied in a disc, tape, film, sound track or other device whatsoever, by means of ... (c) any sound recording, or any electronic magnetic, mechanical or other recording

---

2. Order 24 Rules of the High Court 1980, PU(A) 50/1980 (RHC).
3. *Ong Boon Hua @ Chin Peng & Anor v. Menteri Hal Ehwal Dalam Negeri, Malaysia* (2008) 3 MLJ 625.
4. Order 24 r.1 (1) RHC.
5. Order 24 r.1(2) RHC.
6. Order 24 r.3 RHC.
7. Order 24 r.10 RHC.
8. Order 24 r.11 RHC.
9. Section 3 of the Evidence Act 1950 (Act 56) (EA).

whatsoever and howsoever made, or any sounds, electronic impulses, or other data whatsoever.

The explanation provided within the definition goes on to state that *'A matter recorded, stored, processed, retrieved or produced by a computer is a document'*. The Interpretation Act[10] ('IA') defines 'document' to mean:

> any matter expressed or described upon any substance by means of letters, figures or marks, or by more than one of those means, intended to be used or which may be used for the purpose of recording that matter.

The Electronic Commerce Act[11] (ECA) has given legal recognition to information that is wholly or partly in electronic form and goes further to even give legal recognition to information that may not form part of the electronic message but that was referred to in the electronic message, as long as the person against whom the information referred to might be used is able to have access to the said information. The ECA applies to 'any commercial transaction conducted through electronic means'.

An 'electronic message'[12] is defined in the ECA as 'information generated, sent, received or stored by electronic means'. 'Commercial transactions' are defined as:

> a single communication or multiple communications of a commercial nature, whether contractual or not, which includes any matters relating to the supply or exchange of goods or services, agency, investments, financing, banking and insurance.

As such, although the RHC does not provide any definition of the term 'documents', the definitions provided by the EA, IA, as well as the ECA are wide enough to include ESI, and as such ESI may be subject to the discovery process.

C.   'POSSESSION, CUSTODY, OR POWER'

Whilst the RHC provisions state that the discovery of documents covers those that are in the possession, custody, or power of the litigant, the Court of Appeal has held that 'the court has the jurisdiction to order discovery of a document referred to in an affidavit, whether or not the document is in the possession, custody or power of the party in whose affidavit the reference to that document is made'. The discretion is vested in the court as to whether or not to make an order for discovery. An order will not be made if good cause to the contrary is shown. The absence of possession custody or power may amount to a good cause, but this is not always so. At the end

---

10. Section 3 of the Interpretation Acts 1948 and 1967 (Consolidated and Revised 1989) (Act 388) (IA).
11. Section 6 of the Electronic Commerce Act 2006 (Act 658) (ECA).
12. Section 5 of the Electronic Commerce Act 2006.

of the day, the decision to order discovery is dependent on the facts of each particular case.[13]

D.   'RELATING TO MATTERS IN QUESTION IN THE ACTION'

Parties may obtain discovery in respect of all matters that relate to the action between the parties. Determining the matters in question would depend on the pleadings.[14] Parties have to ensure that they keep in mind the objective of discovery to matters that are necessary for disposing fairly of the matter or case and to ensure savings of costs.[15] A document is relevant if it contains information that may (not that must) either directly or indirectly enable the party requiring the discovery either to advance its own case or to damage the case of his or her adversary or that may fairly lead to a train of inquiry that may have either of those two consequences.[16] The court will disallow the use by a party of the discovery process that is used simply as a fishing expedition to formulate the party's claim or counterclaim.[17]

An order for pre-action discovery, commonly known as the *Norwich Pharmacal*[18] Order, would only be allowed to serve the purpose of finding the identity of wrongdoers. Pre-action discovery orders will not be given for the purpose of simply obtaining documents to support an action against another party.[19]

E.   MUTUAL DISCOVERY BY PARTIES WITHOUT ORDER

Parties to an action between whom pleadings are closed must make discovery by exchanging lists of documents and, accordingly, each party must, within fourteen days after the pleadings in the action are deemed to be closed as between him or her and the other party, make and serve on that other party a list of the documents that are or have been in his or her possession, custody, or power relating to any matter in question between them in the action.[20]

In the absence of any specific procedures relating to discovery of ESI, it is left to the parties who undertake a mutual discovery process to decide on the mechanics

13. See n. 3 *supra*. Abdul Malek Ishak SCJ in delivering the judgment of the Court of Appeal followed the English decisions of *Rafidain Bank v. Agom Universal Sugar Trading Co Ltd & Anor* (1987) 1 WLR 1606 and *Quilter v. Heatly* (1883) 23 Ch D 42, at 48–51 (CA).
14. *Manilal & Sons (Pte) Ltd v. Bhupendra KJ Shan (T/A JB International)* (1990) 2 MLJ 282 at 288.
15. Order 24 r.13(1) RHC.
16. See note 14 *supra*.
17. *ABX Logistics (Malaysia) Sdn. Bhd. v. Overseas Bechtel (Malaysia) Sdn. Bhd.* (2003) 7 CLJ 357.
18. *Norwich Pharmacal Co & Ors and Customs v. Excise Commissioners* (1974) AC 133.
19. *K Anandaraj A/L Krishnasamy v. Dato' Dr Vijayasingam & Anor* (2005) 7 MLJ 120.
20. Order 24 r.2(1) RHC.

in respect of discovery related to ESI. Further, since the general rules on discovery encompass ESI, a party would necessarily be under a duty to preserve all discoverable ESI documents.

Either party may apply to the court for an order for discovery in the event that they feel the other party has failed to disclose relevant documents or ESI for purposes of discovery. In such event the court will take into account the principles as set out above before granting the order for discovery.

F. HAGUE CONVENTION ON THE TAKING OF EVIDENCE

Malaysia is not a signatory to the Hague Convention on the Taking of Evidence.[21]

G. OBTAINING EVIDENCE FOR FOREIGN COURTS

It is not necessary for a litigant seeking production of documents to seek the assistance of the Malaysian court for doing so, provided, of course, that the party being subject to produce the documents consents to the same. In such circumstances, a foreign court or tribunal may appoint a person to take evidence of witnesses or to ensure that witnesses produce documents.

In the event that consent cannot be obtained voluntarily, the High Court may issue an order for examination of witnesses and for attendance and for production of documents for purposes of being used outside the jurisdiction, provided it is in relation to a matter that is pending before a court or tribunal in such jurisdiction. The relevant rules are contained within the RHC.[22]

The application of this order would be subject to the requirement for there to be a pending matter before a foreign court or tribunal and the court in making the order will take into account that the request is within and in accordance with the laws of the requested state,[23] that the request is not made as a 'fishing expedition' to find evidence to support a claim, and that it relates to the matter pending before the foreign court or tribunal.

H. PROCEDURE FOR OBTAINING EVIDENCE BY FOREIGN LITIGANT

An application for an order has to be made *ex parte* by a person authorized to make the application on behalf of the court or tribunal in question and must be supported by an affidavit. The affidavit in support has to exhibit the Letter of Request, certificate, or other document evidencing the desire of the court or tribunal to

---

21. Hague Convention on the Taking of Evidence Abroad in Civil or Commercial Matters, concluded 18 Mar. 1970.
22. Order 66 of the RHC.
23. *Rio Tinto Zinc Corp. & Ors v. Westinghouse Electric Corp.* (1978) AC 547.

obtain for the purpose of a matter pending before it the production of any documents.

The RHC also provides for instances where the application to the court would have to be made by the Attorney General of Malaysia, such as when the Letter of Request, certificate, or any other document is received by the Minister charged with the responsibility to receive such requests from foreign tribunals and forwarded to the Registrar of the High Court with a request that the application need not be made by an agent of either party to the matter pending before the foreign court or tribunal.

Whilst the RHC also provides for the Attorney General to make the application if a request is made pursuant to a Civil Procedure Convention and no person is named in the document who will make the application, Malaysia has, however, yet to accede to the Hague Convention related to the taking of evidence.

III.   DATA PRIVACY PROTECTION: BACKGROUND

Malaysia is currently in the process of legislating an act to protect personal data privacy. Presently the protection of an individual's privacy is largely regulated by contract. Hence unless there was a contract by a data user or service provider that the privacy of the data of an individual will be protected and not used for any other purpose, an individual had no recourse to prevent the dissemination or sale of his or her private data.

The Personal Data Protection Bill 2009 ('the Bill') has at the time of writing this chapter been submitted in the Malaysian Parliament for first reading. Whilst there is no certainty to what extent of the Bill will be passed into law, a brief outline of the Bill is provided below.

The Personal Data Protection Act 2009 that has been proposed by the Bill ('the Proposed Act') seeks to regulate the processing of personal data of individuals involved in commercial transactions by data users so as to provide protection to the individual's personal data and thereby safeguard the interests of the individual.[24]

A.   APPLICATION OF THE PROPOSED ACT

The Proposed Act is intended to apply to any person who processes personal data or who has control or authorizes the processing of personal data of individuals in respect of commercial transactions. It contains seven essential principles that will govern an individual's personal data: the General Principle, Notice and Choice Principle, Disclosure Principle, Security Principle, Retention Principle, Data Integrity Principle, and Access Principle. A data user contravening any of the said principles commits a criminal offence.

---

24. Explanatory Statement of the Personal Data Protection Bill 2009.

The term 'personal data' is defined as any information in respect of commercial transactions that relates directly or indirectly to a data subject, who is identifiable from that information or from that and any other information in the possession of a data user, including any sensitive personal data and expression of opinion about the data subject, but excludes information that is processed for the purpose of credit reporting business carried on by a credit reporting agency. A 'data subject' is defined as an individual who is the subject of the personal data. 'Commercial transactions' includes any transaction of a commercial nature relating to supply or exchange of goods or services, agency, investments, financing, banking, and insurance.[25]

As such the Proposed Act would apply only to personal data relating to an individual in relation to his or her involvement in commercial transactions.

B.　　　　　DISCLOSURE OF PERSONAL DATA

Whilst the Proposed Act prevents a data user from disclosing the personal data of a data subject other than for the purposes for which the data were collected, an exception is provided in circumstances where either the data user consents to the disclosure or where it is necessary for the prevention of any crime or is authorized by law or by order of a court, where the data user is under a reasonable belief that he or she had a right to do so, or where he or she reasonably believes that he or she would have had the consent of the data subject, or if it is in the public interest to do so in circumstances defined by the Minister.[26]

Further, a data user need not comply with the requirement of obtaining consent of a data subject before obtaining the personal data of an individual, notifying the individual that his or her data are being used, allowing the individual to have control over the personal data, having access to the personal data, or disclosing the personal data of the individual when it is necessary for the purpose of or in connection with any order or judgment of a court.[27]

In the context of discovery, therefore it would seem that a party to a litigation may be required to provide discovery of the personal data of its customers by a court order requiring the party to do so.

C.　　　　　TRANSFER OF PERSONAL DATA

The Proposed Act specifically prohibits the transfer by a data user of personal data outside Malaysia. However, among the exceptions to this provision is if the transfer is either consented to by the individual or the data are being transferred for the

---

25.　Section 4, Personal Data Protection Bill 2009.
26.　Section 8 and s.39, Personal Data Protection Bill 2009.
27.　Section 45(2)(d), Personal Data Protection Bill 2009.

purpose of obtaining legal advice or for the establishing, exercising, or defending of legal rights.[28]

D.   ACCESSING ELECTRONIC FILES OF EMPLOYEES

Presently there is no legislation that affords employees protection against their employers' accessing and searching through their e-mails and electronic files stored on computers used in the course of their work. The situation is largely governed by contract. As such, any privacy protection would necessarily have to be included as part of the contract, failing which the employee is powerless to act against an employer who wishes to access electronic data stored within the computers used in the course of work.

IV.   CONCLUSION

Despite the existence of discovery provisions in the RHC that by definition would also extend to ESI, in practice, litigants would usually only resort to producing documents that are directly related to and that support their case. It also remains to be seen how the Proposed Act will affect the discovery process when it comes into effect.

---

28.   Section 129(1) and s.129(3)(d), Personal Data Protection Bill 2009.

Chapter 6.4

Singapore

*Sukumar Karuppiah and Justin Blaze George**

I.   INTRODUCTION

The process of mutual discovery by parties in court proceedings is a fundamental feature in civil litigation in Singapore, as it is in common law jurisdictions around the world. In general terms, discovery allows a party in a litigation to obtain information that he or she does not have but that is relevant to the issues in the suit so that the party may be able to effectively prepare his or her case for trial and will not be caught by surprise by the introduction of new evidence at the trial itself.

Given that that many documents are generated and stored electronically, the courts have increasingly had to deal with issues specific to the disclosure and inspection of electronic documents. With the objective of providing guidance on the discovery and inspection of electronically stored information and the supply of copies of discoverable electronic documents within the boundaries of established principles on discovery, the Singapore courts recently issued Practice Direction 3 of 2009 (the 'E-discovery PD').[1]

---

*   Sukumar Karuppiah is a partner at the law firm of Ravindran Associates and Justin Blaze George is a senior associate at the same firm.
1.   'Discovery and Inspection of Electronically Stored Documents: A Commentary on Practice Direction No. 3 of 2009 (Part 1)' by Yeong Zee Kin, Senior Assistant Registrar of the Supreme Court, published in the November issue of the *Singapore Law Gazette*.

Catrien Noorda & Stefan Hanloser, *E-Discovery and Data Privacy*, pp. 333–347.
© 2011 Kluwer Law International BV, The Netherlands.

II.   DISCOVERY REGIME IN SINGAPORE

The parties to a suit have an obligation and duty to disclose documents[2] on which they rely, those that adversely affect their case, and those that support or adversely affect another party's case and that are or have been in their possession, custody, or power. This is referred to as a party's general discovery obligation.

Further, an application may be made by a party for discovery of specific documents or classes of documents that are not directly relevant in themselves but that may lead the party making the application to a train of inquiry that may either advance his or her own case or damage that of the party against whom the application is sought.[3] However, to succeed in such an application the party making the application must show that the said documents are or have been in the possession, custody, or powers of the party against whom the application is made and that the specified documents are necessary for the fair disposal of the matter or for saving costs. In the circumstances, the applicant seeking discovery is not entitled to undertake a fishing expedition in the off-chance that he or she may find a document that may be relevant.[4] The party making the application for specific discovery must also show the way in which the specified documents may lead to a relevant document.[5]

It should be noted that a party's discovery obligations extend not only to documents in his or her possession, custody, or control but to such documents that he or she had previously but that are no longer in his or her possession, custody, or control – the party would be required to explain what had become of those documents.

Where discovery is ordered (whether general discovery or specific discovery), inspection of the discoverable documents is generally granted unless the party against whom the order is made objects to the inspection, for example, on grounds that the documents are privileged or consist of confidential information and the documents are not necessary for the fair disposal of the matter or for saving costs. It should be noted that inspection generally involves the examination of the original discoverable documents.[6]

---

2. The word 'document' is defined in s. 3(1) of the Evidence Act as 'any matter expressed or described upon any substance by means of letters, figures or marks or by more than one of those mans intended to be used or which may be used for the purpose of recording that matter' and has been held to include e-mails, databases, sound recordings, various electronic media (e.g., CD-ROMs and hard disks), and recording devices.
3. The provision for the disclosure of 'train of inquiry' documents is set out in Order 24, rule 5 of the Rules of Court. The disclosure obligation of such indirectly relevant documents is derived from the United Kingdom case of *Compagnie Financière et Commerciale du Pacifique v. Peruvian Guano Co.* Q.B.D. 11 (1882): 55 at 63, CA.
4. In *Thyssen Hunnebeck Singapore Pte Ltd v. TTJ Civil Engineering Pte Ltd* (2003) 1 SLR 75, Justice Choo Han Teck at para. 6 remarked that 'a fishing expedition in the context of discovery refers to the aimless trawling of an unlimited sea. Where, on the other hand, the party concerned knows a specific and identifiable spot into which he wishes to drop a line (or two), I would not regard that as a fishing expedition'.
5. *Tan Chin Seng & Ors. v. Raffles Town Club Pte. Ltd.* (2002) 3 S.L.R. 345.
6. However, parties may agree to inspect copies as opposed to the original documents, and this is regularly done where the parties do not object to the authenticity of the documents discovered.

A. DISCOVERY REGIME IN SINGAPORE: SANCTIONS

Where a party to the proceedings fails to comply with its disclosure obligations, the court may, in certain circumstances, strike out the claims and/or defences of the defaulting party. In *K Solutions Pte Ltd v. National University of Singapore,*[7] K Solutions sued National University of Singapore ('NUS') for wrongful termination of a contract to develop an integrated student information system for NUS. During general discovery, K Solutions disclosed 1,303 e-mails. However, none of these e-mails were internal e-mails between the staff of K Solutions. On requests for further discovery by NUS of e-mails as well as audio recordings of project management and steering committee meetings, K Solutions disclosed e-mails from only one of its staff and did not disclose any audio recordings. It was revealed that e-mails that were more than six months old had been deleted. According to K Solutions, this was done 'for housekeeping reasons and also to avoid breach of confidentiality and non-disclosure obligations'. It was also revealed that the audio recordings were erased or destroyed 'as would be in the ordinary course of business'. NUS applied to strike out K Solutions' claims and defence to counterclaims on the ground that K Solutions had suppressed discovery. Justice Woo Bih Li held that if a party deliberately[8] destroys a document in order that it may not be used against him or her in a pending or anticipated litigation, a striking-out order would be an appropriate sanction unless 'evidence of the contents of the document is otherwise available or the contents are not critical in the totality of all the available evidence'.[9] The Court, on the strength of certain disclosed e-mails, found that K Solutions had anticipated litigation some time before its action was filed and had collated e-mails in anticipation of such proceedings. Given the anticipation of proceedings by K Solutions, the Court found that K Solutions' explanation, that the relevant documents were deleted because of an alleged house-keeping policy or that the relevant documents were misplaced, was unbelievable. In the circumstances, the Court held that K Solutions was suppressing documents and struck out K Solutions' claims and defence to NUS's counterclaims.

B. DISCOVERY REGIME IN SINGAPORE: DISCOVERY AGAINST A THIRD PARTY

The court has the power to order a person who is not a party to the proceedings to disclose documents where it appears to the court that the documents are relevant and necessary for the fair disposal of the matter or for saving costs and that the said

---

7. [2009] 4 SLR 254.
8. The learned Judge defined the word 'deliberate' at para. 107 to mean 'that the destroyer intends to put the document out of reach of the other party in pending or anticipated litigation'.
9. As stated at para. 129. See also para. 126, where the learned Judge states that the appropriate test in deciding to strike out a party's pleadings where there has been a deliberate destruction of documents is not whether a fair trial is possible.

non-party is likely to have those documents in his or her possession, custody, or power.

C. DISCOVERY REGIME IN SINGAPORE: PRE-ACTION DISCOVERY

The court may order discovery before the commencement of proceedings where the prospective plaintiff is unable to commence proceedings as he or she does not know whether he or she has a viable claim and requires the discovery to ascertain the gaps in the case. An application for discovery of documents before the commencement of proceedings can only be made where the applicant for discovery and the party against whom the order is sought appear to be likely to be parties to subsequent proceedings in the High Court and where the party against whom the order is sought appears to be likely to have or to have had in his possession, custody, or power any relevant documents.

D. DISCOVERY REGIME IN SINGAPORE: NORWICH PHARMACAL ORDER[10]

A court may assist a prospective plaintiff who claims to have been wronged by ordering a third party (i.e., a party who may not incur any liability in respect of the claims made by the prospective plaintiff) to disclose the identity of the wrongdoers and other relevant details of the wrongdoers, where the third party 'through no fault of his own gets mixed up in the tortuous acts of others so as to facilitate their wrongdoing'.[11] Norwich Pharmacal orders are used commonly by proprietors of copyright content against telecommunication companies and Internet service providers to obtain the identity of individuals or companies who download copies of their content without authorization.

E. DISCOVERY REGIME IN SINGAPORE: DISCOVERY AND INSPECTION IN PRACTICE[12]

Generally, discovery of documents is given by filing with the courts and serving on the other party or parties an enumerated list of documents together with an Affidavit Verifying List of Documents to be affirmed or sworn by the litigant confirming that he or she has fully complied with his or her obligations to provide

---

10. See *Norwich Pharmacal Co. v. Commissioners of Customs and Excise* (1974) A.C. 133 ('Norwich Pharmacal'), which is a decision from the United Kingdom House of Lords. In practice an application is made under the common law jurisdiction of the court citing Norwich Pharmacal and under Order 24, rule 6(5) of the Rules of Court, which at least overlaps with the principle set out in Norwich Pharmacal.
11. *Upmann v. Elkan* (1871) L.R. 12 Eq. 140 *per* Lord Romilly M.R.
12. The practice of discovery in Singapore has been succinctly set out by Senior Assistant Registrar Yeong Zee Kin in *Fermin Aldabe v. Standard Chartered Bank* (2009) SGHC 194 at paras 27 to 30.

general discovery. At an appointed time and place the documents set out in the list are produced for physical inspection and the inspecting party is entitled to take a copy of the inspected documents.

However, there is a common practice for parties to agree that copies of all documents are to be exchanged first and for the physical inspection of the documents to be deferred. The parties, if they feel it is necessary, may subsequently rely on the agreement to defer and request for the physical inspection of specified documents.

F.   DISCOVERY REGIME IN SINGAPORE: TAKING OF EVIDENCE IN
         FOREIGN CIVIL PROCEEDINGS

Singapore is a signatory to the Hague Convention on the Taking of Evidence Abroad in Civil or Commercial Matters ('Hague Convention'), subject to certain notified reservations.

To give effect to the principles of the Hague Convention, Singapore enacted the Evidence (Civil Proceedings in Other Jurisdictions) Act (Cap. 98, 1985 Ed.) ('the Evidence (CPOJ) Act'). The procedure for the taking of evidence for use in foreign proceedings is set out under Order 66 of the Rules of Court.

The Evidence (CPOJ) Act and Order 66 set out comprehensively the law and procedure relating to the taking of evidence in aid of foreign proceedings. Of course, the Evidence (CPOJ) Act and Order 66 are only applicable where a foreign litigant requires the assistance of the Singapore courts in obtaining evidence for use in foreign civil proceedings. As such, where evidence is given voluntarily, there is no requirement to apply to the Singapore courts for the taking of such evidence.

Procedure for the Taking of Evidence for Use in Civil Proceedings
Where the assistance of the courts is required for obtaining evidence for use in foreign civil proceedings, the following four conditions must be satisfied before a Singapore court may exercise its jurisdiction to make an order for the taking of evidence to be used in foreign civil proceedings:

(1) An application to the High Court should be made.
(2) The application must be made pursuant to a request made by or on behalf of a foreign court or tribunal ('the requesting court').
(3) The application is restricted to the taking of evidence for use in civil proceedings[13] that have been instituted before the requesting court or whose institution is contemplated.[14]

---

13. The foreign proceedings for which the evidence is required must be a civil proceeding according to both the laws of the requesting court and the laws of Singapore
14. Proceedings that are contemplated are generally taken to mean that the institution of the proceedings is imminent as opposed to the institution of proceedings that are merely possible or probable. Generally, the courts are not keen to exercise their jurisdiction in cases where

(4) Such an application should be made by way of *ex parte* summons together with an affidavit in support of the application.

Powers of the Court

The courts are given wide-ranging powers to give effect to requests from foreign courts or tribunals,[15] including:[16]

(a) the examination of witnesses, either orally or in writing;
(b) the production of documents;
(c) the inspection, photographing, preservation, custody, or detention of any property;
(d) the taking of samples of any property and the carrying out of any experiments on or with any property;
(e) the medical examination of any person; and
(f) the taking and testing of samples of blood from any person.

Limits to the Powers of the Court in Giving Effect to a Request by a Foreign Court

The Singapore courts are only allowed to grant an order for the taking of evidence for use in foreign proceedings where the evidence required is in the nature of proof to be used for the purposes of the trial.[17] The court will refuse to grant an order where it appears that the evidence requested is in the nature of a roving pretrial discovery where the litigant seeks to 'fish' for evidence that may eventually lead to obtaining evidence that is admissible at trial. This is the case even where the procedure of the foreign court allows for such pretrial discovery.

Further, the court is not allowed to give an order requiring a person to give general discovery[18] or discovery of documents other than particular documents that appear to the court to be or to likely be in his or her possession, custody, or power.[19]

Privilege

The Singapore courts generally give effect to a request from the foreign court in the face of claims of privilege as such claims should be taken up at the time of

---

proceedings have yet to be instituted but that are contemplated, unless there are strong grounds to support such a request.

15. Section 4(1) of the Evidence (CPOJ) Act.
16. Section 4(2) of the Evidence (CPOJ) Act.
17. Section 4(3) of the Evidence (CPOJ) Act provides that 'An order under this section shall not require any particular steps to be taken unless they are steps which can be required to be taken by way of obtaining evidence for the purposes of civil proceedings in the High Court'. As such, reference should be made to the discovery obligations of parties as explained above.
18. Section 4(4)(a) of the Evidence (CPOJ) Act provides that a court may not order a person 'to state what documents relevant to the proceedings to which the application for the order relates are or have been in his possession, custody or power'.
19. Section 4(4)(b) the Evidence (CPOJ) Act provides that a court may not order a person 'to produce any documents other than particular documents specified in the order as being documents appearing to the High Court to be, or to be likely to be, in his possession, custody or power'.

examination or when the relevant document is required to be produced. A witness may claim privilege from giving evidence on any ground recognized under Singapore law or the law of the requesting court. A Singapore court will not compel a person to give evidence of privileged information.[20]

Manner of Taking Examination

The manner for examining the witness is set out under Order 39 rules 5 to 10 and rule 11(1) to (3). However, the courts will generally allow examination of the witness in accordance with any particular manner requested by the requesting court if it is stated in the request, unless the requested manner is contrary to established procedures.

G.   E-DISCOVERY

The E-discovery PD came into effect on 1 October 2009 and provides a framework for dealing with issues arising from the discovery of electronically stored information.

One of the main characteristics of the E-discovery PD is that it establishes an opt-in scheme,[21] as e-discovery issues may not be relevant in all cases. The E-discovery PD may be triggered in the following manner:

(a) During general discovery, parties may agree to adopt an electronic discovery protocol. Where parties are unable to agree either to adopt an electronic discovery protocol or on the text of the protocol, the party seeking electronic discovery may apply to the courts under the E-discovery PD.

(b) Where a party seeks specific discovery of electronically stored documents, the party may apply under the E-discovery PD.

(c) The court may direct that the E-discovery PD be applied in a suitable case.

The E-discovery PD provides default protocols that highlight issues that generally arise in the discovery of electronic documents and that would need to be considered and discussed by the parties.[22] Further, the E-discovery PD encourages the parties to collaborate in good faith and to agree on issues relating to the discovery and inspection of electronically stored documents after the close of pleadings.[23]

---

20. Section 5(1) of the Evidence (CPOJ) Act. The additional requirements that need to be fulfilled in claiming privilege under a ground recognized by the requesting court are set out at s. 5(2) of the Evidence (CPOJ) Act.
21. Paragraph 43A(1) of the E-discovery PD.
22. Appendix E, Part 1 provides an agreed protocol for discovery. Appendix E, Part 2 provides a protocol for the inspection of discoverable electronic documents. Appendix E, Part 2 provides a list of reasonably usable formats.
23. Paragraph 43B of the E-discovery PD.

In *Fermin Aldabe v. Standard Chartered Bank* (2009) SGHC 194[24] ('Fermin Aldabe'), one of the issues raised was the format in which copies of discoverable e-mails ought to be given to the plaintiff. The plaintiff had requested that the e-mails be given in PDF format as opposed to the native format of the documents. However, the solicitors for the defendant were not sure whether it was feasible to provide copies of the e-mails in PDF format. SAR Yeong was of the view that it was necessary for the parties to have met for the purpose of discussing these technical issues and provided a warning to litigants confronted with the need to discover electronic documents that if parties were to fail to engage in bona fide discussions on issues relating to electronic discovery, parties will face a wastage of time, resources, and costs.[25]

H. SOME OF THE KEY ISSUES COVERED BY THE E-DISCOVERY PD

1. Definition of Metadata

Paragraph 43A(3) of the E-discovery PD defines metadata information as referring to 'the non-visible and not readily apparent information embedded in or associated with electronically stored documents'. The E-discovery PD appears to contemplate the discovery of both application metadata[26] and system metadata.[27] Metadata may be stored as part of the document or in a separate file. Metadata information stored as part of the discoverable document should not be deleted or altered. Metadata information stored separately is discoverable as separate documents.

2. Location of Electronically Stored Documents

The E-discovery PD envisions that temporarily deleted files (such as files that are stored in the 'Trash' folder) and deleted files that reside in file sectors that have not been over-written by another file or that reside in file sectors that have not been completely over-written may be discoverable. However, the default position suggested by the E-discovery PD is that deleted files (i.e., files that are not merely deleted by moving the files to the 'Trash' folder) do not form part of a party's obligations under general discovery. Disclosure may, nonetheless, be sought by way of an application for specific discovery.

---

24. The applications in this matter were heard before the coming into effect of the E-discovery PD but after the PD was issued on 30 Jul. 2009. Despite the E-discovery PD not having been in effect at the time, SAR Yeong made considerable reference to the E-discovery PD.
25. Paragraph 36 of *Fermin Aldabe*.
26. The term 'application metadata' refers to metadata information created by the relevant application (e.g., Microsoft Word) and includes formulae and comments and deleted text.
27. The term 'system metadata' refers to metadata information created by the operating or storage system and includes the identity of the author and the date of creation.

I.   DISCOVERY, INSPECTION, AND PRODUCTION OF COPIES
       UNDER THE E-DISCOVERY PD

General Discovery

As indicated above, the E-discovery PD encourages parties to collaborate and agree on e-discovery issues immediately after pleadings. Parties should consider issues such as 'the scope and/or any limits on documents to be given in discovery, whether parties are prepared to make voluntary disclosures, and the giving of discovery in stages according to an agreed schedule, as well as the format and manner in which copies of discoverable documents shall be supplied'.[28] As indicated above, if parties are unable to agree on an e-discovery protocol, an application may be made to the courts by the party seeking discovery of electronically stored documents.

Copies of Electronic Documents Are to Be Inspected and Supplied in Their Native Format

The E-discovery PD provides that electronic documents supplied for inspection should preferably be given in their native format.[29] Likewise, copies of the inspected documents should be supplied in their native format.[30] The rationale for this is that the parties should have the opportunity to inspect and take copies of electronic documents with metadata information intact. However, where the native format is not reasonably usable – for example, as in the case of Fermin Aldabe where the plaintiff requested that copies be given in PDF format as opposed to the native format, as he did not have access to the relevant programme[31] – an alternative format may be acceptable.

Specific Discovery and Discovery and Inspection of Database, Electronic Media, and Recording Devices

Specific discovery for a class of documents may be described with reference to certain terms or phrases to be used in a reasonable search for electronically stored documents.[32] The scope of the reasonable search must be limited at least by specifying the storage location or media and by prescribing a period during which the document was created, received, or modified.[33] A party may also apply for discovery of deleted files or file fragments that may be discovered through the use of computer forensics. Paragraph 43C(3) of the E-discovery PD sets out the

---

28. Paragraph 43B(1) of the E-discovery PD.
29. 43F(1) of the E-discovery PD.
30. 43G(1) of the E-discovery PD.
31. However, it should be noted that the plaintiff in that case was a litigant in person and SAR Yeong clearly took into consideration the plaintiff's comparable lack of financial resources in granting the plaintiff's request.
32. Paragraph 43C(2) of the E-discovery PD.
33. Paragraph 43C(2) of the E-discovery PD.

procedure for making such an application and states that the electronic medium or recording device should first be discovered and then a request for forensic inspection is to be made. The request for inspection must be accompanied by an inspection protocol.

Discovery and inspection of databases, electronic media, and recording devices are treated in the same manner as applications for discovery of deleted files as set out above, given the intrusive nature of such inspection. Discovery of the database or storage device must first be made followed by a request for forensic inspection and must be accompanied by an inspection protocol. In a request for discovery by reasonable search of databases and storage media, the search terms are specified by the requesting party and the reasonable search is conducted by the party giving discovery. The party giving discovery will review the results for the purpose of asserting privilege and give discovery of the remainder of the documents. The inspection of the database or storage media is conducted by the party requesting disclosure by a reasonable search. In discovery of information residing in deleted files or file fragments in a database or storage media, inspection is to be carried out by forensic examination and will involve the appointment of a joint computer expert to carry out the forensic examination.

The methodology for the inspection of databases and storage media envisioned by the inspection protocol appended to the E-discovery PD contemplates the acquisition of an image of the database or medium as a first step. The inspection is carried out on the image of the said database or medium. Where a discovery order is made for the discovery of a hard disk, the disclosing party will need to produce the said hard disk or, with the leave of the court, a forensically imaged copy of the hard disk.[34] Where a forensically imaged copy of the hard disk is made, care should be taken to record the details of the chain of custody of the hard disk and the imaged copy.

J.   THE TEST OF NECESSITY

As it is with the discovery of physical documents, the overall test for whether discovery of electronically stored documents should be granted is whether such discovery is necessary for the fair disposal of the cause or matter or for the saving of costs. Paragraph 43D of the E-discovery PD provides the following list of matters that a court should consider in determining whether the application for discovery of electronically stored documents should be granted:

    (a) The number of electronic documents involved.
    (b) The nature of the case and complexity of the issues.
    (c) The value of the claim and the financial position of each party.

---

34. As held in *Alliance Management SA v. Pendleton Lane P and Another Suit* (2008) 4 SLR 1, a mere copy of the hard disk is not sufficient.

(d) The ease and expense of retrieval of any particular electronically stored document or class of electronically stored documents, including:
  (i)   the accessibility, location, and likelihood of locating any relevant documents;
  (ii) the costs of recovering and giving discovery and inspection of any relevant documents; and
  (iii) the likelihood that any relevant documents will be materially altered in the course of recovery, or the giving of discovery or inspection.
(e) The significance of any particular electronically stored document or class of electronically stored documents that are likely to be located to the issues in dispute.

Cost-Shifting Orders
The E-discovery PD provides for the possibility of cost-shifting orders.[35]

III.   DATA PROTECTION

Singapore does not have an omnibus legislation dealing with data protection or privacy rights generally. In general, the protection of personal information is commonly regulated by common law remedies for breach of confidence, contract, and the tort of defamation.

Singapore does, however, have a patchwork of statutory provisions in various acts or subsidiary legislation dealing with data protection in respect of certain types of information, for example, banking secrecy. Singapore also has a Model Data Protection Code ('the Code') that seeks to provide minimum guidelines for the protection of personal information in the form of electronic media. The Code does not have the force of law and its adoption is entirely voluntary.

A.   REQUIREMENTS FOR DATA COLLECTION, PROCESSING, AND USE

Singapore does not have statutory provisions that set out formal requirements for the collection, processing, and use of personal data and that are generally applicable. The Code, however, recommends that personal information should be collected with the consent of the individual concerned and only for purposes specified at the time of collection and that the information be processed and used only in accordance with the specified purposes.

B.   STORAGE AND DISCLOSURE OF PERSONAL DATA

There is no general prohibition for the disclosure of personal data in the context of discovery. A party to litigation is generally required to provide discovery of

---

35. Paragraph 43I of the E-discovery PD.

personal data to comply with its discovery obligations, unless discovery would not be in the interests of national security. The Code also provides that an organization may disclose personal data for the 'purposes of establishing, exercising or defending legal rights'.[36]

C.   TRANSFER OF PERSONAL DATA ABROAD

Similarly, there is no general prohibition for the transfer of personal data abroad to fulfil disclosure obligations or for the purpose of determining whether such data fall under the scope of a party's disclosure obligations.

D.   ACCESSING ELECTRONIC FILES OF EMPLOYEES

The main issue to be considered when accessing electronic files of employees for the purpose of fulfilling disclosure obligations is whether such information is confidential in nature. In determining whether information stored on computers belonging to the employer by employees is confidential, the question to be addressed is whether the employees have an expectation of confidentiality of any personal information on the computers.

Generally, where the computers or storage media are company property and within the premises of the company, it would be difficult for an employee to claim that he or she has exclusive right to any personal information and that the employer does not have a right to access the information. Nevertheless, it would be prudent for companies to clearly set out in their employee handbooks that all documents residing in computers or storage media owned by the company are company property and are subject to review without notice to employees.

E.   SANCTIONS

1.   The Possible Sanctions (Fines; Imprisonment)

a.   *Criminal*

As stated earlier, Singapore does not have an omnibus legislation dealing with data protection or privacy rights generally.

However, there are statutory provisions in various acts or subsidiary legislation dealing with data protection in respect of certain types of information, breaches of which carry criminal sanctions. These include the Official Secrets Act (Cap 213), the Computer Misuse Act (Cap 50A), and the Banking Act (Cap 13). The sanctions provided under these acts include fines as well as imprisonment.

---

36. Paragraph 4.5 of the Code.

The mere fact that the information was already in the public domain does not mean that it ceased to be protected information. If the information reached the public domain as a result of unauthorized disclosure, that information did not cease to be secret official information.[37]

b.   *Civil*

As for civil liability, it is governed by common law, which includes breach of confidence, contract, and the tort of defamation. The remedies in the main are injunction and damages.

2.   Sanctions Actually Taken in Singapore

a.   *Criminal*

Criminal sanctions are imposed stringently by the courts. An illustration of this is the case of *Navaseelan Balasingam v. Public Prosecutor.*[38] The appellant, a British national, had committed, *inter alia*, offences under the Computer Misuse Act by causing various automated-teller machines ('ATMs') to access data held in the central computer systems of a bank and committed theft of money, when he was visiting Singapore engaged on a social-visit pass.

His unauthorized activities were found out. He was arrested and he pleaded guilty before a district judge to five charges under the Computer Misuse Act as well as five charges under the Penal Code (Cap 224) for theft of money from the bank through such unauthorized transactions. Another 258 similar charges were taken into consideration for the purpose of sentencing. The district judge sentenced the appellant to six months' imprisonment on each of the five theft charges under the Penal Code and to eighteen months' imprisonment on each of the five charges under the Computer Misuse Act. Part of the sentence required the term of imprisonment of certain charges to run concurrently, with the aggregate sentence being five and a half years.

The appellant appealed to the High Court. Not only was his appeal dismissed, the High Court felt the aggregate sentence of five and a half years did not quite reflect the severity of the offences in question and was manifestly inadequate in the circumstances. The Court opined that the district judge sentencing resulted in an error of law, which resulted in a serious injustice, which warranted the exercise of revisionary power by the High Court. The High Court decided to enhance the sentence by an additional two years despite the appeal being lodged by the accused person and not the public prosecutor. The Court observed that the security of Singapore's financial institutions and protection of public interest against electronic financial scams were paramount.

---

37. *Bridges Christopher v. Public Prosecutor* (1997) 1 SLR(R) 156.
38. (2007) 1 SLR(R) 767.

b.   *Civil*

Insofar as civil liability is concerned, the issue of breach of data protection, trade secrets, is a common issue in post-employment, particularly when an ex-employee joins a competitor of the ex-employer or starts a business in competition with the ex-employer.

The applicable law is the common law. The Singapore courts have accepted and apply the principle enunciated by the English Court. The Singapore Court of Appeal[39] had reiterated the principle as follows, quoting the observations of the judge in the leading English authority of *Faccenda Chicken Ltd v. Fowler* (1987) Ch 117 ('Faccenda Chicken'):

Insofar as *trade secrets* are concerned, the observations by Neill LJ *Faccenda Chicken*, although not directed at an express covenant in restraint of trade as such, are nevertheless apposite insofar as they constitute guidelines that would aid the court in ascertaining whether or not something constitutes a trade secret (or its equivalent). The factors to take into consideration are:

(a) *The nature of the employment* – where the employee habitually handles confidential information, a higher obligation of confidentiality may be imposed.

(b) *The nature of the information itself* – in this regard, the information concerned must be a trade secret or material that, whilst not properly described as a trade secret as such, is, having regard to all the various circumstances, 'of such a highly confidential nature as to require the same protection as a trade secret'.

(c) *Whether the employer impressed on the employee the confidentiality of the information* – on this point, Neill LJ was of the view that, in order to prevent the use or disclosure of the information in question, it was insufficient for the employer to merely tell the employee that the information was confidential. The employer's attitude toward the information itself had to be considered as well.

(d) *Whether the relevant information can be easily isolated from other information that the employee is free to disclose* – where the information alleged to be confidential is 'part of a package' and the remainder of the package is not confidential, this factor, although not conclusive in itself, can shed light on whether the information in question is truly a trade secret.

The Court of Appeal also endorsed the view in *Faccenda Chicken* that where the confidential information in question fell *short* of constituting a trade secret, such information, although not permitted to be disclosed or used by the employee whilst still *within the employ* of the employer, could be disclosed or used *after* the contract of employment came to an end. The Court of Appeal was of view that the duty

---

39. *Man Financial (S) Pte Ltd (formerly known as E D & F Man International [S] Pte Ltd) Wong Bark v. Chuan David* (2008) 1 SLR(R) 663.

imposed during the period of employment is wholly consistent with the duty of fidelity owed by the employee to the employer whilst in the latter's service.

The Court of Appeal stated that a line must be drawn between a covenant that seeks to protect a legitimate proprietary interest on the one hand and one that merely seeks to prevent the employee in question from exercising his or her own natural skill and talent, even if such skill and talent are acquired by the employee in the course of his or her employment, and that the courts will not sanction the latter. It concluded that much would depend on the facts of each case.

The Singapore High Court[40] has held that former employees who start their own businesses cannot be prevented from applying their ex-employers' policy to their businesses. Citing *Faccenda Chicken*[41] and *Tang Siew Choy*,[42] the Court opined that: 'Employees who acquire knowledge of the products that they deal with do not have to abandon the knowledge when they resign. They are entitled to make the best use of their experience and knowledge in their subsequent employment or ventures, even if that involves their former employers' confidential information – so long as they do not steal and use their trade secrets or information of such high confidentiality as to amount to a trade secret'.

Therefore, the mere fact that non-compete terms may be incorporated in a contract of employment is no guarantee that the clause can be successfully enforced in every case.

IV.   CONCLUSION

As documents these days are in the vast majority of cases created and stored electronically and parties to litigation are increasingly faced with issues relating to the discovery of electronically stored documents, the E-discovery PD is a very welcome development; the guidelines set out in the E-discovery PD are likely to provide much desired certainty when addressing e-discovery issues.

With respect to the interplay between discovery and data protection or privacy rights, it appears that any conflict would be very limited, and in the usual case the discovery obligations prevail. However, it should be stated that the courts regularly take into consideration the confidentiality of information in determining whether an order for discovery of such information should be made. The courts also take into consideration privacy laws of foreign jurisdictions where the information is subject to such foreign laws in ordering disclosure. However, such considerations are left to the discretion of the courts to deal with, and more direction on the disclosure of private information may be beneficial.

---

40.   *Universal Westech (S) Pte Ltd v. Ng Thiam Kiat & Ors* (1997) 2 SLR 139 at 148.
41.   *Supra*, No. 420.
42.   *Supra*, No. 409.

Chapter 6.5

Taiwan

*Jill Niu and Katherine Juang**

I. INTRODUCTION

In common law jurisdictions such as the United States, parties to a civil suit are mutually obligated to disclose in the pretrial discovery process any facts, documents, or materials that are pertinent to the suit.[1] A party will expose itself to risks if it fails to comply with a discovery request served by an opposing party.[2] When asked to produce documents and materials in electronic form stored on corporate networks, the provision of such information or documents is subject to the relevant regime for discovery of electronic evidence. If such information or documents are held by an affiliate in Taiwan and contain personal data of employees or other third parties in Taiwan, the obligation to comply with the discovery request will be subject to legal or regulatory restrictions under Taiwanese law.

To explicate on the reconciliation between the mandatory disclosure requirements of common law jurisdictions and the regulatory rules and requirements for data or privacy protection in Taiwan, we will first provide an analytical context through general introduction of the procedure for evidence investigation for civil

---

*   Jill Niu, Esq., and Katherine Juang, Esq., Lee and Li Attorneys-at-Law, Taipei, Taiwan.
1. Federal Rules of Civil Procedure (F.R.C.P.), Rule 26.
2. According to Rule 37(a) and (b), a litigant can apply for a court order compelling disclosure or discovery of the information in question. If the motion is granted, a party's continued failure to disclose might result in an order of contempt of court and heavy fines, an award of attorney's fees and costs, or even dismissal of a claim or an unfavourable judgment.

Catrien Noorda & Stefan Hanloser, *E-Discovery and Data Privacy*, pp. 349–359.
© 2011 Kluwer Law International BV, The Netherlands.

litigation and personal data protection in Taiwan. We will then analyse how, within that context, a party can respond to or cope with a request for transfer of personal data in electronic form to the relevant jurisdiction.

II.   EVIDENCE INVESTIGATION FOR CIVIL LITIGATION IN TAIWAN

As Taiwan's civil law system is based on that of Germany and Japan, discovery is an unknown concept within its civil litigation procedure. The absence of such a concept is a notable difference between common law and civil law jurisdictions. Generally speaking, in a civil law jurisdiction, the judge hearing a suit is in charge of evidence investigation. A party must file a motion with the court for an order requesting that the opposing party submit evidence, as the opposing party has no obligation to voluntarily disclose documents to the court.[3] In addition, the Taiwanese Code of Civil Procedure limits the disclosure of evidence to what is necessary for the trial. The judge has discretion to decide on the materiality of a disputed fact and the justifiability of the motion before granting such an order.[4] Disclosure of certain documents, however, does not fall under the above-described judicial discretion when explicitly required by law.[5]

There are no blocking statutes restricting cross-border discovery of information intended for disclosure in foreign jurisdictions. In fact, the Taiwanese Act Governing the Provision of Judicial Assistance to Foreign Courts (hereinafter the 'Judicial Assistance Act') provides procedures[6] for foreign courts intending to seek judicial assistance from a Taiwanese court. However, when the Judicial Assistance Act was enacted on 12 April 1963 (no amendment has been made to this Act to date), the legislature's focus was on safeguarding Taiwan's sovereignty and maintaining legal order in Taiwan when delivering such judicial assistance. On the basis of the above concern, the Judicial Assistance Act states that if the request involves evidence investigation for civil litigation, the evidence investigation must comply

---

3. For example, according to Arts 341 to 343 of the Code of Civil Procedure, if a party would like to motion for the court's order compelling the opposing party to submit a document, it must file a brief with the court, specify the document required, specify the disputed fact to be proved by and the contents of such document, and explain the fact that such document is in the opposing party's possession and the reason why the opposing party has a duty to produce such document.
4. Article 343 of the Code of Civil Procedure.
5. According to para. 1, Art. 344 of the Code of Civil Procedure, such documents include: (1) documents to which the party has made reference in the course of the litigation proceeding; (2) documents that the opposing party is entitled to have delivered or inspect pursuant to relevant laws; (3) documents that are created in the interests of the opposing party; (4) commercial accounting books; and (5) documents that are created for the purpose of matter related to the action.
6. According to Art. 3 of the Judicial Assistance Act, a foreign court must, through its country's diplomatic institution, issue a Letter Rogatory, along with related information/documents, to the ROC Ministry of Foreign Affairs ('MOFA') to ask for such assistance.

with relevant provisions under the Code of Civil Procedure.[7] Therefore, filing a request for such assistance might not be practical for discovery purpose under the common law.

III.   TAIWAN'S DATA PROTECTION ACT

The Computer-Processed Personal Data Protection Act, which came into effect on 11 August 1995 (hereinafter the '1995 Act'), is the major legislation for personal data protection in Taiwan. Its scope of operation, however, is rather limited. For example, the 1995 Act applies only to government agencies and a limited group of private entities and concerns only computer-processed personal data (see further discussion in sections A and B below). In practice, effective privacy protection requires recourse to the Civil Code, the Criminal Code, and the Communication Protection and Interception Act (see section F below for further explanation of this Act). However, with a bill to amend the 1995 Act having been promulgated in May 2010 and expected to come into force two years in the future (see details in section E below), a more rigorous legal regime for protection of personal data can be expected.

A.   TAIWAN'S DATA PROTECTION ACT – COMPUTER-PROCESSED
            PERSONAL DATA AND LIMITED SCOPE

According to Item 1, Article 3 of the 1995 Act, personal data refers to any data that may identify a specific person, including but not limited to name; date of birth; identification number; characteristics; fingerprints; marital status; family, educational, and occupational background; file of medical history; financial condition; and social activities of a natural person. As can be seen, the 1995 Act affords protection to personal data in general and does not impose different restrictions on collection, use, or disclosure by category of data. On the other hand, Article 1 of the 1995 Act provides that only personal data that are, or will be, *processed by computer*[8] are protected under the 1995 Act. In short, discovery of electronic evidence clearly falls within the scope of the 1995 Act if personal data are involved.

However, the 1995 Act is only applicable to government agencies and private entities in the businesses specified under Item 7, Article 3 of the 1995 Act. According to Items 7(i) and 7(ii), Article 3 of the 1995 Act, private entities include credit investigation businesses, organizations, and individuals whose main business is to collect or process personal data of computers, hospitals, schools,

---

7. Article 6 of the Judicial Assistance Act.
8. The term 'computer-processed' is defined by Item 3 of Art. 3 of the 1995 Act to mean any act that involves the use of computers or automated machinery to key in, store, compile, correct, search, delete, output, transmit, or otherwise process data.

telecommunication businesses, financial businesses, securities businesses, insurance businesses, and mass media. Furthermore, Item 7(iii) empowers the Ministry of Justice (hereinafter 'MOJ') to designate certain private entities to be governed by the 1995 Act after consultation with other central government authorities in charge of the industries to which such entities belong (hereinafter 'Central Government Authority[ies]').[9]

B.   TAIWAN'S DATA PROTECTION ACT – REQUIREMENTS FOR DATA
          COLLECTION, PROCESSING, AND USE

Under the 1995 Act, the above-mentioned private entities must have a specific purpose for collecting or processing personal data by computer, and must fulfil one of the following requirements: (1) written consent is obtained from the data subject; (2) the collecting/processing party enters into an agreement or quasi-contractual relationship with the data subject to ensure that the rights and interests of the data subject will be protected; (3) the information to be collected/processed is publicly available and there will be no material adverse effect on the data subject; (4) the collection/processing is for the purpose of academic study and there will be no material adverse effect on the data subject; or (5) the collection/processing is performed in accordance with relevant laws or regulations.[10]

If a private entity intends to use the personal data that it has collected, it must do so for the specific purpose for which it undertook the collection. Any use beyond such specific purpose is prohibited, except under any of the following circumstances: (1) to improve public interests; (2) to protect the life, body, freedom, or property of the data subject from imminent danger; (3) to prevent another person from sustaining any significant loss; or (4) upon written consent of the data subject.[11]

An entity of the businesses specified under Item 7, Article 3 of the 1995 Act must register with the Central Government Authorities and obtain a license to collect, process, use, or internationally transmit personal data.[12]

C.   TAIWAN'S DATA PROTECTION ACT – INTERNATIONAL TRANSMISSION

In addition to the above requirements, the competent authority has the power to limit international transmission or utilization of personal data by a private entity under any of the following situations: (1) where major national interests are

---

9. Currently, private cram schools, real estate agents, and employment service providers are included among the designated parties subject to the 1995 Act, due to the volume and importance of the personal data at their disposal.
10. Article 18 of the 1995 Act.
11. Article 23 of the 1995 Act.
12. Article 19 of the 1995 Act.

involved; (2) where international treaties or agreements so require; (3) where the laws of the country to which personal data are to be transmitted cannot protect the rights of the data subject; or (4) where international transmission and utilization of personal data are made or will be made in such a way as to evade the requirements or restrictions of the Act.[13]

D.   TAIWAN'S DATA PROTECTION ACT – SUPERVISORY
         AUTHORITY; ENFORCEMENT

The MOJ, as provided under Article 42 of the 1995 Act, shall be responsible for coordinating matters relevant to the enforcement of this Act; however, implementation of this Act in specific cases should be handled by the Central Government Authorities.

Violations of the 1995 Act are subject to both criminal liability and administrative sanction as follows:

(1) Criminal liability: According Article 33, a person who intends to earn profits for him- or herself by violating the provisions on requirements for data collection, processing, and use, thereby causing injury to another, shall be punished with imprisonment of less than two years, detention, or, in lieu thereof or in addition thereto, criminal fine of less than New Taiwan Dollars (TWD) 40,000 (US Dollars (USD) 1,300[14]). Furthermore, Article 34 provides that a person who intends to make unlawful gains for him- or herself or for a third party or intends to infringe upon the interests of another by illegally outputting, interfering with, changing, or deleting personal data or by other illegal means to impede the accuracy of personal data, thus causing damages to another, shall be punished with imprisonment for less than three years, or detention, or a fine of less than TWD 50,000 (USD 1,700). If a government official takes advantage of his or her position, or opportunity, or means available to him or her to commit the offences prescribed in Articles 33 and 34, half of the above-prescribed penalties can be added to such official's punishment. If a more severe punishment is provided for in other laws with respect to the offences indicated above, according to Article 37, the more severe punishment shall apply.

(2) Administrative sanction: According to Article 38 of the 1995 Act, violation of requirements for data collection, processing, and use will be subject to an administrative fine of from TWD 20,000 (USD 650) to TWD 100,000 (USD 3,400) on the responsible person of such entity, and said responsible person shall be ordered to take corrective measures within a

---

13. Article 24 of the 1995 Act.
14. All US dollar amounts mentioned in this article are approximate figures based on the current exchange rate.

prescribed period. In the event the responsible person fails to take corrective measures within the prescribed period, the Central Government Authority may continue to impose a fine for each violation. In addition, violation of the registration obligation will be subject to an administrative fine of from TWD 10,000 (USD 325) to TWD 50,000 (USD 1,700) imposed upon the responsible person for each violation.

(3) Punishment and sanctions in actual cases: The current body of court judgments shows that most criminal defendants violating the 1995 Act are responsible persons of credit investigation companies. In cases where the responsible person violated the requirements for collecting personal data, the punishments are from twenty to fifty days' detention, in lieu of which a criminal fine of TWD 10,000 (USD 325) to TWD 20,000 (USD 650).[15] In a particular case where the responsible person committed repeated offences while simultaneously violating the requirements for both collecting personal data and the registration obligation, more severe punishment of eight months' imprisonment was handed down.[16]

As to the administrative sanctions, the competent authorities' decision, if not appealed to the court, might not be accessible to the public. Past news reports indicate that three banks were each sanctioned by the Financial Supervisory Commission ('FSC') with administrative fine of TWD 20,000 (USD 650) for disclosing clients' personal data to a third party without obtaining prior consent of the clients. The FSC is the most aggressive Central Government Authority in monitoring businesses under its supervision and in imposing sanctions.

E.   TAIWAN'S DATA PROTECTION ACT – AMENDMENT PASSED IN 2010

Since the 1995 Act only applies to government agencies and a limited group of private entities and only concerns computer-processed personal data, the protection afforded to individuals is rather limited. In order to expand the scope of protection and eliminate unreasonable limits, the MOJ started to draft an amendment bill in 2001, which it completed in early 2005.[17] The bill was passed by the legislative body on 27 April 2010 and promulgated on 26 May 2010.[18] Set forth below are the major revisions broadening the scope of Taiwan's personal data protection.

---

15. Taoyuan District Court's Judgment No. 86-Y-2260 (12 Sep. 1997); Taoyuan District Court's Judgment No. 87-Y-1161 (19 Apr. 2000); Taiwan High Court's Judgment No. 93-SY-1896 (10 May 2005).
16. Taiwan High Court's Judgment No. 94-SY-1237 (16 Nov. 2005).
17. Legislative Yuan's Letter No. TLS-0974300315 dated 3 Jun. 2008.
18. Taiwan President's Order No. HZ1Y-09900125121 on 26 May 2010.

1. Change of Scope of Personal Data and Applicable Private Entities

The new law was renamed 'Personal Data Protection Act' (hereinafter the '2010 Act') to reflect an expanded scope of protection of personal data, which now additionally covers non-computer-processed personal data. In addition, the 2010 Act now applies to all private entities, according to Item 8, Article 2.

2. Sensitive Personal Data

According to Article 6 of the 2010 Act, medical history, genetic data, sex life, health examination, and criminal record are now categorized as sensitive personal data, which, in principle, are not allowed to be collected, processed, or used unless such action meets certain requirements.[19]

3. Requirements for Data Collection, Processing, and Use

Notification obligations are added in paragraph 1, Article 8 of the 2010 Act, which provides that, prior to collection of personal data, private entities are required to notify the data subject that they intend to collect his or her personal data; detailed information related to such collection must be provided[20] unless exempted by paragraph 2 of Article 8.[21] In addition, according to Article 9 of the 2010 Act, if a private entity collects personal data from a third party, it should inform the data subject of the source of data and the above detailed information before processing or using such data.

If a private entity intends to collect or process personal data by obtaining written consent from the data subject, such written consent is valid only when the notification obligation mentioned above is duly performed.[22] If a private entity

---

19. The proviso includes the situation where: (1) the action is provided for in the laws and regulations; (2) the action is necessary for the government agency or the private entity to perform its legal obligation and appropriate data security measures have been adopted; (3) the data are already made publicly available by the data subject or through other legal means; (4) the personal data have been collected, processed, or used through certain procedures by government agencies or academic institutions for the purposes of medical treatment/care, hygiene, or crime prevention and are necessary for statistical or academic research.
20. The items that the data subject must be informed of include: (1) the name of the government agency or private entity; (2) purpose of collection; (3) category of personal data; (4) when, where, by whom, and how the personal data will be used; (5) the data subject's rights; and (6) the data subject's right to freely choose whether to provide his or her personal data, and how his or her rights and interests will be affected if he or she refuses to provide such data.
21. The notification obligation will be exempted under the following circumstances: (1) as provided by laws or regulations; (2) as necessary for government agencies or private entities to perform their legal obligations; (3) when such notification will impede performance of a government agency's legal obligations; (4) when such notification will damage a third party's material interests; or (5) the data subject is already aware of the contents of the notification.
22. Paragraph 1, Art. 7 of the 2010 Act.

intends to use the personal data that it has collected for a purpose exceeding that which it had originally indicated, it must obtain another independent and specific written consent upon providing further notification of such new purpose and scope of use.[23]

On the other hand, the private entities' obligation of registration with the Central Government Authorities to obtain a license to collect, process, use, or internationally transmit personal data is removed.

4.   Supervisory Authority; Enforcement

The MOJ, in accordance with its position that it should not assume general supervisory authority, abdicates its previous position as coordinator of matters relevant to the enforcement of the 2010 Act and is now only responsible for defining categories of the specific purposes and personal data in conjunction with Central Government Authorities. Implementation of the 2010 Act should now be handled by the central or regional competent authority overseeing the private entities.

Both criminal liability and administrative sanction for violating the requirements on collecting, processing, or using personal data are much more significant in the 2010 Act. Criminal liability is now subject to imprisonment of less than five years, detention, or, in lieu thereof or in addition thereto, criminal fine of less than TWD 1 million (USD 30,000), while administrative sanction is now subject to administrative fine of not less than TWD 50,000 (USD 1,700) but not more than TWD 500,000 (USD 17,000).

5.   Timeline for Enactment

According to Article 56 of the 2010 Act, the date on which the Act takes effect will be determined by the administration and is currently uncertain. A press release suggests that, due to the expansive scope of the amendment, the administration might delay the effective date by two years to afford government and private entities time to adapt. Article 54 of the 2010 Act further provides a one-year grace period for all private entities to retroactively fulfil notification obligations for illegitimately obtained personal data.

F.   Taiwan's Data Protection Act – Other Related Laws

The Civil Code and the Criminal Code impose civil and criminal liabilities on privacy violations. Under Article 195 of the Civil Code, a person who illegally intrudes on the privacy of another is liable for compensation for the damage caused. According to Article 318-1 of the Criminal Code, disclosure without justifiable cause of another's private information obtained or otherwise learned via a computer system or other relevant equipment is subject to criminal sanction.

---

23.   Paragraph 2, Art. 7 of the 2010 Act.

In addition, the Communication Protection and Interception Act (the 'Communication Act') prohibits any government agency, person, or private entity[24] from monitoring or intercepting the communication of any person unless the person being monitored or intercepted is a suspect of a serious crime,[25] and unless such monitoring or interception is necessary.[26] Furthermore, the information or data obtained through monitoring or interception in accordance with the Communication Act cannot be provided to another government agency, entity, or person unless otherwise permitted by other laws.[27] Communication is defined by the Communication Act as signals, words, pictures, sounds, or other messages sent, stored, transferred, or accepted through telecommunication equipment.[28] Most important, the definition of such communication indicates that it is presumed private or confidential by the person being monitored or intercepted.[29]

G.   TAIWAN'S DATA PROTECTION ACT – EMPLOYEE E-MAIL

Before the enactment of the 2010 Act, the law was silent on whether an employer can monitor, search, download, or transfer the contents of an employee's computer or whether such acts violate the employee's privacy. A landmark judgment[30] rendered in 2003 first addressed the issue of whether an employer can monitor its employee's e-mail correspondence where the e-mail system is provided by the employer. In the judgment, two issues were discussed in determining whether violation of employee privacy was at stake: (1) whether the employee can reasonably expect that his or her e-mail correspondence will be kept private and (2) whether the law prohibits the employer from monitoring the employee's e-mails. The Court held as follows:

(1) If the employer has notified its employees of its policy of monitoring their e-mail at work for the purpose of maintaining the confidentiality of internal e-mail or documents, and if none of the employees objects to the policy, then the employees should not expect that their e-mail will be kept private when utilizing the e-mail system provided by the employer.

(2) The employer's policy did not violate any law, as Taiwanese law does not prohibit the employer from monitoring its employees' e-mail.

It can be inferred from the above that the employer can monitor its employees' e-mail correspondence if it has notified its employees of its monitoring policy and

---

24. According to Interpretation Letter No. 2000-Law-000805 published by the MOJ on 16 Jun. 2000, the Communication Protection and Interception Act also applies to individuals and private entities.
25. Paragraph 1, Art. 2 and Arts 5 to 7 of the Communication Act.
26. Paragraph 2, Art. 2 of the Communication Act.
27. Article 18 of the Communication Act.
28. Paragraph 1, Art. 3 of the Communication Act.
29. Paragraph 2, Art. 3 of the Communication Act.
30. Taipei District Court Judgment No. 91-LS-139 Katherine Juang 19 Oct. 2010 (8 Dec. 2003).

if no employee objects to the policy. In addition, the employees' acquiescence will be deemed as consent to the monitoring policy. If an employee uses the e-mail system for personal matters, he or she should be fully aware that he or she is being monitored and such monitoring does not violate the law.

Moreover, although both academic and judicial views on the employee's privacy in the workplace focus only on the employer's monitoring of the employee's e-mail, the above rule can reasonably apply to the situation where the employer intends to monitor, search, download, or transfer contents on the employee's computer provided by the employer if it has duly notified the employee of its policy without any objection from the employee.

However, after the enactment of the 2010 Act, even if the employer obtains the employee's consent, no sensitive personal data on the employee's computer can be collected, downloaded, or transferred unless any circumstance set forth in the proviso of Article 6 is met. In addition, for other personal data, if the purpose of discovery of electronic evidence (hereinafter 'e-discovery') is not set forth in the original consent provided by the employee, an independent written consent with prior notification of detailed information of such e-discovery should be obtained by the employer before any downloading or transferring of data takes place.

IV. PRETRIAL DISCOVERY OF ELECTRONIC EVIDENCE IN TAIWAN

Below is an analysis of how Taiwan deals with requests to transfer personal data to another jurisdiction for use in civil litigation.

A. MONITORING, SEARCH, DOWNLOAD, OR TRANSFER OF PERSONAL DATA ON EMPLOYEES' COMPUTERS

According to the 2003 judgment mentioned above, as long as an entity has notified its employees that company-owned computers are provided to them for work purposes and are subject to monitoring, the entity may search the contents of such computers. Additionally, if the entity's policy notice further specifies that such contents might be downloaded or transferred for any legally justifiable reasons, including but not limited to a discovery procedure of foreign litigation, then the employees will be deemed to have given their consent to the policy.

However, Article 30 of the Enforcement Rules of the 1995 Act ('1995 Enforcement Rules') provides that as long as a written statement sufficiently indicates the data subject's consent, it constitutes the written consent required by Item 4, Article 23 of the 1995 Act. In order to obtain the data subject's consent for a specific purpose, a private entity can give the principal the relevant information about the collection, computer processing, and utilization for a specific purpose when it first contacts the data subject, along with a form for the data subject to express his or her disagreement to such collection, processing, or utilization within a specified time. If the data subject does not express disagreement within the specified time, it can be presumed that the data subject has given consent. Therefore, for the entity subject to the 1995 Act, the implied consent to be obtained from the employee must meet the requirements under Article 30 of the 1995 Enforcement Rules.

However, after the enactment of the 2010 Act, a general consent provided by the data subject is not allowed. If the e-discovery purpose is not clearly set forth in the original employee consent, an independent written consent with prior notification of detailed information regarding such e-discovery should be obtained by the employer before any downloading or transferring takes place. In addition, it is currently unclear whether the Enforcement Rules of the 2010 Act to be drafted and promulgated by the MOJ will adopt an implied consent as set out in Article 30 of the Enforcement Rules of the 1995 Act.

In addition, if the electronic evidence searched involves a third party's personal data, such third party's consent must be obtained prior to the transfer or disclosure of such information. Otherwise, transferring or disclosing such information will be deemed to have violated the 2010 Act and be subject to civil and criminal liabilities.

B. INTERNATIONAL TRANSMISSION OF PERSONAL DATA ON EMPLOYEES' COMPUTERS

As mentioned above, if an entity is subject to the 1995 Act, it must register with the competent authorities and obtain a license to legally collect, process, use, or internationally transmit personal data. However, such registration requirement is removed in the 2010 Act. Nonetheless, both the 1995 Act and the 2010 Act provide the Central Government Authority the power to limit international transmission or utilization of personal data by a private entity under certain circumstances.

V. CONCLUSION

In short, under the 1995 Act and other privacy protection laws, an entity's right to search, download, transfer, or internationally transmit personal data depends on whether it has the data subject's consent to such acts. Except that the competent authority may limit or forbid the international transmission of personal data in certain circumstances, Taiwanese law does not stipulate any express restrictions on accommodating the common law pretrial discovery procedure. However, after the enactment of the 2010 Act, even if the employer obtains employee consent, no sensitive personal data on the employee's computer can be collected, downloaded, or transferred unless any circumstance set out in proviso of Article 6 is met. In addition, for other personal data, if the e-discovery purpose is not set out in the originally provided employee consent, an independent written consent with prior notification describing in detail the information regarding such e-discovery should be obtained by the employer before any downloading or transferring takes place.

Annex 1

Directive 95/46/EC of the European Parliament and of the Council of 24 October 1995 on the Protection of Individuals with Regard to the Processing of Personal Data and on the Free Movement of Such Data*

THE EUROPEAN PARLIAMENT AND THE COUNCIL OF THE EUROPEAN UNION,

Having regard to the Treaty establishing the European Community, and in particular Article 100a thereof,

Having regard to the proposal from the Commission,[1]

Having regard to the opinion of the Economic and Social Committee,[2]

Acting in accordance with the procedure referred to in Article 189b of the Treaty,[3]

---

1. OJ No C 277, 5. 11. 1990, p. 3 and OJ No C 311, 27. 11. 1992, p. 30.
2. OJ No C 159, 17. 6. 1991, p 38.
3. Opinion of the European Parliament of 11 March 1992 (OJ No C 94, 13. 4. 1992, p. 198), confirmed on 2 December 1993 (OJ No C 342, 20. 12. 1993, p. 30); Council common position of 20 February 1995 (OJ No C 93, 13. 4. 1995, p. 1) and Decision of the European Parliament of 15 June 1995 (OJ No C 166, 3. 7. 1995).

Catrien Noorda & Stefan Hanloser, *E-Discovery and Data Privacy*, pp. 361–391.
© 2011 Kluwer Law International BV, The Netherlands.

Annex 1

(1) Whereas the objectives of the Community, as laid down in the Treaty, as amended by the Treaty on European Union, include creating an ever closer union among the peoples of Europe, fostering closer relations between the States belonging to the Community, ensuring economic and social progress by common action to eliminate the barriers which divide Europe, encouraging the constant improvement of the living conditions of its peoples, preserving and strengthening peace and liberty and promoting democracy on the basis of the fundamental rights recognized in the constitution and laws of the Member States and in the European Convention for the Protection of Human Rights and Fundamental Freedoms;

(2) Whereas data-processing systems are designed to serve man; whereas they must, whatever the nationality or residence of natural persons, respect their fundamental rights and freedoms, notably the right to privacy, and contribute to economic and social progress, trade expansion and the well-being of individuals;

(3) Whereas the establishment and functioning of an internal market in which, in accordance with Article 7a of the Treaty, the free movement of goods, persons, services and capital is ensured require not only that personal data should be able to flow freely from one Member State to another, but also that the fundamental rights of individuals should be safeguarded;

(4) Whereas increasingly frequent recourse is being had in the Community to the processing of personal data in the various spheres of economic and social activity; whereas the progress made in information technology is making the processing and exchange of such data considerably easier;

(5) Whereas the economic and social integration resulting from the establishment and functioning of the internal market within the meaning of Article 7a of the Treaty will necessarily lead to a substantial increase in cross-border flows of personal data between all those involved in a private or public capacity in economic and social activity in the Member States; whereas the exchange of personal data between undertakings in different Member States is set to increase; whereas the national authorities in the various Member States are being called upon by virtue of Community law to collaborate and exchange personal data so as to be able to perform their duties or carry out tasks on behalf of an authority in another Member State within the context of the area without internal frontiers as constituted by the internal market;

(6) Whereas, furthermore, the increase in scientific and technical cooperation and the coordinated introduction of new telecommunications networks in the Community necessitate and facilitate cross-border flows of personal data;

(7) Whereas the difference in levels of protection of the rights and freedoms of individuals, notably the right to privacy, with regard to the processing of personal data afforded in the Member States may prevent the transmission of such data from the territory of one Member State to that of another Member State; whereas this difference may therefore constitute an obstacle to the pursuit of a number of economic activities at Community level, distort competition and impede authorities in the discharge of their responsibilities under Community law; whereas this difference in levels of protection is due to the existence of a wide variety of national laws, regulations and administrative provisions;

(8) Whereas, in order to remove the obstacles to flows of personal data, the level of protection of the rights and freedoms of individuals with regard to the processing of such data must be equivalent in all Member States; whereas this objective is vital to the internal market but cannot be achieved by the Member States alone, especially in view of the scale of the divergences which currently exist between the relevant laws in the Member States and the need to coordinate the laws of the Member States so as to ensure that the cross-border flow of personal data is regulated in a consistent manner that is in keeping with the objective of the internal market as provided for in Article 7a of the Treaty; whereas Community action to approximate those laws is therefore needed;

(9) Whereas, given the equivalent protection resulting from the approximation of national laws, the Member States will no longer be able to inhibit the free movement between them of personal data on grounds relating to protection of the rights and freedoms of individuals, and in particular the right to privacy; whereas Member States will be left a margin for manoeuvre, which may, in the context of implementation of the Directive, also be exercised by the business and social partners; whereas Member States will therefore be able to specify in their national law the general conditions governing the lawfulness of data processing; whereas in doing so the Member States shall strive to improve the protection currently provided by their legislation; whereas, within the limits of this margin for manoeuvre and in accordance with Community law, disparities could arise in the implementation of the Directive, and this could have an effect on the movement of data within a Member State as well as within the Community;

(10) Whereas the object of the national laws on the processing of personal data is to protect fundamental rights and freedoms, notably the right to privacy, which is recognized both in Article 8 of the European Convention for the Protection of Human Rights and Fundamental Freedoms and in the general principles of Community law; whereas, for that reason, the approximation of those laws must not result in any lessening of the protection they afford but must, on the contrary, seek to ensure a high level of protection in the Community;

(11) Whereas the principles of the protection of the rights and freedoms of individuals, notably the right to privacy, which are contained in this Directive, give substance to and amplify those contained in the Council of Europe Convention of 28 January 1981 for the Protection of Individuals with regard to Automatic Processing of Personal Data;

(12) Whereas the protection principles must apply to all processing of personal data by any person whose activities are governed by Community law; whereas there should be excluded the processing of data carried out by a natural person in the exercise of activities which are exclusively personal or domestic, such as correspondence and the holding of records of addresses;

(13) Whereas the activities referred to in Titles V and VI of the Treaty on European Union regarding public safety, defence, State security or the activities of the State in the area of criminal laws fall outside the scope of Community law, without prejudice to the obligations incumbent upon Member States under Article 56 (2), Article 57 or Article 100a of the Treaty establishing the European

Community; whereas the processing of personal data that is necessary to safeguard the economic well-being of the State does not fall within the scope of this Directive where such processing relates to State security matters;

(14) Whereas, given the importance of the developments under way, in the framework of the information society, of the techniques used to capture, transmit, manipulate, record, store or communicate sound and image data relating to natural persons, this Directive should be applicable to processing involving such data;

(15) Whereas the processing of such data is covered by this Directive only if it is automated or if the data processed are contained or are intended to be contained in a filing system structured according to specific criteria relating to individuals, so as to permit easy access to the personal data in question;

(16) Whereas the processing of sound and image data, such as in cases of video surveillance, does not come within the scope of this Directive if it is carried out for the purposes of public security, defence, national security or in the course of State activities relating to the area of criminal law or of other activities which do not come within the scope of Community law;

(17) Whereas, as far as the processing of sound and image data carried out for purposes of journalism or the purposes of literary or artistic expression is concerned, in particular in the audiovisual field, the principles of the Directive are to apply in a restricted manner according to the provisions laid down in Article 9;

(18) Whereas, in order to ensure that individuals are not deprived of the protection to which they are entitled under this Directive, any processing of personal data in the Community must be carried out in accordance with the law of one of the Member States; whereas, in this connection, processing carried out under the responsibility of a controller who is established in a Member State should be governed by the law of that State;

(19) Whereas establishment on the territory of a Member State implies the effective and real exercise of activity through stable arrangements; whereas the legal form of such an establishment, whether simply branch or a subsidiary with a legal personality, is not the determining factor in this respect; whereas, when a single controller is established on the territory of several Member States, particularly by means of subsidiaries, he must ensure, in order to avoid any circumvention of national rules, that each of the establishments fulfils the obligations imposed by the national law applicable to its activities;

(20) Whereas the fact that the processing of data is carried out by a person established in a third country must not stand in the way of the protection of individuals provided for in this Directive; whereas in these cases, the processing should be governed by the law of the Member State in which the means used are located, and there should be guarantees to ensure that the rights and obligations provided for in this Directive are respected in practice;

(21) Whereas this Directive is without prejudice to the rules of territoriality applicable in criminal matters;

(22) Whereas Member States shall more precisely define in the laws they enact or when bringing into force the measures taken under this Directive the general

circumstances in which processing is lawful; whereas in particular Article 5, in conjunction with Articles 7 and 8, allows Member States, independently of general rules, to provide for special processing conditions for specific sectors and for the various categories of data covered by Article 8;

(23) Whereas Member States are empowered to ensure the implementation of the protection of individuals both by means of a general law on the protection of individuals as regards the processing of personal data and by sectorial laws such as those relating, for example, to statistical institutes;

(24) Whereas the legislation concerning the protection of legal persons with regard to the processing data which concerns them is not affected by this Directive;

(25) Whereas the principles of protection must be reflected, on the one hand, in the obligations imposed on persons, public authorities, enterprises, agencies or other bodies responsible for processing, in particular regarding data quality, technical security, notification to the supervisory authority, and the circumstances under which processing can be carried out, and, on the other hand, in the right conferred on individuals, the data on whom are the subject of processing, to be informed that processing is taking place, to consult the data, to request corrections and even to object to processing in certain circumstances;

(26) Whereas the principles of protection must apply to any information concerning an identified or identifiable person; whereas, to determine whether a person is identifiable, account should be taken of all the means likely reasonably to be used either by the controller or by any other person to identify the said person; whereas the principles of protection shall not apply to data rendered anonymous in such a way that the data subject is no longer identifiable; whereas codes of conduct within the meaning of Article 27 may be a useful instrument for providing guidance as to the ways in which data may be rendered anonymous and retained in a form in which identification of the data subject is no longer possible;

(27) Whereas the protection of individuals must apply as much to automatic processing of data as to manual processing; whereas the scope of this protection must not in effect depend on the techniques used, otherwise this would create a serious risk of circumvention; whereas, nonetheless, as regards manual processing, this Directive covers only filing systems, not unstructured files; whereas, in particular, the content of a filing system must be structured according to specific criteria relating to individuals allowing easy access to the personal data; whereas, in line with the definition in Article 2 (c), the different criteria for determining the constituents of a structured set of personal data, and the different criteria governing access to such a set, may be laid down by each Member State; whereas files or sets of files as well as their cover pages, which are not structured according to specific criteria, shall under no circumstances fall within the scope of this Directive;

(28) Whereas any processing of personal data must be lawful and fair to the individuals concerned; whereas, in particular, the data must be adequate, relevant and not excessive in relation to the purposes for which they are processed; whereas such purposes must be explicit and legitimate and must be determined at the time of collection of the data; whereas the purposes of processing further to collection shall not be incompatible with the purposes as they were originally specified;

(29) Whereas the further processing of personal data for historical, statistical or scientific purposes is not generally to be considered incompatible with the purposes for which the data have previously been collected provided that Member States furnish suitable safeguards; whereas these safeguards must in particular rule out the use of the data in support of measures or decisions regarding any particular individual;

(30) Whereas, in order to be lawful, the processing of personal data must in addition be carried out with the consent of the data subject or be necessary for the conclusion or performance of a contract binding on the data subject, or as a legal requirement, or for the performance of a task carried out in the public interest or in the exercise of official authority, or in the legitimate interests of a natural or legal person, provided that the interests or the rights and freedoms of the data subject are not overriding; whereas, in particular, in order to maintain a balance between the interests involved while guaranteeing effective competition, Member States may determine the circumstances in which personal data may be used or disclosed to a third party in the context of the legitimate ordinary business activities of companies and other bodies; whereas Member States may similarly specify the conditions under which personal data may be disclosed to a third party for the purposes of marketing whether carried out commercially or by a charitable organization or by any other association or foundation, of a political nature for example, subject to the provisions allowing a data subject to object to the processing of data regarding him, at no cost and without having to state his reasons;

(31) Whereas the processing of personal data must equally be regarded as lawful where it is carried out in order to protect an interest which is essential for the data subject's life;

(32) Whereas it is for national legislation to determine whether the controller performing a task carried out in the public interest or in the exercise of official authority should be a public administration or another natural or legal person governed by public law, or by private law such as a professional association;

(33) Whereas data which are capable by their nature of infringing fundamental freedoms or privacy should not be processed unless the data subject gives his explicit consent; whereas, however, derogations from this prohibition must be explicitly provided for in respect of specific needs, in particular where the processing of these data is carried out for certain health-related purposes by persons subject to a legal obligation of professional secrecy or in the course of legitimate activities by certain associations or foundations the purpose of which is to permit the exercise of fundamental freedoms;

(34) Whereas Member States must also be authorized, when justified by grounds of important public interest, to derogate from the prohibition on processing sensitive categories of data where important reasons of public interest so justify in areas such as public health and social protection - especially in order to ensure the quality and cost-effectiveness of the procedures used for settling claims for benefits and services in the health insurance system - scientific research and government statistics; whereas it is incumbent on them, however, to provide specific

and suitable safeguards so as to protect the fundamental rights and the privacy of individuals;

(35) Whereas, moreover, the processing of personal data by official authorities for achieving aims, laid down in constitutional law or international public law, of officially recognized religious associations is carried out on important grounds of public interest;

(36) Whereas where, in the course of electoral activities, the operation of the democratic system requires in certain Member States that political parties compile data on people's political opinion, the processing of such data may be permitted for reasons of important public interest, provided that appropriate safeguards are established;

(37) Whereas the processing of personal data for purposes of journalism or for purposes of literary of artistic expression, in particular in the audiovisual field, should qualify for exemption from the requirements of certain provisions of this Directive in so far as this is necessary to reconcile the fundamental rights of individuals with freedom of information and notably the right to receive and impart information, as guaranteed in particular in Article 10 of the European Convention for the Protection of Human Rights and Fundamental Freedoms; whereas Member States should therefore lay down exemptions and derogations necessary for the purpose of balance between fundamental rights as regards general measures on the legitimacy of data processing, measures on the transfer of data to third countries and the power of the supervisory authority; whereas this should not, however, lead Member States to lay down exemptions from the measures to ensure security of processing; whereas at least the supervisory authority responsible for this sector should also be provided with certain ex-post powers, e.g. to publish a regular report or to refer matters to the judicial authorities;

(38) Whereas, if the processing of data is to be fair, the data subject must be in a position to learn of the existence of a processing operation and, where data are collected from him, must be given accurate and full information, bearing in mind the circumstances of the collection;

(39) Whereas certain processing operations involve data which the controller has not collected directly from the data subject; whereas, furthermore, data can be legitimately disclosed to a third party, even if the disclosure was not anticipated at the time the data were collected from the data subject; whereas, in all these cases, the data subject should be informed when the data are recorded or at the latest when the data are first disclosed to a third party;

(40) Whereas, however, it is not necessary to impose this obligation of the data subject already has the information; whereas, moreover, there will be no such obligation if the recording or disclosure are expressly provided for by law or if the provision of information to the data subject proves impossible or would involve disproportionate efforts, which could be the case where processing is for historical, statistical or scientific purposes; whereas, in this regard, the number of data subjects, the age of the data, and any compensatory measures adopted may be taken into consideration;

(41) Whereas any person must be able to exercise the right of access to data relating to him which are being processed, in order to verify in particular the

accuracy of the data and the lawfulness of the processing; whereas, for the same reasons, every data subject must also have the right to know the logic involved in the automatic processing of data concerning him, at least in the case of the automated decisions referred to in Article 15 (1); whereas this right must not adversely affect trade secrets or intellectual property and in particular the copyright protecting the software; whereas these considerations must not, however, result in the data subject being refused all information;

(42) Whereas Member States may, in the interest of the data subject or so as to protect the rights and freedoms of others, restrict rights of access and information; whereas they may, for example, specify that access to medical data may be obtained only through a health professional;

(43) Whereas restrictions on the rights of access and information and on certain obligations of the controller may similarly be imposed by Member States in so far as they are necessary to safeguard, for example, national security, defence, public safety, or important economic or financial interests of a Member State or the Union, as well as criminal investigations and prosecutions and action in respect of breaches of ethics in the regulated professions; whereas the list of exceptions and limitations should include the tasks of monitoring, inspection or regulation necessary in the three last-mentioned areas concerning public security, economic or financial interests and crime prevention; whereas the listing of tasks in these three areas does not affect the legitimacy of exceptions or restrictions for reasons of State security or defence;

(44) Whereas Member States may also be led, by virtue of the provisions of Community law, to derogate from the provisions of this Directive concerning the right of access, the obligation to inform individuals, and the quality of data, in order to secure certain of the purposes referred to above;

(45) Whereas, in cases where data might lawfully be processed on grounds of public interest, official authority or the legitimate interests of a natural or legal person, any data subject should nevertheless be entitled, on legitimate and compelling grounds relating to his particular situation, to object to the processing of any data relating to himself; whereas Member States may nevertheless lay down national provisions to the contrary;

(46) Whereas the protection of the rights and freedoms of data subjects with regard to the processing of personal data requires that appropriate technical and organizational measures be taken, both at the time of the design of the processing system and at the time of the processing itself, particularly in order to maintain security and thereby to prevent any unauthorized processing; whereas it is incumbent on the Member States to ensure that controllers comply with these measures; whereas these measures must ensure an appropriate level of security, taking into account the state of the art and the costs of their implementation in relation to the risks inherent in the processing and the nature of the data to be protected;

(47) Whereas where a message containing personal data is transmitted by means of a telecommunications or electronic mail service, the sole purpose of which is the transmission of such messages, the controller in respect of the personal

data contained in the message will normally be considered to be the person from whom the message originates, rather than the person offering the transmission services; whereas, nevertheless, those offering such services will normally be considered controllers in respect of the processing of the additional personal data necessary for the operation of the service;

(48) Whereas the procedures for notifying the supervisory authority are designed to ensure disclosure of the purposes and main features of any processing operation for the purpose of verification that the operation is in accordance with the national measures taken under this Directive;

(49) Whereas, in order to avoid unsuitable administrative formalities, exemptions from the obligation to notify and simplification of the notification required may be provided for by Member States in cases where processing is unlikely adversely to affect the rights and freedoms of data subjects, provided that it is in accordance with a measure taken by a Member State specifying its limits; whereas exemption or simplification may similarly be provided for by Member States where a person appointed by the controller ensures that the processing carried out is not likely adversely to affect the rights and freedoms of data subjects; whereas such a data protection official, whether or not an employee of the controller, must be in a position to exercise his functions in complete independence;

(50) Whereas exemption or simplification could be provided for in cases of processing operations whose sole purpose is the keeping of a register intended, according to national law, to provide information to the public and open to consultation by the public or by any person demonstrating a legitimate interest;

(51) Whereas, nevertheless, simplification or exemption from the obligation to notify shall not release the controller from any of the other obligations resulting from this Directive;

(52) Whereas, in this context, ex post facto verification by the competent authorities must in general be considered a sufficient measure;

(53) Whereas, however, certain processing operation are likely to pose specific risks to the rights and freedoms of data subjects by virtue of their nature, their scope or their purposes, such as that of excluding individuals from a right, benefit or a contract, or by virtue of the specific use of new technologies; whereas it is for Member States, if they so wish, to specify such risks in their legislation;

(54) Whereas with regard to all the processing undertaken in society, the amount posing such specific risks should be very limited; whereas Member States must provide that the supervisory authority, or the data protection official in cooperation with the authority, check such processing prior to it being carried out; whereas following this prior check, the supervisory authority may, according to its national law, give an opinion or an authorization regarding the processing; whereas such checking may equally take place in the course of the preparation either of a measure of the national parliament or of a measure based on such a legislative measure, which defines the nature of the processing and lays down appropriate safeguards;

(55) Whereas, if the controller fails to respect the rights of data subjects, national legislation must provide for a judicial remedy; whereas any damage which

a person may suffer as a result of unlawful processing must be compensated for by the controller, who may be exempted from liability if he proves that he is not responsible for the damage, in particular in cases where he establishes fault on the part of the data subject or in case of force majeure; whereas sanctions must be imposed on any person, whether governed by private of public law, who fails to comply with the national measures taken under this Directive;

(56) Whereas cross-border flows of personal data are necessary to the expansion of international trade; whereas the protection of individuals guaranteed in the Community by this Directive does not stand in the way of transfers of personal data to third countries which ensure an adequate level of protection; whereas the adequacy of the level of protection afforded by a third country must be assessed in the light of all the circumstances surrounding the transfer operation or set of transfer operations;

(57) Whereas, on the other hand, the transfer of personal data to a third country which does not ensure an adequate level of protection must be prohibited;

(58) Whereas provisions should be made for exemptions from this prohibition in certain circumstances where the data subject has given his consent, where the transfer is necessary in relation to a contract or a legal claim, where protection of an important public interest so requires, for example in cases of international transfers of data between tax or customs administrations or between services competent for social security matters, or where the transfer is made from a register established by law and intended for consultation by the public or persons having a legitimate interest; whereas in this case such a transfer should not involve the entirety of the data or entire categories of the data contained in the register and, when the register is intended for consultation by persons having a legitimate interest, the transfer should be made only at the request of those persons or if they are to be the recipients;

(59) Whereas particular measures may be taken to compensate for the lack of protection in a third country in cases where the controller offers appropriate safeguards; whereas, moreover, provision must be made for procedures for negotiations between the Community and such third countries;

(60) Whereas, in any event, transfers to third countries may be effected only in full compliance with the provisions adopted by the Member States pursuant to this Directive, and in particular Article 8 thereof;

(61) Whereas Member States and the Commission, in their respective spheres of competence, must encourage the trade associations and other representative organizations concerned to draw up codes of conduct so as to facilitate the application of this Directive, taking account of the specific characteristics of the processing carried out in certain sectors, and respecting the national provisions adopted for its implementation;

(62) Whereas the establishment in Member States of supervisory authorities, exercising their functions with complete independence, is an essential component of the protection of individuals with regard to the processing of personal data;

(63) Whereas such authorities must have the necessary means to perform their duties, including powers of investigation and intervention, particularly in cases of

complaints from individuals, and powers to engage in legal proceedings; whereas such authorities must help to ensure transparency of processing in the Member States within whose jurisdiction they fall;

(64) Whereas the authorities in the different Member States will need to assist one another in performing their duties so as to ensure that the rules of protection are properly respected throughout the European Union;

(65) Whereas, at Community level, a Working Party on the Protection of Individuals with regard to the Processing of Personal Data must be set up and be completely independent in the performance of its functions; whereas, having regard to its specific nature, it must advise the Commission and, in particular, contribute to the uniform application of the national rules adopted pursuant to this Directive;

(66) Whereas, with regard to the transfer of data to third countries, the application of this Directive calls for the conferment of powers of implementation on the Commission and the establishment of a procedure as laid down in Council Decision 87/373/EEC;[1]

(67) Whereas an agreement on a modus vivendi between the European Parliament, the Council and the Commission concerning the implementing measures for acts adopted in accordance with the procedure laid down in Article 189b of the EC Treaty was reached on 20 December 1994;

(68) Whereas the principles set out in this Directive regarding the protection of the rights and freedoms of individuals, notably their right to privacy, with regard to the processing of personal data may be supplemented or clarified, in particular as far as certain sectors are concerned, by specific rules based on those principles;

(69) Whereas Member States should be allowed a period of not more than three years from the entry into force of the national measures transposing this Directive in which to apply such new national rules progressively to all processing operations already under way; whereas, in order to facilitate their cost-effective implementation, a further period expiring 12 years after the date on which this Directive is adopted will be allowed to Member States to ensure the conformity of existing manual filing systems with certain of the Directive's provisions; whereas, where data contained in such filing systems are manually processed during this extended transition period, those systems must be brought into conformity with these provisions at the time of such processing;

(70) Whereas it is not necessary for the data subject to give his consent again so as to allow the controller to continue to process, after the national provisions taken pursuant to this Directive enter into force, any sensitive data necessary for the performance of a contract concluded on the basis of free and informed consent before the entry into force of these provisions;

(71) Whereas this Directive does not stand in the way of a Member State's regulating marketing activities aimed at consumers residing in territory in so far as such regulation does not concern the protection of individuals with regard to the processing of personal data;

---

1. OJ No L 197, 18. 7. 1987, p. 33.

(72) Whereas this Directive allows the principle of public access to official documents to be taken into account when implementing the principles set out in this Directive,

HAVE ADOPTED THIS DIRECTIVE:

CHAPTER I GENERAL PROVISIONS

Article 1

Object of the Directive

1. In accordance with this Directive, Member States shall protect the fundamental rights and freedoms of natural persons, and in particular their right to privacy with respect to the processing of personal data.

2. Member States shall neither restrict nor prohibit the free flow of personal data between Member States for reasons connected with the protection afforded under paragraph 1.

Article 2

Definitions

For the purposes of this Directive:

(a) 'personal data' shall mean any information relating to an identified or identifiable natural person ('data subject'); an identifiable person is one who can be identified, directly or indirectly, in particular by reference to an identification number or to one or more factors specific to his physical, physiological, mental, economic, cultural or social identity;

(b) 'processing of personal data' ('processing') shall mean any operation or set of operations which is performed upon personal data, whether or not by automatic means, such as collection, recording, organization, storage, adaptation or alteration, retrieval, consultation, use, disclosure by transmission, dissemination or otherwise making available, alignment or combination, blocking, erasure or destruction;

(c) 'personal data filing system' ('filing system') shall mean any structured set of personal data which are accessible according to specific criteria, whether centralized, decentralized or dispersed on a functional or geographical basis;

(d) 'controller' shall mean the natural or legal person, public authority, agency or any other body which alone or jointly with others determines the purposes and means of the processing of personal data; where the purposes and means of processing are determined by national or

Community laws or regulations, the controller or the specific criteria for his nomination may be designated by national or Community law;

(e) 'processor' shall mean a natural or legal person, public authority, agency or any other body which processes personal data on behalf of the controller;

(f) 'third party' shall mean any natural or legal person, public authority, agency or any other body other than the data subject, the controller, the processor and the persons who, under the direct authority of the controller or the processor, are authorized to process the data;

(g) 'recipient' shall mean a natural or legal person, public authority, agency or any other body to whom data are disclosed, whether a third party or not; however, authorities which may receive data in the framework of a particular inquiry shall not be regarded as recipients;

(h) 'the data subject's consent' shall mean any freely given specific and informed indication of his wishes by which the data subject signifies his agreement to personal data relating to him being processed.

Article 3

Scope

1. This Directive shall apply to the processing of personal data wholly or partly by automatic means, and to the processing otherwise than by automatic means of personal data which form part of a filing system or are intended to form part of a filing system.

2. This Directive shall not apply to the processing of personal data:

– in the course of an activity which falls outside the scope of Community law, such as those provided for by Titles V and VI of the Treaty on European Union and in any case to processing operations concerning public security, defence, State security (including the economic well-being of the State when the processing operation relates to State security matters) and the activities of the State in areas of criminal law,

– by a natural person in the course of a purely personal or household activity.

Article 4

National law applicable

1. Each Member State shall apply the national provisions it adopts pursuant to this Directive to the processing of personal data where:

(a) the processing is carried out in the context of the activities of an establishment of the controller on the territory of the Member State; when the same controller is established on the territory of several Member States, he must take the necessary measures to ensure that each of these establishments complies with the obligations laid down by the national law applicable;

(b) the controller is not established on the Member State's territory, but in a place where its national law applies by virtue of international public law;

(c) the controller is not established on Community territory and, for purposes of processing personal data makes use of equipment, automated or otherwise, situated on the territory of the said Member State, unless such equipment is used only for purposes of transit through the territory of the Community.

2. In the circumstances referred to in paragraph 1 (c), the controller must designate a representative established in the territory of that Member State, without prejudice to legal actions which could be initiated against the controller himself.

CHAPTER II GENERAL RULES ON THE LAWFULNESS OF THE PROCESSING OF PERSONAL DATA

Article 5

Member States shall, within the limits of the provisions of this Chapter, determine more precisely the conditions under which the processing of personal data is lawful.

SECTION I

PRINCIPLES RELATING TO DATA QUALITY

Article 6

1. Member States shall provide that personal data must be:

(a) processed fairly and lawfully;

(b) collected for specified, explicit and legitimate purposes and not further processed in a way incompatible with those purposes. Further processing of data for historical, statistical or scientific purposes shall not be considered as incompatible provided that Member States provide appropriate safeguards;

(c) adequate, relevant and not excessive in relation to the purposes for which they are collected and/or further processed;

(d) accurate and, where necessary, kept up to date; every reasonable step must be taken to ensure that data which are inaccurate or incomplete, having regard to the purposes for which they were collected or for which they are further processed, are erased or rectified;

(e) kept in a form which permits identification of data subjects for no longer than is necessary for the purposes for which the data were collected or for which they are further processed. Member States shall lay down appropriate safeguards for personal data stored for longer periods for historical, statistical or scientific use.

2. It shall be for the controller to ensure that paragraph 1 is complied with.

SECTION II

CRITERIA FOR MAKING DATA PROCESSING LEGITIMATE

Article 7

Member States shall provide that personal data may be processed only if:

- (a) the data subject has unambiguously given his consent; or
- (b) processing is necessary for the performance of a contract to which the data subject is party or in order to take steps at the request of the data subject prior to entering into a contract; or
- (c) processing is necessary for compliance with a legal obligation to which the controller is subject; or
- (d) processing is necessary in order to protect the vital interests of the data subject; or
- (e) processing is necessary for the performance of a task carried out in the public interest or in the exercise of official authority vested in the controller or in a third party to whom the data are disclosed; or
- (f) processing is necessary for the purposes of the legitimate interests pursued by the controller or by the third party or parties to whom the data are disclosed, except where such interests are overridden by the interests for fundamental rights and freedoms of the data subject which require protection under Article 1 (1).

SECTION III

SPECIAL CATEGORIES OF PROCESSING

Article 8

The processing of special categories of data

1. Member States shall prohibit the processing of personal data revealing racial or ethnic origin, political opinions, religious or philosophical beliefs, trade-union membership, and the processing of data concerning health or sex life.

2. Paragraph 1 shall not apply where:

- (a) the data subject has given his explicit consent to the processing of those data, except where the laws of the Member State provide that the

> prohibition referred to in paragraph 1 may not be lifted by the data sub-ject's giving his consent; or
>
> (b) processing is necessary for the purposes of carrying out the obligations and specific rights of the controller in the field of employment law in so far as it is authorized by national law providing for adequate safeguards; or
>
> (c) processing is necessary to protect the vital interests of the data subject or of another person where the data subject is physically or legally incapable of giving his consent; or
>
> (d) processing is carried out in the course of its legitimate activities with appropriate guarantees by a foundation, association or any other non-profit-seeking body with a political, philosophical, religious or trade-union aim and on condition that the processing relates solely to the members of the body or to persons who have regular contact with it in connection with its purposes and that the data are not disclosed to a third party without the consent of the data subjects; or
>
> (e) the processing relates to data which are manifestly made public by the data subject or is necessary for the establishment, exercise or defence of legal claims.

3. Paragraph 1 shall not apply where processing of the data is required for the purposes of preventive medicine, medical diagnosis, the provision of care or treat-ment or the management of health-care services, and where those data are pro-cessed by a health professional subject under national law or rules established by national competent bodies to the obligation of professional secrecy or by another person also subject to an equivalent obligation of secrecy.

4. Subject to the provision of suitable safeguards, Member States may, for reasons of substantial public interest, lay down exemptions in addition to those laid down in paragraph 2 either by national law or by decision of the supervisory authority.

5. Processing of data relating to offences, criminal convictions or security mea-sures may be carried out only under the control of official authority, or if suitable specific safeguards are provided under national law, subject to derogations which may be granted by the Member State under national provisions providing suitable specific safeguards. However, a complete register of criminal convictions may be kept only under the control of official authority.

> Member States may provide that data relating to administrative sanctions or judgements in civil cases shall also be processed under the control of official authority.

6. Derogations from paragraph 1 provided for in paragraphs 4 and 5 shall be notified to the Commission.

7. Member States shall determine the conditions under which a national identification number or any other identifier of general application may be processed.

Article 9

Processing of personal data and freedom of expression
Member States shall provide for exemptions or derogations from the provisions of this Chapter, Chapter IV and Chapter VI for the processing of personal data carried out solely for journalistic purposes or the purpose of artistic or literary expression only if they are necessary to reconcile the right to privacy with the rules governing freedom of expression.

SECTION IV

INFORMATION TO BE GIVEN TO THE DATA SUBJECT

Article 10

Information in cases of collection of data from the data subject

Member States shall provide that the controller or his representative must provide a data subject from whom data relating to himself are collected with at least the following information, except where he already has it:

- (a) the identity of the controller and of his representative, if any;
- (b) the purposes of the processing for which the data are intended;
- (c) any further information such as
  - the recipients or categories of recipients of the data,
  - whether replies to the questions are obligatory or voluntary, as well as the possible consequences of failure to reply,
  - the existence of the right of access to and the right to rectify the data concerning him

in so far as such further information is necessary, having regard to the specific circumstances in which the data are collected, to guarantee fair processing in respect of the data subject.

Article 11

Information where the data have not been obtained from the data subject

1. Where the data have not been obtained from the data subject, Member States shall provide that the controller or his representative must at the time of undertaking the recording of personal data or if a disclosure to a third party is envisaged, no later than the time when the data are first disclosed provide the data subject with at least the following information, except where he already has it:

- (a) the identity of the controller and of his representative, if any;
- (b) the purposes of the processing;

    (c) any further information such as
- the categories of data concerned,
- the recipients or categories of recipients,
- the existence of the right of access to and the right to rectify the data concerning him

in so far as such further information is necessary, having regard to the specific circumstances in which the data are processed, to guarantee fair processing in respect of the data subject.

2. Paragraph 1 shall not apply where, in particular for processing for statistical purposes or for the purposes of historical or scientific research, the provision of such information proves impossible or would involve a disproportionate effort or if recording or disclosure is expressly laid down by law. In these cases Member States shall provide appropriate safeguards.

SECTION V

THE DATA SUBJECT'S RIGHT OF ACCESS TO DATA

Article 12

Right of access

Member States shall guarantee every data subject the right to obtain from the controller:

    (a) without constraint at reasonable intervals and without excessive delay or expense:
- confirmation as to whether or not data relating to him are being processed and information at least as to the purposes of the processing, the categories of data concerned, and the recipients or categories of recipients to whom the data are disclosed,
- communication to him in an intelligible form of the data undergoing processing and of any available information as to their source,
- knowledge of the logic involved in any automatic processing of data concerning him at least in the case of the automated decisions referred to in Article 15 (1);

    (b) as appropriate the rectification, erasure or blocking of data the processing of which does not comply with the provisions of this Directive, in particular because of the incomplete or inaccurate nature of the data;

    (c) notification to third parties to whom the data have been disclosed of any rectification, erasure or blocking carried out in compliance with (b), unless this proves impossible or involves a disproportionate effort.

SECTION VI

EXEMPTIONS AND RESTRICTIONS

Article 13

Exemptions and restrictions

1. Member States may adopt legislative measures to restrict the scope of the obligations and rights provided for in Articles 6 (1), 10, 11 (1), 12 and 21 when such a restriction constitutes a necessary measures to safeguard:

  (a) national security;
  (b) defence;
  (c) public security;
  (d) the prevention, investigation, detection and prosecution of criminal offences, or of breaches of ethics for regulated professions;
  (e) an important economic or financial interest of a Member State or of the European Union, including monetary, budgetary and taxation matters;
  (f) a monitoring, inspection or regulatory function connected, even occasionally, with the exercise of official authority in cases referred to in (c), (d) and (e);
  (g) the protection of the data subject or of the rights and freedoms of others.

2. Subject to adequate legal safeguards, in particular that the data are not used for taking measures or decisions regarding any particular individual, Member States may, where there is clearly no risk of breaching the privacy of the data subject, restrict by a legislative measure the rights provided for in Article 12 when data are processed solely for purposes of scientific research or are kept in personal form for a period which does not exceed the period necessary for the sole purpose of creating statistics.

SECTION VII

THE DATA SUBJECT'S RIGHT TO OBJECT

Article 14

The data subject's right to object

Member States shall grant the data subject the right:

  (a) at least in the cases referred to in Article 7 (e) and (f), to object at any time on compelling legitimate grounds relating to his particular situation to the processing of data relating to him, save where otherwise provided by national legislation. Where there is a justified objection, the processing instigated by the controller may no longer involve those data;

(b) to object, on request and free of charge, to the processing of personal data relating to him which the controller anticipates being processed for the purposes of direct marketing, or to be informed before personal data are disclosed for the first time to third parties or used on their behalf for the purposes of direct marketing, and to be expressly offered the right to object free of charge to such disclosures or uses.

Member States shall take the necessary measures to ensure that data subjects are aware of the existence of the right referred to in the first subparagraph of (b).

Article 15

Automated individual decisions

1. Member States shall grant the right to every person not to be subject to a decision which produces legal effects concerning him or significantly affects him and which is based solely on automated processing of data intended to evaluate certain personal aspects relating to him, such as his performance at work, creditworthiness, reliability, conduct, etc.

2. Subject to the other Articles of this Directive, Member States shall provide that a person may be subjected to a decision of the kind referred to in paragraph 1 if that decision:

(a) is taken in the course of the entering into or performance of a contract, provided the request for the entering into or the performance of the con- tract, lodged by the data subject, has been satisfied or that there are suit- able measures to safeguard his legitimate interests, such as arrangements allowing him to put his point of view; or

(b) is authorized by a law which also lays down measures to safeguard the data subject's legitimate interests.

SECTION VIII

CONFIDENTIALITY AND SECURITY OF PROCESSING

Article 16

Confidentiality of processing

Any person acting under the authority of the controller or of the processor, includ- ing the processor himself, who has access to personal data must not process them except on instructions from the controller, unless he is required to do so by law.

Article 17

Security of processing

1. Member States shall provide that the controller must implement appropriate technical and organizational measures to protect personal data against accidental or unlawful destruction or accidental loss, alteration, unauthorized disclosure or access, in particular where the processing involves the transmission of data over a network, and against all other unlawful forms of processing.

Having regard to the state of the art and the cost of their implementation, such measures shall ensure a level of security appropriate to the risks represented by the processing and the nature of the data to be protected.

2. The Member States shall provide that the controller must, where processing is carried out on his behalf, choose a processor providing sufficient guarantees in respect of the technical security measures and organizational measures governing the processing to be carried out, and must ensure compliance with those measures.

3. The carrying out of processing by way of a processor must be governed by a contract or legal act binding the processor to the controller and stipulating in particular that:

- the processor shall act only on instructions from the controller,
- the obligations set out in paragraph 1, as defined by the law of the Member State in which the processor is established, shall also be incumbent on the processor.

4. For the purposes of keeping proof, the parts of the contract or the legal act relating to data protection and the requirements relating to the measures referred to in paragraph 1 shall be in writing or in another equivalent form.

SECTION IX

NOTIFICATION

Article 18

Obligation to notify the supervisory authority

1. Member States shall provide that the controller or his representative, if any, must notify the supervisory authority referred to in Article 28 before carrying out any wholly or partly automatic processing operation or set of such operations intended to serve a single purpose or several related purposes.

Annex 1

2. Member States may provide for the simplification of or exemption from notification only in the following cases and under the following conditions:

FROM
OTIFICATION

- where, for categories of processing operations which are unlikely, taking account of the data to be processed, to affect adversely the rights and freedoms of data subjects, they specify the purposes of the processing, the data or categories of data undergoing processing, the category or categories of data subject, the recipients or categories of recipient to whom the data are to be disclosed and the length of time the data are to be stored, and/or
- where the controller, in compliance with the national law which governs him, appoints a personal data protection official, responsible in particular:
- for ensuring in an independent manner the internal application of the national provisions taken pursuant to this Directive
- for keeping the register of processing operations carried out by the controller, containing the items of information referred to in Article 21 (2),

thereby ensuring that the rights and freedoms of the data subjects are unlikely to be adversely affected by the processing operations.

3. Member States may provide that paragraph 1 does not apply to processing whose sole purpose is the keeping of a register which according to laws or regulations is intended to provide information to the public and which is open to consultation either by the public in general or by any person demonstrating a legitimate interest.

4. Member States may provide for an exemption from the obligation to notify or a simplification of the notification in the case of processing operations referred to in Article 8 (2) (d).

5. Member States may stipulate that certain or all non-automatic processing operations involving personal data shall be notified, or provide for these processing operations to be subject to simplified notification.

Article 19

Contents of notification

1. Member States shall specify the information to be given in the notification. It shall include at least:

   (a) the name and address of the controller and of his representative, if any;
   (b) the purpose or purposes of the processing;
   (c) a description of the category or categories of data subject and of the data or categories of data relating to them;
   (d) the recipients or categories of recipient to whom the data might be disclosed;
   (e) proposed transfers of data to third countries;

382

(f) a general description allowing a preliminary assessment to be made of the appropriateness of the measures taken pursuant to Article 17 to ensure security of processing.

2. Member States shall specify the procedures under which any change affecting the information referred to in paragraph 1 must be notified to the supervisory authority.

Article 20

Prior checking

1. Member States shall determine the processing operations likely to present specific risks to the rights and freedoms of data subjects and shall check that these processing operations are examined prior to the start thereof.

2. Such prior checks shall be carried out by the supervisory authority following receipt of a notification from the controller or by the data protection official, who, in cases of doubt, must consult the supervisory authority.

3. Member States may also carry out such checks in the context of preparation either of a measure of the national parliament or of a measure based on such a legislative measure, which define the nature of the processing and lay down appropriate safeguards.

Article 21

Publicizing of processing operations

1. Member States shall take measures to ensure that processing operations are publicized.

2. Member States shall provide that a register of processing operations notified in accordance with Article 18 shall be kept by the supervisory authority.

The register shall contain at least the information listed in Article 19 (1) (a) to (e).

The register may be inspected by any person.

3. Member States shall provide, in relation to processing operations not subject to notification, that controllers or another body appointed by the Member States make available at least the information referred to in Article 19 (1) (a) to (e) in an appropriate form to any person on request.

Member States may provide that this provision does not apply to processing whose sole purpose is the keeping of a register which according to laws or regulations is intended to provide information to the public and which is open to consultation either by the public in general or by any person who can provide proof of a legitimate interest.

CHAPTER III JUDICIAL REMEDIES, LIABILITY AND SANCTIONS

Article 22

Remedies

Without prejudice to any administrative remedy for which provision may be made, inter alia before the supervisory authority referred to in Article 28, prior to referral to the judicial authority, Member States shall provide for the right of every person to a judicial remedy for any breach of the rights guaranteed him by the national law applicable to the processing in question.

Article 23

Liability

1. Member States shall provide that any person who has suffered damage as a result of an unlawful processing operation or of any act incompatible with the national provisions adopted pursuant to this Directive is entitled to receive compensation from the controller for the damage suffered.

2. The controller may be exempted from this liability, in whole or in part, if he proves that he is not responsible for the event giving rise to the damage.

Article 24

Sanctions

The Member States shall adopt suitable measures to ensure the full implementation of the provisions of this Directive and shall in particular lay down the sanctions to be imposed in case of infringement of the provisions adopted pursuant to this Directive.

CHAPTER IV TRANSFER OF PERSONAL DATA TO THIRD COUNTRIES

Article 25

Principles

1. The Member States shall provide that the transfer to a third country of personal data which are undergoing processing or are intended for processing after transfer may take place only if, without prejudice to compliance with the national provisions adopted pursuant to the other provisions of this Directive, the third country in question ensures an adequate level of protection.

2. The adequacy of the level of protection afforded by a third country shall be assessed in the light of all the circumstances surrounding a data transfer operation or set of data transfer operations; particular consideration shall be given to the nature of the data, the purpose and duration of the proposed processing operation or operations, the country of origin and country of final destination, the rules of law, both general and sectoral, in force in the third country in question and the professional rules and security measures which are complied with in that country.

3. The Member States and the Commission shall inform each other of cases where they consider that a third country does not ensure an adequate level of protection within the meaning of paragraph 2.

4. Where the Commission finds, under the procedure provided for in Article 31 (2), that a third country does not ensure an adequate level of protection within the meaning of paragraph 2 of this Article, Member States shall take the measures necessary to prevent any transfer of data of the same type to the third country in question.

5. At the appropriate time, the Commission shall enter into negotiations with a view to remedying the situation resulting from the finding made pursuant to paragraph 4.

6. The Commission may find, in accordance with the procedure referred to in Article 31 (2), that a third country ensures an adequate level of protection within the meaning of paragraph 2 of this Article, by reason of its domestic law or of the international commitments it has entered into, particularly upon conclusion of the negotiations referred to in paragraph 5, for the protection of the private lives and basic freedoms and rights of individuals.

Member States shall take the measures necessary to comply with the Commission's decision.

Article 26

Derogations

1. By way of derogation from Article 25 and save where otherwise provided by domestic law governing particular cases, Member States shall provide that a transfer or a set of transfers of personal data to a third country which does not ensure an adequate level of protection within the meaning of Article 25 (2) may take place on condition that:

   (a) the data subject has given his consent unambiguously to the proposed transfer; or
   (b) the transfer is necessary for the performance of a contract between the data subject and the controller or the implementation of precontractual measures taken in response to the data subject's request; or

(c) the transfer is necessary for the conclusion or performance of a contract concluded in the interest of the data subject between the controller and a third party; or

(d) the transfer is necessary or legally required on important public interest grounds, or for the establishment, exercise or defence of legal claims; or

(e) the transfer is necessary in order to protect the vital interests of the data subject; or

(f) the transfer is made from a register which according to laws or regulations is intended to provide information to the public and which is open to consultation either by the public in general or by any person who can demonstrate legitimate interest, to the extent that the conditions laid down in law for consultation are fulfilled in the particular case.

2. Without prejudice to paragraph 1, a Member State may authorize a transfer or a set of transfers of personal data to a third country which does not ensure an adequate level of protection within the meaning of Article 25 (2), where the controller adduces adequate safeguards with respect to the protection of the privacy and fundamental rights and freedoms of individuals and as regards the exercise of the corresponding rights; such safeguards may in particular result from appropriate contractual clauses.

3. The Member State shall inform the Commission and the other Member States of the authorizations it grants pursuant to paragraph 2.

If a Member State or the Commission objects on justified grounds involving the protection of the privacy and fundamental rights and freedoms of individuals, the Commission shall take appropriate measures in accordance with the procedure laid down in Article 31 (2).

Member States shall take the necessary measures to comply with the Commission's decision.

4. Where the Commission decides, in accordance with the procedure referred to in Article 31 (2), that certain standard contractual clauses offer sufficient safeguards as required by paragraph 2, Member States shall take the necessary measures to comply with the Commission's decision.

CHAPTER V CODES OF CONDUCT

Article 27

1. The Member States and the Commission shall encourage the drawing up of codes of conduct intended to contribute to the proper implementation of the national provisions adopted by the Member States pursuant to this Directive, taking account of the specific features of the various sectors.

2. Member States shall make provision for trade associations and other bodies representing other categories of controllers which have drawn up draft national

codes or which have the intention of amending or extending existing national codes to be able to submit them to the opinion of the national authority.

Member States shall make provision for this authority to ascertain, among other things, whether the drafts submitted to it are in accordance with the national provisions adopted pursuant to this Directive. If it sees fit, the authority shall seek the views of data subjects or their representatives.

3. Draft Community codes, and amendments or extensions to existing Community codes, may be submitted to the Working Party referred to in Article 29. This Working Party shall determine, among other things, whether the drafts submitted to it are in accordance with the national provisions adopted pursuant to this Directive. If it sees fit, the authority shall seek the views of data subjects or their representatives. The Commission may ensure appropriate publicity for the codes which have been approved by the Working Party.

CHAPTER VI SUPERVISORY AUTHORITY AND WORKING PARTY ON THE PROTECTION OF INDIVIDUALS WITH REGARD TO THE PROCESSING OF PERSONAL DATA

Article 28

Supervisory authority

1. Each Member State shall provide that one or more public authorities are responsible for monitoring the application within its territory of the provisions adopted by the Member States pursuant to this Directive.

These authorities shall act with complete independence in exercising the functions entrusted to them.

2. Each Member State shall provide that the supervisory authorities are consulted when drawing up administrative measures or regulations relating to the protection of individuals' rights and freedoms with regard to the processing of personal data.

3. Each authority shall in particular be endowed with:
- investigative powers, such as powers of access to data forming the subject-matter of processing operations and powers to collect all the information necessary for the performance of its supervisory duties,
- effective powers of intervention, such as, for example, that of delivering opinions before processing operations are carried out, in accordance with Article 20, and ensuring appropriate publication of such opinions, of ordering the blocking, erasure or destruction of data, of imposing a temporary or definitive ban on processing, of warning or admonishing the controller, or that of referring the matter to national parliaments or other political institutions,
- the power to engage in legal proceedings where the national provisions adopted pursuant to this Directive have been violated or to bring these violations to the attention of the judicial authorities.

Decisions by the supervisory authority which give rise to complaints may be appealed against through the courts.

4. Each supervisory authority shall hear claims lodged by any person, or by an association representing that person, concerning the protection of his rights and freedoms in regard to the processing of personal data. The person concerned shall be informed of the outcome of the claim.

Each supervisory authority shall, in particular, hear claims for checks on the lawfulness of data processing lodged by any person when the national provisions adopted pursuant to Article 13 of this Directive apply. The person shall at any rate be informed that a check has taken place.

5. Each supervisory authority shall draw up a report on its activities at regular intervals. The report shall be made public.

6. Each supervisory authority is competent, whatever the national law applicable to the processing in question, to exercise, on the territory of its own Member State, the powers conferred on it in accordance with paragraph 3. Each authority may be requested to exercise its powers by an authority of another Member State.

The supervisory authorities shall cooperate with one another to the extent necessary for the performance of their duties, in particular by exchanging all useful information.

7. Member States shall provide that the members and staff of the supervisory authority, even after their employment has ended, are to be subject to a duty of professional secrecy with regard to confidential information to which they have access.

Article 29

Working Party on the Protection of Individuals with regard to the Processing of Personal Data

1. A Working Party on the Protection of Individuals with regard to the Processing of Personal Data, hereinafter referred to as 'the Working Party', is hereby set up.
It shall have advisory status and act independently.

2. The Working Party shall be composed of a representative of the supervisory authority or authorities designated by each Member State and of a representative of the authority or authorities established for the Community institutions and bodies, and of a representative of the Commission.
Each member of the Working Party shall be designated by the institution, authority or authorities which he represents. Where a Member State has designated more than one supervisory authority, they shall nominate a joint representative. The same shall apply to the authorities established for Community institutions and bodies.

3. The Working Party shall take decisions by a simple majority of the representatives of the supervisory authorities.

4. The Working Party shall elect its chairman. The chairman's term of office shall be two years. His appointment shall be renewable.

5. The Working Party's secretariat shall be provided by the Commission.

6. The Working Party shall adopt its own rules of procedure.

7. The Working Party shall consider items placed on its agenda by its chairman, either on his own initiative or at the request of a representative of the supervisory authorities or at the Commission's request.

Article 30

1. The Working Party shall:

    (a) examine any question covering the application of the national measures adopted under this Directive in order to contribute to the uniform application of such measures;

    (b) give the Commission an opinion on the level of protection in the Community and in third countries;

    (c) advise the Commission on any proposed amendment of this Directive, on any additional or specific measures to safeguard the rights and freedoms of natural persons with regard to the processing of personal data and on any other proposed Community measures affecting such rights and freedoms;

    (d) give an opinion on codes of conduct drawn up at Community level.

2. If the Working Party finds that divergences likely to affect the equivalence of protection for persons with regard to the processing of personal data in the Community are arising between the laws or practices of Member States, it shall inform the Commission accordingly.

3. The Working Party may, on its own initiative, make recommendations on all matters relating to the protection of persons with regard to the processing of personal data in the Community.

4. The Working Party's opinions and recommendations shall be forwarded to the Commission and to the committee referred to in Article 31.

5. The Commission shall inform the Working Party of the action it has taken in response to its opinions and recommendations. It shall do so in a report which shall also be forwarded to the European Parliament and the Council. The report shall be made public.

6. The Working Party shall draw up an annual report on the situation regarding the protection of natural persons with regard to the processing of personal data in the Community and in third countries, which it shall transmit to the Commission, the European Parliament and the Council. The report shall be made public.

CHAPTER VII COMMUNITY IMPLEMENTING MEASURES

Article 31

The Committee

1. The Commission shall be assisted by a committee composed of the representatives of the Member States and chaired by the representative of the Commission.

2. The representative of the Commission shall submit to the committee a draft of the measures to be taken. The committee shall deliver its opinion on the draft within a time limit which the chairman may lay down according to the urgency of the matter.

The opinion shall be delivered by the majority laid down in Article 148 (2) of the Treaty. The votes of the representatives of the Member States within the committee shall be weighted in the manner set out in that Article. The chairman shall not vote.

The Commission shall adopt measures which shall apply immediately. However, if these measures are not in accordance with the opinion of the committee, they shall be communicated by the Commission to the Council forthwith. It that event:

- the Commission shall defer application of the measures which it has decided for a period of three months from the date of communication,
- the Council, acting by a qualified majority, may take a different decision within the time limit referred to in the first indent.

FINAL PROVISIONS

Article 32

1. Member States shall bring into force the laws, regulations and administrative provisions necessary to comply with this Directive at the latest at the end of a period of three years from the date of its adoption.

When Member States adopt these measures, they shall contain a reference to this Directive or be accompanied by such reference on the occasion of their official publication. The methods of making such reference shall be laid down by the Member States.

2. Member States shall ensure that processing already under way on the date the national provisions adopted pursuant to this Directive enter into force, is brought into conformity with these provisions within three years of this date.

By way of derogation from the preceding subparagraph, Member States may provide that the processing of data already held in manual filing systems on the date of entry into force of the national provisions adopted in implementation of this Directive shall be brought into conformity with Articles 6, 7 and 8 of this Directive within 12 years of the date on which it is adopted. Member States shall, however, grant the data subject the right to obtain, at his request and in particular at the time of exercising his right of access, the rectification, erasure or blocking of data which are incomplete, inaccurate or stored in a way incompatible with the legitimate purposes pursued by the controller.

3. By way of derogation from paragraph 2, Member States may provide, subject to suitable safeguards, that data kept for the sole purpose of historical research need not be brought into conformity with Articles 6, 7 and 8 of this Directive.

4. Member States shall communicate to the Commission the text of the provisions of domestic law which they adopt in the field covered by this Directive.

Article 33
The Commission shall report to the Council and the European Parliament at regular intervals, starting not later than three years after the date referred to in Article 32 (1), on the implementation of this Directive, attaching to its report, if necessary, suitable proposals for amendments. The report shall be made public.

The Commission shall examine, in particular, the application of this Directive to the data processing of sound and image data relating to natural persons and shall submit any appropriate proposals which prove to be necessary, taking account of developments in information technology and in the light of the state of progress in the information society.

Article 34

This Directive is addressed to the Member States.
Done at Luxembourg, 24 October 1995.

For the European Parliament
The President
K. HAENSCH

For the Council
The President
L. ATIENZA SERNA

Annex 2

Article 29 Data Protection Working Party

00339/09/EN
WP 158

Working Document 1/2009 on pre-trial discovery for cross border civil litigation*

Adopted on 11 February 2009

This Working Party was set up under Article 29 of Directive 95/46/EC. It is an independent European advisory body on data protection and privacy. Its tasks are described in Article 30 of Directive 95/46/EC and Article 15 of Directive 2002/58/EC.

The secretariat is provided by Directorate C (Civil Justice, Rights and Citizenship) of the European Commission, Directorate General Justice, Freedom and Security, B-1049 Brussels, Belgium, Office No LX-46 01/06.

Website: http://ec.europa.eu/justice_home/fsj/privacy/index_en.htm

Executive Summary

This working document provides guidance to data controllers subject to EU Law in dealing with requests to transfer personal data to another jurisdiction for use in civil litigation. The Working Party has issued this document to address its concern that

---

*   © European Union, 1995–2010. Source: http://ec.europa.eu/justice_home/fsj/privacy/docs/wpdocs/2009/wp158_en.pdf.

there are different applications of Directive 95/46 in part as a result of the variety of approaches to civil litigation across the Member States.

In the first section of this document the Working Party briefly sets out the differences in attitudes to litigation and in particular the pre-trial discovery process between common law jurisdictions such as the United States and the United Kingdom and civil code jurisdictions.

The document goes on to set out guidelines for EU data controllers when trying to reconcile the demands of the litigation process in a foreign jurisdiction with the data protection obligations of Directive 95/46.

Introduction

The issue of transborder discovery, particularly in relation to data held in Europe but required in relation to legal proceedings, for example, in the United States is one which has come to the fore recently. Often companies with a US settlement or subsidiary are under significant pressure to produce documents and materials (including items stored electronically) in relation to litigation and law enforcement investigations brought in the US. The material that is required will frequently contain personal data relating to employees or third parties, including clients or customers.

There is a tension between the disclosure obligations under US litigation or regulatory rules and the application of the data protection requirements of the EU. There is also the issue of the contrast between the geographical and territorial basis of the EU data protection regime and the multinational nature of business where a corporate body can have subsidiaries or affiliates across the globe. This is of particular relevance to the European affiliates of multinational companies which can be caught between the conflicting demands of US legal proceedings and EU data protection and privacy laws which govern the transfer of personal information.

The Working Party recognises that the parties involved in litigation have a legitimate interest in accessing information that is necessary to make or defend a claim, but this must be balanced with the rights of the individual whose personal data is being sought.

Although this paper sets out guidelines it is to be noted that resolving the issues of pre- trial discovery is beyond the scope of an Opinion by the Working Party and that these matters can only be resolved on a governmental basis, perhaps with the introduction of further global agreements along the lines of the Hague Convention.

1. Concept of Pre-Trial Discovery

There are various aspects of US litigation law and procedure where data held by European firms may be affected. Some of the most common include:

- Pre-emptive document preservation in anticipation of proceedings before US courts or in response to requests for litigation hold, known as 'freezing'.
- Pre-trial discovery requests in US civil litigation;

- Document production in US criminal and regulatory investigations;
- Criminal offences in the US relating to data destruction.

This paper will only deal with the first two issues and recognises that these have implications for the litigation process and the question of transfers of personal data to a third country. Pretrial discovery can include not just discovery within the context of legal proceedings but also the preservation of data in relation to prospective legal proceedings.

The aim of the discovery process is to ensure that the parties to litigation have access to such information as is necessary and relevant to their case given the rules and procedures of the jurisdiction in which the litigation is taking place. Within common law countries for example, the disclosure requirements are not limited to personal data or only electronic documents. Information sought may include special sensitive personal data e.g. health data as well as personal emails (the provision of which may conflict with duties under telecoms or secrecy regulations) and the data of third parties, for example, employees or customers.

Although the civil litigation rules in the UK refer to the term 'document', this does include electronic documents including email and other electronic communications, word processed documents and databases, in addition to documents that are readily accessible from computer systems and other electronic devices. It also includes documents stored on servers and back-up systems and electronic documents that have been 'deleted'. It extends to metadata i.e. any additional information stored and associated with electronic documents.

The increasing use of electronic records when previously reliance would have been only on hard copy documents has meant that more information than ever before is available. The ease with which electronic records can be downloaded, transferred or otherwise manipulated has meant that the discovery process in litigation often gives rise to a vast amount of information which the parties need to manage to determine which parts are relevant to the particular case in hand. In contrast with stored paper records, the volume of electronically stored information is vastly greater and the storage capacity of the various memory products now means that more information is obtainable and discloseable with greater ease.[1]

Differences between Common Law and Civil Code jurisdictions

The first issue that arises is the difference in civil code and common law jurisdictions, not just in relation to litigation generally, but, in particular, in relation to pretrial discovery. The scope of discovery differs greatly between common law and civil code jurisdictions and is seen as a fundamental part of the litigation process in the former. The ability to obtain and, indeed, the obligation to provide information

---

1. According to figures from the Advisory Committee on Civil Rules in the US, 92% of all information generated today is in digital form and approximately 70% of those records are never reduced to hard copy. As a result almost all litigation discovery now is e-discovery and the US has taken steps to introduce rules to deal with this area.

in the course of litigation is part of the process in common law jurisdictions. This is based on the belief that the most efficient method for identifying the issues in dispute is the extensive exchange of information prior to the matter being heard by the court. This is particularly the case in the United States where the scope of pre-trial discovery is the widest of any common law country.

Common Law – United States

In the US, once litigation has been commenced, companies must comply with the obligations imposed by US litigation procedure, not just under Federal but also under the State rules of civil procedure which encourage parties to exchange materials prior to trial.[2] This includes not just the discovery of relevant information but also of information that itself may not be of direct relevance but could lead to the discovery of relevant information (the so-called 'smoking gun'). This is in contrast to the situation that exists in many European civil code jurisdictions where 'fishing expeditions' are forbidden.

Rule 26f of the US Federal Rules of Civil Procedure requires that the parties 'meet and confer' to allow both parties the opportunity early in the process to discuss and reach agreement on the issues surrounding discovery. One aim of this meeting is to plan for the preservation of the evidence including data and documents necessary for the litigation.

However, US courts too can restrict via stipulative protective order voluntarily or if one party requests it, the scope of excessively broad pre-trial discovery requests as they have the power under the Rules to limit the frequency or extent of use of discovery methods for various reasons including obtaining the information from a more convenient source, or where the burden or expense of the proposed discovery outweighs its likely benefit. The courts may also make via this Protective Order to protect a person or party from annoyance, embarrassment, oppression or undue burden or expense by, for example, ordering that disclosure or discovery may be had only on specified terms and conditions, including the method or the matters to be considered. It is likely therefore that a judge in a US court will grant a request for discovery as long as that request is reasonably aimed at the discovery of admissible evidence and does not contain impracticable demands.

United Kingdom

A similar but more limited approach is taken in the United Kingdom where, under Rule 31 of the Civil Procedure Rules, a party must disclose documents upon which it intends to rely and any other document which adversely affects its own case or

---

2. For example, Rule 34(b) of the Federal Rules of Civil Procedure provides that

   'Any party may serve on any other party a request to produce and permit the party making the request or someone acting on the requestor's behalf to inspect, copy, test, or sample any designated documents or electronically stored information – including writings, drawings, graphs, charts, photographs, sound recordings, images and other data or data compilations stored in any medium from which the information can be obtained . . . and which are in the possession, custody or control of the party upon which the request is served.'

which affects or supports any other parties' case or which is required to be disclosed by a relevant court practice direction. Unlike the US, the UK (like another common law jurisdiction, Canada) have data protection obligations.

Civil Code countries

By way of contrast with the transparency required discovery process in the US and other common law countries, most civil code jurisdictions have a more restrictive approach and often have no formal discovery process. Many such jurisdictions limit disclosure of evidence to what is needed for the scope of the trial and prohibit disclosure beyond this. It is for the party to the litigation to offer evidence in support of its case. Should the other side require that information, the burden is upon them to be able to know and identify it. The French and Spanish systems, for example, restrict disclosure to only those documents that are admissible at trial. Document disclosure is supervised by the judge who decides on the relevance and admissibility of the evidence proposed by the parties.

In Germany e.g., litigants are not required to disclose documents to the other party; instead a party needs only to produce those documents that will support its case. Those documents must be authentic, original and certified but the party seeking the document must appeal to the court to order the production of the document. This appeal must be specific in the description of the document and must include the facts that the document would prove and the justification for having the document produced. If the document is in the possession of a third party, the document seeker must obtain permission from the third party. If permission is refused, the seeker must commence proceedings against the holder of the documents.

Aside from any data protection issues, it is the contrast between the 'opinion of the truth' compared to the 'truth and nothing but the truth' that emphasises the difference between the approach of the civil code and common law jurisdictions to questions of discovery of information including personal data.

Preventative legislation

Some countries, mainly those in civil law jurisdictions, but also a few common law countries have introduced laws *(blocking statutes)* in an attempt to restrict cross border discovery of information intended for disclosure in foreign jurisdictions. There is little uniformity in how these have been introduced, their scope and effect. Some, for example France, prohibit the disclosure from the country, of certain type of documents or information in order to constitute evidence for foreign judicial or administrative procedures. A party who discloses information may be guilty of violating the laws of the country in which the information is held and this may result in civil or even criminal sanctions.[3]

---

3. One example of this is the French Penal Law No. 80-538 which provides that:

   'Subject to international treaties or agreements and laws and regulations in force, it is forbidden for any person to request, seek or communicate in writing, orally or in any other form, documents or information of an economic, commercial, industrial, financial nature leading to the constitution of evidence with a view to foreign judicial or administrative procedures or in

The US courts have so far not accepted such provisions as providing a defence against discovery in relation to US litigation. Under the Restatement (Third) of Foreign Relations Law of the United States no. 442, a court may order a person subject to its jurisdiction to produce evidence even if the information is not located in the United States.[4] As supported by the decisions of various courts[5] a balancing exercise should be carried out with the aim that the trial court should rule on a party's request for production of information located abroad only after balancing:

(1) the importance to the litigation of the information requested;
(2) the degree of specificity of request;
(3) whether the information originated in the United States;
(4) the availability of alternative means of securing the information;
(5) the extent to which non-compliance would undermine the interests of the United States or compliance with the request would undermine the interests of a foreign sovereign nation.

The recent publication from the Sedona Conference on cross-border discovery conflicts sets out more a detailed analysis of the US jurisprudence and considers the relevant factors when determining the scope of cross border discovery obligations.[6] It stresses that this requires a balancing of the needs, costs and burdens of the discovery with the interests of each foreign jurisdiction in protecting the privacy rights and welfare of its citizens. The Sedona Conference Framework also notes that the French decision in the case of Credit Lyonnais has altered the perception of US courts as to the reality of enforcement of foreign preventative statutes.[7]

The Hague Evidence Convention

Requests for information may also be made through the Hague Convention on the taking of evidence abroad in civil and commercial matters. This provides a standard procedure for issuing 'letters of request' or 'letters rogatory' which are petitions from

---

the context of such procedures.' In 2008 the French Supreme Court upheld the criminal conviction of a French lawyer for violating this statute who had complied with a request from US courts in the case of Strauss v. Credit Lyonnais, S.A., 2000 U.S. Dist. Lexis 38378 (E.D.N.Y. May 25, 2007). The lawyer was fined 10,000 Euro (about 15,000 US $).

4. It is important to note that the US judge considers that if the company is subject to US law and possesses, controls, or has custody or even has authorized access to the information from the US territory (via a computer) wherever the data is 'physically' located, US law applies without the need to respect any international convention such as the Hague Convention.
5. Société Nationale Industrielle Aérospatiale v United States District Court, 482 U.S. 522, 544 n.28 (1987), Volkswagen AG v Valdez [No.95-0514, November 16, 1995, Texas Supreme Court] and In re: Baycol Litigation MDL no. 1431 (Mfd/JGL), March 21, 2003. For a more thorough analysis of the US jurisprudence see the Sedona Conference Framework for Analysis of Cross-Border Discovery Conflicts (note 5 infra).
6. The Sedona Conference Framework for analysis of cross border discovery conflicts – A practical guide to navigating the competing currents of international data privacy and discovery – 23 April 2008 (Public Comment Version), A Project of the Sedona Conference Working Group 6 on International Electronic Information Management, Discovery and Disclosure.
7. Sedona Framework, p. 31.

the court of one country to the designated central authority of another requesting assistance from that authority in obtaining relevant information located within its borders. However, not all EU Member States are parties to the Hague Convention.

A further complication is provided by Article 23 of the Convention whereby 'a contracting state may at the time of signature, ratification or accession declare that it will not execute letters of request issued for the purposes of obtaining pre-trial discovery of documents. Many signatory States, including France, Germany, Spain and the Netherlands have filed such reservations under Article 23 with the effect of declaring that discovery of any information, regardless of relevance, would not be allowed if it is sought in relation to foreign legal proceedings. In France, it is allowed for the competent judge to execute letters rogatory in case of pre-trial discovery if requested documents/information are specifically listed in the letters rogatory and have a direct and precise link with the litigation in case.

According to the Hague Convention, pre-trial discovery is a procedure which covers requests for evidence submitted after the filing of a claim but before the final hearing on the merits. It is of interest to note that there is a wider interpretation under UK law as an application may be made where the evidence is to be obtained for the purposes of civil proceedings which either have been instituted before the requesting court or whose institution before that court is contemplated.[8] This would therefore appear to allow for a greater scope for information to be provided in the UK than in other Member States.

The United States Supreme Court has ruled that the procedure foreseen by the Hague Evidence Convention is an optional but not a mandatory way of collecting evidence abroad for litigants before US courts.[9] Since then US courts have largely followed this line but occasionally they have required litigants to resort to the Hague Convention procedure.[10]

Other difficulties

One of the main difficulties with cross border litigation is the control of the use, for litigation purposes, of personal data which has already been properly transferred for example to the US for other reasons under BCR or Safe Harbour. This is not a question that will be dealt with in this paper but the Working Party recognises that this may lead more readily to the disclosure of data.

2. Opinion

The working party sees the need for reconciling the requirements of the US litigation rules and the EU data protection provisions. It acknowledges that the Directive does not prevent transfers for litigation purposes and that there are often

---

8. Evidence (Proceedings in Other Jurisdictions) Act 1975
9. Société Nationale Industrielle Aérospatiale v United States District Court, 482 U.S. 522, 544 n.28 (1987)
10. See the Compendium of reported post-Aérospatiale cases citing the Hague Evidence Convention compiled for the American Bar Association by McNamara/Hendrix/Charepoo (June 1987– July 2003)

conflicting demands on companies carrying on international business in the different jurisdictions with the company feeling obliged to transfer the information required in the foreign litigation process. However where data controllers seek to transfer personal data for litigation purposes there must be compliance with certain data protection requirements. In order to reconcile the data protection obligations with the requirements of the foreign litigation, the Working Party proposes the following guidelines for EU data controllers.

Guidelines
It should be recognised that there are different stages during the litigation process. The use of personal data at each of these stages will amount to processing, each of which will require an appropriate condition in order to legitimise the processing. These different stages include:

- retention;
- disclosure;
- onward transfer;
- secondary use.

Various issues are raised in relation to retention as the Directive provides that personal data shall be kept for the period of time necessary for the purposes for which the data have been collected or for which they are further processed. It is unlikely that the data subjects would have been informed that their personal data could be the subject of litigation whether in their own country or in another jurisdiction. Similarly given the different time limits for bringing claims in different countries, it is not possible to provide for a particular period for retention of data.

Controllers in the European Union have no legal ground to store personal data at random for an unlimited period of time because of the possibility of litigation in the United States however remote this may be. The US rules on civil procedure only require the disclosure of *existing* information. If the controller has a clear policy on records management which provides for short retention periods based on local legal requirements it will not be found at fault with US law. It should be noted that even in the United States there has recently been a tendency to adopt restrictive retention policies to reduce the likelihood of discovery requests.

If on the other hand the personal data is relevant and to be used in a specific or imminent litigation process, it should be retained until the conclusion of the proceedings and any period allowed for an appeal in the particular case. Spoliation of evidence may lead to severe procedural and other sanctions.

There may be a requirement for 'litigation hold' or pre-emptive retention of information, including personal data. In effect this is the suspension of the company's retention and destruction policies for documents which may be relevant to the legal claim that has been filed at court or where it is 'reasonably anticipated'.

There may however be a further difficulty where the information is required for additional pending litigation or where future litigation is reasonably foreseeable.

The mere or unsubstantiated possibility that an action may be brought before the US courts is not sufficient.

Although in the US the storage of personal data for litigation hold is not considered to be processing, under Directive 95/46 any retention, preservation, or archiving of data for such purposes would amount to processing. Any such retention of data for purposes of future litigation may only justified under Article 7(c) or 7(f) of Directive 95/46.

Legitimacy of processing for litigation purposes

In order for the pre-trial discovery procedure to take place lawfully, the processing of personal data needs to be legitimate and to satisfy one of the grounds set out in Article 7 of the Data Protection Directive. In addition, for transfers to another jurisdiction the requirements of Article 26 would have to be met in order to provide a basis for such transfer.

There appear to be three relevant grounds, namely consent of the data subject, that the compliance with the pre-trial discovery requirements is necessary for compliance with a legal obligation under Article 7(c) or further purposes of a legitimate interest pursued by the controller or by the third party to whom the data are disclosed under Article 7(f). For the reasons set out below the Working Party considers that in most cases consent is unlikely to provide a proper ground for such processing.

Consent

Whilst consent is a ground for processing under Article 7, the Working Party considers that it is unlikely that in most cases consent would provide a good basis for processing. Article 2(h) defines data subject's consent as 'any freely given specific and informed indication of his [the data subject's] wishes by which the data subject signifies his agreement to personal data relating to him being processed'. The main argument underlying the US jurisprudence since the Aérospatiale case is that if a company has chosen to do business in the United States or involving US counterparts it has to follow the US Rules on Civil Procedure. However, very often the data subjects such as customers and employees of this company do not have this choice or have not been involved in the decision to do business in or relating to the United States.

Consequently exporting controllers in the European Union should be able to produce clear evidence of the data subject's consent in any particular case and may be required to demonstrate that the data subject was informed as required. If the personal data sought is that of a third party, for example, a customer, it is at present unlikely that the controller would be able to demonstrate that the subject was properly informed and received notification of the processing.

Similarly, valid consent means that the data subject must have a real opportunity to withhold his consent without suffering any penalty, or to withdraw it subsequently if he changes his mind. This can particularly be relevant if it is employee consent that is being sought. As the Article 29 Working Party states in its paper on the interpretation of Article 26(1): 'relying on consent may . . . prove to be a 'false good solution', simple at first glance but in reality complex and cumbersome'[11].

The Working Party does recognise that there may be situations where the individual is aware of, or even involved in the litigation process and his consent may properly be relied upon as a ground for processing.

Necessary for compliance with a legal obligation

An obligation imposed by a foreign legal statute or regulation may not qualify as a legal obligation by virtue of which data processing in the EU would be made legitimate. However, in individual Member States there may exist a legal obligation to comply with an Order of a Court in another jurisdiction seeking such discovery.

In those Member States where there is no such obligation (e.g. because a reservation under Art. 23 of the Hague Evidence Convention has been made), there may still be a basis for processing under Article 7(f) for the data controller who is required to make a pre-trial disclosure.

Necessary for the purposes of a legitimate interest

Compliance with the requirements of the litigation process may be found to be necessary for the purposes of a legitimate interest pursued by the controller or by the third party to whom the data are disclosed under Article 7(f). This basis would only be acceptable where such legitimate interests are not 'overridden by the interests for fundamental rights and freedoms of the data subject'.

Clearly the interests of justice would be served by not unnecessarily limiting the ability of an organisation to act to promote or defend a legal right. The aim of the discovery process is the preservation and production of information that is potentially relevant to the litigation. The aim is to provide each party with access to such relevant information as is necessary to support its claim or defence, with the goal of providing for fairness in the proceedings and reaching a just outcome.

Against these aims have to be weighed the rights and freedoms of the data subject who has no direct involvement in the litigation process and whose involvement is by virtue of the fact that his personal data is held by one of the litigating parties and is deemed relevant to the issues in hand, e.g. employees and customers.

This balance of interest test should take into account issues of proportionality, the relevance of the personal data to the litigation and the consequences for the data subject. Adequate safeguards would also have to be put in place and in particular, there must be recognition for the rights of the data subject to object under Article 14 of the Directive where the processing is based on Article 7(f) and, in the absence of national legislation providing otherwise, there are compelling legitimate grounds relating to the data subject's particular situation.

As a first step controllers should restrict disclosure if possible to anonymised or at least pseudonymised data. After filtering ('culling') the irrelevant data – possibly

---

11. Working document on a common interpretation of Article 26(1) of Directive 95/46/EC of 24 October 1995 (WP 114), p. 11.

by a trusted third party in the European Union – a much more limited set of personal data may be disclosed as a second step.

Sensitive Personal Data and other special categories
Where the information in question is sensitive personal data, a ground for processing under Article 8 of the Directive must be found. Instead, the appropriate ground would be to rely on the explicit consent of the data subject under Article 8(a) or where the processing is necessary for the establishment, exercise or defence or legal claims under Article 8(e). There may be specific requirements in the different Member States relating to the processing and transfer of personal data overseas with which there would need to be compliance by the data controller.

Data protection is not the only issue surrounding the use of an individual's personal data. Where, for example, the personal data sought is health data, there may be other duties of confidentiality between doctor and patient. There may also be other requirements of secrecy or subsisting duties of confidentiality in relation to the information, for example legal professional privilege between lawyer and client or the secrecy of confession to a priest. In addition there may be legal protection for certain types of information, e.g. the e-Privacy Directive. In those circumstances it may not be fair or lawful to process that personal data in a way that is incompatible with the other obligations. Furthermore violations of telecommunications secrecy may carry criminal sanctions in a number of Member States.

Proportionality
Article 6 of the Directive provides that personal data must be processed fairly and lawfully, collected for specified, explicit and legitimate purposes and not used for incompatible purposes. The personal data must be adequate relevant and not excessive in relation to the purposes for which they are collected and/or further processed.

In relation to litigation there is a tension in the discovery process in seeking a balance between the perceived need of the parties to obtain all information prior to then determining its relevance to the issues within the litigation and the rights of the individuals where their personal data is included within the information sought as part of the litigation process.

It is clear from the US civil procedure rules and the principles expounded by the Sedona Conference that the approach of both the US and the EU legal systems place importance on the proportionality and the balance of the rights of the different interests.

There is a duty upon the data controllers involved in litigation to take such steps as are appropriate (in view of the sensitivity of the data in question and of alternative sources of the information) to limit the discovery of personal data to that which is objectively relevant to the issues being litigated. There are various stages to this filtering activity including determining the information that is relevant to the case, then moving on to assessing the extent to which this includes personal data. Once personal data has been identified, the data controller would need to consider whether it is necessary for all of the personal data to be processed, or for example, could it be produced in a more anonymised or redacted form. Where the identity of the individual data subject's is not relevant to the cause of action in the litigation, there is no need to provide such information in the first instance. However, at a later stage it may be required by the court which may give rise to another 'filtering' process. In most cases it will be sufficient to provide the personal data in a pseudonymised form with individual identifiers other than the data subject's name.

When personal data are needed the 'filtering' activity should be carried out locally in the country in which the personal data is found before the personal data that is deemed to be relevant to the litigation is transferred to another jurisdiction outside the EU.

The Working Party recognises that this may cause difficulties in determining who is the appropriate person to decide on the relevance of the information taking into account the strict time limits laid down in the US Federal Rules of Civil Procedure to disclose the information requested. Clearly it would have to be someone with sufficient knowledge of the litigation process in the relevant jurisdiction. It may be that this would require the services of a trusted third party in a Member State who does not have a role in the litigation but has the sufficient level of independence and trustworthiness to reach a proper determination on the relevance of the personal data.

Throughout the discovery process including freezing, the Working Party would urge the parties to the litigation to involve the data protection officers from the earliest stage. It would also encourage the EU data controllers to approach the US courts in part to be able to explain the data protection obligations upon them and ask US courts for relevant protective orders to comply with EU and national data protection rules. As the Supreme Court stressed in the Aérospatiale case 'American courts, in supervising pre-trial proceedings, should exercise special vigilance to protect foreign litigants from the danger that unnecessary, or unduly burdensome, discovery may place them in a disadvantageous position.'[12]

Transparency
Articles 10 and 11 of the Directive address the issue of information that should be provided to the data subject.

In the context of pre-trial discovery this would require advance, general notice of the possibility of personal data being processed for litigation. Where the personal data is actually processed for litigation purposes, notice should be given of the identity of any recipients, the purposes of the processing, the categories of data concerned and the existence of their rights.

Article 11 requires that individuals are informed when personal data are collected from a third party and not from them directly. This is likely to be a common scenario where the personal data is held by one of the parties to the litigation or by a subsidiary or affiliate of such a party.

In such cases the data subjects should be informed by the data controller as soon as reasonably practicable after the data is processed. Under Article 14 the data

---

12. 482 U.S. 522, 546 (No.15, 16a).

subject also has a right to object to the processing of their data if the legitimacy of the processing is based on Article 7(f) where the objection is on compelling legitimate grounds relating to the person's particular situation.

As was discussed in the Opinion of the Working Party on internal whistleblowing schemes[13] there is however an exception to this rule where there is a substantial risk that such notification would jeopardise the ability of the litigating party to investigate the case properly or gather the necessary evidence. In such a case the notification to the individual may be delayed as long as such a risk exists in order to preserve evidence by preventing its destruction or alteration by that person. This exception however must be applied restrictively on a case by case basis.

Rights of access, rectification and erasure
Article 12 of the Directive gives the data subject the right to have access to the data held about him in order to check its accuracy and rectify it if it is inaccurate, incomplete or outdated. It is for the data controller in the EU to ensure that there is compliance with the individual's rights to access and rectify incorrect, incomplete or outdated personal data prior to the transfer.

The Working Party would suggest that such obligations are imposed on a party receiving the information. This could be achieved by way of a Protective Order. This has the merit of allowing a data subject to check the personal data and to satisfy himself that the data transferred is not excessive.

These rights may only be restricted under Article 13 on a case by case basis for example where it is necessary to protect the rights and freedoms of others. The Working Party is clear that the rights of the data subject continue to exist during the litigation process and there is no general waiver of the rights to access or amend.

It should be noted however that this right could give rise to a conflict with the requirements of the litigation process to retain data as at a particular date in time and any changes (whilst only for correction purposes) would have the effect of altering the evidence in the litigation.

Data security
In accordance with Article 17 of the Directive, the data controller shall take all reasonable technical and organisational precautions to preserve the security of the data to protect it from accidental or unlawful destruction or accidental loss and unauthorised disclosure or access. These measures must be proportionate to the purposes of investigating the issues raised in accordance with the security regulations established in the different Member States. These requirements are to be imposed not just on the data controller but such measures as are appropriate should

---

13. Opinion 1/2006 on the application of EU data protection rules to internal whistleblowing schemes in the fields of accounting, internal accounting controls, auditing matters, fight against bribery, banking and financial crime (WP 117 00195/06/EN)

also be provided by the law firms who are dealing with the litigation together with any litigation support services and all other experts who are involved with the collection or review of the information. This would also include a requirement for sufficient security measures to be placed upon the court service in the relevant jurisdiction as much of the personal data relevant to the case would be held by the courts for the purposes of determining the outcome of the case.

External service providers
Where external service providers are used for example as expert witnesses within the litigation process, the data controller would still remain responsible for the resulting processing operations as those providers would be acting as processors within the meaning of the Directive.

The external service providers will also have to comply with the principles of the Directive. They shall ensure that the information is collected and processed in accordance with the principles of the Directive and that the information is only processed for the specific purposes for which it was collected. In particular they must abide by strict confidentiality obligations and communicate the information processed only to specific persons. They must also comply with the retention periods by which the data controller is bound. The data controller must also periodically verify compliance by external providers with the provisions of the Directive.

Transfers to third countries
Articles 25 and 26 of the Directive apply where personal data are transferred to a third country.

Where the third country to which the data will be sent does not ensure an adequate level of protection as required under Article 25 the data may be transferred on the following grounds:

(1) where the recipient of personal data is an entity established in the US that has subscribed to the Safe Harbor Scheme;
(2) where the recipient has entered into a transfer contract with the EU company transferring the data by which the latter adduces adequate safeguards, for example, based on the standard contract clauses issued by the European Commission in its Decisions of 15 June 2001 or 27 December 2004;
(3) where the recipient has a set of binding corporate rules in place which have been approved by the relevant data protection authorities.

Where the transfer of personal data for litigation purposes is likely to be a single transfer of all relevant information, then there would be a possible ground for processing under Article 26(1)(d) of the Directive where it is necessary or legally required for the establishment, exercise or defence of legal claims. Where a significant amount of data is to be transferred the use of Binding Corporate Rules or Safe Harbor should be considered. However, the Working Party reiterates its earlier opinion that Art. 26 (1)(d) cannot be used to justify the transfer of all employee files to a group's parent company on the grounds of the possibility that legal proceedings may be brought one day in US courts.[14]

The Working Party recognises that compliance with a request made under the Hague Convention would provide a formal basis for a transfer of personal data. It does recognise that not all Member States however have signed the Hague Convention and even if a State has signed it may be with reservations.

Whilst there may be some concerns about the length of time such a procedure could take, the courts, for example in the US, are experienced in the use of the Hague Convention and such timescales can be built into the litigation process. Where it is possible for The Hague Convention to be used, the Working Party urges that this approach should be considered first as a method of providing for the transfer of information for litigation purposes.

Conclusion

This working document is an initial consideration of the issue of the transfer of personal data for use in cross border civil litigation. It is an invitation to public consultation with interested parties, courts in other jurisdictions and others to enter a dialogue with the Working Party.

Done at Brussels, on 11/02/2009

For the Working Party
The Chairman
Alex TÜRK

---

14.   WP 114, p. 15.